ROYSTER MEMORIAL STUDIES

# ROYSTER
# MEMORIAL STUDIES

EDITED BY

Louis B. Wright        Dougald MacMillan
N. B. Adams            Raymond Adams
G. A. Harrer

CHAPEL HILL
THE UNIVERSITY OF NORTH CAROLINA PRESS
1931

COPYRIGHT 1931 BY
THE UNIVERSITY OF NORTH CAROLINA PRESS

Reprinted from *Studies in Philology*, Volume XXVIII, Number 4.

TO THE MEMORY OF

## JAMES FINCH ROYSTER
1880-1930

KENAN PROFESSOR OF ENGLISH PHILOLOGY

DEAN OF THE GRADUATE SCHOOL
THE UNIVERSITY OF NORTH CAROLINA

EDITOR OF STUDIES IN PHILOLOGY

# DEDICATION

This issue of *Studies in Philology* is made up of contributions from former pupils, colleagues, and friends of James Finch Royster. Such a tribute to his memory is prompted not only by his gifts as a teacher, his capacity for friendship, and his eminence in scholarship, but because of his long connection with the journal. He watched it grow from modest beginnings to its present position as one of the leading journals in the world in linguistic and literary scholarship, and to this growth he contributed. My own first perception of the fact that the University of North Carolina was not just another college, but an institution in which research was fostered and its results published, came from copies of *Studies in Philology* sent me, many years ago, by Dr. Royster.

At that time the journal appeared only at long intervals. A publication of the Philological Club of the University, its contents were limited to papers read at meetings of the Club. It was slender in size, and was badly printed because income was small and costs were high. But it contained things worth reading. In a day when university presses were almost unknown and the publication of research was limited to only a few of the larger institutions, it did pioneer work. It helped to further the conception, dimly held in those times, that a prime function of a university is the fostering of research and the publication of its results.

In that early time Dr. Royster aided the young journal by his contributions, his faith, and his rare power to transmit his own enthusiasm to others. In later years, by his sympathy and his contributions when he was associated with another university, by his service as associate editor upon his return to Chapel Hill, and, from 1926 to his death, by his work as editor, he continued to influence the program and development of the journal.

With the history of *Studies in Philology*, therefore, the name of James Finch Royster will forever be associated. To the memory of an inspiring teacher, an acute scholar, and a friend of the propagation of learning, this number of the journal is dedicated.

EDWIN GREENLAW

# PREFACE

The Editorial Board of *Studies in Philology* has designated the October number as a memorial to Professor James Finch Royster. It has been edited by a committee, consisting of Louis B. Wright, Dougald MacMillan, N. B. Adams, Raymond Adams, and G. A. Harrer, elected by a group of Professor Royster's students to receive contributions to a memorial volume and to see it through the press. The committee has been aided in the selection of contributors and in other matters by Professor John M. Manly, Professor Edwin Greenlaw, and Professor George R. Coffman, who consented to act as advisory editors.

The articles are arranged in three groups: first, those dealing with philology, Professor Royster's main interest, second, those dealing with English literature, and third, those dealing with literatures other than English. Numbers at the top of the page are for this number only, the page numbers of the volume of *Studies in Philology* appearing at the foot of the page in brackets.

To the Editorial Board of *Studies in Philology* and to the University of North Carolina Press the present editors are indebted for valuable assistance. They wish also to acknowledge the generosity of Scott, Foresman and Company, Professor Royster's publishers, J. H. Furst Company, printers of *Studies in Philology* for many years, and the Alumni Loyalty Fund of the University of North Carolina, who have contributed towards the expense of issuing this memorial number.

D. MacM.

## CONTENTS

|  | PAGE |
|---|---|
| GREENLAW, EDWIN—Dedication, | v |
| WOOD, FRANCIS A.—Indo-European Bases Derivable from Skt. *Áva* 'Down', | 1 |
| TOY, WALTER DALLAM—*Whether* and *If*, | 14 |
| STEADMAN, JOHN M., JR.—Phonetic Differentiation in English, | 19 |
| HOLMES, URBAN T., JR.—French *gnaff*, Scottish *nyaff*, | 37 |
| MALONE, KEMP—On Wulfstan's Scandinavia, | 42 |
| COFFMAN, GEORGE R.—A Note on Saints' Legends, | 48 |
| TATLOCK, J. S. P.—Irish Costume in Lawman, | 55 |
| BROWN, CARLETON—An Early Mention of a St. Nicholas Play in England, | 62 |
| HULBERT, J. R.—The Text of *The Siege of Jerusalem*, | 70 |
| MANLY, JOHN MATTHEWS—Tales of the Homeward Journey, | 81 |
| CRAIG, HARDIN—Shakespeare and Wilson's *Arte of Rhetorique*, | 86 |
| LAW, ROBERT ADGER—Shakespeare's Earliest Plays, | 99 |
| THRALL, WILLIAM FLINT—*Cymbeline*, Boccaccio, and the Wager Story in England, | 107 |
| TAYLOR, GEORGE COFFIN—Some Patristic Conventions Common to Shakespeare and Milton, | 120 |
| HARD, FREDERICK—Lamb on Spenser, | 124 |
| WRIGHT, LOUIS B.—The Reading of Renaissance English Women, | 139 |
| ADAMS, JOSEPH QUINCY—*Eastward Hoe* and its Satire against the Scots, | 157 |
| MAXWELL, BALDWIN—The Date of *Love's Pilgrimage* and its Relation to *The New Inn*, | 170 |
| HOWELL, A. C.—A Note on Ben Jonson's Literary Methods, | 178 |
| MILLICAN, CHARLES BOWIE—The First English Translation of the *Prophecies of Merlin*, | 188 |

|                                                                                   | PAGE |
|-----------------------------------------------------------------------------------|------|
| POTTER, RUSSELL—Three Jacobean Devil Plays,                                       | 198  |
| GRIFFITH, R. H.—A Piracy of Pope's *Iliad*,                                       | 205  |
| BOND, RICHMOND P.—Shenstone's Heroi-Comical Poem,                                 | 210  |
| HUDSON, ARTHUR PALMER—The Hermit and Divine Providence,                           | 218  |
| JONES, HOWARD MUMFORD—The Importation of French Literature in New York City, 1750-1800, | 235  |
| MARSH, GEORGE L.—Some Notes on Pierce Egan,                                       | 252  |
| MACMILLAN, DOUGALD—Planché's Fairy Extravaganzas,                                 | 258  |
| PAINE, GREGORY—Cooper and *The North American Review*,                            | 267  |
| REYNOLDS, GEORGE F.—Literature for an Audience,                                   | 278  |
| LONG, O. W.—Goethe and Bancroft,                                                  | 288  |
| HARRER, G. A.—Sparsus, A Friend of Pliny,                                         | 298  |
| LYONS, J. CORIDEN—Notes on Mathurin Regnier's *Macette*,                          | 301  |
| DEY, WILLIAM M.—A Note on Stendhal and Victor Hugo,                               | 306  |
| CRAWFORD, J. P. WICKERSHAM—Gutierre De Cetina: Notes on the Date of his Birth and the Identity of Dorinda, | 309  |
| LEAVITT, STURGIS E.—Notes on the Gracioso as a Dramatic Critic,                   | 315  |
| ADAMS, N. B.—Hartzenbusch's "Sancho Ortiz De Las Roelas",                         | 319  |
| STOUDEMIRE, S. A.—A Spanish Play on the Fair Rosamond Legend,                     | 325  |

# INDO-EUROPEAN BASES DERIVABLE FROM SKT. ÁVA 'DOWN'[1]

## By Francis A. Wood

1. The original form of Skt. *áva* 'down, down from' was probably *\*awe,* with *a* from schwa. The IE ablaut-forms of the underlying base may be set down as *\*ēwe-, ōwe-, awe, ū, u-,* with by-forms *awā-,* etc. Closely related to Skt. *áva* are AV., OPers. *ava* 'weg, ab', Gr. αὐ-, Lat. *au-* 'away, from', *vē-,* indicating negation, Lett., Lith. *au-,* OB *u-* 'weg, ab', etc.

Compare further Skt. *aváḥ* adv. 'down', prep. with the instr. 'down from, under': Goth. *us* 'out of, from', *us-, uz-, ur-* in composition denoting the absence or lack of something, OHG *ur, ar* 'aus, aus — heraus, aus — hervor, von — her, von — weg', in composition *ur-, ar-, ir-, er-,* OE *or-,* 'un-, ex-, free from, without', etc. Perhaps here also Lat. *auscultāre* (excolere, diligenter colere, obsequi, ὑπακούειν) 'give heed to, listen attentively or furtively', from *aus-* (Skt. *aváḥ*) and *-cultāre* : *cultus, colere.*

The comparative and superlative give added meanings: *ávara-ḥ* 'der untere; geringer, nachstehend, jünger, näher, später, westlich', *avamá-ḥ* 'der unterste, nächste, letzte, jüngste'. With various additions to the original base arise the enlarged *\*ēwex-; \*awāx-; \*wix-*. For this last form compare Skt. *vi* 'apart' (*\*w-i*), Av. *vĭ*. From the idea of separation came that of duality, two-ness, Lat. *vīginta* etc., also words for 'we two' and then, by extension, for 'we' (three or more). The idea of separation can be followed through many bases *\*wēix-, wāix-*.

2. The idea of separation contained in these words gave others

---

[1] The limits of this article prevent any attempt to make this discussion exhaustive.

[533]

for 'spread out, open, wide; hollow, empty, lacking, deficient'.
For this early meaning compare Skt. *āviḥ* (\**ōwis*) adv. 'offenbar,
bemerkbar', OBulg. *javĕ* 'offenbar', *javiti* 'zeigen', OE *ēowian,
īewan* 'show, reveal', *ēawunga* 'openly, publicly', OFris. *auwa*
'zeigen', *au-ber, ā-ber* 'offenbar', OHG *awi-zoraht* 'openly clear,
evident'; OE *open* 'open; evident', *yppe* 'evident, known; show,
spectacle'; Gr. εὐρύς 'wide, broad'; Lat. *vacuus;* Skt. *vi* 'apart,
away from', OE *wīd* 'wide', and many others. The different ideas
coming from \**upo* 'sub; super', occurring even in the same word,
are constantly repeated in bewildering multifariousness. A few
of the many examples are here given.

3. Base \**ēwe-, awe-* 'rise, arise, spring; grow, swell, increase,
prosper': Skt. *ávati* 'fördert, erregt, labt, sättigt, schützt, behütet,
hat gern', with *upa* 'stimmt zu, ruft zu' ( : Lat. *avē* 'hail'), *áva-ḥ*
'Gunst, Huld', *ūma-, ōmán-* helfend, schützend', *ōmyā* 'Gunst,
Schutz', Goth. *iumjō* 'multitude', Lett. *aumakan* 'in Menge, mit
Gedränge, rasch, eilig', Lith. *ūmaī* 'plötzlich, sogleich' (with a
spring), *ūmyti* 'drängen, treiben' (cf. Bezzenberger, Bezz. Beitr.
21, 316), OE *wōma* 'tumult; terror', *wēman* 'sound; announce,
persuade, entice, seduce', Skt. *vāmá-ḥ* 'hold, lieb, schön; strebend
nach, versessen auf', *vāmám* 'Reichtum, Gut, Glück, Heil'; *avanam*
'Begünstigung, Gunst', *ávant-* 'freundlich, gern', *vánati, vanáti*
'erstrebt, wünscht, hat gern', *vaní-ḥ* 'Verlangen, Wunsch', OHG
*wunna* 'Wonne, Freude, Lust', Lat. *venia* 'favor, indulgence',
*venus,* etc. (cf. No. 12) : Lat. *avēre* 'strive after, long for, desire
earnestly'; Skt. *ávaḥ* (stem \**awos-*) 'Förderung, Hilfe, Labung,
Lust, Verlangen', *avasám* 'Nahrung' (Fick I, 502), *úṣa-ḥ* 'begierig, verlangend', *ōṣám* 'geschwind, sogleich' compare Lith. *ūmaī*
above), Goth. *iusiza* 'better', *wisan* (with and without *waila*) 'be
merry, make merry, fare sumptuously', OHG *wist* 'Nahrung',
OE *wist* 'sustenance, food; luxury', *ge-wistian* 'feast', *wistfull*
'productive', NE *wistful* 'wishful, longing', OBulg. *veselŭ* 'merry',
Skt. *vásu-ḥ* 'gut, heilsam', neut. 'Gut, Besitz', *vasura-ḥ* 'wertvoll,
reich', *vasnám* 'Wert, Kaufpreis', *vasnayáti* 'feilscht', *vásnya-ḥ*
'wertvoll, verkäuflich', Gr. ὠνή 'a purchasing, buying', ὠνέομαι
'bargain or bid for a thing; buy', Lat. *vēnus* 'sale'; Skt. *ūti-ḥ*
'Förderung, Hilfe; Helfer; Labung, Erquickung', Russ. *vytī*
'Anteil' (Uhlenbeck Ai Wb. 32), ON *auðinn* 'vergönnt, gewährt,
bestimmt', OS *ōdan,* OE *ēaden* 'granted', Lat. *autumnus* 'year's

growth, harvest; autumn' (Walde s. v.), also *autumo* (make strong, corroborate) 'affirm, assert, say; hold, think', ON *vǫðvi* (outgrowth) 'muscle', OHG *wado* 'Wade'; Russ. *úditi* 'anschwellen', Lat. *ūber* 'rich, full, fertile, plentiful, copious, productive; stout, plump, fat', 'udder, breast; a cluster or mass; richness, fertility', Gr. οὖθαρ 'udder', Skt. *údhar* (*rn* stem), *ūdhas-* neut. 'udder, breast, cloud', OHG *ūtar*, OE *ūder* 'udder', ON *júr, júgr,* OFris. *iader*, MLG *jeder* 'udder' (IE *ūdh-, ōudh-, ēudh-*), with which compare Gr. εὐθένεια, εὐθηνία 'ubertas, abundance; well-being, weal', εὐθενής: εὐπαθοῦσα, ἰσχυρά Hesych., εὐθενέω 'thrive, flourish, prosper; abound', Goth. *audags* 'blessed', *auda-hafts* 'highly favored' OS *ōdag* 'reich', *ōd* 'Glück', OE *ēad* 'prosperity, wealth, happiness, (eternal) bliss', *ēadig* 'prosperous, rich, happy, blessed, perfect', Gr. ἔθνος (**wedhno-* 'a swelling, mass', for parallels compare Lat. *tumeo* and its congeners) 'a body of men, throng, crowd; nation, people; race, family, tribe, class, sex; a part, number; a flock (of birds), a swarm (of bees)'; Lat. *augeo, auxilium* (No. 20); Skt. *óha-ḥ* 'Darbringung, Gefälligkeit', *ōgha-ḥ* 'Flut, Strom, Menge', *āughá-ḥ* 'Flut', OE *ēagor* 'flood, tide; sea', OS, OHG *wāg* 'Flut, Woge', Skt. *vāhá-ḥ* 'fliessend', *váhati* 'fliesst; führt zu, verschafft, bringt dar', *váhni-ḥ* 'Zuführer, Darbringer (bes. Agni), Feuer, Feuergott', Lith. *ugnìs* 'Feuer', Lat. *vehemens* 'violent, furious, ardent; vigorous, strong, powerful', base **awegh-* (which has become confused with **aweĝh-* 'vehere', cf. No. 22), to which belongs Lat. *voveo* (from **woghw-,* not **wog*ʷ*h-*) 'promise solemnly, dedicate, consecrate, vow; wish for', Skt. *vāghát-* (Darbringer) 'der Opferveranstalter, der Gelobende, Beter', Gr. εὔχομαι 'offer vows or prayers, pray; pray for, long or wish for; vow, promise; profess loudly, boast, vaunt; declare', εὐχή 'prayer or vow; wish; imprecation', εὖχος 'thing prayed for; boast, vaunt; votive offering', αὐχέω 'boast; declare loudly, say, confidently', αὔχη 'boasting, pride', Av. *aog-* 'verkünden, sagen, sprechen': Goth. *augjan* 'zeigen', OHG *ougen* 'vorbringen, zeigen', *ar-ougnessī* 'ostensio, Erscheinung', NHG *Ereignis* [: Skt. *váhati* 'führt zu, bringt dar', *ūḍhá-* (**ūgh-to-*) 'geäussert, entstanden'], OE *wōgian, ā-wōgian* 'woo', NE woo 'solicit, sue, ask with importunity; seek to obtain or bring about; court, seek the favor of, esp. with a view to marriage' (: Skt. *ā-vaha-* 'herbeiführend, bewirkend', *ā-váhiti* 'führt, bringt, herbei', *upa-váhati* 'führt, bringt, herbei, verleitet jemand zu etwas', *ud-váhati* 'führt heim, heiratet', *vāghát-* 'vower'), OHG *wegōn*, MHG *wegen* 'gewogen sein, helfen, sich verwenden für, beistehn', etc.; base *ēwe-s-, awes-* (rather than *āwes-*), giving words for 'dawn, east; spring (the time of flowing water and springing vegetation); blaze, burn, etc.'

That all these words are one in origin is incapable of proof. But if they are not, then we have a most extraordinary parallelism in the development of different bases. Of course, we must count on the possibility of crossing and confusion of different words. But when we consider the marvelous adherence to type evidenced by the development of a multitude of words of IE origin, coming down through many milleniums, we are forced to admit that a development of language such as is indicated in this paper is at least not beyond the bounds of credibility.

4. Base *awe-s-, wes-* 'subside, settle down: dwell, abide; be, exist': Skt. *vásati, -tē* 'wohnt, übernachtet, weilt, befindet sich; widmet sich (acc. einer Sache)', *vāsáyati* 'lässt wohnen, beherbergt; lässt warten, hält hin', *pra-vásati* (Goth. *fra-wisan*, No. 5) 'bricht auf, zieht fort, verreist, entfernt sich, verschwindet', Goth. *wesan* 'weilen, bleiben; wohnen; zubringen (Winter)', 'endure, dwell, abide, remain; be', OHG *werēn* 'währen, dauern, bleiben', Goth. *wis* 'calm (on the sea)', Lat. *ves-per*, OE *west*, etc.: Skt. *aváḥ* 'herab; herab von, unter', *avástād* 'unten, diesseits; unter'. Cf. Walde s. v. *vesper*.

Gr. ἕσπερος, Lat. *vesper* are probably comparatives from an adj. *wespo-* 'low, late'. Compare Skt. *ávara-* 'der untere; später, westlich'; *ápara-* 'der hintere, später, westlich'. Similarly OBulg. *večeru* 'evening' is derivable from a synonymous adj. *weqo-*, from *awe-q-* 'settle, subside; dwell' in Skt. *ókaḥ* 'Behagen, Gefallen, Heimat, Wohnung, Zufluchtsort', *úcyati* 'findet Gefallen, pflegt, ist gewohnt', OBulg. *vyknǫti* 'sich gewöhnen' (cf. No. 18). Other points of the compass are expressed as comparatives: Lat. *auster* 'south'; Skt. *úttara-* 'higher; north of', *uttaráḥ* 'upward; toward the north'.

5. Base *awe-s-, wes-, wā-s-* 'subside, diminish, wane; become or make empty, exhaust, lay waste': ON, NIcel. *ausa* 'bale, scoop, dip, draw; squander', pret *jós* (*ēuse*), *austr* 'baling, scooping; bilgewater, *eysill* 'ladle', MLG *ōsen* 'schöpfen', *ōse* 'Schöpfgefäss, Giesser', MDu. *ōsen* 'dip out; wet, besprinkle', Gr. αὔω

'haurio', ἐξ-αῦσαι· ἐξελεῖν, ἐξ-αυστήρ : κρεάγρα, κατ-αῦσαι· καταντλῆσαι, καταδῦναι Hesych., Lat. *h-aurio* (? cf. Boisacq 105 with lit.); Goth. *fra-wisan* 'vergeuden, verbrauchen', MHG *ver-wesen* 'zu nichte werden, vergehen, herunterkommen; zunichte machen, verderben, aufbrauchen, consumere', *wesel* 'schwach, matt, abgestorben', OHG *ar-, ir-weran* 'affectus, decoctus, confectus, decrepitus', OE *for-weren, -weoren, -woren* 'decayed, worn out', *for-werian* 'wear out', NE *wear* 'waste, consume, exhaust', ON *vesall* 'wretched, poor, miserable', *veslask* 'pine or waste away', *vás* 'toil, fatigue, exposure to bad weather', etc. (or see Post-Cons. W in IE 15. 11); *wās- in Lat. *vāstus* 'laid waste, ravaged, destroyed; empty, desert, desolate; uncultivated, rude, harsh', OE *wēste* 'waste, uninhabited', OHG *wuosti* 'wüst, öde, leer; verschwenderisch', etc., Skt. *vāsáyati* 'schneidet ab'.

6. Base *awe-d-, awā-d-: Skt. *úd* 'up, out', *úttara-ḥ* 'the upper, higher; north; left; latter, later', *uttamá-ḥ* 'the upmost, highest, outmost', probably also *avadyám* (a falling short of, lack) 'Fehler, Tadel, Schmach, Schande', Gr. ὑστερίζω 'come after; fall short of, be inferior to; be in want of, lack', ὑστερέω 'be behind or later; come short of, be inferior to; be in want of; fail, be wanting or deficient', ὑστέρημα 'deficiency, need', ὕστερος 'latter, later; following, next (day); inferior (in age, worth, quality)', Goth. *ūt* 'out, out of', OE *ūt* 'out, outside, abroad', *ūte* 'outside, in the open air; away from home, abroad', *ȳtemest, ūtemest* 'outermost, outmost, utmost, extreme; last', *ūtian* 'expel; alienate (property)'; *ȳtan* 'expel', *ȳting* 'outing, journey', NE *out, utter*, etc., ON, NIcel. *ūt* 'out', *úti* 'out, out of doors, abroad, in the open air; at an end, over, finished', *ȳta* 'push, shove', OHG, MHG *ūz* 'aus, heraus, hinaus, fort, hindurch; hervor aus, weg von', *ūzar, ūzer* 'äusser, äusserlich, aussen wohnend, auswärtig', *ūzōn* 'einen wovon ausschliessen; refl. verzichten auf, sich entäussern', MHG *ūzerunge* 'Äusserung, Rede; Ausweisung, Entfernung', MLG *uten* 'herausgeben, herauskehren; äussern, effari; beweisen, dartun; nicht anerkennen, verwerfen', *uteren* 'hinaustreiben, verjagen, verstossen, exterminare; ausmustern, ausscheiden, verwerfen; von sich tun, herauskehren, veräussern (verkaufen), ausgeben; herausfordern; äussern, zeigen; beweisen, erklären', *uteringe* 'Befreiung, Reinigung; Losschwören', etc.: Skt. *úditi-ḥ* (utterance) 'Rede', *vádati* 'erhebt die Stimme, redet, singt, schallt, tönt', Gr. αὐδή 'the

human voice, speech; sound, twang; report, account; oracle', αὐδάω 'utter sounds, speak; of oracles, utter, proclaim, tell; speak to, accost, invoke, call', etc.; Skt. *undati, unátti* 'quillt, benetzt', *uda-, udan-, udakám* 'water', *ódatī* 'gushing', Gr. ὕδωρ, Lat. *unda*, Goth. *watō* 'water', ON *vátr* 'wet', Goth. *wintrus* 'winter; year', MHG *wāz* 'Wehen, Sturm; Atem, Hauch; Duft, Geruch', *wāzen* 'duften, riechen', OHG *ūz-wāzzen* 'herausblasen, hervorstürmen': Gr. ἄημι 'breathe, blow', ἀήτης 'blast, gale, wind' (*\*awē-* 'issue forth or out; expel: breathe, blow'), Skt. *vắta-ḥ* 'wind', Lith. *vétra* 'Sturm, Unwetter', OE *weder* 'air, breeze, weather; season, time of day', Ir. *feth* 'air': Gr. ἔτος (*\*wetos* 'weather, winter', used in reckoning time) 'year' (cf. Walde s. v. *tempestas*). Here would belong many other words for 'water; wind' from bases *\*awe-x-, awā-x-*.

From such meanings as occur here may also have developed the base *\*awe-* 'weave, wind, envelop, clothe', with its enlarged forms *\*awes-, \*awebh-, \*awedh-, \*aweg-*, etc., as well as many other words for 'wave, wag, wallow, wander, etc.'

7. Bases *\*awe-dh-, we(n)dh-* 'lack, need, suffer hardship, struggle, etc.': Skt *vandhya-, -ā-* 'unfruchtbar, unnütz, vergeblich', fem. 'ein unfruchtbares Weib', *vádhri-ḥ* 'verschnitten, impotent', Gr. ἄθρις 'a castrated ram' (*\*wṇdhri-* 'deficient, εὐνοῦχος'), Skt. *vadhá-ḥ* 'Vereitelung, Vernichtung, Verletzung, Tötung; Mörder, Todeswaffe', *vadhati, vadhayati* 'schlägt, vernichtet, tötet', Goth. *wunds* 'wounded', OE *wund* 'wounded', fem. 'wound', *wundiht* 'ulcerous', etc.; Gr. ἔθρις: τομίας κριός Hesych., also ὄθρις Zonaras 1428, ἄθλιος 'unhappy, pitiful, wretched' (*\*awedhlio-* 'lacking, wanting, suffering, struggling, contending', cf. Persson Beitr. 537), same as the older ἀέθλιος 'running for or winning the prize, of a horse; of contention (apple)', ἄθλος 'struggle, conflict, toil, trouble; contest in war or sport', ἄεθλον, ἄθλον 'struggle, contest; prize of contest, prize', ἀθλεύω 'contend for a prize; struggle, suffer', Ir. *feidm* 'effort', *fedil* 'persevering' (Zupitza KZ 37, 405 ff., cf. Boisacq 15). Since the idea of want, need, hardship, toil, struggle leads over easily to 'struggle for, contend, gain by contest, etc.', or 'strive, struggle' may equally well give 'suffer hardship, toil, be wretched', the above combinations may be made whichever end of the line we start from. In either case we may properly add here the base *\*wedh-* 'win, capture: lead home, marry': Skt. *vadhū́-ḥ* 'bride,

wife, daughter-in-law (primarily 'rapta, booty', as in Skt. váhati 'vehit; carry off, rob; take home, marry', ūḍhám 'booty', -ā́ 'wife'), Av. vāḍayeiti 'flührt, führt heim', Lith. vedù, vèsti 'lead (as the blind by the hand, a cow by the horns or on a tether); carry on, wage (war); take home, marry' vedlỹs, védys 'bridegroom'.

Compare the base *wi-dh- (from *wi 'separated, apart'): Skt. vídhyati 'durchbohrt, durchsticht, verwundet', Gr. ἴθρις· σπάδων, τομίας, εὐνοῦχος Hesych., Skt. vidhú-ḥ 'vereinsamt', vidhávā 'vidua', vidhura-ḥ 'beschädigt, beraubt, allein; gedrückt, traurig; mangelhaft, widrig, ungünstig', vidharayati 'nieder drückt', Lat. dī-vido, etc.

8. Bases *wā-dh-, wōdh- 'push, shove': Gr. ὠθέω 'thrust, push, shove, force onwards or away; expel, banish; push out from land (so NIcel. ýta); pass. be pushed or thrust, rush or fall violently, force one's way; crowd, throng; burst forth (of sweat)', Lat. vādo 'go hastily, rush, advance', in-vādo 'go or get into, rush upon, assail, assault, invade; fall upon, seize, usurp; accost, address', OE wadan 'go, advance', gewadan 'penetrate', OHG watan 'schreiten, gehen, dringen, durchdringen', MHG waten 'vadere, run (of a horse); pierce (a spear through the brain); flow, gush (of blood)', wetten 'treiben; niedertreten', MDu. waden 'pierce, of a weapon through the body; flow, gush, of blood from the body' (Gr. ὠθεῖσθαι 'burst forth, of sweat'), wade 'a break or leak in a dike', wadich 'broken through, of a dike' (not the same as wade, vadāre, vadum, on which see Post-Cons. W in IE, 8. 32). These last words bring us back to the meaning underlying Gr. ὄθρις above. In meaning if not in form they may also be compared with Lett. wāts 'wound', Lith. votìs 'a malignant open sore', Gr. ὠτειλή 'wound, esp. a fresh, open wound; a scar; an ulcer', βωτάζειν· βάλλειν Hesych. Compare also NIcel. vana 'castrate', No. 11.

9. Goth. auþeis 'desert; desolate', OE íeþe 'waste, desolate', íeþan 'lay waste, ravage, depopulate, kill', OHG ōdi 'öde, wüst, leer', Gr. αὔτως 'in vain', perhaps also αὐτός 'alone, by oneself; self' (*au-to-, -tio- 'separated: alone; empty'), ἐτός (*we-tos) 'in vain, without reason', ἐτώσιος 'fruitless, useless', Lat. veto (turn back) 'hinder, forbid' (cf. Boisacq 104, 293 with lit.). With these compare *wēt- in ON váði 'Schaden, Unheil', OE wēþl, wǣdl 'poverty', -a 'pauper', OHG wādal 'bettelnd, arm'; also

*ōut-* in Lat. *ōtium* (vacuum) 'vacant time, leisure, idle life, ease', *ōtiōsus* 'free, idle; useless, unprofitable; calm, gentle', OE *ēaþe, īeþe* 'easy; indulgent, kind', OHG *ōdi* 'leicht, facilis, possibilis (Schade 664).

Compare *\*wi-t-* in Lat. *vitium* 'defect, fault, blemish, vice', *\*witio-* 'a falling away, waning', OE *wīdl* 'defilement, impurity', *inwidd* 'deceitful, wicked, malicious', *inwid* 'guile, deceit, malice', OS *inwid* 'Bosheit, Tücke, Übeltat': Skt. *vāyati* 'erschöpft sich, wird müde', *nir-vāṇa-* 'erloschen, untergegangen; beruhigt', *nir-vāpayati* 'löscht aus, tilgt; stillt; erquickt', *abhi-vāta-* 'siech, krank'. Cf. No. 10.

10. ON *aumr* 'elend, unglücklich' (Norw. dial. 'verlassen, leer', Persson Wurzelerw. 230), NIcel. *aumur* 'wretched, miserable, unhappy; aching, sore', *aumungi* 'poor fellow, wretch', *eymd* 'misery, wretchedness', *eymsli* neut. pl. 'soreness, sore place, sore', Lith. *ūmyti* 'drängen, treiben', Goth. *un-wamms* 'without spot, without blemish, without blame', noun gen. pl. 'spot', OS *wam* 'böse; Böses, Übles, Verbrechen', OE *wamm* 'wicked; crime, injury; stain, defilement', *wemman* 'injure, destroy; profane, pollute, defile', *ā-wemman* 'curtail, shorten; defile', pre-Germ. *\*wamwo-* 'wanting, vitiosus', Skt. *vāmanā-ḥ* 'klein, kurz, gebeugt; Zwerg': *avamá-ḥ* 'lowest, last', *ávara-ḥ* 'lower, inferior', *áva* 'down': *vāyati* 'erschöpft sich, wird müde, erliegt': Lett. *wājsch* 'schwach, krank, schlecht, mager', *wājums* 'Schwäche, Krankheit' (cf. Persson Beitr. 535 f.). Cf. No. 11.

11. Gr. εὖνις 'bereft of, bereaved', Skt. *ūnā-ḥ* 'incomplete, lacking; less', Av. *unā* 'hole in the ground', NPers. *vang* 'empty, poor', Lat. *vānus* 'empty, void, vacant; fruitless, delusive; false, deceptive, ostentatious, vain', Goth. *wans,* ON *vanr* 'wanting, lacking', OHG *wan* 'mangled, mangelhaft, leer', MHG *er-wanen* 'leer machen, empty', MDu. *wanen* 'become empty (of vessels); diminish, decreases; wane (of the moon or other light)', Du. *wan* 'leak', OE *wan* 'lacking', *wanian* 'diminish, curtail, give away (property); deprive, take as plunder; injure, infringe, annul; intr. diminish, wane, fade' (cf. Boisacq 296 with lit.): OE *wann* (*\*wanwo-*) 'dark', *wanniht* 'pale', *ā-wannian* 'become pale', NE *wan* (author Color-Names 98). Add also MLG *wōne* 'eine ins Eis gehauene Öffnung', NHG *wuhne* 'a hole in the ice', Germ. *\*wōnō-* ( : Av. *unā* 'hole, gap in the ground' Franck Et. Wb. 774). Since

the bed as well as the abode of primitive man was a protected hollow or hole in the rocks, here may belong Gr. εὐνή ' bed or resting-place of men and animals', εὐνάζω, εὐνάω ' lay or place in ambush; put to bed, put to sleep', from *ēunā- ' hollow, hole, cave'.

NIcel. *vana* (: OE *wanian*) ' castrate', *vanaður* ' castrated; disabled, sick' would indicate that here belong Goth. *wunds* ' wund', *wundufni* ' Geissel, Plage', OE *wund* ' wounded; wound', etc. (or cf. No. 8). Compare *wā- in Skt. *vắyati* ' erschöpt sich, erliegt', *vāyú-* ' matt', Lith. *vójęs* ' leidend', etc., No. 10.

12. The IE base *wen-, which certainly did not mean originally ' wish' (as given by Walde s. v. *venus*), might well have developed its various significations from ' struggle'. However, this meaning may have come from ' be in want' (Gr. εὖνις). The full form *ēwe-n-, awe-n-, and *awā-n-, etc., if derived from the root of Skt. *áva* ' ab, herab', OPers. *au-*, OB *u-* ' weg, ab', Lat. *au-*, etc., would have had some such meaning as ' subside, settle; fall away, wane'. This naturally gives the words for ' empty, vanus, vacuus; vacuum, opening, hole, etc.' From this could come words for ' dwelling, resting-place, εὐνή', though it is more probable that ' dwell, wohnen, gewohnt sein' came from ' settle down'. It is certain, however, that ' win' means ' gain by struggles'; and ' wish, desire' is easily derivable from ' struggle for, strive for, streben', as is probably the case, though even here the primary meaning might have been ' lack, want'. In any case we have the meaning ' be empty, lack' and from this could come ' weariness, toil, struggle', with the other meanings as noted above. Compare Goth. *winnan* (*wenwo-) ' Schmerz leiden, leiden, arbeiten', *winna* ' πάθος, Leiden', *winnō*, *wunns* ' πάθημα, Leiden', MHG *winnen*, OHG *winnan* ' sich abmühen und abarbeiten, wüten, toben, rasen, streiten', *gi-winnan* ' durch Anstrengung erreichen, erwerben, erobern, besiegen, gerichtlich überführen', OE *winnan* ' strive after, struggle, toil; endure hardship, suffer', *ge-winnan* ' gain, win, conquer', etc., Skt. *vanóti*, *vánute*, *vanati*, *vanáti* ' (erstrebt) hat gern, wünscht, verschafft, erlangt, bezwingt, siegt, gewinnt', *vanúḥ* ' eifrig; Feind', *vanúḥ* ' verlangend, eifrig, anhänglich; Nachsteller, Feind', *vanuṣyáti* ' ist eifrig, greift an', with which may be compared directly Lat. *venus-tus* ' winning, winsome, charming, lovely', stem *wenus-, wenu-* as well as *wene-, wenos-* in Lat. *venus* ' love, loveliness; the highest throw at dice (winner?); Venus', Skt. *vánaḥ* ' Verlangen,

Lieblichkeit', *vaní-ḥ* 'Verlangen, Wunsch', *vanīyati* 'bettelt',
OHG *wini* Geliebter, Freund', *wunnia* 'Wonne', OE *wine* 'friend;
protector, lord', etc., with which compare Gr. ἄνακες ϝάνακες 'Castor
and Pollux', either as 'the friends, mates, Gemini' or as 'the
winners, victors, rulers', as the use of the word otherwise would
indicate: ϝάναξ, ἄναξ 'lord, master, of gods and sons of gods, of
heroes, of kings, of brothers, or sons of kings; master of the house,
dominus, herus; chief leader', ἄνασσα 'queen, lady, mistress', ἀνάσσω
'be lord, master, owner, rule, sway'. For the ablaut-grade compare Skt. *vanáti* (*vánati*) 'bezwingt, besiegt, gewinnt', OHG
*wonēn* 'bleiben, hausen, wohnen'.

13. ON *jóli,* Norw. dial. *jōl* 'Rohr, Stengel', pre-Germ. *ēul-
'hollow', Gr. αὐλή 'an open court before the house; any hall or
court; dwelling, abode, chamber', *aulā* 'opening, open spaces',
αὖλις 'a tent; a roost of birds', αὔλιον 'a cottage; a stable, fold; a
chamber, cave, grotto', αὐλός 'any hollow body, tube, pipe, groove,
flute', αὐλών 'a hollow way, defile, glen; canal, aqueduct, trench;
channel, strait; pipe, conduit', Lith. *avilȳs, aulȳs* 'gehöhlter Stock
für Bienen', *aũlas* 'Stiefelschaft', Pruss. *aulis* 'Schienbein',
OBulg. *uliji* 'alveus', etc. (cf. Persson Beiträge 540 f.) : Skt.
*valá-ḥ* 'Höhle', Lith. *volẽ* 'ein ausgehauenes Schöpfloch im Eise,
Wuhne', OHG *wuolen* 'wühlen', etc.

14. Gr. εὐρύς 'wide, broad, spacious, esp. of heaven, earth and
sea; far-reaching, far-spread', Skt. *uru-ḥ,* comp. *váriya-ḥ* 'weit,
geräumig, gross', *urum* 'das Weite, der freie Raum', *urvī* 'die
Erde', dual 'Erde und Himmel', *váraḥ* 'Weite, Breite, Raum',
*váruṇa-ḥ* 'ocean, water; Varuna', Gr. οὐρανός, Dor. ὠρανός
(*o-ϝορανος) 'heaven, sky', primarily 'expanse, open space', Lesb.
ὄρανος 'sky', *ϝορανος, OE *wǣr* 'sea', *ēar* 'sea; earth', base *ewer-
(*ēwe-r-). Compare *wā-r- 'spread out' in Lat. *vārus* 'bent,
stretcht, or grown apart, bent or stretcht outward; diverse, different', *varius* 'diverse, different; changing, various', OE *wōrian*
'wander'.

15. Norw. dial. *op* 'opening, hole, free space', NIcel. *op* 'opening, mouth', Faer. *opa* 'split up a skinned sheep', ON *opinn,*
OSwed. *opin, upin, ypin,* OFris. *open, epen,* OS *opan,* OHG *offan,*
OE *open* 'open; evident', pre-Germ. *ubono-, ubeno-,* OE *openian*
'open; become manifest; tr. open; disclose, manifest, discover',
MHG *offenen, öffnen* 'öffnen, eröffnen; offenbar machen, zeigen,

verständlich machen', MDu. *ope* 'mouthful, bite; kiss', *open* 'opening; open sea', OE *geyppan* 'make manifest, disclose, betray', *yppe* 'evident, known' (or these may belong to No 16), MLG *uppen* 'vorbringen, verlauten lassen, kundgeben, offenbaren; eine Sache von neuen wieder anfangen'.

These imply a pre-Germ. *\*ubo* by the side of *\*upo*. To a form with -*b*- as well as a -*p*- may be referred Goth. *iup* 'up, upward', *iupa* 'upward', *iupana* 'ἄνωθεν, again, anew', OE *ūp* 'above, up, upward', OHG *ūf* 'auf', etc. Compare Lat. *s-ub* (which may have original *b*, cf. Fick III, 31) 'under, below, beneath; immediately after, just after' (like NE thereupon, whereupon, upon this). Compare *\*ubo* in Gr. ὑβός 'humped, humpbacked', ὕβος 'hump on a camel', ὑβάζω 'stoop forward and vomit (throw up)', Suid., ὑβάλης· λάγνος Hesych., ὕβρις (uppishness, Üppigkeit) 'wanton violence, insolence; lust, lewdness; fermentation', ὑβρίζω 'wax wanton, run riot; of overfed horses and asses, neigh, bray and prance about; of plants, grow rank and luxuriant, üppig wachsen; outrage, maltreat, insult; beat and insult, ravish; maul', ὑβρίσθαι 'be mutilated, of eunuchs'. Compare the ablaut forms in OFris. *wapul* 'swamp, mire' (low place), OE *wapol* 'bubble, froth' (:ὑβάλης 'loose, lewd'), Lith. *vėbanas* 'leichtsinnig, leichtfertig', Goth. *wōpjam* 'cry, call; crow, of the cock' (ὑβρίζειν).

16. ON *ofn*, OE *ofen*, OHG *ovan* 'oven', pre-Germ. *\*úpno-* 'hole, hollow place' : Goth. *uf*; 'under', Gr. ὑπό 'under', ὕπτιος 'the under (parts of the body); laid back, supine; turned (upside) down; of land, sloping; of language, flat, tedious', Skt. *úpa* '(under), less than (acc.); (over), more than (loc.); up to, near to', *úpara-* 'the under, lower, later, nearer', etc. (: *ává* 'down, down from'), Icel. *ýfa* 'rip up; ripple, ruffle; tease', Av. *vī- vap-* 'veröden', Skt. *vápati* (pull off) 'schert, grast ab; (scatter out, spread) wirft, streut, sät', pp. *upta-, vapra-ḥ, -m* (a slope) 'Abhang, Ufer, Erdwall', *vāpī* (low place) 'ditch, trench', OBulg. *vapa* 'pool' (cf. Uhlenbeck Ai. Wb. 282).

17. Goth. *auhns*, ONorw. *ogn*, OSwed. *ugn* 'oven', Skt. *ukhá-ḥ, ukhā́* 'cooking-pot', Lat. *auxilla, aulla, ōlla* 'pot' probably imply the primary meaning 'hollow object'. A base *\*awāqh-* may be represented by Gr. αὐχή 'neck, throat, gullet; mountain-pass, defile; narrow sea, strait', ἀχήν (*ϝᾱχήν?) 'poor, needy' (empty), ἀχηνία

'need, want', ἠχάνω· πτωχεύω Suid., ἠχῆνες: κενοί, πτωχοί Hesych. Cf. No. 18.

18. Lat. *vaco* ' be empty, void, vacant; be without, lack, want; be free from labor, be idle, at leisure; have leisure or time for a thing '; *vacuus* ' empty, void, clear, free from, devoid of, wanting; at leisure, idle; single, unmarried; ownerless, vacant; open, public, accessible, of places; useless, unprofitable, vain', *vacuum* ' an empty space, an open or vacant place, a void, vacuity ', Umb. *vaçetum, uasetom* ' vacatum, vitiatum ', *uas* ' vitium ', Ir. *uain* (*ukni) ' Musse, Gelegenheit ' (cf. Walde with lit.) : Skt. ókaḥ ' Behagen, Gefallen, Wohnung, Zufluchtsort ', úcyati ' findet Gefallen an etwas, ist gewohnt ', etc.

19. ON *vǫk* ' hole or opening in the ice ', *vaka isinn* ' make a hole in the ice ', MLG *wake* ' open water in the ice, esp. a hole broken in the ice ', Du *wak* ' hole in the ice ', Gr. ἀγή ' a fragment, piece, splinter; (κύματος) the place where the waves break, beach; a curve, bending; a wound' ἄγνυμι ' break, shiver ', ἀγμός ' a breakage, fracture (of a bone); a broken cliff, crag ', ἰωγή (*ϝιϝωγη) ' shelter (from the north wind), windbreak ', κυματ-ωγή ' (wave-breaking), beach ', Ir. *fān* (*wagno-) ' abrupt, steep ' (cf. Franck Et. Wb. 771): Lat. *vāgīna* ' scabbard, sheath; hull, husk ', Lith. *vožti* ' etwas Hohles über etwas decken, stülpen ', Lett. *vāft* ' einen Deckel auflegen ', base * *wā-ǧ-* ' open; open place; be in the open, wander ': Lat. *vagus* ' rambling, roving, wandering ', *vagor* ' ramble, rove ', etc.

20. Base *aweg-* ' augere ' : Lat. *augēre* ' increase, enlarge; exalt, honor, enrich, bless; honor or worship by offerings; grow become greater ', *auctor* ' a begetter, father, ancestor; founder, builder; originator, author ', *auxilium* ' help, aid, support, succor; remedy , *auxilior* ' give aid, help; heal, cure ', Gr. ἀέξω, αὔξω ' increase, enlarge, foster, strengthen, glorify, magnify, exaggerate ', αὐξάνω ' make large, strengthen, exalt, extol, amplify; rear (a child); sacrifice (ἔμπυρα); pass. grow, increasing in size, number, strength, power; grow up, grow taller ', Skt. *vā́ja-ḥ* ' Opferspeise ', *vakṣayati* ' lässt wachsen ', *ójas-, ōjmán-* ' Kraft ', *ugrá-ḥ* ' gewaltig, gross, streng ', Lith. *áugti* ' gross werden, wachsen ', *auga* ' Wachstum ', *augìnti* ' erziehen, bes. von Kindern ', *áugyvė* ' die Gebärerin, Mutter ', *ūgys* ' Jahreswuches ' (Persson Beitr. 651), ON, NIcel. *auka* (pret. *jók, *ēuge*) ' augment, increase; join, piece (one thing

to another), add to', *auki* 'eking piece; addition, increase', *auk,* OE *ēac* 'in addition to, besides', *ēac* 'auch, also' ( : Skt. *ōja-* 'uneven, of a number' i. e. one added to an even number), *ēaca* 'increase, addition; usury', *ēacen* 'increased, enlarged; endowed; strong, mighty, vast, great; pregnant', *ēacnian* 'augment; conceive, be pregnant, be with child', OS *ōkan* 'pregnant', Goth. *aukan* 'sich mehren', *ana-aukan* 'hinzufügen; fortfahren', *wōkrs* 'τόκος, Zins', OE *wōcor* 'progeny, living creatures; usury, Wucher', *wacan* 'originate; be born', *wæcnan* 'be born; have origin', *weccan* 'cause', *weccend* 'instigator, auctor', MDu. *waken* 'be born', Du. *verwekken* 'bring forth, beget (children); cause'.

A synonymous *\*aweq-* or *awek-* occurs in Goth. *auhuma* 'higher', *auhumists* 'highest, chief', OE *ȳmest* 'higher, upper'.

21. Base *\*ēweǵ-, aweǵ-* 'vegere': Lat. *vegēre* 'move excite, quicken, arouse; be active, lively', Skt. *vā́ja-ḥ* 'Raschheit, Wettlauf, -kampf; Kampf, Kampfpreis, Beute, Gewinn, Lohn, Gut', *vājáyati, -yáti* 'läuft um die Wette, kämpft, eilt; spornt an, fördert', *vájra-* masc. and neut. 'Donnerkeil (Blitzstrahl); Diamant; ein best. Mörtel', Av. *vazra-* 'Haukeule', OE *wacor* 'watchful, vigilant', *wacol* 'awake, watchful, vigilant, attentive', *wacian* 'be awake, keep watch', *weccan* 'awake, arouse; refresh, encourage; stir up, move', Goth. *wakan* 'wachen; wachsam sein', *us-wakjan* 'erwecken', *wōkains* 'das wachen', etc. Cf. No. 20.

22. Compare also *\*aweǵh-* and *\*awegh-* in Lat. *veho,* Skt. *váhati* 'fährt, bewegt sich, weht, fliesst; zieht; verschafft, bringt dar; führt weg, raubt, führt heim, heiratet; trägt, erduldet, empfindet', part. *ūḍhá* 'geraubt; geheiratet; geäussert, entstanden', *ūḍhám* 'der Raub', *ūḍhá* 'Gattin', Lith. *vèžù* 'veho', *vagiù* 'steal', *vagìs* 'thief', etc. Here belong Skt. *ūhati* 'schiebt, schafft weiter, verändert', with *apa* 'fortstossen, verscheucht, entfernt', *ūha-ḥ* *ūhanam* 'Hinzufügung, Veränderung; Überlegung, Prüfung' (Erwägung), *ōhatē, ūhati* 'beachtet, begreift, setzt voraus, erschliesst', *vāhatē* 'drängt, drückt', etc. Cf. No. 3.

*The University of Chicago.*

# WHETHER AND IF

## By Walter Dallam Toy

### I

The purpose of this note is to compare the methods employed by a group of related languages or dialects in the statement of indirect questions other than those introduced by an indirect interrogative.

The languages considered are Greek, Latin, Gothic, O. H. G., O. E., modern German (Luther), modern English (King James).

The texts selected are taken from the four Gospels, since the passages quoted are with few exceptions found in the versions of all the languages in question.

Outside of the Gospels a few examples of indirect question occur in the N. T., but they are not considered here, since the material for comparison is not complete.

### II

The passages quoted are as follows:

#### Mat. 26, 63

Greek. ἵνα ἡμῖν εἴπῃς, εἰ σὺ εἶ ὁ Χρίστος.
Latin. ut dicas nobis si tu es Christus.
Gothic. lacking.
O. H. G. (Tatian). thaz du uns quedes oba thu sis Crist.
O. E. þæt ðu secge us gyf þu sy Crist Godes sunu.
Luther. —dass du uns sagest, ob Du seiest Christus.
King James. —that thou tell us whether thou be the Christ, the Son of God.

#### Mat. 27, 49

Greek. ἴδωμεν εἰ ἔρχεται Ἡλίας σώσων αὐτόν.
Latin. videamus an veniat Helias leberans eum.
Gothic. ei saihvam qimaiu Helias nasjan ina.
O. H. G. (Tatian). gisehemes oba come Helias losenti inan.
O. E. utun geseon hwæþer Helias cume, and wylle hyne alysan.
Luther. lass sehen, ob Elias komme, und ihm helfe.
King James. let us see whether Elias will come to save him.

## Mark 3, 2

Greek. καὶ παρετήρουν αὐτὸν εἰ τοῖς σάββασι θεραπεύσει αὐτόν.
Latin. Et obseruabant eum, si sabbatis curaret.
Gothic. jah witaidedun imma, hailidediu sabbato daga.
O. H. G. lacking.
O. E. And hi gymdon, hwæþer he on reste-dagum gehælde.
Luther. Und sie hieltun auf ihn, ob er auch am sabbath ihn heilen würde.
King James. And they watched him, whether he would heal etc.

## Mark 15, 44

Greek. ὁ δὲ Πιλᾶτος ἐθαύμασεν εἰ ἤδη τέθνηκε· καὶ προσκαλεσάμενος τὸν κεντυρίωνα, ἐπηρώτησεν αὐτὸν εἰ πάλαι ἀπέθανε.
Latin. Pilatus autem mirabatur si jam obisset. Et accersito centurione, interrogauit eum si jam mortuus esset.
Gothic. Iþ Peilatus sildaleikida ei is juþan gaswalt, jah athaitands þana hundafaþ frah ina juþan gadauþnodedi.
O. H. G. Pilatus wuntrota, oba her iu entoti, inti gihalotemo uualtambahte frageta inan oba her iu entoli.
O. E. Ða wundrode Pilatus gif he þa gyt forðferde—and hine ahsode hwæþer he dead wære.
Luther. Pilatus aber verwunderte sich, dass er schon todt war; und rief den Hauptmann, und fragte ihn, ob er längst gestorben wäre.
King James. And Pilate marvelled if he were already dead; and calling unto him the centurion, he asked him whether he had been any while dead.

## Luke 6, 7

Greek. παρετήρουν δὲ αὐτὸν οἱ γραμματεῖς καὶ οἱ φαρισαῖοι, εἰ ἐν τῳ σαββάτῳ θεραπεύσει.
Latin. Obseruabant autem scribae et Pharisaei, si sabbato curaret.
Gothic. Witaidedunuh þan þai bokarjos jah Fareisaieis, jau in sabbato daga leikinodedi.
O. H. G. In bihieltun tho thie scribara inti thie Pharisei, oba her in sambaztag heilti.
O. E. Ða gymdon þa boceras and Farisei hwæþer he on restedæge hælde.
Luther. Aber die Schriftgelehrten und Pharisäer hielten auf ihn, ob er auch heilen würde am Sabbath.

King James. And the scribes and Pharisees watched him, whether he would heal on the sabbath-day.

## LUKE 23, 6

Greek. Πιλᾶτος δὲ ἀκούσας Γαλιλαίαν ἐπηρώτησεν εἰ ὁ ἄνθρωπος Γαλιλαῖός ἐστι.
Latin. Pilatus autem audiens Galilaeam, interrogauit si homo Galilaeus esset.
Gothic. Lacking.
O. H. G. Pilatus gihorenti Galileam frageta oba ther man wari Galilaeus.
O. E. Ða Pilatus gehyrde Galileam, he ahsude hwæðer he wære Galileisc man.
Luther. Da aber Pilatus Galiläa hörete, fragte er ob er aus Galiläa wäre.
King James. When Pilate heard of Galilee, he asked whether the man were a Galilean.

## JOHN 7, 17

Greek. γνώσεται περὶ τῆς διδαχῆς, πότερον ἐκ τοῦ θεοῦ ἐστιν, ἢ ἐγὼ ἀπ' ἐμαυτοῦ λαλῶ.
Latin. ... cognoscet de doctrina, utrum ex Deo sit, an ego a me ipso loquor.
Gothic. ... ufkunnaiþ bi þo laisein framuh guda sijai, þau iku fram mis silbin rodja.
O. H. G. ... uorstentit uon leru, uuedar fon gote si odo ih fon mir selbomo spreche.
O. E. he gecnæwð be þære lare, hwæþer[1] heo si of Gode, hwæþer þe ic be me sylfum spece.
Luther. Der wird inne werden, ob diese Lehre von Gott sei, oder ob ich von mir selbst rede.
King James. ... he shall know of the doctrine, whether it be of God or whether I speak of myself.

---

[1] My colleague, Professor E. E. Ericson, has called my attention to the fact that the use of hwæðer-hwæðer þe is not so common in Old English as hwæðer-þe: Cynewulf's *Christ* 1306. 1332. 1553. *Guthlac* (Goodwin) 70, 17. *Blickling Homilies* 177, 19; or hwæþer-þe-þe: Ælfric's *Genesis* 42, 16. *Pastoral Care* 427, 31.

## JOHN 9, 25

Greek. εἰ ἁματωλός ἐστιν, οὐκ οἶδα.
Latin. Si peccator est, nescio.
Gothic. Jabai frawaurhts ist, ik ni wait.
O. H. G. oba her suntig ist, ni uueiz.
O. E. Gif he synful is, þæt ic nat.
Luther. Ist er ein Sünder, das weiss ich nicht.
King James. Whether he be a sinner or no, I know not.

### III

1) Greek. Of the 8 passages examined the Greek employs the conditional particle εἰ 7 times. For the disjunctive question, John 7, 17, it has πότερον ... ἤ. Model Greek and Latin prose have other methods of introducing indirect questions.

2) Latin uses *si* 6 times. *An* occurs once. For the disjunctive question it has *utrum ... an*. In classical Latin *si* is not common in indirect questions.

3) Gothic has only 6 passages recorded. Enclitic ... *u* occurs 3 times. In Mark 15, 44 *ei* is used, probably in imitation of the Greek εἰ; otherwise *ei* means *that, in order that*. For the disjunctive question we have ... *u ... þau ... u*. In John 9, 25 *jabai* is used in a purely conditional sense. Otherwise Ulfilas uses no conjunction in these questions.

4) O. H. G. One passage is lacking in Tatian. *Oba* occurs 6 times. For the disjunctive question we have *wedar ... odo oba*.
   Note. In Otfrid IV, 30, 27 *oba* occurs in a double sense, as *whether* in an indirect question, and as *if* in the protasis of a conditional sentence: Dua unsih uuis, oba thu unser kuning sis, so stig nidar, uuir giloubeN thir.

5) O. E. *Gyf (gif)* occurs 3 times; *hwæþer*, 5 times. Other methods possible in Old English are not used.

6) Luther has *ob* 7 times. In John 9, 25 there is an inverted clause, which might be either a conditional protasis or an indirect question.

7) King James has *whether* 7 times; *if*, once. Otherwise in modern English *if* is common. In John 9, 25 this version

[549]

has an indirect question while the others interpret the subordinate clause as a purely conditional protasis.

## IV

An inspection of this material shows that the Greek prefers the conditional particle εἰ; and Latin, *si*. Gothic does not use any conjunction at all.

In O. H. G. *oba* is the prevailing form and it is in its origin conditional, *if*.

Old English prefers *hwæþer*. Luther regularly writes *ob*, corresponding to the O. H. G. *oba*. King James prefers *whether*.

Both *whether* and *if* are historically warranted; if, as seems likely, the preference is in favor of *if*, we may infer that the basis of the construction was a conditional protasis, to which an apodosis was to be supplied from the governing verb.

*The University of North Carolina.*

PHONETIC DIFFERENTIATION IN ENGLISH

By J. M. Steadman, Jr.

I

English, like many other languages, possesses a number of meaningless phonetic variants. Different individual habits, speed of utterance, differences in sentence stress, analogy, dialect differences, and contamination of words lead to the creation of non-significant differences in form which correspond to no differences in meaning or in function.[1] Often when two pronunciations of the same word arise, only one of the variant pronunciations survives. But such is not always the case. Just as virtual synonyms often become sharply differentiated in meaning or in connotation, so two pronunciations, at first meaningless and interchangeable phonetic variants, come to be associated each with its distinct meaning. One word splits into two.[2]

Paul, in discussing the phenomenon of phonetic variation, says that it is common for a language to develop a superabundance of words, forms, and constructions of similar or identical meanings, but, he adds, "Language abhors luxury."[3] The inventor of new forms forgets for the moment or is ignorant of older parallel forms. But other persons, hearing one form from one person and another form from another, use both, either indiscriminately, or with differentiation in meaning. We cannot assume for a common language the coexistence of meaningless double forms. Simplification is unconscious and is due to the desire to avoid purposeless overloading of the memory.

One remedy for this excess of linguistic material is for one form, pronunciation, or construction to drive out all competitors. The individual, of course, chooses one form and continues to use it;

---

[1] See Edwin Sapir, *Language*, p. 105.

[2] See Maetzner, *Englische Grammatik* (Murray: London, 1874), I, 213-216, and Morris, *Historical Outlines*, p. 32.

[3] This paragraph and the next two summarize Paul's discussion, *Principien der Sprachgeschichte*, 272 ff., translation of H. A. Strong. As will be shown later, Paul's statement that language abhors luxury is too broad a generalization.

and the more often he uses this form, the more natural it is for him to continue using it.

Another positive remedy is to keep both forms and utilize this superfluity of material by a differentiation in meaning between the variant forms. The safest assumption is that the accidental creation of variant forms precedes the utilization of this difference for the purpose of showing a difference in meaning. This differentiation in meaning may be individual, dialect, or general.[4]

But, as Jespersen's discussion shows, it is unsafe to assume that differentiations in meaning are first made by the most subtle minds. Jespersen explains what I consider to be the chief cause of phonetic differentiation: the hearing of two pronunciations of a word in two different contexts and from two different people. Jespersen says:[5] "Linguistic 'splittings' or differentiations, whereby one word becomes two, may also be largely due to the transmission of the language to a new generation. The child may hear two pronunciations of the same word from different people, and then associate these with different ideas. Thus Paul Passy learnt the word *meule* in the sense of 'grindstone' from his father, and in the sense of 'haycock' from his mother; now the former in both senses pronounced [moel], and the latter in both [møl], and the child thus came to distinguish [moel] 'grindstone' and [møl] 'haycock.' (Ch. 23)

" Or the child may have learnt the word at two different periods of its life, associated with different spheres. This, I take it, may be the reason why some speakers make a distinction between two pronunciations of the word *medicine,* in two and in three syllables;

---

[4] Paul quotes Behagel (*Germania*, 23, 257): "In living language there is no such thing as a voluntary conscious differentiation of form for the purpose of differentiation of meaning." Bréal (*Essai de Sémantique*, p. 37 of Mrs. Henry Cust's translation) likewise stresses the fact that the creation of excess linguistic material precedes the differentiation. "Obviously it [differentiation] must first find a material in which to work. As it does not create, but only attaches itself to what is, in order to use it and perfect it, the terms to be differentiated must already exist in the language. . . . Distinctions are first made by a few minds that are more subtle than others: they then become the common property of all."

[5] *Language*, pp. 176-77.

they take [medsin] but study [medisin].⁶ . . . I do not doubt that a number of differentiations of words are to be ascribed to the transmission of the language to a new generation. Others may have arisen in the speech of adults, such as the distinction between *off* and *of* (at first the stressed and unstressed form of the same preposition), or between *thorough* and *through* . . . But complete differentiation is not established till some individuals from the very first conceive the forms as two independent words."

Though sentence stress, speed of utterance, spelling pronunciations, analogy, emotional exaggeration of important words in the sentence may all be factors in word splitting, the chief factors are hearing the two forms of the word in different contexts, or learning them at widely separated intervals from different persons.

II

Phonetic differentiation produces many doublets. This study, however, is concerned, not with doublets in general,⁷ but with a special, very definite type of doublet: *doublets arising within the English language itself*. Since the following types of doublets and related pairs of words are not due to any differentiation within the English language itself, they do not come within the scope of this study.

1. Borrowings from two different foreign languages. In such cases the two words have been distinct in English from their first appearance in the language. Examples are:

*Camera*⁸ (from Latin *camera*): *chamber* (from Fr. *chambre*).
*Legal* (fr. Latin *legalis*): *loyal* (fr. Fr. *loial*. G. & K.).

---

⁶ Jespersen gives some interesting examples of "how the child can itself split words." See also Nicklin, *The Sounds of Standard English*, p. 13 for differentiations made by adults.

⁷ For lists of doublets in English see Skeat, *Concise Etym. Dict.*, Appendix V; Morris, *Hist. Outlines*, p. 32; Maetzner, *Eng. Gram.*, I, 221 ff.; and especially Edward A. Allen, "English Doublets," *PMLA*, XXIII, 184-239.

⁸ Where no citation of authority is given, the information has been taken from the *New English Dictionary*. Other references cited are Sk., Skeat, *Concise Etym. Dict.*; Wk. Ernest Weekley, *An Etym. Dict. of Mod. Eng.*; C, the *Century Dictionary*; W, Webster's *New Internat Dict.*; and G. & K., Greenough and Kittredge, *Words and Their Ways in Eng. Speech*.

2. Borrowings from two foreign dialectal or other variant forms of the same foreign word. In such words the differentiation took place in the foreign language, and English borrowed both variants:

*Convey* (fr. O. N. F. *convei-er*) : *convoy* (fr. Fr. *convoy-er,* Central Fr. variant of *convei-er*).

*Vertex* (fr. Lat. *vertex*—Sk. and NED.) : *vortex* (Lat. variant of *vertex*—Sk. and NED.)

3. Successive English borrowings from the same foreign word, usually a Latin or a French word. In words of this class, the later borrowing was differentiated from its first appearance in the language and so was never interchangeable with the earlier borrowing. Such cases are exceptions to the principle stated by Paul, Behagel, and Bréal that the creation of excess linguistic material in the language always precedes the use of this material to express differences in meaning.[9] Examples are:

*Gállant* (fr. *galant* in 14th cent.) : *gallánt* (fr. the same Fr. word in the 17th cent.—G&K.)

*Gentle* (fr. Fr. *Gentil* by the 13th cent.) : *genteel* (fr. the same Fr. word at the end of the 16th cent. to express a different meaning from that of *gentle*.)

4. Variants with the same meaning. Some variants are different only in pronunciation or, more rarely, in spelling, with no differentiation in meaning. In such cases we have an excess of linguistic material that has been turned to no useful purpose in the language and that thus contradicts Paul's dictum that " language abhors luxury." In these words the difference in form corresponds to no difference in meaning or function. Examples are:

*gray: grey; neb: nib; jostle: justle;*[10] *jole: jowl; faze* (U. S.

---

[9] It is possible, however, that the pronunciations were at first interchangeable and that the differentiation was made later. But most of the later borrowings seem to have been introduced with a distinct meaning from the first appearance of the word. Many of the later borrowings are learned and literary.

[10] Some of these words are provincial. In general I have omitted pairs in which one of the words is obsolete, provincial, or highly technical; only the most significant examples are included in this discussion. Pairs in which one member is obsolete, provincial, or technical are: *cud* (dial. var. of *quid* [of tobacco] : *quid; shay* (U. S. dial. var. of *chaise*) : *chaise;*

variant of *feeze*): *feeze* (fr. O. E. *fesian* [?], 'drive,' 'frighten,' 'threaten,' worry ').

5. Pairs in which the differentiation is due to separate phonetic histories, to the operation of different phonetic laws. Such pairs as *bath: bathe* are only apparent, not real, doubtlets. At no stage of their development were the two forms meaningless or interchangeable variants of one and the same original word. Such Old English pairs as *baþ : baþian, cealf : cealfian*, etc. developed differently according to the position of the consonants þ, f, etc. Between vowels or between a vowel and a voiced consonant þ, s, f were voiced to ð, z, v. For this reason the nouns *bath, calf, glass, grass,* and *house* contain voiceless consonants, whereas the corresponding verbs *bathe, calve, glaze, graze,* and *house* contain the corresponding voiced consonants. The difference between the vowel sounds in some of these pairs is likewise due to the fact that the words in each pair have had separate phonetic histories.

6. Cognate words, such as O. E. *thrill* and Dutch *drill*; Scand. *egg* [verb] and English *edge*; Scand. *saga* and English *saw*; Dutch *spoor* and English *spur*.

7. Ablaut forms, such as *song, sung, fleet* and *float*.

These exclusions leave one narrowly defined type of doublets, the true phonetic variants, divergent forms of what was originally one and the same English word. The splitting or differentiation of this word into two took place within the English language itself.

### III

Many words which once had a single pronunciation developed one or more variant pronunciations. These variant pronunciations were, in all probability, accidental, or at least non-significant, alternate forms. But with some of the words in the course of time each pronunciation came to be associated with its distinct meaning, and the useless variations in speech were thus utilized by the speakers of the language and turned to a practical account. Such a utilization of originally interchangeable forms for the expression of a difference in meaning, in connotation, or in function illustrates the principle of economy in language.

*thrid* (dial. or poetic var. of *thread*): *thread*, 'to make one's way'; *roil: rile*.

Phonetic differentiation takes many forms. The following rough classification will, however, indicate the more important types of phonetic differentiation in the English language.

1. DIFFERENTIATION BY A CHANGE IN ACCENT. Greenough and Kittredge, in their discussion of doublets, say: "Our language often shows considerable diversity of usage in the pronunciation of the same word, especially with regard to accent. . . . Occasionally, the language has taken advantage of such diversity to make two words out of one by attaching different meanings to the different pronunciations." [11]

In the case of dissyllabic adjectives derived from Latin adjectives that were accented on the penult, there was, as late as the Elizabethan age, a variable accent according to the position of the adjective in the word-group or sentence. "As time went on, the accent became settled. In some instances however, both pronunciations were retained, each with its special set of meanings, and thus the single term split into two distinct words. *Húman* carries the literal sense of the Latin *humanus*: *humáne,* the other pronunciation, is specialized to the ethical meaning. *Antíque* is literal; *ántic,* simply another accentuation of the same word, means first 'fantastic' (as *old* things seem to the moderns), and then 'a fantastic caper'."

The following words illustrate the same kind of development:

*Divers: diverse* (fr. Fr. *divers,* fem. *diverse*). Both spellings are found in Middle English. The stess was originally on the last syllable, but the word was early naturalized. But, as in the case of many other words from French, both pronunciations long coexisted, especially in verse. When *dívers* was established as the regular prose form, especially in the sense of 'various,' 'sundry,' 'several,' in which the word was always plural, the final -*s* was treated like the final -*s* of plural nouns and came to be pronounced [z]. To-day *diverse* is always distinctly associated with *diversity* and no longer possesses the vague numerical sense of *divers*.

*Ínvalid: inválid. Inválid* (fr. Latin *invalidus*) appears in the early 17th century; *invalid,* as noun and adjective, is an 18th century modification of Latin *invalidus* after the French *invalide.* The

---

[11] *Op. cit.,* 354-56. I have taken several examples from this discussion: *chew, clench, conjure,* and *negro.*

early pronouncing dictionaries, e. g., Bailey's, 1727, give the pronunciation *inválid*. The word *invalid* thus appears to have been originally only a special sense of the adjective *inválid* (= 'not valid').

*Secret: secrete. Secret* (fr. Fr. *secret*) is from the 14th century; *secrete* is an 18th century alteration of the now obsolete verb *secret*.

*Urban: urbane* (fr. Latin *urbanus*). *Urbane* is the older form (16th century); *urban* first appears in the 17th century. The differentiation in spelling, pronunciation, and meaning is parallel to the development of *human* and *humane*.[12]

A second variety of differentiation through accent is seen in the distinction between the past participial use of *áged* (ag'd) and the adjective use of the same word, *ágèd*. At the beginning of the Modern English period the *e* of the preterit and the past participial ending *-ed* began to be dropped in pronunciation. During the 16th century and possibly even later, usage seems to have varied on this point. In some words or by some speakers (perhaps also in different positions in the sentence) the *-ed* was pronounced as a separate syllable, and in other words or by other speakers the *e* was not sounded. *Looked,* for example, was pronounced either [lóokèd] or [lookt]. The dropping of the *e* probably took place first in colloquial speech and then gradually spread into general use. To-day, of course, the *-ed* is pronounced as a separate syllable only with verbs whose stems end in a dental, or in poetry.[13] The following words illustrate the differentiation between the participial and the adjective use of *-ed: aged, beloved, blessed, cursed, learned, linked*.[14]

---

[12] See Jespersen, *Mod. Eng. Gram.*, I, 5.54, 5.75, for a discussion of *urbane* and other end-stressed words of recent introduction. A parallel development is seen in *ravin; ravine*, both from Fr. *ravine*. *Ravin* 'robbery,' 'rapine,' and *ravine,* 'gorge,' were once identical in meaning. The differentiation is later than the 15th century, when *ravine* meant 'violence,' 'force.'

[13] Suggested by Lounsbury, *History of the Eng. Lang.*, 359-60. See also Ripman, *Sounds of Spoken English*, 24.13.

[14] This verbal ending *-ed* is distinct in both origin and use from the ending *-ed* which is added to a noun to form an adjective meaning 'possessing, provided with, characterized by.' *The New Eng. Dictionary* treats these two suffixes separately. The adjective suffix is seen in such words as *bearded* (16th century), *crooked* (1225), *delighted* (meaning 'delightful'

Differentiation by accent is found most frequently in Modern English, however, as a means of distinguishing between the nominal and the verbal use of a word. In the case of native pairs consisting of a noun (or adjective) and the corresponding verb, the difference of accent has existed from the very beginning of the English language. In Old English, compounds consisting of a preposition and a noun (or adjective) had the accent on the first element of the compound, whereas compounds of preposition or adverb plus a verb had the accent on the last element.[15] The following are survivals of native nouns and verbs which are distinguished only by accent:

| Nouns | Verbs |
| --- | --- |
| fórecast | forecást |
| fóretaste | foretáste |
| úndercut | undercút |
| úndress (undréss in NED.) | undréss |

But, although such native pairs as *fórecast* and *forecást* are now rare, the long existence of such pairs has left its imprint upon the English speech habits. Most of the pairs of noun and verb now differentiated by accent are of Romance origin. The difference in accent in these borrowed pairs is due chiefly, I think, to analogy

---

in Shakespeare), *dogged* (14th century), and *winged*. This adjective suffix may have been a factor in the preservation of *ed* as a separate syllable in participles used as adjectives.

[15] See Jespersen, *Mod. Eng. Gram.*, I, 5.71, 5.72. The number of such native pairs in Modern English is very small. Instead of using a difference in accent to distinguish between noun and verb pairs Modern English has often substituted a borrowed word for the noun or verb or has developed new means of expression. This loss of any formal distinction between noun and verb is, of course, in line with the persistent tendency in the language to drop inflections and other formal signs of the parts of speech and to rely upon function and context to indicate the meaning and use of a word. In some cases a new noun is formed, however: the old nouns *foreshadow, gainsay, inflow*, listed by Jespersen, are now obsolete or archaic, *foreshadowing, gainsaying, a flowing in of* — being used instead. On the other hand, such verbs as *outcry, outleap, upcast, upstart* have been replaced by the increasingly popular verb-adverb combinations *cry out, leap out, cast up, and start up*, or by adverb and preposition, *start up* the stairs.

to native pairs like *fórecast* and *forecást*.¹⁶  Typical examples of words of Romance origin which are differentiated by accent are:

*Advocate* (from Lat. *advocatus* or M. Fr. *advocat*.—Sk.) first used as a noun; the verb was derived from the noun in the 17th century.

*Conduct* (fr. Lat. *conductus; conduyt(e)* [fr. Fr. *conduit*] appears in M. E. as an alternate spelling. But in the 16th century the Latin spelling *conduct(e)* was used for some meanings of the word, and *conduit* was specialized in other senses.

*Contract* (fr. Middle Fr. *contract*). The English noun was originally accented on the last syllable, but a later shift of accent differentiated the noun from the verb.

*Project* (fr. Mid. Fr. *project*, Fr. *projet*.—Sk.). In Shakespeare the verb was accented on the first syllable. The verb is apparently derived from the participial adjective *project* which is recorded earlier than the finite verb.¹⁷

2. DIFFERENTIATION BY ABBREVIATION. Many phonetic variants arise from the dropping of a syllable. These aphetic forms are due to carelessness, economy, speed of utterance, or sentence stress. Many of the variants thus arising are still freely interchangeable in meaning, or the two pronunciations represent merely the colloquial and the formal utterance of the same word. But

---

¹⁶ Jespersen, *op. cit.*, 5.73 ff. suggests other explanations, such as the position of the verb at the end of the sentence where it was not followed by a word that might cause a rhythmical forestress. See also Ripman, *op. cit.*, 51.2, 51.3, and Krapp, *The Pronunciation of Standard English in America*, p. 43.

¹⁷ The dialect verb *project*, as in "He is *prójecting* around," is derived from the verb *projéct* by a change in accent, or the noun has become a verb by functional change. The colloquial or dialectal nouns *invite* and *cómbine* also illustrate the differentiation by accent between the nominal and the verbal uses of the same word. Greenough and Kittredge, *op. cit.*, 356, discuss the splitting of the verb *conjúre* into two verbs: *cónjure*, 'to use charms or incantations,' and *conjúre*, 'to call upon one solemnly.' The noun *batten* and the noun *baton* are both derived from an original noun *baton, batoon*. *Batten*, 'a bar or strip or ledge of wood,' is a 17th century variant of this word. Other examples of similar differentiations are seen in *aggregate, alternate, content, converse, convict, digest, envelop(e), frequent, incense, minute, perfect, perfume, prelude, premise, presage, prostrate, purport, refuse, relay, retail*, etc.

in the following typical examples a difference in meaning, in connotation, or, less commonly, in function has been developed to correspond to the difference in form. The special peculiarity of this type of differentiation is that the long form and the clipped form of the word usually represent the same part of speech; that is, there is a difference in meaning between the two forms, but only rarely a difference in function.

Most of the clipped forms are due to the loss of an initial syllable, most commonly *a* or *e,* which on account of the weak sentence stress is pronounced [ə].[18] Examples of differentiation by abbreviation are:

*Abate: bate* (from the 14th century, 'lower, lessen in force').

*Accrue: crew* (possibly an aphetic form of *accrue*).

*Acute: cute* (listed in Bailey, 1731).

*Amend: mend.*

*Appall: pall,* 'lose color, lose force, satiate.'

*Apert,* 'open, evident': *pert* (from the 14th cent.), 'bold, impertinent.' During the 15th century a form with long vowel is found; this is probably the ancestor of the modern provincial [pjęrt], 'lively, saucy.'

*Astray: stray* (partly an aphetic form of *astray* and partly an adj. use of the noun *stray;* from the 17th century).

*Defence: fence* (from the 14th century in the sense 'defence'; now means 'barrier' or 'self-defence with the sword').

*Despite* (once a noun and a verb): *spite* (a 15th cent. aphetic form of *despite*).

*Display: splay,* 'dislocate.' The adj. use of *splay* arose in the 18th century. Cf. *splayfoot.*

*Disport* (now archaic as a noun): *sport* (from the 15th century).

---

[18] "Many words which had aphesis in the sixteenth and seventeenth century pronunciation now have the full forms through the influence of the spelling, and sometimes both forms have survived with differentiation in meaning." — Joseph and Elizabeth Wright, *Elem. Hist. New Eng. Gram.,* p. 90. Wright cites, among others, the following pairs: *live* (ai): *alive; lone; alone; venture: adventure; sample: ensample, example; fend: defend; special: especial; spy: espy; squire: esquire; strange: estrange; vie: envy.*

*Escheat: cheat* (probably an aphetic form of M. E. *achete*), Falstaff puns on the double meaning of *cheat:* (1) 'reversion of lands to the Crown,' (2) 'fraud, deceit.'

*Especially: specially.* See Fowler, *The King's English*, p. 11.

*Estate: state:* the two words are used indifferently in early English.—WK. Partly a variant of *estate.*—*NED.*

*Etiquette: ticket* (probably from *etiquette*. French *etiquette* meant 'note, label, etc. stuck on a post.'

*Madame: dame.*[19]

3. DIFFERENTIATION THROUGH A CHANGE IN CONSONANT SOUND. As explained above, such pairs as *bath: bathe; glass: glaze,* and (a) *house:* (to) *house* are the result of the divergent and distinct development of Old English final and medial consonants, the former being voiceless in Modern English, the latter voiced. This divergent development is due to different phonetic histories. *Bath* and *bathe* are not derived from the same original English word; the noun and the verb have always been pronounced differently. But on the basis of the pattern *bath*-noun: *bathe*-verb new pairs have been formed analogically by changing a noun to a verb or a verb to a noun. Speakers of the language have thus utilized the *bath: bathe* pattern as a model for other pairs. Both native and foreign words have been differentiated by a change in the consonant sound. Representative examples are:

*Close,* adj. and verb; *diffuse,* adj. and verb; *excuse,*[20] *grease; mouse, mouse* [mauz], the verb from the noun in the 13th century; *mouth, mouth* [mauð], the verb from the noun in the 14th century;

---

[19] Examples of the loss of syllables other than initial syllables are seen in *cab,* from *cabriolet,* which has been recently revived in full form as the name of an automobile body; *cad,* from *caddie, caddee,* a variant form of *cadet; mob,* from *mobile vulgus; ordnance,* var. of *ordinance,* used since the 17th century; *curtsy* from *courtesy; specialty,* from *speciality; tarnal* (dialect variant of *eternal; etarnal*), like *varsity* (from *university*) with the common pronunciation of *er* as *ar.*

[20] "The pronunciation with *s* instead of *z*, as in the verb, is due to the analogy of pairs of words like *use, abuse,* vbs. and sbs. *advise, advice,* etc., where the sb. was in O. F. masc., and ended in *s*."—*NED.* Note, however, that many of these nouns when used as verbs changed the voiceless consonant to the voiced equivalent on the analogy of native pairs like *bath: bathe.*

*rise* (noun with *s* or *z* sound), *rise* (verb with *z* sound), *sheath, sheathe* (the verb from the noun in the 15th century).

The divergent development of Old English consonants is in some cases dialectic: the word developed differently in the different dialects. In some cases the standard language has adopted the dialect form to express a meaning different from the meaning of the standard form of the word as in

*Fat* (Biblical, 'vessel'; cf. *winefat*): *vat* (the Southern and now standard variant).

*Lurch*, 'to shirk' (as of a dog in coursing) is a Midland or Southern form: *lurk,* originally meaning 'to shirk,' but now meaning 'to hide in ambush,' is a Northern variant of *lurch.*

*Hack,* 'framework, grating, feeding rack,' etc: *hatch,* 'lower half of a divided door, opening in a floor or deck.' *Hack* is a North. form.

A difference in function is sometimes indicated by a difference in the pronunciation of the consonant. Sentence stress results in strong and weak forms of the same original word: *off, of; too, to; than, then; that* (as a demonstrative pronounced [ðaet], as a relative [ðət].[21] Many speakers pronounce the verbs *have, used,* and *going* in two ways, giving them a strong form when the words are used as independent verbs, a weak form when they are used as auxiliaries. Compare "I have two books" and "I have to go." Some speakers also make a distinction between *why* as an adverb or conjunction [hwai] and *why* as in interjection [wai].[22]

---

[21] Sweet, *History of Language,* p. 26, comments on *that:* "This last is an instance of how language utilizes new distinctions of sound which are the result of mechanical causes—in this case of difference of stress—to express distinctions of meaning or grammatical function." For the two forms of *your* see Kenyon, *American Pronunciation,* p. 157 and p. 160, note 8.

[22] I have observed a few cases of individual, personal differentiations of this kind. One of my friends says that [grīsi] is a more refined pronunciation than [grīzi], the latter indicating a greater degree of greasiness! Another (probably because he heard the two pronunciations at different times from different speakers) pronounces *cordial* [kɔdiəl] when it means 'a beverage' and [kɔdʒəl] when it means 'hearty.' My unconscious and naturally acquired pronunciation of *humor* is without the *h,* but for one meaning of the word I pronounce the *h.* The first time I heard the phrase "the comedy of humours," the speaker pronounced the *h.*

4. DIFFERENTIATION THROUGH A CHANGE IN VOWEL OR IN VOWEL AND CONSONANT. The largest number of phonetic variants are due to a change in vowel or in both vowel and consonant. One class of variants is due to the divergent development of the same word in different local or class dialects. Some of these dialectal variants have been adopted by the standard speech; others are still illiterate, technical, or provincial.

The differentiation in the following group of words was probably due to divergent development in different dialects:

*Band: bond,* at first merely phonetic variants, like M. E. *land; lond; man: mon,* but now largely differentiated in sense, *bond* being used figuratively for moral or legal bonds, 'restraint' (senses in which *band* is now obsolete), and keeping more distinctly the connection with *bind, bound.*

*Chew: chaw.* "*Chaw* is a dialectic variety of *chew,* and does not appear in literature before the sixteenth century. For a time it was interchangeable with *chew* in dignified speech."—G&K, *op. cit.,* 354. Cf. also *chow,* Krapp, *Hist. of Eng. Lang. in Amer.,* I, 154.

*Clench: clinch.* "*Clench* and *clinch* are dialectic variations of the same word, and were formerly interchangeable. In present usage, however, there is a strong inclination to distinguish them. We '*clench* our fists,' but '*clinch* a bargain.'" G&K, 354.

*Dike: ditch.* Weekley derives both words from O. E. *dīc,* but the *NED.* says it is not clear how the Old English word gave both forms. Whatever the origin of the words may be, however, they were once interchangeable and have since been differentiated.

*Dent: dint,* dialectic variants; M. E. *dint, dynt, dent, dunt,* from O. E. *dynt,* 'blow, stroke.' To-day *dent* is specialized in the sense 'indentation, to make a dent.' Though *dint* is interchangeable with *dent* in most senses, it is the only form used in the expression "by dint of", where it has the now archaic meaning 'force, power.'

Learning the words in two different contexts and on widely separated occasions, I have unconsciously differentiated the two pronunciations, each being applied to its own distinct meaning. Some speakers make a similar distinction between "first version" [vɜsiən] and *version* (with z) in any other context.

*Hale: whole.* *Hale*,²³ the North. form of *whole*, was borrowed into the literary language in the sense 'robust.'

*Kale* (Nth. form): *cole*, 'any plant of the cabbage family.' *Cole* is also the botanical form.

*Negro: nigger.* "*Negro* and *nigger* are interesting examples of the tendency to utilize variant pronunciations for the increase of our vocabulary." Greenough and Kittredge, *op. cit.*, p. 356. The whole comment should be read.

*Pond: pound,* 'enclosure'; probably variants of O. E. *pund,* 'enclosure'; *pound* originally meant also 'an enclosed body of water.' *Pound* is still used for *pond* in some English dialects.

*Raid: road.* *Raid,* the Nth. form of O. E. *rād,* originally meant 'riding, a hostile incursion.' The word was revived by Scott and was subsequently adopted into general use.

*Ramp,* 'to rear, to be in rampant position': *romp,* 'play, sport,' but originally 'creep, crawl,' fr. Fr. *ramper.* *Ramp* is recorded from 1390; *romp* in the sense 'play' from 1709.

*Shade: shed: shad* (variant of *shade* in the sense 'shelter.') All from O. E. *sceadu,* M. E. *schade.*

*Shred: screed* ('strip of plaster,' 1315, 'strip of land,' 1615, 'border,' 1828). Dialect variants of O. E. *scrēad,* 'strip, fragment.'—Wk.

---

²³ The verbs *hale* and *haul* are from Fr. *haler.* The two words are only partly differentiated today. Popular speech has made some differentiations not accepted in standard speech. Miss Wright (*Rustic Speech and Folklore,* p. 19) says: "Fine shades of meaning are often expressed in the dialects by some slight variation in pronunciation. . . . For example, *drodge* and *drudge* both mean a person who works hard, but the difference is this: a *drudge* is always kept working by a superior, a *drodge* is always working because she cannot get forward with her work; the word *drodge* implies blame, and *drudge* none." Ida C. Ward (*The Phonetics of English,* p. 78) makes a similar observation on English dialects: "There are certain words in which many Northern [British] speakers use *a* or *ae*, which in the South are pronounced with [broad *a*]. . . . Certain words, however, do not follow this rule . . . and a few have two pronunciations with some speakers, indicating different meanings: e. g. *mass* **maes,** heap; **ma·s,** the religious service; *ass,* **aes,** the animal; and **a·s,** a term of friendly abuse." These dialectic forms are included here because they throw considerable light on the process of phonetic differentiation.

*Shrub: scrub* ('a low tree,' from 1398 on).

*Sleek: slick. Sleek* is a later variant of M. E. *slike; slick,* the earlier form, is now chiefly dialectal and U. S.

*Snob: snub.* The *NED* describes *snob* as of slang or obscure origin; Weekley says *snob* is an 18th century vulgarism derived from *snub.*

*Strap: strop.* The dialect form *strap* appears in the 17th century beside the original form *strop.* Later *strap* appears in all senses of *strop* and in many modern meanings it is now the usual form.

*Tamper: temper. Tamper* is probably an early (1573) dialectal or workman's pronunciation of *temper,* 'mix or moisten' [as clay], which later became established in the senses 'meddle with, alter.'

*Thrash,* 'flog, sail to windward in a lively sea': *thresh,* 'to beat out grain.' *Thresh* is the historically regular form, from M. E. *ðreschen, ðreshen,* O. E. *ðerscan,* 'beat, pound.' *Thrash* is a dialect variant that came into literary use near the end of the 16th century and became established in its modern meanings during the next century. Some speakers, however, do not pronounce the two words differently. (See Krapp, *Comprehensive Guide.*)[24]

The other words in this section admit of no logical classification. In a few of them (*corps: corpse; flour: flower, salon: saloon*) the differentiation in sound may be due to the variant spellings, but it is impossible to tell whether the differentiation in spelling or the differentiation in pronunciation came first. Some of the changes in pronunciation (possibly in *mode: mood, pass: pace, plat: plot*) may be due to contamination with words similar in sound and meaning. Some are colloquial differentiations. In all cases, however, the differentiation is marked by a change in vowel or in vowel and consonant:

*Alarm: alarum. Alarm* is from the 14th century (fr. Fr. *alarme*); *alarum* is a 16th century variant, formerly used in all senses of *alarm,* but now, except in poetry, restricted to the meanings 'the peal or chime of a warning bell or clock, the mechanism that produces it.'

[24] In some cases the technical pronunciation of a word differs from the general pronunciation; for example in military contexts *oblique* and *route* are pronounced [oblaik] and [ru:t], pronunciations which are rarer in general use than are [oblīk] and [raut]. For two pronunciations of *salve* see Krapp, *op. cit.*

*Arrant: errant.* Arrant is a variant of *errant*, 'wandering, vagrant,' which from its frequent use in connection with *thief* became an intensive with the meaning 'thorough, notorious, downright.' The old phrase 'thief errant' is common; "knight errant" is recorded as early as 1340. The vowel change is similar to the change seen in *university: varsity, arrand: errand, clerk, merchant: Clark, Marchant.*

*Born: borne.* Originally interchangeable. In the early 17th century *borne, born* and *bore* were all used as past participles. About 1660 *borne* was generally given up and *born* (occasionally *bore*) was used in all senses. Johnson lists only *bore* and *born* as past participles. But about 1775 *bore* ceased to be used as a past participle; *borne* was reinstated as the regular form; and *born* was specialized in the sense *natus*. In modern times the connection between *bear* and *born* is scarcely felt: *to be born* has virtually become an intransitive verb.

*Bilge: bulge.* The former is probably a corruption of the latter, which is from M. E. *bulge,* O. Fr. *boulge,* 'bag, a bulging.' *Bilge* in the sense 'bottom of a boat' is recorded in 1513; in the sense of "foulness collected in the hull" from 1829.

*Chirp: chirrup. Chirrup* is a later pronunciation with sharply trilled *r;* contaminated with *cheer up* and so expressing a more sprightly or cheery notion than *chirp.* Chiefly English slang.— *NED.* This explanation does not seem plausible. Cf. *alarm* above and the frequent development of a vowel between *r* and a consonant: *Hen(e)ry, p(e)rairie,* etc. I question the original association with *cheer up.*

*Cleanly: cleanly,* listed as two words in Webster, with different pronunciation. See Kenyon, *Amer. Pron.* Section 152.

*Corps: corpse. Corpse* was originally a variant spelling of *corps,* from M. E. *corse,* fr. Fr. *cors.* In the 14th century French *cors* was changed to the spelling *corps* after the Latin *corpus.* This new spelling was also introduced into English. By 1500 *corps,* which was originally interchangeable with *cors,* became prevalent, and *cors* was changed to *corse.* By 1500 the *p* of *corps* was pronounced. Thus *corpse,* which was at first a variant and rare spelling of *corps,* became the only form for the meaning 'dead body.' It is thus completely differentiated from *corps,* which is given the French pronunciation in military contexts.

*Daft: deft,* fr. O. E. *gedæfte,* 'fitting,' M. E. *dafte, defte,* both meaning 'meek, silly.' Webster suggests that *daft* got its present meaning through contamination with M. E. *daffe, daf,* 'fool, coward.'

*Flour: flower,* pronounced differently by some speakers (Ripman, *op. cit.* 38.2). *Flour* is a specialized sense of *flower,* 'flower of wheat.' The difference in spelling probably preceded the differentiation in pronunciation.

*Jet: jut. Jet,* from Fr. *jeter,* means 'to spout, spurt, send forth jets,' or 'to build out' [as a part of a house]. *Jut* is a phonetic variant meaning 'to project, to protrude.' Contrast *jut* out and *jets* of water.

*Jutty* and *jetty,* though spelled and pronounced differently, mean the same thing.

*Ma'am: madam. Ma'am, ma'm,* is a colloquial contradiction of *madam* and is now the unaccented form and the usual oral form; it is preferred as the common title of address. It also enters into compounds like *school- ma'am,* in which *madam* could not be used.

*Master: mister.* In ordinary use to-day *mister* is the oral form of *Mr. Mister* may have arisen as a weakened form of *master* on account of the proclitic use of the word. The usual written form remained *master* to the end of the 17th century. From that time the two words have been practically differentiated in form and function.

*Mood: mode. Mode,* fr. Fr. *mode,* Lat. *modus,* was the original form. Fr. *mode* developed the meaning 'fashion,' and this sense was adopted into English during the 17th century beside the earlier meanings 'measure, form,' etc. *Mood* is an altered form of *mode* and is due probably to association with *mood,* 'feeling,' which is from O. E. *mōd.*

*Parlous: perilous. Parlous* is a syncopated form of *perilous* with *er* pronounced *ar.* It is recorded from the 14th century on, but is now chiefly dialectic or archaic. Cf. *vermin* and *varmint, person: parson.*

*Pace: pass.* The noun *pace* is from M. E. *pace* Fr. *pas;* by the 16th century the verb *pace* was derived from the noun. *Pass* as a noun is the same word as *pace,* but its meaning has been changed by association with the verb *pass,* fr. Fr. *passer,* 'to advance.'

*Peck: pick,* variants of M. E. *picken; pick* is the earlier form.

*Parson: person,* M. E. *persone, parson, person,* O. Fr. and A. F. *persone, parson(e).* *Person* in the sense of 'parson' is found as early as 1250. The words are now completely differentiated.

*Plat,* 'plan, outline': *plot,* 'piece of ground.' *Plat* (recorded from the 16th century) is a variant of plot and has been contaminated with *plat,* 'flat.'

*Saloon: salon,* both from Fr. *salon.* *Salon* has retained a narrower meaning, whereas *saloon* has been greatly extended in meaning, especially in the United States.

*Sham: shame.* *Sham* is "probably" late 17th century slang for *shame.*—Wk. "not impossible."—*NED.*

*Travel: travail,* pronounced alike by many speakers, but given different pronunciations in the *NED,* which calls *travel* " originally the same word as *travail.*"

*Triumph: trump.* *Trump* is a variant of *triumph,* due, possibly, to confusion with *trump,* 'to deceive.'—*Cent. Dict.* Shakespeare plays on the double meaning of *triumph.*—Wk. *Triumph,* fr. O. Fr. *triumphe,* fr. *triomphe; trump,* "corruption of triumph." —*NED.*

*Troth: truth,* from O. E. *trēōwð.* The *Cent. Dict.* derives the words from different M. E. words. But Wk., Sk., and *NED.* regard the words as variants of the same M. E. word: *treuðe, trouðe.*

*Whit: wight.* "Both descended from the Anglo-Saxon *wiht,* though they have become differentiated in the period that intervenes between the Anglo-Saxon times and the present day." Greenough and Kittredge, *op. cit.,* 346. The *Cent. Dict.* suggests that the difference in the initial consonant may be due to a difference in emphasis. Cf. *why* with *hw* and *w* pronunciations and the strong and weak forms (*hw: w*) of *which, what,* etc. Why the vowel varies in length is not explained. The *NED* states that *whit* is "apparently an alteration of *wight.*"[25]

*Emory University.*

---

[25] Krapp, *Comprehensive Guide,* cites the following words that have two pronunciations each specialized in meaning: *ensign, irony, patent, piazza, rigor, route.* In addition to some of the words I have discussed above, Krapp discusses the pairs *fount: font, resin: rosin, sac: sack, slack: slake, Sir: sire,* and *broach: brooch.*

# FRENCH *gnaf*, SCOTTISH *nyaff*

## By Urban T. Holmes, Jr.

The standard dictionaries[1] which record Scottish dialect words list a word *nyaff* with many variant spellings and derivatives: *nyaff, gnaff, naff, nyaffet, nyaffle, neaphle, njafək, njafin, nyauchle, neffit, nyeffit,* in which the sense hesitates between "a small or stunted object, thread ends which project, a dwarf, a talkative person, or a diminutive and conceited chatterer," when used as a noun; the same forms as verbs mean rather "to yelp, to bark, to snap, to eat in a gluttonous manner."[2] This last occurs as *nyaffle* in an isolated text. It becomes obvious from the cross references in Wright's dialect dictionary, and from the *NED*, that authorities consider these forms as variants of another series, *gnap, nyap,* "to bite, to talk affectedly, hungry," also of *gnip, nip* "to bite" and possibly of *snap, nap*. Wright gives a single occurrence of a present participle *gnafeen* "chopping." Jamieson considers "protruding thread ends, that which protrudes" as the primary meaning and postulates an Islandic etymon *gnaf-er, prominet, gnoef nasus prominens;* q. "any small object that juts out."

So far as I have been able to discover no Anglicist has ever connected this Scottish word, and its numerous variants, with another group of words of very similar form occurring primarily in the northern and eastern dialects of France, as well as in Switzerland.[3] These forms are *gnaf, niaffe, gniafe, gnafe, gnafre* meaning

---

[1] I refer to such references as *The English Dialect Dictionary* of Wright, John Jamieson's *An Etymological Dictionary of the Scottish Language* (Paisley, 1879), David Donaldson's *Supplement to Jamieson's Scottish Dictionary* (Paisley, 1887), and the *NED*. The manuscript material for the Modern Scots Dictionary which is being directed by William Grant of Aberdeen has not been available to me. Sir William Craigie writes that the word is not as old as 1700 and does not occur, therefore, in his *Middle Scots Lexicon* (still unpublished).

[2] Perhaps the meaning "to bark, to yelp" is due to confusion with *yap*, an echo word which ordinarily has no connection with either *gnap* or *nyaff*. We do not need to assume this, as we shall show.

[3] Also in Swiss-Romance; see *Ce fas tu?*, IV, 4: "e lu si vedĭ quant che gnûfs barbars (todescs par la plui gran part) . . ." In this passage the reference is to "crude barbarians, Germans for the most part" who invaded Friulia. This reference was given to me by my friend Dr. Aloys Nikl of the Oriental Institute, University of Chicago.

"a petty shoemaker, a bad shoemaker, a bungler, a blockhead, a coarse man." We also find *gniafre* (the exact phonetic equivalent of Scottish *nyaffle*) meaning "a glutton, a guzzler," and in addition, in Lyons, *gniaffron* "the glutton in a puppet show," and in Provençal *gnaflá* "to guzzle." There is a Picard *gnafrée* "much food in a heap," and such adjectives as *gnoufe* "a man of limited intelligence" and *gnife* "rusé."[4] A careful examination of the meanings shows basic resemblance between the French and Scottish series. Apparently the idea of "biting, guzzling, working the mouth steadily and rapidly" is common to both. The "thread ends" and the concept of "dwarf, that which is stunted, trifling" can both be explained as extensions of the sense "bitten off." How familiar we are with such current slang expressions as "little bit" for a diminutive person or "sawed-off," or "chewed off" runt. To explain the concept of "a petty shoemaker, a repair shoemaker" (in contrast to one who actually manufactures shoes) requires more subtlety. Many trades have a special significance in European folklore. We have only to read Alphonse Daudet's *Le Curé de Cucugnan* to realize that the miller is, because of his trade, a gay devil. Proverbs and tale motifs, to illustrate this characterization, abound. In many folktales, particularly Irish, the tailor has the ability to deal with fairies and recognize a changeling. The shoemaker, on the contrary, is proverbially a man of limited intelligence. "Schuster bleib bei deinem Leisten" is doubtless older than Frederick the Great; the story by which we commonly explain it was made to illustrate an earlier saying. A *Schusterarbeit* in modern German is "patchwork, work ill done";[5] and in Scotland and England that word of mysterious

---

[4] The French forms are cited by A. C. Thorn in the *Archiv f. d. St. d. neueren Spr. u. Lit.*, new series XXIX (1912), 130-132, and by Lazare Sainéan in *Le Langage Parisien au XIXe Siècle* (Paris, 1920), 197, and in numerous dialect dictionaries. The *ALF* records *gnaf* once as an epithet for the *cordonnier*. *Carte* 326, no. 284 (in Pas-de-Calais).

[5] The English etymologists are in doubt over the origins of *shyster* "a roguish lawyer." Some have proposed a doubtful connection with *shy*. I have not yet encountered the suggestion that *shyster* might be an anglicized slang form of German *Schuster* (*Schuester* in Switzerland and Bavaria) which the Grimm's in their monumental *Wörterbuch* attest with the meaning "rogue." "Sie hat ihm den Schuster gegeben" means "You have given him the slip."

eighteenth century origin *snab, snob,* which once meant a cobbler, has now taken on a special sense of criticism and ridicule.[6] If the cobbler in France were conceived of as " an idle talker, a blow-hard, one who works his jaws and says nothing " it is possible to understand how he would win this epithet of *gnaf*. On the other hand the idea of repair shoemaker, and not manufacturing shoemaker, occurs so prominently in the spread of the word that we might agree with A. C. Thorn and the *Dictionnaire Général* in the belief that *gnaf* is connected in some way with the shoemaker's repair thread. Perhaps his constant biting of the thread may be responsible for the epithet of *gnaf*. A repair tailor is sometimes called a *gnaf du drap*.[7]

Sir William Craigie assures me that Scottish *nyaff* did not come into use till some time after seventeen hundred. The exact date has not been determined. The earliest example recorded by Jamieson dates as late as 1866. French *gnaf* is not found in print before the *Dictionnaire du Bas Langage* (1808) of Hautel, although Wilfrid Challemel claims that it was common in 1691.[8] The presence of *gnaf* in the New Orleans dialect of French [9] would lead me to believe that the word was current in the first half of the eighteenth century, when New Orleans received most of her colonization. As both the Scottish and the French forms are slang and do not go back far into history we must examine their phonology in that light. Sainéan has indicated that a characteristic of slang and child speech, in French, is the alternation of the vowels *i-a-o* (or *ou*) as we find in *gnife, gnafe, gnoufe*. In the same way an alternation of final *p-v-f* is possible. We could expect a \**gnap*, \**gnav, gnaf*.[10] In both the Scottish and the French forms which we are considering initial *gn-* alternates with *ny-*. Does this

---

[6] Could this word, first attested by the *NED* for the eighteenth century, be a folk derivative of the series *Schnabel, schnaben, snaven, snavel, snap?* These forms are so common in German, Dutch, and Flemish. Such a suggestion would parallel the facts in our discussion of *gnaf*.

[7] L. Rigaud, *Dictionnaire de l'Argot Moderne* (Paris: Ollendorff, 1881).

[8] *Tailleurs et cordonniers de Domfront, 1691* (Flers-de-l'Orne, 1909), p. 10, note 1.

[9] This information was given me by Dr. Aloys Nikl, who heard the word in use there.

[10] *Les Sources Indigènes de l'Etymologie française* (Paris: Boccard), I, 394-399.

mean that the *gn-* in *gnaf* should be pronounced as a palatal
*n* or that it is a stage in phonetic development before the
arrival at palatal *n*? I have heard only the pronunciation with a
palatal *n* in both Scottish and French, but it is not impossible that
the *g* was once pronounced hard in *gnaf*. Both the Scottish and
the French dictionaries show that such a *gn-* usually is derived
from a German *kn-*. I have an example in Dutch *knicker* becoming
*gniko* (beside *kaniko*) in modern Provençal; the corresponding
results given for Picard and Wallon are *knek, knik* (beside *kenek*
and *kinik*).[11] Note that in these French dialects the intercalated
*e* is not unavoidable as A. C. Thorn believed in discarding such an
etymon as *knabe*.[12] Ernst Tappolet has shown that in German
words taken into Swiss French, *kn-* becomes *gn-* or simply *n-*; e. g.
*knöpfli > gnèfle*.[13]

I have cited the suggestions already offered to explain the origin
of Scottish *nyaff*. I have also mentioned for the French *gnaf* such
suggested etyma as *knabe* and imitation from the snap of the shoemaker's thread. Other etymologists have brought forth English
*knave* and the Latin *ignavus* in their search for a solution. As I
believe that the Scottish and the French forms have a common
origin, somewhere in their history, I am making another suggestion. The meaning of the common etymon must have been that
of " snap, bite, move the jaws rapidly, chew the rag (Amer.)" and
thence " bitten off, stunted, talkative, chatterer, a biter of threads,
threads thus bitten, a patching shoemaker, a dolt, a glutton."
There exists in both Low and High German a term *knappen, knap-
fen, gnapfen* which according to the Grimms, Kluge, and others,
has the meanings " *wackeln, schnalzen, klatschen, von kurzen Be-
wegungen schnappen, kurz zufahrend beissen, essen, hurtig zugrei-
fen.*" As the Grimms say, the word is " ganz heimisch " in Dutch,
and I should suppose the same to be true for Flemish. This Germanic word could have entered the underground road of French
slang, like so many other Germanic words, through Switzerland,
Lorraine, and the Low Countries; we should expect to find it most
common, therefore, in Picardy and down the eastern border of

---

[11] *REW* no. 4722.

[12] *Op. cit.*, 132.

[13] *Alemanischen Lehnwörter in d. Mund. d. Franz. Schweiz* (Basel, 1916),
90.

France, including eastern Provençal territory. It is precisely in these districts that our form *gnaf* is most frequent, although it has spread farther, as far as Paris. It is quite possible that the Scots borrowed the term independently from the Low Countries; but we know that the Scots borrowed many dialect words from France during the period 1100-1800 and a large number were borrowed as late as the eighteenth century. Sir William Craigie once remarked that he thought the number of these borrowed words unduly exaggerated; but a count which I undertook myself some five years ago, when I went carefully through Jamieson's *Dictionary* and certain minor Scottish word lists, noting all words whose French provenance could scarcely be doubted, yielded me approximately 1289 words of this class. If we estimate about twenty thousand Scottish dialect words in all it is evident that Sir William Craigie is correct in his criticism, but these thousand odd French words are there nonetheless, and they are common words: such as *ashet* < *assiette, giggot* < *gigot, tassie* < *tasse,* etc. It is not impossible that the forms in *-f*: *nyaff, gnaf* (if not those in *-p*: *gnap, gnip*) were brought from France, perhaps before the term was used so commonly to denote a shoemaker in northern France.

And now a few words about a compound of *gnaf, gnoufe,* namely *pignouf,* which is common in French slang for " an apprentice shoemaker, a rustic, a booby." Sainéan believes this to be a compound of *pignou* (Swiss) " rag-picker " and *gnoufe* " simple." [14] There is a slang use of *pigeon* which is very old and very common, that of ' dupe, gull." We know many such crossings as *Alboche* from *Allemand* plus *Boche,* and *sagrolle* from *sabot* plus *grole,* which are in colloquial use.[15] Why is *pignouf* not a crossing of *pigeon* and *gnoufe?*

*The University of North Carolina.*

---

[14] *Le Langage Parisien,* 198.
[15] *Ibid.,* 112. Also *Les Sources Indigènes,* etc., II, 337.

# ON WULFSTAN'S SCANDINAVIA

## By Kemp Malone

King Alfred the Great includes in his *Orosius* an account of a voyage which a certain Wulfstan made from Hæthum to Truso (i. e. from Schleswig to East Prussia). The passage in Wulfstan's account which I wish to discuss reads as follows:

Wulfstan sæde þæt he gefóre of Hæðum, . . . Weonoðland him wæs on steorbord, and on bæcbord him wæs Langaland, and Lǽland, and Falster, and Scóneg; and þas land eall hyrað to Denemearcan. And þonne Burgendaland wæs us on bæcbord, and þa habbað him sylf cyning. Þonne æfter Burgendalande wæron ús þas land, þa synd hatene ærest Blecinga-ég, and Meore, and Eowland, and Gotland on bæcbord; and þas land hyrað to Sweon.[1]

In this passage Wulfstan gives us a number of place-names not without interest from various points of view. I will take a few of them up for discussion. The name *Hæðum* is the first place-name we meet here. It occurs also in the last passage of the narrative of Ohthere, a narrative which immediately precedes the account of Wulfstan's voyage. Ohthere uses the name twice. First he tells us that he sailed to a port called *æt Hæþum* 'at the heaths.' Then he speaks of passing certain districts before he came *to Hæþum* 'to the heaths.' And Wulfstan says that he went *of Hæðum* 'from the heaths.' Evidently the name of the port must appear in the dat. pl., and if the construction of the sentence does not call for a dative, then the preposition *æt* is used to throw the name of the port into the requisite dative form. This peculiarity is not the only thing of interest about the name. If we turn to other records, we find that the oldest Danish record of the name reads *Haiþabu*,[2] i. e. 'heath town.' Ethelwerd in his *Chronicles* records the name as *Haythaby*,[3] i. e. he tries to give it in its Danish form. Not so Alfred, who uses a form obviously English and apparently ancient. One may indeed suppose that *Hæðum* is a translation from the Danish, but the highly idiomatic use of prepositions and dat. pl.

---

[1] *King Alfred's Orosius*, ed. H. Sweet, EETS 79 (London, 1883), 19 f.

[2] P. G. Thorsen, *De Danske Runemindesmærker*, I (Copenhagen, 1864), 139 ff.

[3] *Mon. Hist. Brit.* I (London, 1848), 502.

has no counterpart in Danish usage, and the translation theory seems hardly tenable.

Wulfstan next gives the names of three Danish islands: Langaland, Lǽland and Falster. The last of these names appears in Anglian rather than West Saxon form, and this peculiarity may indicate that Wulfstan was an Angle. The -eg of the names Scóneg and Blecinga-ég points in the same direction. Professor Sir William Craigie has argued on other grounds that Wulfstan was an Angle,[4] and the Anglian characteristics of the names cited tend to confirm his theory.

The name Lǽland answers to Danish Laaland. Here as in Hæðum we seem to have an ancient English name-form, although, alternatively, Wulfstan may be supposed to have observed that Scandinavian á usually answers to English ǽ (thus, ON mál = OE mǽl 'meal') and, in accordance with this correspondence, to have englished Láland by changing it to Lǽland. The second alternative strikes me as distinctly the less plausible, and I am inclined to believe that Lǽland is a name which the English brought with them when they migrated to England and which they held fast to through the centuries. If so, Wulfstan here used a West Saxon, not an Anglian form, unless we suppose that his scribe, or some later copyist, turned the name into good West Saxon.

I have already mentioned the second element of the name Scóneg. The ó of the first element is not easy to account for. We obviously have to do with ON Skáney or Skánøy, a name which Wulfstan did not try to anglicize, so far as its first element was concerned, but simply took over as it stood. Our name thus ought to be *Scáneg, and I am strongly inclined to think that this was in fact the reading of the Lauderdale MS. The present passage, however, has come down to us in the Cotton MS only, and this MS dates from the middle of the eleventh century.[5] By that time OE á was already beginning to become ME ǭ, and this phonetic change may well have had its effect on the copying of the Cotton scribe. If *Scáneg was a living name for the scribe (and, as we shall see, there is good reason to think it was), the vowel of its first syllable might be expected to become ǭ in his pronun-

---

[4] Journal of English and Germanic Philology, XXIV (1925), 396 ff.
[5] C. Plummer, Two of the Saxon Chronicles Parallel, II (Oxford, 1899), xxxi.

ciation along with OE *á* in general.⁶ Traditional spelling held our scribe in general to *a*, in spite of his pronunciation, but tradition would hardly have had much weight in the case of a proper name taken from the Scandinavian.⁷

*Blecinga-ég* is an English formation which must be taken to mean 'coastland of the Blecings,' the first element of the name being interpreted as a gen. pl. The long mark in the MS over the *e* of *-eg* proves that the scribe at least had in mind the English word *ég*, not a phonetic transcription of ON *-ey*. In Scandinavia, moreover, so far as I know, the element *-ey* was not added to the name *Bleking*, which regularly stood alone. The *-e-* of *Blecinga-* is not original, but goes back to the ON diphthong *ei*, which in the latter part of the tenth century underwent smoothing in Danish and Swedish territory.⁸ The smoothed vowel recorded in the Cotton MS thus cannot have originated with Wulfstan, and presumably would not have appeared in the Lauderdale MS if this part of that MS had survived to us. The spelling with *-e-* is best attributed to the Cotton scribe, who no doubt got his up-to-date pronunciation from contemporary Danish speakers, and corrected accordingly the manuscript which he was copying.⁹

The spelling *Meore* belongs to a different category. Here we are dealing, not with a Scandinavian but with an English change (purely orthographical, it is true). At the beginning of the eleventh century the OE diphthong *eo* underwent smoothing, and became a monophthong with the value [ö].¹⁰ From A. D. 1000 or thereabouts, then, *eo* was a suitable spelling with which to rep-

⁶ For the chronology of this sound-change, see K. Luick, *Hist. Gram. der engl. Sprache* (Leipzig, 1914—), I, 363 (§ 369, Anm. 9). There are indications that this change began *circa* 1000. Thus, we find OE *sácerd* 'priest' spelt *socerd* in the *Letter of Alexander* (ed. S. Rypins, p. 41, l. 9). See also *sole* (for *sále*) in *Beowulf* 302.

⁷ For other attempts at explaining the *ó* of *Scóneg*, see A. Kock, *Arkiv för nordisk Filologi* XXXIV (1918), 74 and E. Björkman, *Namn och Bygd* VI (1918), 168, note 2.

⁸ A. Noreen, *Geschichte der nord. Sprachen*³ (Strassburg, 1913), p. 137.

⁹ It is possible, of course, that Wulfstan used a native English form of this name. If so, it probably took the form *Blácinga-* or (with umlaut) *Blǽcinga-*. In such case one would have to suppose that the Cotton scribe substituted the Scandinavian for the English vowel when he came to copy this proper name.

¹⁰ Luick, *op. cit.*, I, 336 (§ 357, Anm. 7).

resent in English the stem vowel of Swedish *Möre*. The form *Meore* of the Cotton MS obviously reflects eleventh-century, not ninth-century conditions. The Lauderdale spelling for this name was doubtless either \**Mére* (West Saxon) or \**Moere*; the latter spelling would represent equally well the Scandinavian pronunciation or a dialectal (Anglian) Old-English pronunciation. Had the term been (or become) a living English word, its eleventh-century form would have been \**Mére* in any case, and one would have expected this spelling in the Cotton MS. The Cotton scribe, however, knew the name as the Scandinavians of his day pronounced it, and he spelt it accordingly. It seems unlikely that an English as distinct from a Scandinavian pronunciation of the provincial name was current in eleventh-century England.

Wulfstan's name-form *Eowland* wants phonetic correspondence, in its first element, with the cognate ON *Eyland*, *Øyland*. The first syllable of the ON forms goes back to a primitive \**aujō-* which in English developed into the familiar words *ég* (Anglian) and *ieg, ig* (West Saxon). Wulfstan's *Eow-* therefore cannot be a native English development of \**aujō-*. It can no better be explained as an imitation of ON *ey-* or *øy-*.[11] If we interpret the *eo* of *Eowland* as we interpreted that of *Meore*, we can say that the *eo* of the Cotton MS reflects an Old Danish *Øland*, but this would involve the assumption that the Cotton scribe's Danish was exceedingly up-to-date,[12] and even so the *-w-* of the OE form would remain without an explanation. It therefore seems advisable to seek a solution by attacking the problem from a different angle. If we start with the primitive nom. sg. \**awi*[13] instead of the oblique case-stem \**aujō-* we reach, through regular phonetic stages, an OE \**Eweland*, which would then undergo syncope of the middle vowel[14] and by way of \**Ewland* would end up as *Eowland* (cf. *meowle* 'maiden'). I take it, therefore, that out of the nom. sg. \**awi* developed an i-stem \**awi-* which existed (in English, at least) alongside the jō-stem \**aujō-* and survived in the proper name

---

[11] Cf. E. Björkman, *Scandinavian Loan Words in Middle English*, Part I (*Studien zur engl. Philologie*, ed. L. Morsbach, vol. VII), pp. 63 ff.

[12] According to Noreen, *loc. cit.*, the sound-shift $øy > ø$ took place in Danish "probably about 1050."

[13] Noreen, *op. cit.*, p. 165.

[14] Luick, *op. cit.*, I, 283 (§ 305).

*Eowland.* Wulfstan's *Eowland* thus seems to be the native English name of the island. As a name it is supported by the tribal name *Eowum* (dat. pl.) of *Widsith* 26. This name, in its English form, is obviously based on the *Eow-* of *Eowland*. The Tacitean form *Aviones* (i. e. *Aujōnes*) goes rather with the *Ey-* of ON *Eyland*. The tribe of *Widsith* 26 has long been connected with the *Aviones* of Tacitus,[15] but its localization in Eowland was thought to be inconsistent with the Tacitean account, the general assumption being that Tacitus named the tribes of the Nerthus amphictyony in a fixed geographical order, proceeding from the south. In an earlier study I made a vigorous but only partially successful attempt to get away from this old mistake.[16] It now seems to me self-evident that *Eowland* was the home of the *Eowan*. Everyone agrees that the *Eowan* were islanders, and *Eowland* by virtue of its name is obviously the proper island for them to live in. So long as the English form of the name of the island could be regarded as an attempt to indicate the pronunciation of ON *Eyland*, one might well hesitate to connect it with so ancient a name-form as the *Eowum* of *Widsith*. But Wulfstan's *Eowland* in fact cannot be explained from any Scandinavian form, while it can be explained as a native development. *Eowland* is therefore as old as *Eowum* in the English language, and the two names can only with violence be separated.

Summing things up, we find that the proper names attributed to Wulfstan in our passage fall into two distinct groups. On the one hand we have a number of names, definitely English in form, and some of them, at least, hardly explicable as anglicized loan-words. On the other hand are *Scóneg, Blecingaég* and *Meore*. The first two of these have an English second element, but otherwise all three are essentially Scandinavian in form, and must be classified as loan-words. Moreover, these three words appear in what must be called Middle-English rather than Old-English form. The *ó* of *Scóneg* and the *eo* = *ö* of *Meore* are highly characteristic of the Middle-English period, while the *-e-* of *Blecinga-*, though it reflects a foreign sound-shift, belongs to the same period. We may conclude that the Cotton scribe, though usually faithful to his original, did not hesitate to improve upon it (or bring it up to

---

[15] See R. W. Chambers, *Widsith* (Cambridge, 1912), pp. 73, 197.
[16] *Literary History of Hamlet*, I (Heidelberg, 1923), 4 ff.

date) when for any reason he thought such a thing desirable. More specifically, in dealing with Scandinavian place-names which, in the eleventh century, had no well-established English forms he might change the spelling of his original in order to bring the names into conformity with the Scandinavian pronunciation then current (*Blecinga, Meore*). Moreover, in place-names his own pronunciation now and then won expression in the spelling, quite apart from his nordicizing tendencies (*Denemearcan, Scóneg, Sweon*). This is not the place to present an extensive study of the spelling of proper names in the Cotton MS, but our gleanings from a single short passage indicate that such a study might well be worth the making.

*The Johns Hopkins University.*

# A NOTE ON SAINTS' LEGENDS

## By George R. Coffman

In the matter of historical continuity and literary tradition and of imitation and adaptation of material, saints' legends offer an interesting and significant field for study. They have been widely and zealously collected through the ages. This task, however, was first carried on by churchmen for immediate liturgical ends; then because of the intrinsic interest and value of some of the legends, they became an accepted genre in the field of mediaeval literature; later, in the hands of the Bollandists,[1] who combined a pious and a scientific purpose in their attempt to sift the authentic from the bizarre and the meretricious in the vast body of the materials, the work assumed gigantic proportions; and finally modern hagiographers and other scholars have made valuable contributions to the study of saints' legends in various aspects. But the enriching of the stories of their lives, the impulse to create new legends or traditions, the conventionalized nature of some of the martyrdoms, the imitation or adaptation of miracles or miraculous events all still offer a fertile field for study. Such possible study ranges from literary evaluation to analysis and synthesis, for those interested in the significance and continuity of literary forms.[2]

---

[1] See Hippolyte Delehaye, *L'Oeuvre des Bollandistes, 1615-1916* (*à travers trois siècles*) (Brussels, 1920), translated, *The Work of the Bollandists Through Three Centuries* (Princeton, 1922), *passim*.

[2] The following are a few of the representative studies in this field and illustrate typical approaches to the materials. For a general survey by one of the Bollandists, with an analysis of methods and an exposition of some of the critical problems involved, see Hippolyte Delehaye, *Les Légendes Hagiographiques* (Brussels, 1906); translated by Mrs. V. M. Crawford, *The Legends of the Saints: An Introduction to Hagiography* (Longman, Green & Co., 1907). For a consideration of the cult of the saints from the point of view of origins, see Ernst Lucius, *Die Anfänge des Heiligenkults in der christlichen Kirche* (Tübingen, 1904). For a comprehensive classification and discussion of motifs and types, see Peter Toldo, "Das Leben und die Wunder der Heiligen im Mittelalter," *Zeitschrift für Vergleichende Litteraturgeschichte* (Berlin, 1901), vol. XIV, pp. 267-288; and *Studien zur Vergleichenden Litteraturgeschichte* (Berlin, 1901-1909), vol. I, pp. 320-353; vol. II, pp. 87-103, 304-353; vol. IV,

Though more specialized in range and appeal than are ballads or other types of popular stories whose sources and analogues have been traced from the extreme Orient to the limit of the Occident, they are just as essentially of the folk. This, in fact, is their basis. They arose out of the sufferings of a cult which developed in opposition to established religion, government, and society and which later became the dominant force in Western civilization. Their validity for over a thousand years consisted in the universal acceptance of them as the authentic records of the lives, martyrdoms, and miracles of the leaders of the Christian Church. And their vitality resided in the fact that the saints themselves were accepted as the official, divine intercessors for the human race. These legends are, then, the literary record of the cult of the saints. This brief paper is not the place for an extended historical resumé of that cult. A statement which I have made in another connection suffices here: [3]

> The beginnings of the cult of the saints are to be sought in the cult of the martyrs. To possess the crown of martyrdom was for this epoch of faith the desire of the most simple and enthusiastic of men. They wished

pp. 48-83; vol. V, pp. 337-353; vol. VI, pp. 289-333; vol. VIII, pp. 18-74; vol. IX, pp. 451-460. Toldo's point of view is indicated in the opening sentence of his first article (*Zeitschrift*, etc., p. 266): "Diese Untersuchungen sollen zwei verschiedene Zwecke erfüllen: eine wissenschaftliche Einteilung der Wunder der Heiligen im Mittelalter und das allgemeine Studium der Beziehungen dieser Wunder zu der Bibel und den religiösen, dem Christentum vorangehenden Mythen." A related work, much more accessible for the average student, is Heinrich Günter's *Die Christliche Legende des Abendlandes* (Heidelberg, 1910). A sentence from his "Vorwort" expresses well the significance of such studies (p. v): "Wenn die Legende ein Stück vom mittelalterlichen Menschen ist, muss sie auch das Leben mitbestimmt eingegriffen haben; die kulturgeschichtliche Bedeutung der Legende reicht über Kunst, Dichtung und Reise weit hinaus." For the subject matter of saints' legends considered as folklore, see Stith Thompson's forthcoming bibliography, *Motif-Index of Folk-Literature: A Classification of narrative elements in Folk-Tales, Ballads, Myths, Fables, Mediaeval Romances, Exempla, Fabliaux, Jest-Books, and Local Legends*. Folklore Fellows Communications, No. 98 ff. (Helsingfors, 1932———). Section V, of his classification under the letters of the alphabet, has to do with Religion and includes saints' materials.

[3] *A New Theory Concerning the Origin of the Miracle Play* (1914), pp. 25-27.

to live again in Christ. And the wishes of large numbers were gratified through the persecutions of the early emperors. The martyrdom of these heroes made a profound impression upon the faithful; and they could not forget them. Moreover, the leaders proposed them for models. Soon the faithful each year celebrated the anniversaries of martyrs and rejoiced in their happy birth in Christ. No churches were yet raised to them on or near their tombs, which the faithful visited only on the day of the anniversary. That represents a later development. But the cult was born; the people prayed for the martyrs and bore them oblations for the safety of their souls.

Then with the popular movement into the church during the third century the cult increased and the bishops counseled the believers to note exactly the anniversary of martyrs. Calendars were drawn up to keep a record of those who died in the faith. Each large community preserved such a calendar of martyrs. The next step was the transformation of the Christian religion. The new converts came to regard these martyrs as divine intercessors before God and Christ. In its turn arose the conception that martyrdom gave to the one who endured it a supernatural virtue. After that, everything which the martyr had touched became a precious talisman for the faithful. Thus came into existence the cult of the relics.

It was at this period that the doctrine of Christ penetrated more and more into the Occident, and that evangelization progressed rapidly but superficially. It was necessary that the converts find in the Christian sanctuary that which paganism had given them: protection from the destructive forces in nature and the support of the Divinity in their times of trouble. The popular conception of martyrs gave these converts the assurance of such divine intermediators as they had found in their gods. The crowds flocked to the suburban cemeteries of Rome to celebrate the anniversaries of Christian heroes at their tombs and to implore their aid. So great did these crowds become that churches were erected beside the cemeteries to accommodate them. " In the liturgies, prayers for the saints were now displaced by invocations for their intercessions. In this the people found a compensation for the loss of hero, genius, and *manes* worship."

But the cult of the martyrs is only the first step toward the cult of the saints. In the fourth century, with the triumph of the Church, martyrdom became rare. Soon there were added to the cult, ascetic monks, who passed their lives in continued internal struggle. These came to be known through the ascetic literature of the fourth century. After this there came to be included as saints, bishops of exemplary life—men who had rendered themselves dear to the people by their almsgiving and other acts of helpfulness. Miracles proved their supernatural power. Thus all these —martyrs, ascetics, and holy confessors—came early to form the cult of the saints. And by the Merovingian epoch there was a fixed popular conception concerning them. At the celestial court they surrounded the thrones of God and Christ, discussing before them the demands of mortals and pleading their cause. They spoke without ceasing in favor of the inhabitants where their cult was honored and prayed God to spare the faithful who addressed prayers and presented gifts to them. It was the saints who watched over men, guided and counseled them.

My purpose in this *Note* is to offer from the literature of the cult of the martyrs a single illustration of some of the varied themes for study indicated in the opening paragraphs above.

It is a well known fact that Matthew Paris in his lives of the Abbots of St. Albans tells of a miracle play of St. Catherine of Alexandria which was presented at Dunstable, England, about the year 1100 by a certain Geoffrey, who later became abbot of St. Albans.[4] The play is lost. Matthew Paris gives the only record of its presentation. On the basis of what we know concerning the subject matter of early saints' plays and concerning the legends of St. Catherine, the theme of the play was almost certainly her martyrdom. According to the tradition she was put to death A. D. 310. Her legend, the essence of which is her martyrdom, runs as follows:[5]

St. Catherine, a Christian girl of eighteen, learned in philosophy beyond the scholars of her day, lived in Alexandria at the time of the Emperor Maximinus. During his reign he sent out an edict that all his subjects should appear with sacrifices and worship the god of their country. St. Catherine, from her house, heard the noise outside of people coming to worship; aroused she hastened to the Emperor, and boldly spoke against his gods in behalf of the true God. He was unable to argue against her successfully, but had her imprisoned, and sent out another edict ordering the wisest men of the land to appear and defend the religion of his gods. On the day appointed they came. But as a result of a dramatic debate, in which Catherine quoted in her defense passages from Homer, Plato, and the Sibyl, prophesying the birth of Christ, she overcame them all, and persuaded them, fifty in number, to accept her belief. The emperor, enraged, ordered them burnt to death at once. On the evening of the same day some of the pious who went out to collect the remains of the martyrs found the bodies sound and whole, not a hair consumed. Then Maximinus tried to win Catherine over by flattery and promises; but since he was unsuccessful in this, he ordered her flogged and thrown into prison again. Soon Augusta, his wife, heard of this defender of Christianity, and through the assistance of Porphyrius, the general of the army, visited her

---

[4] *Vitae Abbatum St. Albani* (London, 1684), p. 1007.

[5] See *Patrologia Graecia*, CXVI, col. 275-302. (Latin translation by Surius). Cf. also Mombritius, *Sanctuarium seu Vitae Sanctorum* (Paris, 1910), I, 283-287; and *Aurea Legenda* (ed. Dr. Th. Graesse, 1890), pp. 789-797: For this summary see *A New Theory, op. cit.*, pp. 76-77.

in prison one night. As a result, the Empress, Porphyrius, and the soldiers were converted. After some time the Emperor had St. Catherine brought before him again. When despite his command she refused to renounce faith in the true God, at the suggestion of a prefect, he ordered made, as an instrument of torture, a four-wheeled car with each wheel having nails pointing outward, and threw her in front of this. It passed over her without doing any harm, for an angel protected her; but it killed many infidels standing near. Just at this time the Empress ran out from the palace, ordered the council dismissed, and the persecution stopped. The Emperor did stop long enough to have his wife put under the most brutal and fiendish tortures, and then beheaded. Upon a protest from Porphyrius because of this atrocious deed, he had him and his soldiers put to death also. Finally, on November 25th St. Catherine was beheaded. At the execution, milk instead of blood flowed from her body. Angels carried her remains to Mt. Sinai.

It is also well known that about one hundred and fifty years before the time of the St. Catherine play, in Gandersheim, Germany, a nun, Hrotswitha, to offset the fascination and charm of Terence, wrote in imitation of him, as she says, six legends of miracles and martyrdoms in the form of dialogues. *Sapientia,* the last of these six is of immediate interest to us. The situation of the so-called play is conveniently presented in summary by Dr. Coulter:[6]

> The scene of *Sapientia* is laid in Rome in the time of Hadrian, but the principal characters (Wisdom and her three daughters, Faith, Hope, and Charity) are allegorical, and the philosophical element so predominates that there is little of the dramatic left. Sapientia and the three maidens are examined before the emperor; and Sapientia, in giving the ages of the three children . . . , goes through an elaborate discourse on number, based on the *Institutio Arithmetica* of Boëthius. Hadrian orders them all to worship the gods of Rome and, on their refusal, puts them into custody; later, he bids Fides sacrifice to Diana and, when she remains steadfast, has her flogged and burned; Spes meets with a similar fate; Karitas is told merely to say "Magna Diana" but refuses to do even this. She is thrown into a fiery furnace, where, although the flames are so intense that they kill 5000 men, she is seen walking about uninjured, with three shining

---

[6] Cornelia C. Coulter, "The 'Terentian' Comedies of a Tenth-Century Nun", *The Classical Journal*, XXIV, p. 526. For Hrotswitha's works see Paul de Winterfeld, *Scriptores Rerum Germanicarum Hrotsvithae Opera* (Berlin, 1902); K. Strecker, *Hrotsvithae Opera* (Leipzig, 1906). For Hrotswitha in relation to her period, see my article "A New Approach to Mediaeval Latin Drama", *Modern Philology*, XXII, pp. 238-271; esp. pp. 256-264.

ones beside her. She is then beheaded, and Sapientia and other maidens take the three bodies and bury them at the third milestone from the city. Sapientia offers a long prayer and then dies.

Incidentally, these two legends have an intrinsic interest for all students of mediaeval drama and mediaeval culture. But my fundamental reason for selecting them is their integral relationship to one another, as I shall now proceed to show. The summaries just given indicate kinship of theme and treatment in the wisdom of St. Catherine and Sapientia and in the tortures which the martyrs have to undergo. But the striking quality of the conventionalized pattern, some details of which are undoubtedly authentic from the period of martyrdom, is best shown by a parallel summary of similarities:

| *St. Catherine* | *Sapientia* |
|---|---|
| 1. On her first appearance before Maximinus, she confuses him by her arguments against his gods and in favor of the one true God. | 1. Sapientia confuses Hadrian by posing a mathematical problem the solution of which gives the ages of her three daughters. Then she turns the discussion to the "sapientia Factoris", who "omnia in numero et mensura et pondore posuit." |
| 2. St. Catherine asserts herself of noble birth. | 2. Sapientia says she is descended from princes. |
| 3. She is imprisoned to appear later for real argument when the fifty wise men will be present. | 3. Sapientia and daughters imprisoned for three days to consider the matter. |
| 4. Roman prefect suggests device of torture—spiked wheels—to be used on St. Catherine. | 4. Antioch—villian—suggests various diabolical tortures for Hadrian to use on Fides, Spes, and Caritas. |
| 5. Tortures and martyrdom:<br>a.) Wise men burned to death; hair and flesh not marred;<br>b.) Augusta, Empress, has breasts cut off; subjected to further torture beheaded;<br>c.) Porphyrius and his soldiers beheaded;<br>d.) St. Catherine flogged, thrown in front of car (unhurt); (ultimately beheaded). | 5. Tortures and martyrdom:<br>a.) Fides' breasts cut off (milk instead of blood flows); thrown into boiling pitch; unhurt; beheaded;<br>b.) Spes, suspended and flayed until her flesh is in shreds; thrown into boiling pitch, (unhurt); beheaded;<br>c.) Caritas thrown into a furnace that has been heated three days and nights (unhurt); three men in white seen with her; beheaded. |

| St. Catherine | Sapientia |
|---|---|
| 6. Emperor offers to make Catherine his wife. | 6. Emperor Hadrian offers to take Spes as his daughter if she will honor and worship Diana. |
| 7. Miraculous destruction of pagans: Car made to torture St. Catherine broken by the angel of the Lord. Many spectators killed. Some versions have number indefinite; others give different numbers—as many as four thousand. | 7. Miraculous destruction of pagans: <br> a.) Vat into which Spes is thrown bursts and destroys Roman ministers; <br> b.) Furnace into which Caritas is thrown explodes and kills five thousand spectators; |
| 8. Angel protects St. Catherine but destroys car. | 8. Three men in white are present with Caritas in furnace as she composes praises to the Lord. |
| 9. Milk instead of blood flows when St. Catherine is beheaded. | 9. Same phenomenon occurs in the case of Fides when her breasts are cut off. |

Though the study suggested by these legends and by a comparison of them may include a consideration of sources and influences in the conventional sense of those words, it really transcends them. It includes in its range the literary fashion of the martyr's cult, first popularized by Prudentius (348-405) in his *Songs of the Martyrs' Crown* (ΠΕΡΙΣΤΕΦΑΝΩΝ), especially the passion of St. Eulalia (Hymn No. 3) and of St. Agnes (Hymn No. 14);[7] the themes of the learned maidens and the virgins as a part of the legends of martyrdom; the relation of authentic and pseudo-authentic stories of martyrdom to the essence of tragedy and tragic romance as literary genre; and the place of such themes in the life of a people who placed their trust in the efficacy of saints. But that which is of immediate interest for us is the dominance of literary tradition as evidenced in the analogous or identical character of the patterns and details of these two legends.

*University of North Carolina.*

---

[7] Manitius (*Geschichte der Lateinischen Literatur des Mittelalters*, Erster Teil, 1911, p. 627) states that Hrotswitha selected from the Peristephanon of Prudentius, the tortures she employed. An examination of the fourteen epic-lyric hymns reveals that in such an event she was not imitating, but creating largely from suggestions received.

# IRISH COSTUME IN LAWMAN

## By J. S. P. Tatlock

If the peoples of Britain and their descendants possess an ancient national epic, it is the earliest English poem on King Arthur and King Lear; and when this has been made more intelligible and accessible than it is now, it may be regarded as not utterly unworthy of such an imposing position; all this in spite of Freeman's Saxon fanaticism.[1] It is high time therefore to rid it of stumbling-blocks as to nomenclature. For the poet's name there are three defensible forms, Laȝamon, Lagamon, and Laweman or Lawman. To the first there are objections on grounds of convenience and pronunciation, to the second on the ground of excessive archaism. Convenience and analogy alike favor *Lawman*. Further, there was no justification for renaming the poem *Brut;* its oldest title is *Hystoria Brutonum*.[2]

The poet was not learned or bookish. He owed little to reading except in that volume which lay open before him while he wrote, Wace's *Roman de Brut*. The immense vitality of his poem is due to his vigorous and racy wording, his visual and dramatic imagination, his enthusiastic hair-trigger emotions, his charming and singularly un-English temperament; and also to his wide experience of the more primitive parts of his world. He was no gentle old priest sitting by his fireside on a highroad to Wales and picking up Celtic tradition from benighted travelers. What I have in mind at the moment is certain concrete evidence of a close knowledge of Ireland and of what had been happening there during the generation before 1200 or a little earlier, when he was writing. It suffices to remember that while mutual knowledge and intercourse between Britain and Ireland had existed time out of mind, extensive relations began with the Norman-English expeditions of 1169-71 and 1185. Irish matters appear at various points in the poem, but especially at and after the raid on Ireland by Uther, and at its

---

[1] *Norman Conquest*, V (1876), 584-94. He preferred the honest English of that sacred poet, Orm (or, shall we say, that Soliloquizer in a Spanish Cloister). How much had he read of either?

[2] I use of course Sir Frederic Madden's *Laȝamons Brut* (London, 1847), an admirable edition for its day; references later are to volume and page.

subjugation by Arthur. The essentials and more or less of the detail in each episode are in his original, and even in Wace's original, Geoffrey of Monmouth. We are concerned of course only with such of the detail as was not. About this we have a substantial certainty. While Leroux de Lincy's edition of the *Roman de Brut* leaves much to be desired, his text and notes allow us to state that this or that was not in Lawman's source; this I say after an extensive examination of all known MSS of it but two, and also on the word of the chief living authority on Wace. With unsparing actuality and no friendliness, and of course with no appreciation of Irish culture, Lawman shows among other matters just how the Irish were clothed and equipped.

At their first appearance his eye is on their sordid dress. In Wace (3321 ff.) the first settlers of Ireland under Pantalous have suffered hardships on their voyage of a year and a half from their home in Spain, but prosper after their arrival. Lawman (I, 267-8) on their arrival at the end of seven years irrelevantly adds grotesque details about the state of their clothes,—

>Heore claðes weoren iwerede,
>and vuele heo weoren igærede.
>nakede heo weoren,
>and naðing ne rohten
>wha heore leomen sæʒe,
>alle þe on heom weoren;
>& þus heo ladden heore laʒen,
>and longe heo ilæsten.

These customs long continued, says he. The tatters and rags which travelers in Ireland have commented on for many a day [3] are given a highly respectable history; the Irish are ragged because their forefathers' clothes wore out,—in very truth, *Patres comederunt uvam acerbam, et dentes filiorum obstupescunt*. It is a fair conjecture that Lawman did not invent this, but is retailing a current excuse. At any rate, the poverty-stricken look of Ireland antedates the hated Saxon.

---

[3] *E. g.*, in a French poem on the deposition of Richard II, in the appendix to J. A. Buchon's edition of Froissart's *Chroniques*, in *Collection des Chroniques*, XXIII (Paris, 1826), p. 326:
>En Yrlande, où gens vys laide et orde,
>L'un deschiré, l'autre chaint d'une corde.

Cf. Gerald de Barri, *Top. Hib.*, iii, 10.

He is more interested in their accoutrements in war. When
Uther invades Ireland to carry off gigantic stones for his memorial
at Stonehenge,

>  þa Irisce weoren bare,
>  & Bruttes iburnede.   (II, 303)

Wace merely says the Irish were ill-armed, and unaccustomed to
the combat (8317-8),—a remark ignorant enough. The Irish
presently pursue the Britons into Wales:

>  þer isah Gillomar
>  Whar him com Vther,
>  & hæhde his cnihtes
>  to wepne forð rihtes.
>  & heo to biliue,
>  & gripen heore cniues,
>  & of mid here breches,
>  seolcuðe weoren heore leches;
>  & igripen an heore hond
>  heore speren longe;
>  hengen an heore æxle
>  mucle wi-æxe.   (II, 332)
>
>  and þa Irisce weoren nakede.   (II, 333)

None of this, except the fact of a battle, is in Wace (8558 ff.).
When Arthur invades Ireland,

>  Arðures men weoren
>  mid wepnen al bi-þehte,
>  þa Irisce men weoren
>  nakede neh þan,
>  mid speren & mid axen,
>  & mid swiðe scærpe sæxen.
>  Arðures men letten fleon
>  vnimete flan,
>  and merden Irisc folc,
>  & hit swiðe ualden.
>  ne mæhten heo iþolien
>  þurh nanes cunnes þingen,
>  ah flu3en awai s[w]iðe
>  swiðe uæle þusend.   (II, 514-5)

In Wace, 9916 ff., the Irish are "trop nu," without armor, and
unacquainted with bows and arrows, but their weapons are not
mentioned.

[589]

In spite of the difficulties in making clean-cut statements about early Ireland, the direct knowledge shown here, abundant and significant, is verified by many later authorities. It is verified especially by the earliest foreign describer of the country, Gerald de Barri, Lawman's contemporary, who was there with Prince John in 1185-6; and also by a later Englishman who had spent years in Ireland, Henry Cristede, who in 1395 gave Froissart a vivid and highly diverting account of his observations there. First, Lawman shows the Irish as fighting only with spears, battle-axes and knives. The battle-axe was the characteristic weapon of the Irish, whether borrowed from the Norse, as Gerald says, or not, as is Joyce's opinion. It is repeatedly mentioned by Gerald as the weapon of the foot-soldiers, and was carried by the Irish even in peace, he says,[4] as a staff, which accounts for it in the hands of the trousered figures in two thirteenth-century pictures given by Joyce.[5] It would naturally be hung over the shoulder, as the poet says, when the hands were otherwise engaged. Axes, javelins and darts appear in the "Song of Dermot and the Earl" (about 1225)[6], and long darts in the poem already cited on the deposition of Richard II.[7] Knives or daggers appear often enough, mentioned by Sullivan, and also by Cristede; — "coutiauls agus devant, à largue alumelle à deux taillans à la manière de darde."[8] Further, in Monstrelet's pathetic account of the Irish auxiliaries of Henry V at the siege of Rouen in 1418, they have merely little javelins and "gros couteaulx d'estrange façon," no saddles for their horses, scanty clothes and no armor but targets, so that they were at the mercy of the French.[9]

That in war, as Monstrelet says, the Irish wore little or no armor, and were lightly dressed, is a familiar fact, touched by Wace but

---

[4] *Topographia Hibernica*, iii, 10; *Expugnatio Hibernica*, i, 4, 21 and 41, ii, 13, 39 (*Gir. Cambrensis Opera*, Rolls Series, 1861-91, vol. V); also Eugene O'Curry, *Manners and Customs of the Ancient Irish* (London, 1873), and W. K. Sullivan's Introduction, I, ccccxlix ff.; II, 348 ff.

[5] P. W. Joyce, *Social Hist. of Anc. Ireland* (London, 1903), I, 123, II, 208, and cf. I, 118 ff., 107 ff.

[6] Ed. G. H. Orpen (Oxford, 1892), ll. 2428, 2444-7, 3197.

[7] Buchon, *Collection*, XXIII, 330, 335.

[8] Froissart, *Chroniques* (ed. K. de Lettenhove), XV, 169; Sullivan in O'Curry, *Manners and Customs*, I, ccccxxxviii.

[9] *Chronique* (Soc. de l'Hist. de France), III, 284-5.

enlarged on by Lawman. A generation before the conquest, Geoffrey of Monmouth at Arthur's invasion (ix, 10) calls them "gens nuda et inermis." According to Gerald de Barri they fought "nudi et inermes."[10] In *Dermot and the Earl* they are "nues," wear neither "haubers ne bruines."[11] Their "nakedness" in war and peace is constantly spoken of by later writers.[12] They are mentioned by Saxo Grammaticus, not far from 1200, as using "leui et parabili armatura."[13] Even chiefs wore little defensive armor before the tenth century, and though they may have acquired some use of it from the Norse, they continued on the whole to disregard it out of gallant bravado. At the time of the English invasion they wore no metallic armor, and nothing over their linen tunics; an Irish poet contrasts the Irish chiefs in linen shirts with the English in iron at a battle near Down in 1260.[14] They maintained later than the rest of Europe the ideality of heroic poetry; we remember Beowulf's refusal to bear sword and armor against Grendel (671 ff.). Whether or not in these particular cases, such customs reflect the training of boys among primitive peoples in bravado and stoicism.

The most curious touch is in the third passage; they "off with their breeches." Since the world began, did any poet of battle ever draw such a picture from his own fancy? Here we seem closest to the memories of an eye-witness, and find an actual contribution as to a point in social history which moderns have discussed with more feeling than completeness. It is enough here first to make two brief statements without quoting any passages. It is quite certain that long before and long after Lawman's day some of the Irish sometimes wore close-fitting trews from waist to ankle, and equally certain that sometimes some of them wore nothing of the sort. It is evident that these were rather tight. Now the Irish method of warfare was frequently that of the guerilla, rapid unexpected attack followed by rapid flight; with their fighting in

[10] *Top. Hib.*, iii, 10; *Exp. Hib.*, ii, 38.

[11] Ll. 672-3 and p. 268; cf. Orpen's *Ireland under the Normans* (Oxford, 1911-20), I, 339.

[12] Cf. Spenser's *View of the State of Ireland* (Dublin, 1633), p. 37; (ed. Todd, 1805) VIII, 368.

[13] *Gesta Danorum*, ed. Alfred Holder (Strasbourg, 1886), bk. V, p. 169.

[14] Joyce, *Social Hist. of Ireland*, I, 122 ff., 535, II, 368; Sullivan in O'Curry's *Manners and Customs*, I, cccclxxv, but cf. II, 253.

woods and swamps, and their dependence on agility, says Gerald, "semper in primo fere impetu vel parta est statim vel perdita victoria."[15] If ever there was an occasion on which trews would be discarded, it would be in such fighting. This is easily shown. The Heruli of Germany, either for freedom of movement or to show contempt for wounds, fought practically naked, according to Paulus Diaconus' *Historia Langobardorum* (i, 20). The Galli of Macedonia in the second century B. C., says Livy (xxxviii, 21), stripped naked for battle, showing clear white skin because uncovered only then. The Red Indians (if my Irish friends will forgive me) in the fight often wore only a slight girdle. As to more immediate evidence, Henry Cristede described how nimbly the Irish would spring up on their enemies' horses from behind and pull off the riders:[16]

> ... ne pèvent nuls hommes d'armes montés à cheval si tost courir, tant soient bien montés, que ils [*sc.* les Yrlandois] ne les rattaindent, et saillent de terre sur ung cheval, et embrachent ung homme par derrière et le tirent jus. ...

A man wearing long tight trews could hardly be so agile. According to Monstrelet, Henry V's Irish auxiliaries mentioned above were mostly footmen, with one foot shod and the other bare, wretchedly clad and without breeches,—"sans braies." With the isolation and the extraordinary persistence of manners in medieval Ireland, it is right to fit into a whole these scraps from several centuries. But only Lawman tells of men taking off their trews just before combat, and thereby he completes the picture. Gillomar's wild fighters are now ready for the exploits of those of Richard II's time. Their breeches off,—

> seolcuðe weoren heore leches.

The word *leches* was archaic; rare in other writers, in each of the dozen cases recorded in Madden's very ample glossary it is omitted or altered by the later text of the poem. It can seldom mean "glances," as rendered by Madden. Though it may be a coalescence of more than one word, it goes back to *lǽcan* rather than to anything else, and rather vaguely means "quick movements,"

---

[15] *Exp. Hib.*, ii, 38 (vol. V, p. 396); cf. Cristede's account, pp. 169, 171.
[16] Froissart's *Chroniques*, XV, 169; tr. by Johnes (London, 1839), II, 580.

"behavior." Hengest's slayer gripped him "mid grimme his læchen" (II, 267); Arthur thrust out his shield "mid feondliche lechen" (584); Gawain even leaps on his horse "mid grimliche lechen" (III, 52).[17] Marvelous no doubt were the leaps and antics of Gillomar's men thus released.

Various other passages in Lawman's poem on his early heroes allow glimpses of Irish life as it was in his own day,—of usages in war, in peace, in religion. All poems on the remote past owe much of what is picturesque and vital in them to what the poet has seen in the life around him. That it is more difficult to embody this congruously in our times is why satisfying long poems on the remote past are now few. In the middle ages a poet's imagination was untrammeled, and drew on what he saw in his own day more than at any time before or since; Lawman to a less extent but perhaps not less successfully than some others. As to the significance of his Irish touches for his personal history, that would be a part of a longer discussion of the Geoffrey of Monmouth tradition.

*University of California.*

---

[17] In II, 532, it means impulse of feeling, — " Ælc hafede an heorte leches heʒe."

# AN EARLY MENTION OF A ST. NICHOLAS PLAY IN ENGLAND

## By Carleton Brown

The well-known thirteenth-century manuscript, Trinity College Cambridge B. 14. 39 (No. 323 in James's Catalogue), contains, among other pieces of English verse not hitherto printed, a homily composed, as I hope to show, for the anniversary of St. Nicholas. The homilist mentions a "pleye," which was to follow after the conclusion of the sermon:

> yf ye wollet stille ben
> in þis pleye ye mowen isen.

The reference apparently is to a dramatic performance of one of the Miracles of St. Nicholas. Sir Edmund Chambers,[1] referring to the St. Nicholas plays on the Continent, remarks that it is "curious that no mention should be found of any English parallel." It is most interesting now to find definite evidence that usage in England was not out of line in this respect with that on the Continent. Moreover, the Trinity MS.—dated about 1250—belongs to the same period as the Fleury play-book which preserves the text of four St. Nicholas plays.

Trinity MS. 323, as I am endeavoring to show elsewhere,[2] was compiled in a convent of friars, probably of the Dominican order. A number of hands appear in the manuscript, but the article with which we are here concerned was written by the same hand as the "Life of St. Margaret" and the so-called "Ballad" of Judas. Dr. James in listing the contents of MS. 323 makes only the following brief mention of the present article: "Latin text followed by English verse equivalents." This statement, while not incorrect, is hardly adequate, and completely ignores the fact that we have here a formal sermon, beginning with a text and a prelocution and concluding with the Latin formula of benediction and doxology: "Quod nobis & uobis prestare dignetur qui uiuit & regnat deus per omnia secula seculorum."[3]

---

[1] E. K. Chambers, *Mediæval Stage* II, 132.

[2] *English Lyrics of the XIII century*, Oxford Univ. Press, to appear shortly.

[3] For a useful discussion of the plan and divisions of the Medieval

In presenting the text of this homily I have availed myself of a transcript made by a former student, Miss Gertrude H. Campbell, now deceased. Her transcript I have collated with the M. L. A. rotograph of this manuscript, deposited in the Library of Congress.

[Trin. Coll. Camb. MS. 323]

*Iustum deduxit dominus per uias rectas* [f. 26ro col. 1]
*& ostendit illi regnum dei.*

   yc ou rede ye sitten stille
   & herknet wel wid gode wille
   of godes wordes ant is werkes
4 boþe þis lewede ant þis clerkes
   for godes children wollet scechen
   euer to heren of godes spechen
      *qui ex deo est verba dei audit* [Joannem 8: 47]
   Alle þat leued on god almitte
8 godes word hit scal hem litte
   ant bringen hem to heuenric blisse
   þer he scullen haue ioye ant lisse
   launterne hit is to monnes fote
12 ant of sunnes hit deyd bote
      *lucerna pedibus meiis verbum tuum & lumen* [Ps. 118: 105]
   ant yet ic wille ou sigge more
   alle þat heret godes lore
   ant witet hit wel in stable þout
16 he wort him leyf þat al hat wrout
   ant edi scal euere boe
   ase me may in þe boc ysoe
      *beati qui audiunt uerbum dei & custodiunt illud* [Lucam 11: 28]
   euerhuych mon þat hauet his munde
20 godes word he clepet his cuynde
   for so þe bred fed fleys ant blod
   also his word is soule fod
      *non in solo pane viuit homo, set in omni*
      *uerbo quod procedit de ore dei & cetera* [Matthæum 4: 4]
   huyc mon þat is godes foster

---

Sermon see Harry Caplan, "A Late Medieval Tractate on Preaching" (*Studies in Rhetoric and Public Speaking in Honor of James Albert Winans*, N. Y. 1925, pp. 60-90). I call attention particularly to the following: "First the preacher should pronounce his theme in Latin in a low voice, then introduce one prayer in the vulgar tongue. . . . Now he should resume his theme, using the vulgar tongue for expression. And after this he can draw or elicit one prelocution through similes, moralizations, proverbs, or natural truths, or sometimes even by adducing definite authorities." Our homilist pursues this plan: note lines 23-25 calling upon the congregation to join in saying a *Pater Noster* and *Ave Maria*.

24 þerto sigge a pater noster
ant an aue marie þer to
þat ic is wordes mowe scewe so
þat hit boe god almytte iqueme
28 ant þe deuel henne to fleme
   pater noster
 *Iustum deduxit dominus per vias rectas &c.* [col. 2]
þe mon þa wole rist-wis boe
Sittit stille ant he may soe
Wou god wole for þe gode do
32 þat gode hope hauet him to
it was a king bi olde dawene
þat wel leuede on godes lawe
him he louede suyþe wel
36 þat he yeld him huyc adel
þat he bad he dede him sone
ant þorou senicholas bone
yf ye wollet stille ben
40 in þis pleye ye mowen isen
þis mon hauede lond & lede
ant alle þe men þat heueden nede
at him hoe mistin habbe froure
44 ne hatede noþing godes poure
Sum mon is riche & gederit þing
ant wit hit to is endeing
Suyc richesse preyse ic nout
48 for hoe boet in a sori þout
hoe louet hore moker & hore lif
al ase þe bonde det his wif
 *propter hoc dicuntur viri diuiciarum quia*
 *complexi sunt diuicias in amore sicut viri*
 *vxores & ipsi in-separabiliter adherent &c.*
hoe loued to muchel here catel
52 ne dorren hoe tamen hit neuer adel
hem seluen nabbet þer of no god
ac pinet hem boþe fleis & blod
 *Ecclesiasticis in quinto auarus non implebitur pecunia & qui amat*
 *diuicias non capit fructus ex eiis* [Ecclesiastici 10: 10]
god hoe gederet to oþer men
56 þat lutel þong scal cunnen hem
ant eke hoe neten wat hoe bet [f. 26vo col. 1]
for nout of hem hoe ne seet
 *Tessaurizat & ignorat cui congregabit ea* [Ps. 38: 7]
Such amon þat is riche

---

 36. MS. hym *written after* him *and erased*
 49. moker] " filthy lucre." This form is not recorded in the *NED*, but
  cf. *muck, sb.*¹ 2 fig. " contemptuously applied to money."

60 he is to þe nasse iliche
   þe asse is preked corn to geten
   ant þan ne scal hoe þrof nout heten
   þau hoe scule þer fore suete
64 þe grete schaf scal ben hir mete
   *Ieremias quadragesimosexto. Stumulator ab*
   *aquilone veniet* [Jer. 46: 20] *nam ab aquilone vnde*
   *omne malum pandetur venit stumulator. i.*
   *diabolus qui auarum stumulat ad querendum & portandum onus quod*
      *notatur.*
   yet he is liche to amon
   þat dropesie is fallen on
   þau me yife him nourist drinke
68 eft he mai ase him þunket
   also fart þe coueytous
   þe more he hauet in is hous
   þe more he þenchet to winnen euere
72 so þat suiken nul he neuere
   *Iob viii exardesset contra eos sitis* [Job 18: 9] *& alibi anima calida*
   *quasi ignis ardens nec extinguetur donec.* [Eccli. 23: 22] *i. quam diu*
   *ligna apponuntur*
   of sueche riche speket þe boc
   wer of daui þe wordes toc
   ant seiid þat hem is sclep op on
76 þat hore catel leued op on
   ant habbet al þis worldis þing
   he bet y-nome wid scleping
   *Salmista dormitauerunt qui ascenderunt equos in dormisione duo*
   *sunt operis suspencio & mentis obliuio* [Ps. 75: 7]
   Wile mon sclepet he nis nout
80 for he hauet loren al his þout
   So þe herte of þis riche mon [col. 2]
   awei from god is al idon
   y turnd a is to his catel
84 ant þat þe boc us scewet wel
   *vbi est tesaurus uester ibi cor vestrum erit* [Mattheum 6: 21]
   þer þe riche sit in is sete
   of god ne taket he none gete
   of god ne þenket he no þing þer
88 for we findet iþe sauter
   *obliuioni datur tamquam mortuus a corde* [Ps. 30: 13]
   þat þer is anoþer þing
   mon ne may nout in scleping
   lemen sterien ne werkes don

---

67. nourist = nou riȝt.    82. MS. farom.
74. *Erasure in MS. after* þe.    86. gete] heed, attention < ON gǽtr.

92 þe wile þe sclep is him up on
    quoniam sompnus est retractio spiritus a
membris organicis ad interiora
on þisse manere sclepet þe riche
ant þe false godes iliche
þat saresines bi-leuet oṇ on
96 ant wenet þat hit be wel idon
ha wenet þat hoe godes ben
ant bet ymages imaket of tre
wid honden werc ne dot hoe non
100 ne on hoere fet ne mowen hoe gon
    Manus habent & non palpabunt. pedes habent & non ambulabunt
      [Ps. 113: 7].
So det þe riche þat boc of rad
from gode dede hoe bet ilad
ant lenere werkes ha wollet don
104 of hem speket salomon. in parabolis
    Non dormierunt nisi malefecerint [Prov. 4: 16]
leue frend þenket wel
wid wronge ofte mon winnet catel
betere is lutel wid riste igete
108 þene wid wronge muchel imeten
    Spalmista. melius est modicum iusto super diuicias [Ps. 36: 16]
peccatorum multas
yef þet þou wolt riche ben [f. 27ro col. 1]
yef for him þat yaf hit þe
tressur of heuene þou scalt habbe
112 þat euer wole lasten ant nomon gabbe
he is celi þat hit getet
þer þef ne comet ne worm hit etet
    facite uobis sacculos quos fur non appropiat
    nec tinea corumpit [Lucam. 12: 33]
cloþes he makede for þe colde
116 þat ye ov schulden vnder folde
ant yeue þe poure of oure brede
þe soule hit fint wen ye bed dede
    Quoniam in pauperibus habitat xpc
yeuet on ye findet tuo
120 for þe boc us scewed so
    date & dabitur uobis
þat lutel sowet lutel repet
ase in þe boc þa apostel speket
    Qui parce seminat parce & metet [II Cor. 9: 6]
riche þat habbet þit catel kep

97. þat] t *interlined above.*
103. lenere] more meagre; cf. *NED lean* a 2.
115. cloþes] s *interlined above.*     118. *Erasure in MS. after* bed.

```
124 from gode dedes hoe habbet isclep
    no god ne deden he in þe londe
    ant þat hoe sculen habben an honde
    for nabbet ha nout of here dede
128 þat may þe wreche soule fede
    he þat wole her almes do
    he scal merci vnder fo
    his soule scal into heuene wende
132 ant wonie þer wid outen ende
        Quod nobis & vobis prestare dignetur qui viuit & regnat deus per
    omnia secula seculorum
```

   128. may *interlined above.*

We may first consider the evidence connecting this homily with the anniversary of St. Nicholas. The text which serves as the theme of the sermon finds its ultimate source in the *Liber Sapientie* (10: 10): "Haec profugium iræ fratris justum deduxit per vias rectas, et ostendit illi regnum Dei, et dedit illi scientiam sanctorum; honestavit illum in laboribus, et complevit labores illius." As cited in the homily, however, the first four words of the Vulgate text are lacking, and "Dominus" has been introduced as the subject of the sentence. In both these points the homily agrees precisely with one of the Antiphons included in the Breviaries of York, Sarum, and Hereford "In natalis unius confessoris et pontificis": [4]

  *añ.* Justum deduxit dominus per vias rectas: et ostendit illi regnum dei et dedit illi scientiam sanctorum honestavit illum in laboribus et complevit labores illius.

It is clear, therefore, that the homilist turned for his text to the service-books. The Antiphon *Justum deduxit* occurs also, as one would expect, in the special order of services for the Feast of St. Nicholas (December 6). Thus at Sarum one finds a long and elaborate service with a procession. The following items are to our purpose:

      Ad vesperas:
         Ant. Justum deduxit.
      Ad mat[utinas].
         Hym[nus] Iste confessor.

---

[4] See the *York Breviary* (ed. Surtees Soc., vol. II, col. 37), *Sarum Brev.,* II, 410 ff., *Hereford Brev.,* I, 67.

In pr. nocturno
  Lect. 1. Beatus Nicholaus ex illustri
prosapia ortus, etc.
  R. 1. Confessor Dei Nicholaus nobilis
progenie sed nobilior moribus.
. . . . . . . . . . .
  In sec. noct. Justum deduxit (*Sarum Brev.*, III, 23 ff.)

And similarly at Hereford:

In festo sancti nicholai
  Ad vesperas
. . . . . . . . . . .
Lectio iii. Committebat se quotidie deo que despensat et ordinat omnia quando vult et quomodo vult.
  His itaque transactis mirra metropolis orbata est antistite suo
  In secundo nocturno.
  Vs. Justum deduxit. (*Hereford Brev.*, II, 58).

Finally, the mention, at line 38, of the efficacy of the prayers of St. Nicholas must be accepted as conclusive identification of our homily with the anniversary of this saint.

Inasmuch as Nicholas was the patron saint of school-boys it might be surmised that the play in question was a school play, but the character of the homily itself is wholly opposed to such a suggestion. The homily is not addressed to any special group, either scholars or monks, but to a general audience:

yc ou rede ye sitten stille
& herknet wel wid gode wille
of godes wordes ant is werkes
boþe þis lewede ant þis clerkes.

The form of address which the preacher here employs is very similar to that in the opening lines of the Life of St. Margaret, in this same manuscript.

Olde ant yonge i prei ou oure folies for to lete
Þenchet on god þat yef ou wit oure sunnes to bete
Here i mai tellen ou wid wordes feire ant swete
Þe vie of one meidan was hoten maregrete.

The Life of St. Margaret, as I have already stated, is written in the same hand as the St. Nicholas homily and possibly may have been intended, like the other, for the celebration of the saint's anniversary.

As to the content of the play which was to follow, the references in the sermon are too vague to enable us to draw positive conclusions. In vv. 33-34 we have mention of a pious king whom God loved so that his petitions were promptly granted " þorou senicholas bone." This agrees fairly well with the character of Getron in the fourth of the Fleury St. Nicholas plays, except that Getron, though a person of wealth and influence, is not a king.[5] And it will be observed that our homilist a few lines later (v. 41) states that " þis mon hauede lond & lede " without mentioning his kingly rank. It is possible, therefore, that the homilist may have been alluding to the story of Getron.

Evidently the homilist did not think it necessary to outline the story in his sermon. His main purpose was to condemn the avaricious who heaped up riches and neglected alms to the poor. And this, of course, was a theme specially appropriate for the anniversary of a saint who was renowned for his charitable deeds.

Whatever may have been the miracle presented, at least we have assurance that some play dealing with St. Nicholas was enacted in England by the middle of the thirteenth century.

*New York University.*

---

[5] In the corresponding story in the *Legenda Aurea* (ed. Graesse, p. 29) he is unnamed but is referred to as " vir dives."

# THE TEXT OF *THE SIEGE OF JERUSALEM*

## By J. R. HULBERT

The Middle English alliterative poem *The Siege of Jerusalem* has received little attention from scholars since the appearance in 1891 of G. Steffler's faulty print of the Laud version of it.[1] In 1887 the poem was made the subject of a dissertation by Ferdinand Kopka,[2] which described the manuscripts, attempted to determine their relation to each other and discussed the problem of source. Kopka knew of six versions of the poem but was unable to use the Ashburnham copy. That version is now in the Huntington Library and hence available to scholars. To the list of versions known by Kopka can be added that in Lambeth Ms. 491.[3]

The manuscripts (of which a description can be found in Kopka's monograph) are as follows:

(L.)   Bodleian Library 1059 = Laud Miscellaneous 656.
(V.)   Cotton Vespasian E. xvi (British Museum).
       (Since this version contains only about 400 lines at the end of the poem, it cannot be used often for evidence of relation.)
(U.)   Cambridge University Library, Mm. 5, 14.
(A.)   British Museum Additional 31042.
(C.)   British Museum Cotton Caligula A. II., pp., 111 a to 125.
(La.)  Lambeth 491, pp. 206 a ff.
(H)    Huntington Library = formerly Ashburnham 130.
       (In so many cases this ms. provides merely a paraphrase that it is of little value for determining text.)

In his comparison of the manuscripts Kopka points out the chief agreements and differences, and concludes that the versions fall into two main groups. First he states that L. lacks some lines found manuscripts AVUC. This, he realizes, is not evidence that the four manuscripts constitute a group, because the additional lines

---

[1] See Napier's Collation, Herrig's *Archiv* 88, 214-15. Steffler omits lines which are in L and adds lines which are not there.

[2] *The Destruction of Jerusalem, ein mittelenglisches, alliterierendes Gedicht.* Einleitung. Breslau, 1887.

[3] For description of this manuscript see Herrig's *Archiv* 86, 383 ff.

may have been in the original and may have been omitted by L. Next he points out that L has lines not found in the other four versions.[4] As to this fact he remarks: "Eine zufällige Übereinstimmung (among the Mss. lacking these lines) ist bei der Zahl der Minus-Verse wohl ebenso ausgeschlossen, als die Annahme abzuweisen ist, das wir in diesen Versen einseitige Zudichtungen von L zu sehen hätten. Wir werden vielmehr anzunehmen haben, dass x (the source of the sub-group containing the four versions) diese Versen bereits nicht mehr hatte, während sie dem Original angehörten."[5] A third argument for the view that the four versions constitute one group is the fact that in two places in them two verses are transposed. Again the four are divided into sections in various ways, differing from the division of L, which preserves the original scheme (as evidenced by the fact that its divisions end at points where the poem has a formula suggestive of the end of a canto.) From all these reasons, says Kopka, it is clear that the four manuscripts derive from a common ancestor which is not the source of L . . . "so dass es nicht nötig sein wird, die Varianten der einzelnen Verse zur Vergleichung heranzuziehen."[6] Finally that L cannot be the source of the other versions is clear from the fact that they have lines not found in L, "da sie zum grössten Teil als echt zu bezeichnen sind."[7]

A study of Kopka's reasons for supposing that AVUC go back to a common source, different from that of L, shows that the first, third and fourth are not evidence at all. Kopka admits that the first is not. Similarly, it may be that L and not AVUC transposed the lines in question; they make equally good sense in both arrangements. As to the fourth, a clever scribe could easily notice the formulae which indicate canto-endings and make divisions at those points.

The only real proof that AVUC constitute one group would be common errors. Is the second of Kopka's points—the lines found in L but not in the other versions—evidence of error on the part of AVUC? The lines involved are 311-314, 1230-1232, 1298,

---

[4] Kopka's numbers are those of L. In this article I use Steffler's numbers so that readers can refer to his text.

[5] *Op. cit.*, p. 14.

[6] *Op. cit.*, p. 15.

[7] *Ibid.*

1323-1328, and a line after 420 (omitted in Steffler's print). An examination of the text will show that all of those lines can be omitted without harm to the continuity or completeness of the poem, i. e., that they were not necessarily in the original. Of course they may have been in the original text. If we knew the source from which the poet worked we could tell; but as we know no source for the poem as a whole, we cannot use that method. At first glance, the line after 420 seems necessary to the passage and its omission, therefore, an obvious error. The author has been describing the preparations of the besiegers and shifts to the activities within the city; the line makes clear the transition:

"Riȝt so in þe cite  þey schapte hem þerfore."

Certain considerations, however, indicate that the line is spurious.

One of these is derived from the division of the poem into quatrains. C La U H are subdivided into stanzas:—C and H into quatrains, U into stanzas usually of eight lines, La very irregularly into groups of lines which are usually multiples of four. Gollancz has called attention to a division of *Cleanness* and *Patience* into quatrains, has printed the texts in this form, and has remarked that the same division occurs in our poem.[8] It is curious, to be sure, that if the sub-division is original it does not appear in L (the best version) or AV. Nevertheless a study of the text produces the conviction that the stanza division is original, and that the quatrains are much more strongly marked thought divisions than those in *Cleanness* and *Patience*. Indeed they are of great value in determining the author's sentence structure, and though some of these stanzas are "run-on," the whole poem can be reconstructed into four line stanzas without violence to the text. In this division into stanzas we have a valuable test for the genuineness of such extra lines as the one after line 420. This line occurs as the third of a quatrain. If it is included, the stanza in which it stands must have five lines—or some neighboring one has that number. Without it the four lines beginning line 419 makes a thought-unit; with it, they do not. Moreover the line breaks the apparent parallelism between *strogelyng* (in the line before it) and *armyng* (in the following one) and spoils the construction of the latter word.

[8] See his edition of *Cleanness*, p. x, note.

Another consideration warrants rejection of this line. Schumacher found only two cases in this poem of the alliteration of *s* with *sch* (as he used Steffler's text, he did not know of this one) and hence concluded: "Man darf also als sicher hinstellen, dass *s: sch* in *Seg. Jer.* nicht gilt." [9] The two which he noted (ll. 313, 1327) like the one under discussion are found only in L. Hence it seems clear that the line after 420 is an addition made by L (or more likely by L's source) and that it was inserted in the text because a transitional sentence seemed necessary.

From the foregoing discussion it is apparent that Kopka's evidence for the view that AVUC have common errors as compared with L, is of no value. To this might be added one instance of a possible error of LAV as compared with CLaU. This is in line 1322. Mediaeval tradition couples Pilate with Vienne (either as the place of his banishment or as the one to which his body was sent). C reads *Vyane;* La, *Vyan;* U, *Vian;* but L has *Viterbe;* A, *Vittern;* V, *Vettury,* which, though not identical, point to a common reading.

It is necessary, therefore, to study the versions in detail in order to determine whether there are common errors which make clear their grouping. Kopka was right in his conclusions as to subgroups. To his group CU may be added now LaH which he did not use. AV and L are the other sub-groups. The essential question now is: Do these two main groups go back to one source (as Kopka thought), L: AVCLaUH, or do the three sub-groups go back independently to one source, L : AV : CLaUH? Before making detailed comparisons we must consider what we are to do with the variations that we find. For many years it has been customary to employ the method of Lachmann, which uses "common errors" as basis of classification.[10] Before starting to work with this method, we need to decide what is a common error. In no case, as far as I am aware, is there anything in the material, verified by medieval tradition or a possible source, which enables one in a particular place to be sure that one reading is correct and the

---

[9] K. Schumacher, *Studien über den Stabreim in der mittelenglischen Alliterationsdichtung*, p. 101.

[10] For a clear, brief account of method see W. P. Shepard's article: "Recent Theories of Textual Criticism" in *Modern Philology*, XXVIII, 129-141.

others erroneous, unless it be the one mentioned in the preceding paragraph. Hence one must depend upon apparent errors in sense or in verse, both unsafe as time after time research has proved that in medieval documents passages formerly thought to be faulty in meaning or verse are correct. Since we have no better test in this case, however, let us see what we can do with it. In line 742 where L reads:

" Grayþed of gray steel    and of gold riche."

CALaU have "The grate on þe graye steel" (" was of gray," " of the grey ") which seems senseless. It may be, however, that grate has some technical meaning there; or perhaps after *grayþe* became archaic, two or more scribes independently made the change to *grate*. In line 693, L reads:

"And suþ honget on an hep    upon hye galwes."

For *hep,* CLaU have *hye,* A *highte*. A repetition of *hye* in the line doesn't seem probable; though *highte* isn't quite the same as *hye,* it suggests derivation from the same reading. In line 575, the reading of CLaUH, *hundred* fits the situation better than LA's *vnder*.

Aside from those instances, there seems to be no common error uniting L and AV or L and CLaUH or AV and CLaUH, except instances of faults in alliteration. How much weight we should give to such evidence it is hard to say. Certainly it is not conclusive, for the poem has lines which, in all versions, lack alliteration between the two halves: ll. 430, 577, 1166. Perhaps those indicate that all our versions are derived from a faulty copy, or perhaps the author didn't feel it necessary to provide alliteration always. One of the cases of fault in alliteration which apparently binds A and L together is in l. 253. L reads

" þe kerchief carieþ from hem alle    and in þe eyr hangyþ."

It is possible that alliteration is on *alle* and *eyr,* but the line begins as though it should have a *K* alliteration (and Shumacher distrusts all lines in this poem which do not have two alliterating words in the first half.)[11] At any rate A reads similarly, but CLaU have instead of *in þe eyr, in the cherche*. If the form *cherche* is a

[11] *Op. cit.,* p. 33.

substitution for northern *kyrke* (which is found in alliteration in line 234), the line would be normal. Again line 159 reads:

L  "And þat worliche wif  þat arst was ynempned."
A  " That ilke worthily woman  that j firste neuynede."

but CLaUH agree in:

La  "And þan þis worthi wyf  of whom y ferst tolde." [12]

Similarly in line 394, LA read *wonnen with swerd,* CLaUH *wonnen with werre.* Only one alliteration is required, but note Schumacher's opinion cited above.

All other instances, if they are errors, group AVCLaU together. In line 116 where L reads:

" To take careynes kynde  of a clene mayde,"

CU read *mannes* for *careynes,* La has *to cacche mannys kynde,* A has *carefull manes.* Evidently La and A tried to improve a faulty reading which was similar to that of CU. In line 195, ALaU (C omits this line) lack alliteration but are phrased differently. In line 277, ACL,U read *tuke* (*toke*) instead of *lawȝte,* but as there are already three alliterating syllables in the line, we can't be sure that this is an error. Line 746 in L reads:

"A bryȝt burnesched swerd  he belteþ alofte."

ACLaU read *gyrdeth* instead of *belteþ.* The substitution of the synonym might occur independently, however. In line 820, for *pyble,* C reads *brayne,* A *stone,* La *pomel,* U *polel.* If those aren't errors of coincidence, they may be derived from an illegible word in their common source. In line 988, CALaUV read *lyfe* instead of *herte* (*while my herte lasteþ*)—perhaps independent substitution, as one would naturally say *life* rather than *heart* there, if it were not for alliteration. In line 990, LaUAV do not have *eure* [13] or any common reading. In line 1042, L has *hetterly,* A *etterly,* but CLaUV *sodainly.* In V's case, the substitution is independent of CLaU as V has practically no special agreement with CLaU. Hence this instance shows how cautious we must be in concluding that errors of a single word have value for classification.

[12] The alliteration of *w: wh* occurs in three other places in this poem (Schumacher, *op. cit.,* pp. 79-80).

[13] Steffler prints *cure* erroneously.

From the foregoing evidence it is clear that regarding one set of details one could argue that LA(V) comprise one main group against CLaUH; but if one considered another series one could argue that A(V)CLaUH comprise one group against L. Clearly the theory of Lachmann cannot be applied successfully to this problem, because one cannot be sure which of the agreements have significance for classification. Whether one accepts one of the two conclusions stated above or decides on three independent main groups (L: AV: CLaUH), one must disregard a considerable amount of evidence as due to chance agreement or contamination.

Moreover we must realize that superior readings may be the product of a scribe-editor and need not necessarily represent the author's original. A little observation of these versions shows how freely the scribes treated their originals and how capable they were as editors. That some of them could compose acceptable alliterative verse is demonstrated by the entirely different lines found at the same point in different manuscripts. For instance where L reads (and LaUC agree):

"And many segge at þat saute   souȝte to þe grounde,"

A(V) has:

"And many beryns at þat brayde   birssede to dede."

Again in one place where A has no corresponding line, L reads:

" Was no poynt perschid   of alle her prise armor,"

but LaUH have:

"And no bierne (body) on hem breke   so boldely þei stode."

In another case, L(A) reads

"And riche emperour of Rome   þer redeþ þes lettres,"

but LaUHC read:

"As ye may se by the sele   assay if ȝow likith."

Again L(AV) have:

" þan seiþ sir Sabyn anon   semelich lord,"

LaUH:

" The knyght knelyd anone   and to the kyng sayde."

In each of these pairs one line is not original, unless some of the variations in the manuscripts represent the author's revisions. In view of its general superiority L might lay claim to the distinction of being a revised version, but the fact that its added lines confuse the quatrains of the original diminishes the likelihood. Disregarding that possibility, we must conclude that on any hypothesis some superior readings are to be rejected. Thus, if Kopka's judgment is accepted, the lines which in CLaU read "better" than in LAV cannot be original; if LAV are a group or if there are three main groups, those readings in L which differ from AVCLaU and are "better" than those in the other versions cannot be original. Therefore we cannot use "common errors" mechanically as a means of establishing the main groups in this case. If anything is to be made of Lachmann's method in the study of this poem, the scholar must decide among the body of *apparent* common errors those which really *are* common errors; and that is a hazardous process quite as dependent on the critic's judgment as the old editorial method of adopting the "best" readings.

On the other hand, it is not impossible to construct a text which is at least ninety per cent. "critical." The method would be: (1) to keep before one constantly the existence of three groups, with recognition of the possibility that two of them may be divisions of one group, (2) to take up the text line by line. In many instances, of course, there will be such agreement among the versions as to establish the text on either hypothesis of grouping. In others, alliteration, stanza structure, the principle that archaic diction is likely to be original, will establish the reading. This process may look like eclecticism, but it is not. If one rejects a reading which seems to have the weight of manuscript authority, one does so as result of a reasonable judgment that chance agreement or contamination accounts for it. The likelihood of chance agreement is much greater than anyone who has not studied such a text as this would believe. Any two versions of the seven display such agreements occasionally. For instance, in l. 1030 L and C have "man" for "freke," which alliterates; in l. 1215 V and U read "god" instead of "heuen," which alliterates. As to contamination, it is fairly sure that from about line 900 on C has been conflated with a version belonging to the group AV, and it is possible that A(V) at times has been altered by influence of a text belonging to the same tradition as L.

That the process sketched above will produce a text which is as nearly critical as the extant versions can give us, the following experience shows. Some years ago I made a critical text on the assumption that L, CLaUH and AV constitute three independent groups. I found that there were so many cases in which the three groups have three readings (usually the variation was in single words, not in phrases or lines) that it was necessary to establish an arbitrary rule—to accept the reading of one group (obviously L) when two groups did not agree. Consequently perhaps as often as every other line I had to include a reading which was not "critical." Thus the result was L (with omission of lines found only in L) plus some readings superior to L and a very few (where AVCLaUH agree but do not alliterate) which seem not so good. In making that text, I paid no attention to the quatrains since, noticing that they appeared only in versions of the poorest group, I thought they could not be original.

About a year ago, despairing of the possibility of establishing three main groups, I made a new text, using L as a basis but accepting readings from other versions when they seemed better and omitting most of the lines found only in L. At that time I had become convinced that the quatrain division was original and so divided the text into quatrains. Recently I have compared the two texts thus made and have found to my astonishment that up to l. 1223 they are practically identical. The "critical" text provided exactly the lines needed for the quatrains, if one included a line at places where two of the groups have a line but the diction and alliteration differ. In only a few cases ("the grate on þe graye steel"; "gyrdeth" for "belteþ") does the critical text have a less satisfactory reading than the amended text, and those may perhaps be regarded as due to independent errors.

I have said that at line 1223, my effort at a critical text encountered difficulties. The facts are so curious as to warrant presentation here. After line 1223 CAV add a line which in V reads:

"þe same tyme þe towne was taken and graunted." [14]

If this is retained it is the first line of a quatrain, which ends with

---

[14] Steffler prints this line, but it is not in L. The line number in Steffler's text is, of course, 1224; in my text it would be 1225.

a full stop three lines below. All versions have these three lines, but after them we find confusing variation.

1228. LCLaUH read:

"And haplich was had away how wyst j neuere" (but AV omit)

1229. LLaUH read:

"And þan þey deuysed hem and vengaunce hit helde" (but CAV omit).

Finally L has three lines not found elsewhere. Judging by stanza structure, one must conclude that either AV or L alone is right, since L has two quatrains, AV one quatrain and the other versions one quatrain and odd lines. Against L is the fact that L has a practice of adding lines singly and in groups. But A also occasionally adds a line. Against AV is the fact that C's possession of 1224 cannot be used as an argument in favor of AV, since from about line 900 on, C retains its verbal agreement with LaUH but also agrees at times unexpectedly with A and hence probably has been contaminated. Thus its possession of line 1224 (absent from LaUH) can be discounted. I cannot choose between the two alternatives though I tend to accept AV because I believe that in the poem there is no other instance of omission by all versions but L of a *series* of lines. Unfortunately the solution of another problem depends on this. After l. 1305 CAV have this line:

"Thouȝ euery ferþynge hadde be worth floreyns a hondredde."[15]

If accepted this line makes the last line of a quatrain, and the quatrain ends with a period. If it is not, we must go back and accept a line (printed in Steffler as l. 1298) which is found only in L. The result is not so good for stanza structure as are the rejection of this line and the acceptance of CAV's later line (i. e. the line quoted from CAV immediately above). Acceptance of L's line necessitates reading two "run on" stanzas and no full stop at a stanza's end until l. 1305. Certainly CAV is "superior" to L here, but whether that fact warrants one in accepting CAV's reading (and in logical consequence its reading of the passage considered above) is a puzzle.

The difficulties which we have just been considering begin a

---

[15] Steffler prints this line, but it is not in L. In my text this line would be 1300.

hundred lines before the end of the poem. Even if we could prove a division of the extant versions into three main groups, we could not construct impersonally a critical text at those points, for if we accepted any reading transitional between AV and L the stanzaic division would be broken from line 1227 to the end. Since no similar difficulty appears before l. 1223, however, we can construct a critical text up to that point, by the methods indicated. It would not be a perfect text; we could not assert positively that it is the same as the ancestor of all extant versions, because where three different words appear as the reading of the three groups, and no one of them could be established by alliteration, grammar or sense. as correct, we should have to "take a chance" on L's reading, and in some cases at least that would probably be wrong. But the result would be a text considerably closer than is L to the ancestor from which all extant versions are derived and would not be significantly different from the original.

*The University of Chicago.*

# TALES OF THE HOMEWARD JOURNEY

## By John Matthews Manly

If one should read the Prologue of the Parson's Tale attentively and without preconceptions, it can hardly be doubted that he would derive the impression that it was intended to introduce, not the last tale of the outward journey, told as the pilgrims were approaching Canterbury, but the final tale of the whole series, told as they were approaching London on their return. The words of the Host are very specific:

> Now lakketh us no tales mo than oon;
> Fulfilled is my sentence and my decree.
> Almost fulfild is al myn ordinannce.     (ll. 16-19)

And again, speaking to the Parson he says:

> Thou sholdest knytte up wel a greet mateere;     (l. 28)

to which the Parson replies:

> I wol yow telle a myrie tale in prose
> To knytte up al this feeste and make an ende.     (ll. 46-47)

Finally, the company regards the Parson's tale as the last of all:

> Upon this word we han assented soone,
> For as us semed, it was for to doone,
> To enden in som vertuous sentence.     (ll. 61-63)

The impression conveyed by these passages is definitely and unmistakably that the whole enterprise of the journey is nearing its end; and this is confirmed by a bit of evidence which seems to have escaped the attention of most students. If the Parson's tale is to be placed after the tales of the Canon's Yeoman and the Manciple, on the outward journey, it is difficult to see what can be meant by l. 12:

> As we were entring at a thropes ende;

for there is no village at the Canterbury end that can be referred to in this line.

In the first place, according to the Prologue of the Canon's Yeoman's Tale (G 556) the pilgrims had passed Boughton-under-Blee fairly early in the morning; and if we accept the view that the Manciple's Tale immediately preceded the Parson's, they must also have passed during the morning hours the mysterious little town,

> Which that ycleped is Bob-up-and-down,
> Under the Blee, in Canterbury weye.   (H 1-3)

But if Bob-up-and-Down [1] is Harbledown (two miles from Canterbury), there is no village now and no trace of an ancient village between it and Canterbury; and if we accept the unlikely suggestion of Mr. J. M. Cowper that "Bob-up-and-down" refers to a field called "Up-and-down Field," we are still nearer to Canterbury, with no group of buildings lying between, that Chaucer would have called a "thorp."

On the other hand, if the Parson's Tale is to be told at the close of the return journey, as the pilgrims are approaching London there were many "thorpes"; and four o'clock [2] in the afternoon is a suitable time for beginning the tale that is to last until they reach London at sunset.

The most serious objection to the view that the Parson's Tale was to be the last of the whole series is perhaps that the first line of the Prologue seems to bind it inseparably to the Manciple's Tale. But there are so many suspicious features about the general situation here that the mention of the Manciple cannot be regarded as conclusive.

In the first place, the allusions to the morning in the links of Groups F, G and H make that sequence rather satisfactory. In F 73 the Squire hastens on with his tale, saying:

> I wol not taryen yow, for it is pryme.

---

[1] It is true that "toun" formerly meant the enclosure of a farm house and its yard, but Chaucer seems not to have used the word in this sense; and the place was obviously one that he expected travelers to Canterbury to remember.

[2] The most probable explanation of the error of *ten* for *four* in l. 5 of the Parsons Prologue is that the number 4 was written in Chaucer's rough draft as an Arabic numeral.

This when carelessly written often looks like an x (Roman ten) in fourteenth and fifteenth century MSS. In the present passage Hengwrt, one of the earliest and best of the MSS, has "29" in l. 4, "Ten" in l. 5, "xj" in l. 6, and "6" in l. 9. A fifteenth century scribe might well have mistaken an Arabic four, for a Roman ten.

We can hardly think that Chaucer uses "pryme" here to mean 6 a. m., for the Squire implies that it is not early. The word probably means 9 a. m. here, as it does when the Host is urging the Reeve to get on with his tale:

> Sey forth thy tale and tary not the tyme.
> Lo Depeford, and it is half wey prime.    (A 3905-06)

Then, after the tales of Squire and Franklin and Second Nun have been told—and any others that may have been planned to come between Groups F and G—the day is still so young that the Canon and his Yeoman, riding hard, overtake the Pilgrims within five miles of the place where they had spent the night. After the telling of so many tales it is really astonishing to find the Host suggesting, as he apparently does, in H 4-13, that it is time to begin the sport. Indeed the whole implication of the scene between Host, drunken Cook, and Manciple is that no tales had yet been told and that it was time to begin.

If we assume for the moment that the Manciple's Tale was the first told on the return journey, the whole situation seems simpler. The difficulty about "Bob-up-and-down" disappears; it may well be Harbledown, or some village more deserving of the description "under the Blee" than that hill-crowning village; and the Host's fears for the lagging Cook would seem better justified when the pilgrims were entering the robber-haunted forest than after they had passed through it, as Furnivall suggested.[2] Moreover the Cook's condition seems to be a "hang-over" from heavy drinking the night before (perhaps in Canterbury) rather than the result of stopping too often in the morning at ale-stakes. The Host's questions imply this, and the Manciple's "gourde" of wine, though offered as a jape, may have served as a "bracer."

That Chaucer should have written the links introducing the first and last tales of the homeward journey before completing all the tales and links of the journey outward would not be at all surprising. Even the most systematic of writers might have done this, but Chaucer, as we know from the evidence of the tales themselves, although he may have formed a very careful plan, changed his plan more than once, and worked on it in somewhat desultory fashion. Besides, on the present hypothesis, he was not concerned with writ-

[2] *Temporary Preface*, p. 35.

ing the tales, but only the links, of the Manciple and the Parson. The Manciple's Tale is proved by its literary technique to have been written long before the period of the Canterbury Tales, probably as a sort of rhetorical exercise; the Parson's Tale, on the other hand, was probably never composed by Chaucer, the two uncomposed fragments of penitential treatises found in our MSS under that designation being at best only loose materials, translated by Chaucer for future use, and copied by his literary executor as the Parson's Tale only because Chaucer's chest contained no other piece of prose that seemed appropriate to the Parson. To prepare the links for the first and last tales of the homeward journey would, therefore, have been a simple matter.

These suggestions are, of course, not new. Furnivall long ago discussed the whole matter in his *Temporary Preface* (p. 36) and, speaking of the mention of the Manciple in l. 1 of the Parson's Prologue, said: "But the lines following show, that either the Manciple's name must have been introduced by a copier after Chaucer's death, or that Chaucer himself had not revised this link or prologue." When he wrote these words Furnivall had apparently not observed that in the Hengwrt MS—one of the very earliest and best—"Manciple" is written over an erasure, and that two MSS (Rawlinson Poetry 223 and Glasgow) read "Merchant," and one (Trin. Camb. R. 3.3.) reads "Franklin." The readings of the last three MSS are perhaps not significant of anything except the confused state in which Chaucer left his MS of the Canterbury Tales—though the Rawlinson ancestor seems in some tales to have had access to corrected readings that must have come from Chaucer (notably the insertion of F 1001-06 before l. 999 instead of after l. 1000). There is, however, much evidence to suggest that Hengwrt may have been, in parts, a copy—and one of the earliest—from the imperfectly revised drafts found in Chaucer's chest at his death.

That the MSS of the Canterbury Tales are derived from drafts, and not from more or less imperfect copies of a MS corrected and put into circulation by Chaucer himself, becomes increasingly evident the more one studies the MSS and their interrelations, and is of fundamental importance for the criticism of the text and for all discussions as to what were Chaucer's intentions. We may be reasonably sure that the major inconsistencies are due to Chaucer himself and result from the fact that different fragments of the

Tales belong to different stages in the development of his plan. If he had lived to complete his work, he would no doubt have rearranged, and rewritten, and brought all the parts into harmony. As it is, the arrangements and the attempts at organization into a consistent whole are the work of more or less intelligent copyists. This was understood long ago by Furnivall and others, but Furnivall and succeeding editors and commentators got interested in trying to discover the correct arrangement of the tales and the number of days required for the journey, and neglected the question whether Chaucer had left his work in such condition as to permit intelligent discussion of such matters.

Some one may ask whether any other tales besides those of the Manciple and the Parson were intended for the homeward journey. The reply would seem to be that there are none for which there is clear evidence of such an intention. But it may be remarked that if the Group commonly known as B2 (Shipman, Prioress, Thopas, Melibeus, Monk, Nun's Priest) were so intended, the difficulty about the reference to Rochester (B 3116) would disappear, without resort to the violent and altogether unjustifiable expedient of moving this group up to follow the Man of Law's Tale and regarding the Man of Law's end-link as intended to introduce the Shipman.

Finally it seems that we are justified in regarding each group of tales as a unit in making such inferences as we can with regard to Chaucer's intention concerning the group at the time he wrote it; we are also justified in making inferences from inconsistent features as to changes of his plan; but we are not justified in attempting to force the fragmentary groups that have come down to us into a consistent arrangement conforming to a definite plan.

*The University of Chicago.*

# SHAKESPEARE AND WILSON'S *ARTE OF RHETORIQUE*, AN INQUIRY INTO THE CRITERIA FOR DETERMINING SOURCES

By HARDIN CRAIG

When George Chalmers, provoked by what he considered the arrogancy of Malone, published *An Apology for the Believers in the Shakspeare-Papers, which were exhibited in Norfolk-Street*,[1] he did a good deal more than merely showing that the Ireland forgeries were not without much credible and even verifiable information. He took occasion to treat, from the abundance of his antiquarian knowledge, various aspects of the history of the stage, the office of the Revels, and the "studies of Shakespeare." His reply to what Steevens, Malone's enemy, called "one of the most decisive pieces of criticism that was ever produced," is of relatively small value, but the book as a whole is full of both originality and good sense. It was Chalmers who, so far as I know, was the first to advance the idea that Shakespeare was familiar with Wilson's *Arte of Rhetorique*.[2] It is desirable to quote Chalmers both because one of his parallels is perhaps the best ever adduced and because his manner of reasoning is typical; that is to say, he notes a resemblance between the book and the works of Shakespeare, shows an antecedent probability that Shakespeare knew and used the book, and then lets the case rest as satisfactorily demonstrated.

There is nothing of any importance involved either in accepting or rejecting Shakespeare's dependence on Wilson, and for that

---

[1] London, Printed for Thomas Egerton, 1797. Edmund Malone, *An Inquiry into the Authenticity of certain Miscellaneous Papers and Legal Instruments, published Dec. 24, 1795, and attributed to Shakespeare* (London, 1796).

[2] Published by Richard Grafton in 1553, by J. Kyngston (Newlie sette again) in 1560, 1562, 1563, 1567, 1580, 1584, and by G. Robinson in 1585—all editions in quarto. *Wilson's Arte of Rhetorique. 1560.* Edited by G. H. Mair. Tudor and Stuart Library (Oxford: Clarendon Press, 1909). Review by Max Förster, Sh.-Jb., XLVI (1910), 341-2. The references in the following article are to Mair's edition. For important criticism of Mair's text and information as to texts and editions of *The Arte of Rhetorique*, see Russell H. Wagner, *The Text and Editions of Wilson's "Arte of Rhetorique*," M. L. N., XLIV, 421-428.

very reason it will afford us an opportunity for dispassionate inquiry into the bases of such attributions of source and, if not to arrive nearer the truth, at least to become more able to distinguish it from error. Nobody doubts, for example, the validity of Theobald's discovery that Shakespeare actually knew Samuel Harsnet's *Declaration of Egregious Popish Impostures* (1603), a most unlikely book, and derived from it the names of Edgar's fiends and other minor matters in *King Lear*; and yet there is still debate, except for the one passage in *The Tempest*[3] indicated by Capell a hundred and fifty years ago, about Shakespeare's knowledge and use of Montaigne.

"It is, indeed, more than probable," says Chalmers, "that Shakspeare had studied with great attention, Wilson's *Art of Rhetorique*, which was published, for the *third time*, in 1585. It is sufficiently known to the readers of Shakspeare, that he had unbounded curiosity, from nature, and vigilance of observation, from habit: And, it was natural for such a poet, who early felt the ambition of authorship, to inspect, and to study, the *Art of Rhetorique*, which was popularly known, while his inquisitive mind was on the wing. From this fountain of knowledge, both historical, and critical, such an intellect must necessarily have quaffed abundant draughts of instruction; both of ancient lore, and modern attainments: In it, he must have seen, as in a *specious mirror*, the whole mistery of writing, the good, exemplified, and the bad, exploded. In the *Art of Rhetorique*, he also saw characters pourtrayed, which as a dramatist, he must have viewed with pleasure, and recollected with advantage: Herein, he must have seen *Tymon of Athens*,[4] and the *Pedantick Magistrate*: He, herein, discovered *the character*; but he found, in his own invention, *the constable*. He now became acquainted with *the mayor*; but he afterwards shook hands with Dogberry at Credenton."[5]

In a footnote to the "*Pedantick Magistrate*" Chalmers quotes from Wilson[6] as follows: "Another good fellowe of the countrey,

---

[3] Act II, scene i, lines 147-164.

[4] Footnote reference to *The Arte of Rhetorique*, edition of 1585, p. 56 (Mair's edition, p. 55), and quotation of the passage with the side-note "Tymon a deadly hater of all companie."

[5] *Apology for the Believers*, pp. 558-560.

[6] Edition of 1585, p. 167; Mair's edition, p. 164.

being an *officer* and *mayor* of a toune, and desirous to speak like a fine learned man, having just occasion to rebuke a runnegate fellowe, said after this wise, in a greate heate:—Thou *yngraine* and *vacation* knave, if I take thee any more within the *circumcision* of my *dampnation*; I will so *corrupt* thee, that all other *vacation* knaves shall take *ilsample* by thee." Mair prints "yngrame" instead of "yngraine," which is obviously the original reading, especially since it presents a case of the unexpected happy hit of the wrongly used word, a feature of this type of comicality.

The possibility that Shakespeare had any debt to Wilson's brief reference to Timon of Athens is too slight to be considered. To say nothing of the accounts of Timon in Plutarch's *Life of Mark Antony*, in Lucian's dialogue *Timon the Misanthrope*, in Sir Richard Barckley's *A Discourse of the Felicitie of Man* (1598, 1603), and in Pierre Boaistuau's *Theatrum Mundi*,[7] it is to be noted that Timon the Misanthrope was a stock figure in sixteenth century literature and is frequently alluded to in just the way he is in Wilson. But as regards the "*Pedantick Magistrate*" as the immediate source of Dogberry's speeches at the examination of Conrade and Borachio in *Much Ado about Nothing*, Act IV, scene ii, the case must at the outset be admitted to be a much better one, since the situations in Wilson's story and Shakespeare's play are similar, and in the severity of the magistrate there is a suggestion of Dogberry's fine burst of indignation at being called an ass. The source of the humor is also identical, and it is, moreover, a form of humor which seems to be peculiarly Shakespearean. Clowns of course always misused their words; it is impossible to think of a clown who does not do so. But in this case there is a touch of pedantry. There is a certain amount of ridicule of pedantry in Lyly, but no humor derived from a misunderstanding or misuse of learned terms. There are excellent fantastically talking clowns in Greene, Peele, and Porter; but nowhere in early comedy have I been able to find a malaprop who directly suggests Bottom, Mistress Quickly, and Dogberry. On the other hand, the pedantical misuse of fine language is not a rare form of comicality, as Wilson's story bears witness, and although it seems to have been a favorite method of Shakespeare's, it also seems to have been with

[7] Englished by John Alday and published by T. Hacket, 1566? and 1574, 8°, and by J. Wyght, 1581, 8°.

him a more or less gradual growth. It is not so pronounced in Bottom as in the later characters, and there are touches of it in Launce, Launcelot Gobbo, and Jack Cade. This circumstance would indicate that Shakespeare was not immediately borrowing an idea in his creation of Dogberry. Particularly and, I think, significantly, there is no sign of the direct borrowing of names, words, or circumstances, and with reference to Chalmers's contention the findings are negative. Wilson himself possibly gives a clue to the origin of this kind of comic speech when he introduces a letter full of " ynke horne termes " with the statement that " William Sommer himselfe could not make a better for the purpose." Note also the following passage: " William Somer seeing much adoe for accomptes making, and that the Kinges Maiestie of most worthie memorie Henrie the eight wanted money, such as was due vnto him: and please your grace (quoth he) you haue so many Frauditours, so many Conueighers, and so many Deceiuers to get vp your money, that they get all to themselues. Whether he sayd true or no, let God iudge that, it was vnhappely spoken of a foole, and I thinke he had some Schoolemaster: He should haue saide Auditours, Surueighours, and Receiuers." [8]

Nathan Drake was also firmly convinced that Shakespeare knew and imitated Wilson in his *Arte of Rhetorique*.[9] He quotes Wilson's satire against the Latinizing and Italianizing of the English language to such a degree that it was scarcely intelligible to the common people, and gives as an example the " letter full of ynke horne termes," " deuised by a Lincolnshire man, for a voyde benefice, to a gentleman that then waited vpon the Lorde Chauncellour." [10] Drake thinks it " probable, nay certain, that Shakespeare improved his limited education in the country by inspecting those treatises in philology and criticism which had acquired the popular approbation, and were adapted to the years of his manhood." He " perused with avidity " the *Arte of Rhetorique* of Wilson and the *Scholemaster* of Ascham and " availed himself professionally " of the rhetoric. This he thinks

[8] Mair's edition, pp. 163, 201.

[9] *Shakespeare and his Times.* Two vols. London, 1817, pp. 440-441, 472-473.

[10] Mair's edition, pp. 162-163. The letter begins " Pondering, expending, and reuoluting with my selfe, your ingent affabilitie."

will be evident from the two passages cited above from Chalmers, which he quotes. But Shakespeare's ridicule of pedantry he need not have had suggested to him by Wilson, since it was common to Wilson, Cheke, Ascham, and perhaps a dozen other writers.[11] Halliwell-Phillipps [12] also cites the epistle of the Lincolnshire man in connection with Armado's letter to Jaquenetta in *Love's Labour's Lost*, Act IV, scene i, lines 60-89, but does not regard Armado's effusion as an imitation of Wilson. Furness,[13] who cites Halliwell-Phillipps and quotes the passage from Wilson at length, lends some color to the possibility of influence by citing the participles " illustrate " and " indubitate " from Don Armado's letter for comparison with a number of such forms from Wilson. Many Latin verbs, however, were adopted into English in the sixteenth century in the form of the passive participle, and the resemblances probably have no special significance.[14] It will be necessary for us to say something further on in the paper about a possible connection between Wilson's *Rhetorique* and *Love's Labour's Lost* in its ridicule of pedantry.

The Reverend Joseph Hunter [15] makes a more extensive use of Wilson in the elucidation of Shakespeare (usually to small purpose) than any other commentator and brings forward one of the closest and most convincing resemblances ever cited. Hunter's parallels to Beatrice's " Thus goes every one to the world but I, and I am sun-burnt " (*Much Ado*, II, i, 331), Sir Toby's " passy measures panyn " (*T. Night*, V, i, 206), Juliet's " O, swear not by the moon, the inconstant moon " (*R. & J.*, II, ii, 109), and the First Clown's protest at the privileges of " great folk " more than " their even Christian " (*Hamlet*, V, i, 32) are unimportant; but not so his parallel to the following words of Iago (*Othello*, III, iii, 155-161):

---

[11] George Phillip Krapp, *The Rise of English Literary Prose* (New York, 1915), pp. 287-306.

[12] *Memoranda on Love's Labour's Lost*, London, 1879.

[13] *Love's Labour's Lost*, Variorum edition, pp. 119, 120.

[14] Henry Bradley, "Shakespeare's English," in *Shakespeare's England* (Oxford, 1917), Vol. II, pp. 561-563, and E. A. Abbott, *A Shakespearian Grammar*, par. 342.

[15] *New Illustrations of the Life, Studies, and Writings of Shakespeare.* Two vols. (London, 1845).

> Good name in man and woman, dear my lord,
> Is the immediate jewel of their souls:
> Who steals my purse steals trash; 'tis something, nothing;
> 'Twas mine, 'tis his, and has been slave to thousands;
> But he that filches from me my good name
> Robs me of that which not enriches him
> And makes me poor indeed.

"There are several passages," says Hunter, "in Wilson's *Rhetorique* which remind one of Shakespeare, so many that it might be affirmed to be a book which Shakespeare had at some period of his life not only read but studied. The resemblance of the lines above to the following passage found in the chapter on Amplification is remarkable:—'The places of Logique help oft for amplification. As, where men have a wrong opinion, and think theft a greater fault than slander, one might prove the contrary as well by circumstances as by arguments. And first, he might shew that slander is theft, and every slanderer is a thief. For as well the slanderer as the thief do take away another man's possession against the owner's will. After that he might shew that a slanderer is worse than any thief, because a good name is better than all the goods in the world, and that the loss of money may be recovered, but the loss of a man's good name cannot be called back again: and a thief may restore that again which he hath taken away, but a slanderer cannot give a man his good name again which he hath taken from him. Again, he that stealeth goods or cattle robs only but one man, but an evil-tongued man infecteth all their minds unto whose ears this report shall come.'" [16]

In spite of the fact that the thought is exactly the same, namely, that slander is worse than theft, the two passages are deficient in signs which might tie them together. Wilson is not speaking in actual contempt of wealth or its transitoriness and he lacks the idea with which Shakespeare closes, that the slanderer is not himself enriched by his filchings. There are many aspects of the subject as presented by Wilson not mentioned in Shakespeare, and

---

[16] See Mair's edition, pp. 124-125. Wilson goes on to amplify his proposition "by the places and circumstances," showing that slander is the more heinous offence because the law does not touch it, that it is craftily committed like a poisoning, and that it is an enchantment injuring the mind rather than the body. He repeats his thought more briefly (see page 186) under the heading "Correction."

Wilson's chief interest in the passage as a logical demonstration is not hinted at. To Wilson it was a clever bit of unexpected argument. As used by Iago, it was a facile moral sentiment. The chances are that both Shakespeare and Wilson were doing the same thing; both were choosing an attractive bit of Renaissance learning, a well-rounded moral sentiment, to serve an immediate purpose. Wilson borrowed much from the rhetorical works of Erasmus.[17] It happens that this passage is one of his borrowings. The thought was a favorite one with Erasmus. It occurs in *Lingua* among his precepts concerning moderation in speech,[18] and is alluded to several times in his letters.[19] Wilson's actual source was, however, *De Conscribendis Epistolis*,[20] in which the following passage occurs: *Sapientis est famæ suæ longe diligentius, quam opibus suis, non minus vero diligenter quam vitæ consulere. Minus siquidem damni, & incommodi accipit, qui pecuniam, aut etiam vitam amittit, quam qui famam. Pecunia enim amissa sarciri potest, fama semel amissa, in integrum restituitur nunquam. Et vita quidem corporis, quum certos a natura terminos acceperit, in longum tempus extendi nequit. . . . Quod si homines iis rebus maxime timere videmus, quæ cum sint preciossimæ, facillime tamen perduntur, ac difficillime restituuntur: sapiens existimandus non est, qui famæ, quæ neque restitui potest semel amissa, & qua nihil habet homo preciosius, non multo diligentius consulendum putat quam pecuniæ, aut etiam vitæ. Potest etiam tribus dumtaxat, aut quattuor partibus confici collectio: si vel confirmatio, vel expolitio, vel utraque omittitur.* Erasmus then proceeds to develop the idea as a rhetorical exemplum. Wilson has apparently borrowed the idea, and condensed and adapted it to his own purposes.

Slander was not originally one of the Seven Deadly Sins, but in certain groups of treatises it found a place as one of the sub-headings under Envy.[21] Slander is, therefore, usually treated

---

[17] Russell H. Wagner, "Wilson and his Sources," *Quarterly Journal of Speech*, XV, 525-537.

[18] *Opera Omnia*, Lugduni Batavorum (1703), tom. IV, 66 3 F.

[19] See Ep. CCCCLXXX and DCIII.

[20] Cap. xlvi; *loc. cit.*, tom. I, 407-408.

[21] R. Elfreda Fowler, *Une source française des poèmes de Gower* (Macon, 1905), pp. 59 ff., and "Tableau I, L'Ordre des vices et des vertus," pp. 81-96; Kate O. Petersen, *The Sources of the Pardoner's Tale* (Boston, 1901), pp. 35-81.

under Envy in the moral treatises of the sixteenth century. I have, however, found only one in which this particular example is used. That, with the appearance in the works of Erasmus, is perhaps enough to suggest that it was a moralistic commonplace, and, for that reason, less likely to be derivable only from Wilson. La Primaudaye in his chapter " Of Envie, Hatred, and Backbiting," [22] after inveighing against envy, declaring it like Wilson, to be sorcery (in which he is following Plutarch), and saying that it is hurtful to others " and much more noisome to him that possesseth it," makes this statement: " The occasion whereof is the ill will which naturally he beareth against all them that deserve more than himselfe, wherupon he striveth rather to blame, or to wrest in ill part whatsoever was well meant, than to reape any profit thereby." La Primaudaye's main utterance about backbiting, which follows closely on the sentence quoted, seems to me to be, though briefer than Wilson's description, closer to the Shakesperean passage than is Wilson himself: " Of this wilde plant of envie, backbiting is a branch, which delighteth and feedeth it selfe with slandering and lying, whereupon good men commonly receive great plagues, when they over-lightly give credit to backbiters. . . . For seeing good fame and credit is more pretious than any treasure, a man hath no lesse an injury offered him when his good name is taken away, than when he is spoiled of his substance." Thus La Primaudaye presents all three of the ideas in the Shakespearean passage, namely, that good name is a treasure, that to be slandered is to be robbed, and that slander is without profit to the slanderer. There is of course no question of presenting La Primaudaye as a source for Shakespeare, but there is certainly removed the necessity of regarding Wilson as a source.

The tale of the relations between Wilson and Shakespeare is almost told. The late Sir Walter Raleigh of Oxford [23] make a dexterous and legitimate use of Wilson in the following passage: " Falstaff was never at the end of his resources; and if he had chosen to inveigh against his own manner of life, not without some sidelong depreciation of his companions, might he not have spoken after this

[22] *The French Academie*, Part I. Translated by T. B. Imprinted at London by Edmund Bollifant for G. Bishop and Ralph Newbery, 1586, pp. 432-435.

[23] *Shakespeare* (London, 1907), pp. 50-51.

fashion: 'Now, Lord! what a man is he; he was not ashamed, being a Gentleman, yea a man of good years, and much authority, and the head Officer of a Duke's house, to play at Dice in an Ale house with boys, bawds and varlets. It had been a great fault to play at so vile a game among such vile persons, being no Gentleman, being no Officer, being not of such years; but being both a man of fair lands, of an ancient house, of great authority, an Officer of a Duke, yea, and to such a Duke, and a man of such years that his white hairs should warn him to avoid all such folly, to play at such a game with such Roysters and such Varlets, yea, and that in such an house as none comes thither but Thieves, Bawds, and Ruffians; now before God, I cannot speak shame enough on him'? This speech which is given as an example in Thomas Wilson's *Art of Rhetoric* [24] (1553), has not Falstaff's wit, but it has the rhetorical syntax which he borrows when he rides the high horse." In this Sir Walter makes no claims for dependence by Shakespeare on Wilson and yet indicates pretty clearly that Shakespeare knew the kind of thing that Wilson's book embodies.

The last case of an actual claim of dependence is that put forward by Mr. G. H. Mair in the introduction to his edition of *The Arte of Rhetorique* (pp. xxxiii-xxxiv). He calls attention to Drake's suggestion (really, as we have seen, that of George Chalmers) that the character of Dogberry was derived from Wilson. This we have already considered. Mair finds more certain evidence of Shakespeare's reading of Wilson in *Love's Labour's Lost*. Holofernes remarks (Act IV, scene ii, lines 137-138), "I will look again on the *Intellect* of the letter, for the nomination of the party writing to the person written unto." "The word here," says Mair, "is Wilson's Intellection, which is 'a trope, when we gather or iudge the whole by the part, or part by the whole.'" In point of fact it is not. "Intellect" is an Anglicization of the Latin word *intellectus,* which had and has the meaning "sense or interpretation." It is here used as a technical term in the art of letter-writing. Wilson's word "intellection" is for *intellectio* and means "synecdoche." Wilson probably borrowed it from the *De Ratione dicendi ad C. Herennium,*[25] formerly attributed to Cicero.

[24] Mair's edition, pp. 122-123.
[25] See *Incerti Auctoris de Ratione dicendi ad C. Herennium Libri IV,* edidit Fridericus Marx (Lipsiae, MDCCCCIV), IV, 33, 44e.

There is thus no value in this parellelism, which, incidentally, was first adduced by T. S. Baynes in *Shakespeare Studies* (London, 1896, p. 192). "But," Mair continues, "Holofernes is not the only student of *The Arte of Rhetorique* in the company gathered in Navarre. Don Armado culled some of the splendour of his speech from this source. His letter to Jaquenetta is modeled on one of Wilson's examples. He is writing of King Cophetua (*Love's Labour's Lost,* IV, i, 67-81):

'He it was that might rightly say, Veni, vidi, vici; which to annothanize the vulgar,—O base and obscure vulgar!—videlicet, He came, saw, and overcame: he came, one; saw, two; overcame, three. Who came? the king: why did he come? to see: why did he see? to overcome: to whom came he? to the beggar: what saw he? the beggar: who overcame he? the beggar. The conclusion is victory: on whose side? the king's. The captive is enriched: on whose side? the beggar's. The catastrophe is nuptial: on whose side? the king's: no, on both in one, or one in both. I am the king; for so stands the comparison: thou the beggar; for so witnesseth thy lowliness.'

"All this follows the questions appended to the Example of commending King David given below p. 21." We must see this example, for Mr. Mair adds, "A certain knowledge of it [Shakespeare's acquaintance with Wilson's work] can be proved beyond doubt." The questions referred to, given under the caption "Examining of the circumstaunces," are: i. Who did the deed? ii. What was done? iii. Wherefore did he it? iiii. What help had he to it? v. Wherefore did he it? vi. How did he it? vii. What time did he it?

Although, to begin with, I confess that with the best will in the world I cannot discover an inevitable interdependence, there is yet this behind it, that the passage from Shakespeare is making fun of just such a general rubric as Wilson gives. It is one of the most familiar of logical and rhetorical devices and rests ultimately on the "places" of logic. Aristotle himself had conceived of rhetoric as the counterpart of dialectic and had complained (*Rhet.,* I, i.) that earlier writers on rhetoric had neglected the true basis of oratory, which is persuasion through logical conviction. The *Topica* of Aristotle and of course of Cicero have to do with "places" as forms of reasoning, and both books have as intention the preparation of logical discourses. Quintillian defines a *locus* as "the seat of arguments in which they are latent and from which they are to be derived," and gives many outlines of appropriate *loci*. One of these Wilson himself repeats in this form (p. 132) : i. What is done. ii. By whom. iii. Against whom. iiii. Upon what mind. v. At what time. vi. In what place. vii. After what sort. viii. How much he would have done. The particular rubric to which Mr. Mair refers in Wilson is a mere inquiry into the circumstances as they might apply to persons; and, although he gives further on (p. 112) a still more careful outline for the same inquiry, the matter is much too common to form the basis for any argument of specific reference to Wilson on Shakespeare's part. Quintillian, the Ciceronian works, and various other rhetorical writings were in wide circulation.

Indeed, the whole thing is nothing more than a form of the *methodus* of Aristotelian logic, and the pedantry of both Armado and Holofernes is, to my mind, quite as much logical as rhetorical. Had it been intentionally rhetorical one might have expected a specifically absurd use of the "figures of rhetoric" rather than of the "places" of logic. As it is (and I think this weakens the argument for Shakespeare's dependence on Wilson's *Rhetorique*), what you find ridiculed in *Love's Labour's Lost* might quite as well have come from Wilson's *Rule of Reason* (1551, 1552, 1553, 1563, 1567, 1584?, 1593) as from his *Arte of Rhetorique*. There is indeed one circumstance that connects Shakespeare with *The Rule of Reason*. Not only did Shakespeare have a considerable familiarity with the terminology of formal logic,[26] but it is just possible that he derived a suggestion from that book for the device of mis-punctuation which he uses in Peter Quince's prologue in *A Midsummer-Night's Dream,* Act V, scene i, lines 108-117. It will be remembered that a similar device appears in a letter in *Ralph Roister Doister* (III, iii, 36-70) and that this letter appears as an example in the third edition (1553) of *The Rule of Reason* and is there attributed to Nicholas Udall, thus forming the chief means of dating the play from which it was taken. Copies of *Ralph Roister Doister* were probably none too unmerous, and copies of Wilson were plentiful. *The Rule of Reason* would certainly have been more available than the play, or the poem on *Women,* from Add. MS 17492, printed in Flügel's *Lesebuch* (p. 39), or that in Ebert's

---

[26] See my article, "Shakespeare and Formal Logic" in *Studies in English Philology, a Miscellany in Honor of Frederick Klaeber* (Minneapolis, 1929), pp. 380-396.

Jahrbuch (XIV, 214), or that given by Furness in the Variorum edition of *A Midsummer-Night's Dream* from a manuscript collection of short poems formerly belonging to Dr. Percy; and these are the only cases of mis-pointing for comic effect earlier than *A Midsummer-Night's Dream* which have been cited. I do not insist upon this connection, but merely state it as a possibility slightly more definite than the original contention.

The editor of *Love's Labour's Lost* in the Arden Shakespeare (Methuen, 1906) cites a number of parallels in that play to Wilson's *Arte of Rhetorique* and seems to believe that Wilson was an actual source. There is no doubt that in *Love's Labour's Lost* there is abundant satire on pedantry and that part of it is rhetorical. As the editor cites these parallels he cites others to Chapman, Harvey, and other Elizabethan writers, and I think there can be little doubt that in so doing he is pointing the way to a correct explanation of the stylistic vagaries of that play. In his introduction (pp. xxxiv-xli) the editor makes out a strong case for connecting the play with various living writers, particularly Nashe and Harvey. The idea that *Love's Labour's Lost* was intended to ridicule a particular literary coterie, a fantastic academy of advanced, if not atheistical views, has been vigorously espoused by Sir Arthur Quiller-Couch and Professor J. Dover Wilson and by various other scholars.[27] Whatever may be the value of the identification of particular persons, it is certainly a better idea that the play was meant as a satire against pedantical behavior and speech on the part of a literary coterie, than that it was a new composition made up of various pedantical bits. School learning in England had passed its infancy by the time *Love's Labour's Lost* was composed, and mere rhetoric and logic as learned in the schools had given place to the more complex forms of affectation ridiculed in that play.

We have now examined the case for Shakespeare's acquaintance with Wilson's *Arte of Rhetorique,* all the citations of parallels of importance which have ever been made. They are fairly numerous. We began by admitting that it was inherently probable that Shakespeare had read that popular and genuinely meritorious book, and we know that such books were freely read. We know that Shakespeare read widely. But there is no testimony covering the

---

[27] *Love's Labour's Lost* (Cambridge, 1923), pp. xxviii-xxxiv; Sir E. K. Chambers, *William Shakespeare*, I, 335-337.

case, the argument from antecedent probability is of no value, and the argument from sign—the only one in the whole list of artificial arguments enumerated in Aristotle's *Topica* which could possibly have any weight—fails to establish itself. In every case we have found that the thing supposed to have been borrowed was a thing which might just as well have come from some other quarter. In the case of the borrowings from Harsnet the argument from sign is unmistakable. The names of the fiends are specific things which to any reasonable mind did actually come from *The Declaration of Egregious Popish Imposters*. They belong under the logical category of accident, not to species or proprium or any other category. It cannot be said that the large number of parallels adds to the strength of the case. A case unsupported by testimony is as strong as it can be made by the argument from sign, and in this ideational currency of sixteenth-century humanism which both Wilson and Shakespeare were using, the specific markings of the coins are not sufficient, the proper markings are themselves none too convincing, and the accidental markings are not present.

It is not my intention to imply that Shakespeare knew no formal rhetoric. He uses a number of rhetorical terms, and there is no reason to think that he may not have employed his many rhetorical figures with conscious knowledge. It is at least possible that the difference in style between the speeches of Brutus and Antony in *Julius Caesar* reflects the current rhetorical classification of oratory derived form Cicero and Quintillian. Henry V's denunciation of the traitors (*Henry V,* Act II, scene ii), particularly of Scrope, has points suggestive of the rhetorical invective.[28] I do not mean even to assert that Shakespeare did not know Wilson's *Arte of Rhetorique* but merely that there is no unmistakable evidence that he did so.

*Stanford University.*

---

[28] For a close parallel in form to the invective in *Henry V* see *An Invective ayenste the great and detestable vice, treason,* published by Berthelet in 1539, where the author, Sir Richard Morison, denounces Cardinal Pole.

## SHAKESPEARE'S EARLIEST PLAYS

### By ROBERT ADGER LAW

Before the Shakespeare Group of the Modern Language Association of America, meeting at Cleveland in 1929, Professor Tucker Brooke suggested as a real desideratum the determination by a competent committee of such books and articles on Shakespeare published annually as every Shakespeare scholar ought to know. The number, I think, would be small. Yet had we in operation such machinery to separate the grain from the abundant chaff, I feel sure that one comparatively recent book deserving acclaim as worthy of human consumption would be Peter Alexander's study, *Shakespeare's Henry VI and Richard III,* issued from the Cambridge University Press two years ago. This book has already had marked influence on English and American scholars in its field

In a small volume of 229 pages Mr. Alexander attacks the generally accepted theory as to the composition of the *Second and Third Parts of Henry the Sixth*.[1] Through minute examination of the texts of these two plays as printed in the 1623 Folio, and comparison with the 1594 and 1595 Quarto, usually known as *The Contention* and *The True Tragedy,* the young British scholar has all but demonstrated that the Folio texts preceded the Quartos, instead of being founded on them. To establish his case Alexander has had to combat the views, not only of the vast majority of modern editors of Shakespeare, but also the judgments expressed publicly by Sir Edmund K. Chambers, Mr. A. W. Pollard, and Professor Tucker Brooke. He has undertaken the task without mincing words.

[1] Generally accepted, as introductions to various recent editions of these plays will show. Yet in 1927 T. W. Baldwin in *The Organization and Personnel of the Shakespearean Company,* p. 140, n., had expressed a "hope to show" that the "First and Second *Contentions* are only *2* and *3 Henry VI* printed from damaged manuscript." Again, in 1928, Miss Madeleine Doran contributed to the *University of Iowa Humanistic Studies* an analysis of *Henry VI, Parts II and III,* which reached the same conclusions by a somewhat different line of argument from Alexander's. But Alexander had previously announced his results and his general process in arriving at them through a series of articles in the *Times Literary Supplement* in 1924, and to these Miss Doran acknowledges her debt. Alexander, on the other hand, shows no acquaintance with American scholars on this problem.

As a result, devout worshippers in the Temple of Learning have hastened to confess their faults before the altar. First to declare his mistakes was Mr. Pollard, who acknowledged in the Introduction to Alexander's book that he had been "hypnotized by the old idea of the wicked publisher."[2] Then Tucker Brooke, reviewing the book with chivalric gentleness, pleaded that his own error was venial, to be charged, not "to original sin, but to simple ignorance of what is now known, or at least suspected."[3] Sir Edmund Chambers in his monumental, *William Shakespeare* (1930), puts it more bluntly: "I formerly accepted this view [of Malone], but a recent study, suggested by Alexander's papers and Greg's work . . . has convinced me that it is wrong."[4] And the conservative Dutch scholar, Professor B. A. P. van Dam, reviews the Alexander book under the suggestive title, "Shakespeare Problems Nearing Solution."[5] In response to Alexander's thundering homily a host of sinners is still crying, "Peccavimus, peccavimus."

Yet this very willingness to accept as genuine the main article in the contention of Alexander, namely that the Folio text of the Henry VI plays preceded the Quartos in composition, may easily blind one's eyes to definite weakness in his argument. For he is unwilling to stop there. If *The Contention* and *The True Tragedy* are "bad quartos" of the *Second* and *Third Henry the Sixth*, he assumes without thorough discussion that *A Shrew* is a "bad quarto" of *The Shrew* by Shakespeare, and he even implies belief in some similar explanation of *The Troublesome Reign of King John*, the lost *Hamlet*, which he attributes to Shakespeare, and the early *King Leir*. Such speculation surely darkens counsel. Particularly must one deprecate the hazardous assumptions contained in Alexander's final chapter, "The First Period."

"Although it is not yet possible," writes Alexander in this chapter, "to offer any precise date for the beginning of the first period, *Titus Andronicus* and *The Comedy of Errors* can be placed at its very commencement and dated some considerable time before

---

[2] *Op. cit.*, p. 4.
[3] In *The Journal of English and Germanic Philology*, XXIX, 443 (1930).
[4] *Op. cit.*, I, 281.
[5] *English Studies*, XII, 81-97 (1930).

1589."[6] This statement embraces several conclusions of fact, and every one seems to me erroneous.

To these conclusions Mr. Alexander has apparently been led by his acceptance of four separate assumptions: (1) That the inclusion of any play in the First Folio by its editors, Heminge and Condell, is evidence that each line of it was composed, not merely revised, by Shakespeare, and, therefore, Shakespeare wrote without assistance the three Parts of *Henry the Sixth, Titus Andronicus,* and *The Comedy of Errors;* (2) That Shakespeare was a rural schoolmaster before he became a playwright, and so used classical themes for his first works: *Titus Andronicus, The Comedy of Errors,* and *Venus and Adonis;* (3) That Kyd, Marlowe, and Shakespeare were all writers for Pembroke's company of actors before the plague of 1592-3, that Marlowe was dismissed by Pembroke for his radical religious views, Kyd was imprisoned and tortured without intervention by Pembroke, and Shakespeare may then have left the company in disgust; (4) That resemblances between the Henry VI plays and Marlowe's *Edward the Second* are the result of Marlowe's conscious effort to imitate Shakespeare. Evidence to negate all four of these points is almost overwhelming, but brief discussion of each in turn should make clear the argument.

First, the fundamental weakness of Alexander's entire book is his insistence on Shakespeare's sole authorship of every play in the Folio. One can pardon his refusal to follow the older school of critics in assigning every individual line of the Henry VI plays to Marlowe, to Greene, to Peele, or to Shakespeare. One may likewise approve his good judgment in rejecting the theories of the new school of "disintegrators," who find a mysterious new playwright in every inconsistency of plot, and evidence of revision in every unmetrical line. But it is Mr. Pollard, not a disintegrator, who in his Introduction to this volume expresses doubt of Heminge and Condell's supposed guarantee that the three Henry VI plays and *Richard the Third* "were each and all the unaided work of

---

[6] *Op. cit.*, p. 200. Cf. the statement on p. 198: "Jonson's reference to time . . . undoubtedly strengthens the claim that *The Comedy of Errors* and *Titus Andronicus* are, as their debt to Plautus and Seneca suggests, among the earliest ventures of the schoolmaster who came from Warwickshire, possibly in 1586."

Shakespeare."[7] And it is Sir Edmund Chambers, chief denouncer of "disintegration," who in his latest work sees probably divided authorship in *First Henry the Sixth*,[8] in *Titus Andronicus*,[9] in *The Taming of the Shrew*,[10] in *Macbeth*,[11] in *Timon of Athens*,[12] in *Cymbeline*,[13] and in *Henry the Eighth*.[14] One shows no derogation to the memory of either Master William Shakespeare or Heminge and Condell in holding to the conviction that at least in the beginning and at the close of his dramatic career Shakespeare was a reviser or a collaborative author of plays that now bear his name. Alexander is inconsistent in arguing at one time so strongly that the absence of Shakespeare's name from the title-page of a quarto means nothing, and at another time that the presence of a play under his name in the Folio means everything. For my own part, I am yet to be convinced that Shakespeare wrote any large share of either the *First Henry the Sixth* or *Titus Andronicus*.

Second, Shakespeare may once have been a country schoolmaster, and Professor Joseph Q. Adams has made the early tradition more plausible, but it still remains far from proof. Professor Adams surmised further that the schoolmaster took *The Comedy of Errors* complete with him to London, but Adams knew that this was only a surmise. The objection to it is that no rural schoolmaster without stage experience could write so good an acting play.[15] But Alexander goes several steps beyond Adams in attributing to "the schoolmaster's" classical training *The Comedy of Errors, Titus Andronicus,* and *Venus and Adonis*. Of the plays, which Alexander

---

[7] *Op. cit.*, p. 23.
[8] *William Shakespeare*, I, 290.
[9] *Ibid.*, I, 320.
[10] *Ibid.*, I, 324.
[11] *Ibid.*, I, 472.
[12] *Ibid.*, I, 481.
[13] *Ibid.*, I, 486.
[14] *Ibid.*, I, 497. Since the sentence above was written, I have read with interest Sir Edmund's comment on Alexander's book in *The Year's Work in English Studies for 1929*, pp. 176-177, with a sturdy defence of his position against attacks from both sides.
[15] As shown below, Baldwin's entire argument in *William Shakespeare Adapts a Hanging* (1931) counts against this surmise. Shakespeare must have seen or heard of this hanging in October, 1588, some time after his arrival in London.

dates " some considerable time before 1589," I shall have something more to say presently.  But in connection with *Venus* he writes: " Shakespeare's first poem is *Venus and Adonis,* another work suggested by his Latin reading . . . *Titus Andronicus* . . . is linked to this poem by many internal marks of style, subject matter, and treatment; most arguments against *Titus* can be applied with equal force to *Venus and Adonis.*  The poem, however, cannot be explained away, and it clearly agrees with the tradition that in his youth Shakespeare was a schoolmaster, not with the view that he came to London with everything to seek." [16]  Now *Venus and Adonis* was entered on the Stationers' Register April 18, 1593, and critical opinion to-day agrees in placing its date of composition within a year of its printing.[17]  Almost certainly it owes much to Lodge's *Scillaes Metamorphosis* (1589).  The use, then, of the poem to prove Shakespeare's interest in classical themes on his first arrival in London about 1586 is unfortunate.

Third, Marlowe's *Edward the Second* was acted by Pembroke's company, for we are so informed on the title-page of that drama. But we have no evidence that Marlowe wrote any other plays for those actors.  The one reason for connecting Kyd with the same company is his letter to Sir John Puckering with its reference to a certain "Lord" whom Marlowe served in "writing for his players."  But that this refers to the Lord Pembroke is disputed by Boas, Greg, Chambers, Tannenbaum, and Brooke.[18]  Shakespeare's connection with Pembroke's men at any time is still more doubtful. It is questioned by Pollard in his Introduction to Alexander's book.[19]  Much more reasonable than Alexander's theory as to the relations of the three dramatists is that advocated by Brooke, following Tannenbaum, that Lord Strange probably dismissed Marlowe for his supposed atheistical views.  The marked difference between *Edward the Second* and all earlier plays of Marlowe,

---

[16] *Op. cit.,* pp. 140-141.

[17] See Carleton Brown's clear discussion of the date in his introduction to the poem (Tudor Shakespeare, 1913), pp. vii-viii; Adams, *Life of Shakespeare,* pp. 147-149; Tucker Brooke, *Shakespeare of Stratford* (Yale Shakespeare, 1926), p. 120.

[18] See Brooke's *Life of Marlowe* (1930), pp. 45-47 for a lucid and temperate discussion of the vexed matter.

[19] *Op. cit.,* p. 12.

Brooke plausibly suggests, may be explained if the earlier plays were written with Alleyn in mind for the title rôle, while *Edward the Second* was composed for a rival company with no Alleyn. Shakespeare was at this time probably a Strange's man, as he certainly was later.

Fourth, the belief that Marlowe the rebellious, the Cambridge Master of Arts, the confidential agent of the Queen's Privy Council, the author of *Tamburlaine, Faustus,* and *The Jew of Malta,* should deliberately set himself to imitate that "upstart crow, beautified with our feathers," demands a faith that reason without miracle shall never plant in me. Greene, even after using the phrase just quoted, might have done so, but Marlowe never. That Shakespeare could learn from Marlowe, his *Richard the Third* and *Richard the Second,* both of them surely dated after *Edward the Second,* go far to prove. No sufficient reason has yet been advanced for discarding the long accepted theory that Marlowe at his death in 1593 was a dramatist and a poet of far greater repute than was William Shakespeare.

Unless, then, I have failed to grasp the entire basis of Alexander's claim to a rediscovery of "Shakespeare's First Period," as a result of a new conception of the origin of the Henry VI plays, his whole case must fall to the ground. For Shakespeare is probably not sole author of all the Folio plays, did not begin writing like a schoolmaster on classical themes, was not connected with Pembroke's company along with Marlowe and Peele, and was not imitated by Marlowe. But granted that *The Contention* and *The True Tragedy* were not the first tools used "in the workshop," the workshop still remains. What tools did he use? May it still be true that *The Comedy of Errors* and *Titus Andronicus* were written by Shakespeare alone at the very beginning of his first period "some considerable time before 1589?" Let us discuss the two plays separately.

*The Comedy of Errors,* it so happens, has been critically analyzed by three American scholars within the past five years. In 1926 Professor Allison Gaw of Southern California made a detailed examination of it under the caption "The Evolution of *The Comedy of Errors.*"[20] While I am not ready to accept all of Gaw's conclu-

[20] *PMLA.,* XLI, 620-666.

sions as to antenatal relations of the present text, I find his opening explanation of the structure of the play and its relation to its Latin sources altogether clear and admirable. Professor Gaw cogently argues for the excellent technique of the construction. Further investigation of the dramatist's use of his Plautine sources in characterization and in plot-structure has been made by Dr. Erma Gill of Texas in two published articles.[21] Again the result is to place a higher estimate than has usually been assigned to the author's mastery of technique in this play. More recently still, Professor T. W. Baldwin of Illinois, through his scholarly edition of the comedy in the Arden Shakespeare (1928), supplemented by his *William Shakespeare Adapts a Hanging* (1931), has presented a strong case for the actual composition of the play in December, 1589. Professor Baldwin's argument for that date rests partly on the topography of the enveloping action added by Shakespeare to the plot, partly on the history of Elizabethan theaters, partly on actual events known to have occurred in October, 1588. The upshot of the three independent analyses by competent scholars is to increase respect for the author's technical attainment in construction of the comedy and to disprove any theory which would place the composition before or immediately after Shakespeare's arrival in London.

*Titus Andronicus* was first printed in 1594 and is unheard of before that year. Unfortunately our knowledge of its composition is more circumscribed than that of the comedy just mentioned. But Alexander correctly notes that it has "with its torrent of horrors a smoothness not found in the dramas of Marlowe."[22] He might have added that the same smoothness is not found in other dramas known to have been written by Shakespeare before 1594. The structure of the play and some of its characters are too good, in my opinion, to be the early work of Shakespeare. Inclusion of this play in the Folio is evidence of Shakespeare's hand in it, but not of his sole authorship. To date the play some years before 1589 is utterly unwarranted.

---

[21] "A Comparison of the Characters in *The Comedy of Errors* with Those in the *Menaechmi*," *Texas Studies in English*, No. 5 (1925), pp. 90-94; and "The Plot-Structure of *The Comedy of Errors*," *Texas Studies in English*, No. 10 (1930), pp. 13-65. Professor Gill has other articles on the play in preparation.

[22] *Op. cit.*, p. 205.

But if there is a "smoothness" in *Titus Andronicus,* there is likewise smoothness with mastery of technique in *Richard the Third* and in *Romeo and Juliet,* both dated about 1595, but a notable lack of smoothness or finished technique in the Henry VI plays and in *Love's Labor's Lost.* Granting as we do the skill in putting together the plots of *The Comedy of Errors,* we must acknowledge in that play much beating about of brains and exquisite fooling to interfere with the progress of the action. Unless and until one can give external evidence to the contrary, we are driven to the conclusion that if Shakespeare is responsible for all these plays in their present shape, then the Henry VI plays and *Love's Labor's Lost* are products of " the workshop," while *Romeo* and *Richard the Third* furnish examples of mastered art. Further study of these plays, with perhaps the addition of *A Midsummer Night's Dream,* may yet solve the mystery of " The First Period."

**University of Texas.**

# CYMBELINE, BOCCACCIO, AND THE WAGER STORY IN ENGLAND

## By William Flint Thrall

This paper makes no attempt to discuss in full the vexed problem of Shakespeare's possible indebtedness to *Decameron* ii. 9 for the wager plot in *Cymbeline*. It proposes rather to call to the attention of such students as are not satisfied with the Holinshed-Boccaccio source formula some neglected documents that should be taken into account in case any one ever attempts a frank appraisal of all the evidence pointing toward Shakespeare's use of an English source.

The somewhat summary manner in which such writers as Sir Edmund Chambers, Professor J. Q. Adams, and Professor Tucker Brooke have dismissed the possibility that some non-Boccaccian tradition may have been utilized, seems to justify the effort, since the statements of these scholars may be taken to indicate a prevailing tendency both to rule out of court certain evidence which has seemed to many special students of the problem significant and to ignore at least one important primary document as well as some comparatively recent contributions to the critical literature of the subject.

Professor Adams says: "The plot he [Shakespeare] derived from two sources. In his familiar thumb-worn copy of Holinshed's *Chronicle*, whence he had drawn so many of his plays, he found the story of an early British king, Cunobeline; and in the *Decamerone* of Boccaccio he found the story of Imogen, Posthumus, and Iachimo under the names of Ginevra, Lomellino, and Ambrogiuolo. Boccaccio's work had not yet been printed in an English translation, but Shakespeare could have read it in the original Italian, or in a French version. From these two sources, with important changes suggested by his better taste and with many additions from his brooding imagination, he wove the stories of Cymbeline and Imogen."[1] Chambers remarks upon the widespread character of the wager story and continues: " Stray coincidences of detail are insufficient to show that Shakespeare used any other version of it than

---

[1] Joseph Quincy Adams, *A Life of William Shakespeare* (Boston and New York, 1923), pp. 416-417.

the story of Bernabo of Genoa in Boccaccio's *Decameron,* ii. 9. They are closest in a story called *Westward for Smelts,* but this though dated by Steevens in 1603, was not registered until January 15, 1620. Boccaccio's story was translated into English as *Frederick of Jennen,* and printed by Jan van Doesborgh at Antwerp in 1518." [2] No less pronounced is Professor Tucker Brooke's statement [3] of the adequacy of Boccaccio as sole source: "There appears now no reason to assume that Shakespeare knew any version of the story except that of Boccaccio." [4] Professor W. W. Lawrence, unwilling to commit himself unreservedly to the Boccaccio hypothesis, for the purposes of his argument accepts "with due reservations" the Boccaccio version as Shakespeare's source. Like Chambers, Lawrence is inclined to belittle the evidence of *Westward for Smelts,* and his comments on *Frederick of Jennen* are based upon the assumption that our knowledge of the story is limited to the fragmentary copy in the Douce collection.[5]

No one of these writers and no editor of *Cymbeline,* so far as I know, reflects an adequate knowledge of the facts about *Frederick of Jennen.* Yet it is a close analogue of the Boccaccio version; it appeared in three English editions in the sixteenth century; and it contains features of the story emphasized by Shakespeare and not present in Boccaccio. I do not propose to urge *Frederick* as a direct source for *Cymbeline.* It is, however, a version which Shakespeare may very well have read and it supplies important evidence of the popularity of the wager tale in England in the time of Shakespeare and his forerunners. It yields some data, too, which tend to lessen the force of the Boccaccian argument.

In the late fifteenth century there appeared in Germany a version of the wager story under the title *Historie von vier Kaufmännern* (commonly referred to as *Four Merchants*). It is a close relative

---

[2] E. K. Chambers, *William Shakespeare, A Study of Facts and Problems* (Oxford, 1930), I, 484-487.

[3] Tucker Brooke and others, *Shakespeare's Principal Plays* (New York, 1923), pp. 813-814.

[4] Some editors, of course, have been more cautious, *e. g.,* Furness (variorum edition of *Cymbeline,* Philadephhia, 1913, p. 479) and Neilson (*Shakespeare,* Students' Cambridge edition, 1906, p. 381).

[5] William Witherle Lawrence, "The Wager in *Cymbeline,*" *Shakespeare's Problem Comedies* (New York, 1931), pp. 174-205 and 247-253. See esp. pp. 180-182, and p. 250, Notes 12 and 17.

of *Decameron* ii. 9, though not derived from it.[6] In it the disguised heroine assumes the name of Frederick of Jennen. It was printed first at Nürnberg about 1478, this edition being followed by four others, the last appearing in Hamburg in 1510. Its popularity in Germany appears to have subsided after this date because of the appearance of German translations of Boccaccio. *Four Merchants* and its dramatization in Germany have been studied in a dissertation of Kurt Mechel.[7] Through the 1510 edition the tale spread to the Netherlands, England, Denmark, and Sweden. Mechel shows that Hans Sachs's comedy, *Die unschuldig fraw Genura,* 1548, while based upon a German translation of Boccaccio, makes definite use of *Four Merchants*. It is not without interest to students of *Cymbeline* that this German dramatic predecessor of Shakespeare utilized as sources both the literary version (Boccaccio) and the popular version (*Four Merchants*) available to him. A later German comedy, *Eine schöne Historia von einem frommen Gottfürchtigen Kaufman von Padua* (Breslau, 1596), by Zacharias Leibholdt, a pupil of Sachs's, draws both upon a German translation of Boccaccio and upon Sachs's play, according to Mechel.[8]

An English translation of *Four Merchants,* under the title of *Frederick of Jennen,* was printed in Antwerp by Jan van Doesborgh in 1518. A copy of this edition is in the Pierpont Morgan Library. This publication sometimes has been referred to erroneously as a translation of *Decameron ii. 9*.[9] Another edition, represented by a fragment in the Douce collection in the Bodleian, appeared in England soon afterward. The printer, according to Douce, was Pynson,

[6] Gaston Paris, *Romania* XXXII (1903), 507-508, esp. Note 1; and Mechel's dissertation cited in the following note.

[7] *Die " Historie von Vier Kaufmännern " (Le Cycle de la Gageure) und deren dramatische Bearbeitungen in der deutschen Literatur des XVI und XVII Jahrhunderts* (Halle, 1914). This discussion seems to have failed to attract the attention of *Cymbeline* students.

[8] *Ibid.*, pp. 32 ff.

[9] Chambers, *op. cit.*, p. 487. The error seems to have originated in Steevens' remark that a deformed and interpolated English version of Boccaccio's story had been printed in Antwerp in 1518 (E. Dowden, ed., *Cymbeline,* English Arden edition, 3d edition, London, 1918, Introd., p. xxiii. On p. xxxiii Dowden gives separate notice to the German tale, *Four Merchants*, apparently without realizing that one was a translation of the other).

and the date, according to Furnivall, was before 1537.[10] The fragments are printed by Furnivall.[11] In the "short title" catalogue this edition is hypothetically dated and assigned to Wynken de Worde, 1520. A third English edition of *Frederick* was printed by Abraham Vele about 1560. A copy of this edition is in the British Museum bound up with five other pamphlets dealing with the woman question.[12]

That *Frederick of Jennen* was well known in England in the sixteenth century is attested not only by these three editions but also by its inclusion in the famous list of Captain Cox's story books in *Robert Laneham's Letter,* where it appears seventh in the list of "matters of storie" under the title "Frederick of Gene."[13] Gollancz in the Temple Shakespeare edition of *Cymbeline* commented on the popularity of the *Four Merchants* story in Denmark and Iceland in the sixteenth century and referred to his own possession of transcripts of Icelandic ballads and rimes on the subject. Unaware of *Frederick of Jennen* or not recognizing it as an English translation of *Four Merchants,* Gollancz shrewdly inferred its existence: "Some such English variant of the Imogen story was probably current in England in the sixteenth century, and may account for certain features of the play [*Cymbeline*]; e. g. the introduction in Act I, Sc. iv of the four nationalities."[14]

A brief summary[15] of *Frederick of Jennen* with some comments

---

[10] F. J. Furnivall, ed., *Robert Laneham's Letter, New Shakespeare Society,* Ser. 6, 14 (London and New York, 1907), "Forewords," pp. xxv-xxviii.

[11] *Loc. cit.*

[12] The five are: *The Deceyte of Women; The Schole house of women; The Defence of women and especially of English women, made against the Schole howse of women; The proude wyves pater noster; The seven sorowes that women have when theyr husbandes be deade.* The second, third, and fourth of these pamphlets are dated 1560, a fact which suggests an approximate date for the reprinting of *Frederick.* Vele was printing and publishing from about 1548 to 1586 (E. Arber, "List of Publishers 1553-1640," *Transcript of the Registers of the Company of Stationers of London,* Birmingham, 1894, Vol. V, p. cviii).

[13] Furnivall, ed., *op. cit.,* p. 30.

[14] Israel Gollancz, ed., *The Works of Shakespeare,* Vol. IV (London, 1899), Preface to *Cymbeline.*

[15] Based upon a partial transcript and full summary of the *BM* copy of the Vele edition kindly prepared for me by Mr. C. S. Gentry in 1918. My thanks are also due the director of the *Pierpont Morgan Library,* who

based upon comparisons with other versions follows. I sometimes employ abbreviated titles: *Miracle,*[16] *Violet,*[17] *Smelts,*[18] *Northern Lord,*[19] *Chest,*[20] *Aran,*[21] and *Decam.*

In the year 1424 [22] four merchants of different nationalities, Courant of Spain, Borchard of France, John of Florence, and Ambrose of Jennen (Genoa), meet at a Paris inn. Retiring to their room after a dinner, the four fall to discussing their wives. Borchard and John mention women's frailty [23] and are sure all the four wives are taking advantage of their husbands' absences. Ambrose, however, is sure his own wife is virtuous. John accuses him of over-prizing her and offers to wager 5000 gyldens that he

---

courteously answered some queries as to the readings in the 1518 edition, of which the Vele edition appears to be a reprint (W. C. Hazlitt, *Bibliog. Collections and Notes,* III, London, 1887, p. 88).

[16] *Un Miracle de Nostre-Dame . . . Ostes roy d'Espaigne.* Text in Monmerqué and Michel, *Théâtre français au Moyen-Age* (Paris, 1842), pp. 417-480. Collier's summary is reprinted in Hazlitt, *Shakespeare's Library* (London, 1875), II, 186 ff. Probably fourteenth century.

[17] Gibert de Montreuil, *Roman de la Violette* (13 cen.), pub. by F. Michel, Paris, 1834, and by Douglas Labaree Buffum, Paris, 1928. Analysis in *Shak. Lib.,* II, 179-181 and elsewhere.

[18] The tale told by the fishwife of Standon-the-Green in *Westward for Smelts,* by "Kind Kit of Kingston," 1620. Steevens' assertion that he had seen a copy of a 1603 edition is generally discredited by editors who think the entry in the stationers' register a few weeks before the appearance of the 1620 edition is proof that the book had not been printed earlier. Reprinted by J. O. Halliwell-Phillips, *Percy Society,* Vol. XXII; *Shak. Lib.,* II, 197 ff.; Furness, variorum *Cymbeline,* etc.

[19] *The Northern Lord,* in four parts, a ballad printed by J. P. Collier, *Broadside Black-Letter Ballads* (1868), pp. 48-56.

[20] *The Chest,* a folk-tale collected in Islay, Argyll, in 1859. Printed in J. F. Campbell, *Popular Tales of the Western Highlands,* II (London, 1890), 1-23.

[21] Gaelic folk-tale collected by J. M. Synge and reproduced in *The Aran Islands,* pp. 23-30 of the 1920 (Dublin) edition.

[22] No time-setting specified in *Decam.* It is possible that the dates in *Frederick* (1424-1437) may have suggested the time-setting for *Smelts,* "the troublesome reign of King Henry VI," which began in 1422, though the action in *Smelts* actually takes place in the late days of the reign (1471).

[23] Philosophical discussion of women's frailty more extended in *Decam.* The "general taxation" of women present but not pronounced in *Smelts.* Missing in *Cymb.,* where the patriotic praising of one's own "country mistress" is introduced. The later tirades against women by Posthumus (II. v. 1 ff.) and Cymbeline (V. v. 61 f.) may be noted, however.

can have his will with Ambrose's wife. Ambrose accepts promptly and the host is made stakeholder.

Resolved to win the wager, by right or by wrong, John rides to Jennen. He accosts the lady on her way to church but finds her behavior so perfect that he is shamed out of making his proposal. He conceives the chest idea and makes the box. At a loss how to get the chest conveyed into the lady's room he recalls the saying that an old woman can do what even the devil can't and so resorts to the old clothes market, where he makes friends with an old woman [24] by selling her a coat at a bargain. Next day after dining and wining her he engages her for 200 ducats to contrive the needed means. Feigning a pilgrimage to Saint James, the accomplice gets the lady to promise to keep the chest for her.

In the night John issues from the chest and steals from the lady's coffer three jewels: a purse, a girdle, and a diamond ring. As the moon is shining, he can see every corner of the chamber and observes the lady sleeping in her bed. "And then it fortuned that her left arme lay upon the bed, and on that arm she had a black wart." He retires to the chest. The old woman returns in three days, with a tale of having postponed her pilgrimage because of illness, has chest removed, and collects her fee.

John returns to Paris, seeks a private interview (to save husband embarrassment), shows his tokens, and claims the stakes. Ambrose asks better proof, hears of the wart, and after recovering from a swoon orders the host to pay John the money.

Ambrose returns toward home, stops at one of his country-houses, makes his trusted servant swear to do whatever he may command,[25] and then orders him to bid the lady come to that place, where he is to slay her and bury her body in the sand. In spite of his oath, the servant objects and agrees only when threatened with death.[26] The lady sets out with the servant, carrying with her a pet lamb. In the woods the servant explains his master's orders: he is to slay the lady and return with her tongue and a lock of hair as evidence. The lady protests her innocence and asks the servant to kill the lamb and deliver its tongue together with a lock of her

---

[24] *Decam.*: accomplice a poor woman who works about heroine's house and feigns intent to "be gone" a few days. *Aran:* an old hag who sold small things in the road and who slept in a big box in the heroine's room. *Smelts* and *Cymb.* omit female accomplice.

[25] Swearing of servant also present in *Smelts*, though lacking in *Decam.* and of course in *Cymb.*, where negotiations are by letter. Pisanio's words (III. ii. 13-15), however, are to be noted:

"How? That I should murther her,
"Upon the Love, and Truth, and Vowes; which I
"Have made to thy command?..."

[26] So in *Smelts*. Missing in corresponding scene in *Decam.* but reflected later when servant tells lady his master threatened to have him hung if he did not obey. *Cymb.*: lacking.

hair and some of her clothes smeared with the lamb's blood as evidence. The servant agrees on condition that the lady depart. When Ambrose sees the evidences of his wife's death, he is a bit remorseful and wishes he had spoken to her to find out how John got the jewels.

The lady assumes the dress of a man, gives herself the name of Frederick, secures passage on a ship sailing from Secant, after explaining to the sailor that she had lost friends and goods and is undone. On the ship she is employed as a keeper of hawks consigned to the king of Alkare.[27] When the hawks are delivered to the king, they droop, mourning for Frederick, who is thereupon called into the king's service. She prospers, becoming in turn an officer, a knight, and finally a lord. When a plague threatens, the king leaves Frederick in charge of kingdom. Enemies come and are ravaging the country, but Frederick routs them and on the king's return is made lord protector, ruling thus for seven years.[28]

Meantime John goes to the palace of the king of Alkare to display his goods. Frederick sees among them the stolen things. When she asks him where he got them, he boastfully explains his trick. Feigning a sympathetic interest, Frederick, though condemning the husband's killing of the wife, praises John's shrewdness and urges him to tarry there. She then has a letter sent in the king's name requesting Ambrose to come at once to Alkare. On his arrival she invites him to dinner, also sending for John to show his jewels to the king. When Ambrose sees the jewels, he fears he is to be put to death, but Frederick cheers him and urges John to repeat his story before the king. This done, Frederick asks the king what punishment such a man as John deserves. The king says the wheel and the gallows, for causing murder and for stealing. Frederick asks all the lords to assemble in the hall. She retires for a time and returns virtually nude. She explains all, asserts that she has remained continent,[29] and demands John's death.[30] John's goods are given to Ambrose, and John, after a full confession, is executed. Ambrose asks and receives his wife's forgiveness,[31] the two receive gifts from the king, and go home to live

---

[27] The use in *Cymb.* and *Smelts* of an English historical background and war setting with no overseas journey involved for the heroine decreases the similarity between the two English versions and the *Decam.-Frederick* account in this part of the story.

[28] *Decam.*: heroine much less active—no plague, no fighting. She is merely sent to the fair at Acre as chief of the merchants' guard.

[29] *Decam.*: heroine indignantly asks villain when he had ever lain with her. *Smelts*: "Hadst thou, villain, ever any strumpet's favour at my hands?"

[30] *Decam.*: villain condemned to death at heroine's request. *Smelts*: king passes judgment without suggestion from heroine. *Cymb.*: king, with approval of husband, pardons villain.

[31] So in *Decam. Smelts*: king allows heroine to judge husband, who is forgiven with a kiss. *Cymb.*: heroine gently rebukes husband before embracing him.

happy.³² They have four children, the eldest of whom, Frederick, goes to court, becomes a lord, and is visited by his parents, the tale closing with their return to Jennen on January 8, 1437. The lady becomes ill and dies. "And so endeth this little story of lord Frederick."

While it is obvious that this version closely parallels that of Boccaccio, I can not agree with Mechel ³³ that "what Shakespeare is supposed to have borrowed from Boccaccio he may just as well have found" in *Frederick*. Certain elements present in *Cymbeline* and *Decameron* but lacking in *Frederick* may be noted: similarities in the bedroom scene—light found burning by villain,³⁴ who carefully notes furnishings of room, pictures, etc., and then makes an intimate examination of heroine's person, finding mole under left breast; ³⁵ some effort at peace-making before conclusion of wager; the use of written covenants instead of host-as-stakeholder ³⁶ (though the latter seems reflected in *Cymbeline*); the haggling over terms (present, however, in *Smelts* and other versions); husband's sending the wife a letter asking her to meet him on the way (though the presence of Posthumus in Rome would necessitate this

---

³² As in *Smelts*.

³³ *Op. cit.*, p. 62.

³⁴ *Decam.*: it was heroine's custom to have a light burning by her bed when her husband was absent. *Cymb.*: maid leaves light burning at heroine's request. *Frederick*: moonlight. *Smelts*: maid carries candle to adjoining room, villain presumably accomplishing theft and escape in a dark or partially lighted chamber. *Aran*: villain has "some means" of making a light.

³⁵ *Decam.*: a wart or mole with golden hairs upon the left breast. *Cymb.*: a mole cinque-spotted under left breast "like the crimson drops in the bottom of a cowslip." Ohle regarded the comparison to a flower an evidence of the influence of *Violet*, where there is a purple violet mark on the right breast. But hardly any two versions agree on the character and location of the mark, and the flower comparison occurs elsewhere (a strawberry in a Menton tale, Paris, *op. cit.*, p. 497; a red rose in *Guillaume de Dole*; a violet between breasts in a folk-tale, etc.). The descriptions vary widely: mole under right breast, mole with hairs on left shoulder, three golden hairs, mark with golden hairs between breasts, two black marks with hairs on left breast, black mole on thigh, wart on groin, three grains of coffee on thigh, velvety mouse on back, etc. (Paris, *op. cit.*). The hairs on the mark are perhaps a modification of the primitive mutilation motive (connected with the substitution formula), as they are sometimes to be cut off as evidence.

³⁶ *Frederick* and *Smelts* agree in reflecting host-stakeholder device.

in *Cymbeline* regardless of source); villain reports to husband with others present;[37] a possible verbal parallel.[38] The unique method of punishment administered to the villain in the Boccaccio version, though of course not present in *Cymbeline,* seems to be reflected in *Winter's Tale* (IV. iv. 812-821).

Though I do not think *Frederick* can be urged as a source for all of Shakespeare's "Boccaccian" features, I think it clear that the tale must be added to the list of significant analogues of *Cymbeline,* and it is interesting to note that it shares with *Cymbeline* certain non-Boccaccian features: the representatives-of-four-nations motive (stressed by Shakespeare in both the Rome and the Orleans quarrels and found in no other version so far as I know—it is to be remembered, however, that *Frederick* does not utilize the situation for bringing in the patriotic defence of the ladies of one's own country); villain rather than husband proposes the wager (as in *Smelts* and practically all other versions); the use of a preliminary confrontation scene between the villain and the lady (as in *Smelts, Miracle,* and elsewhere);[39] husband requires servant to produce bloody evidence of wife's death;[40] husband after receiving word of

---

[37] The villain in *Frederick* takes pains to report to husband in private; in *Smelts* he seeks early morning interview in husband's room at the inn. Some confirmation of Paris's belief that *Smelts* was departing awkwardly from its source in the bedroom scene may be found in the fact that the villain, after displaying the stolen crucifix, offers "further proof" if required, though as the story stands he has no further proof, as he did not examine the heroine's person and saw no birthmark. I am inclined to agree with Paris and Brandl (*infra,* Note 49) that the chest and the birthmark may have been present in an earlier form of *Smelts* or in its source. Professor Lawrence, however, thinks otherwise (*op. cit.,* p. 250).

[38] Reference by husband to his wife as a "gift" of God or of Heaven, and use of the word "grace" (*Cymb.* I. iv. 87 ff.; *Decam., Tudor Trans.,* p. 206).

[39] *Smelts:* villain meets lady in field, is received as husband's friend, and for days seeks a private interview with the lady, who avoids him. *Miracle:* very close to *Cymbeline* here (*infra,* Note 44). Professor Greenlaw notes (*PMLA,* XXI, 1906, 616) that Shakespeare's treatment here is also closely paralleled in *Sir Triamour, Erl of Toulous,* as in the Spanish romance *Oliva,* in all of which the villain pretends he was but testing the lady, as in *Cymb.* These stories, of course, do not belong to the wager cycle proper, though related to it.

[40] *Decam:* no mention of lamb or bloody evidence. *Smelts:* lacking. *Cymb.:* though not in text of letter of Posthumus (III. iv. 24 ff.), it is

wife's supposed death and while still convinced of her guilt expresses remorse over having acted hastily in having her killed (*Cymb.* V. i. 7 ff.); villain confesses guilt and agrees that he deserves death (as also in *Smelts*); lady has no bedmate.[41] Also the host-stakeholder motive of *Frederick, Smelts,* etc., though replaced in *Cymbeline* by the device of a written covenant, as found in Boccaccio, nevertheless seems reflected in Shakespeare's play when Philario, at whose home the wager-scene has taken place, formally notifies Iachimo that he is the winner of the bet (II. iv. 150).

Some of these parallels no doubt may be explained reasonably as due to independent creation, but I would point out that those who assert that Shakespeare needed no other source for the wager plot than the *Decameron* must regard as "stray coincidences" all of these *Cymbeline-Frederick* parallels (some of which represent Shakespeare's adherence to the general tradition of the cycle where Boccaccio had departed from it) as well as *all* the similar evidence connecting *Cymbeline* with other tales of the cycle, among which I should cite as particularly difficult to explain away the *Cymbeline-Smelts* parallels [42] and the *Cymbeline-Miracle* parallels.[43]

referred to by Pisanio as part of his orders (III. iv. 140 f.) and Posthumus exhibits the bloody handkerchief in V. i. 1.

[41] Paris says lady had a maid-servant as bedmate in the version of the German *Four Merchants* he used; it is not present, however, in Mechel's summary of *Four Merchants* and is not present in *Frederick*.

[42] Much of the discussion of *Smelts* seems to me to be misdirected. The question of whether there was or was not a 1603 edition is important only in case one is attempting to establish *Smelts* as a direct source. I dare say that few readers who compare the two versions will find it easy to believe either that *Smelts* was a direct source for *Cymbeline* or *vice versa*. I think, however, that the candid reader can hardly fail to see a community of traditional matter here that is not derivable from Boccaccio. Some have recognized this. Even Professor Lawrence, who is inclined to regard the *Smelts* evidence as "fishy," concludes by saying (*op. cit.*, p. 250, Note 12) that Shakespeare and the author of *Smelts* probably used independent versions, each related to the *novella* of Boccaccio.

The most important non-Boccaccian *Cymbeline-Smelts* parallels are: English historical background, with enveloping war action; actors not merchants but of the gentry; wager proposed by villain, who has no accomplice, and who is assisted by husband himself in getting access to heroine for the trial of her virtue, with resultant interview and with the lady repulsing or avoiding the advances; lady sleeps alone and is seen to bed by maid-servant; servant knows why he is to kill his mistress and

The difficulty of considering Boccaccio's version or any other known analogue as an adequate single source for the wager plot in *Cymbeline* seems to me obvious, and I believe that the facts about *Frederick of Jennen* add plausibility to the suggestion that Shakespeare employed an important English source now lost. This was the view reached by Gaston Paris [44] (based partly upon the work of R. Ohle [45]) after what is perhaps the most careful and comprehensive study of the wager cycle yet attempted.[46] Although the skepticism with which lost sources are nowadays viewed is no doubt a wholesome one, I would call attention in this case to the significance of Paris's remark that among the forty-odd versions involved

himself suggests the disguise and escape; heroines throughout this scene are submissive and beg for death, asking that servant report to husband both their innocence and obedience (in speeches embodying a rather striking verbal parallel: the *Smelts* heroine closes her plea for death thus, " I am prepared now; strike prethee home, and kill me and my griefs at once "; cf. *Cymb*. III. iv. 69-71); husband contemplates suicide; heroine and husband both appear in disguise and distress; heroine's wandering about and her extreme weariness stressed; she takes service as a page to a general; denouement after a battle and before a king. The presence of most of these traits in *Miracle* or other versions of the " French " type strengthens their significance.

[43] Chief non-Boccaccian resemblances: dramatic form; social atmosphere courtly; after marriage husband leaves wife at court, giving her a love-token, and goes to Rome, where he wagers with an Italian villain, who boasts that he can succeed if only he has the opportunity of a second interview; villain alleges husband's infidelity in Rome in urging his own suit; ladies repulse villains in similar words; enveloping war action; heroine complains of weariness; heroes rebuked in visions for their incredulity; sleeping draught (function different).

[44] " Le Cycle de la Gageure," *Romania* XXXII (1903), 481 ff.

[45] R. Ohle, *Shakespeares Cymbeline und seine romanischen Vorläufer* (Berlin, 1890).

[46] Professor Edwin Greenlaw's paper, " The Vows of Baldwin," *PMLA* XXI (1906), 616, having to do with a larger cycle of tales is of interest to students of the wager cycle in supplementing Paris's study, esp. the comments on English romances containing parallels with *Cymbeline* (pp. 607 ff.). See also F. J. Child, *English and Scottish Popular Ballads*, V (Boston and New York, 1894), 21 ff.; F. H. von der Hagen, *Gesammtabenteuer*, III (Stuttgart and Tübingen, 1850), ch. lxviii; H. A. Todd, *PMLA* II (1886), 107-157.

in his study, he found but two examples of direct relationship.[47] A vast number of lost versions seems indicated.

The hypothesis of a lost English source seems to me to receive added support from Professor Brandl's study [48] of the three folk versions found in Great Britain which he calls the Imogen-Portia group because they incorporate the pound-of-flesh theme in the wager story: *Northern Lord, Chest, Aran* (*supra*, Notes 19, 20, 21). Building upon the work of Ohle and Paris, Brandl notes that there seems to have occurred in England an amalgamation of (1) the old French type (courtly actors, no chest, wandering about of husband and wife in distress, with final resolution before a king and involving a duel—*Violet* and *Miracle* being representatives) which reached Great Britain by oral tradition and (2) the derivative Italian type (merchant folk replacing courtly, chest device introduced, servant employed to kill wife for husband, overseas journey taken by disguised heroine—*Decam.* and *Four Merchants* being representatives) which reached Britain, Brandl thinks, through such a literary version as Boccaccio's. This commingling took place before Shakespeare's time, the resultant tale (now lost) being reflected in *Smelts, Cymbeline,* and the Portia-Imogen folk versions, the latter having annexed the pound-of-flesh theme from the *Gesta Romanorum*.[49] The *Cymbeline-Smelts* and *Cymbeline-Miracle* parallels are thus explained. Brandl further demonstrates, I think, that the parallels between *Cymbeline* and the folk versions just mentioned can not be explained as borrowings from Shakespeare, a fact which gives added weight to the theory of a lost English source for *Cymbeline*. Though Brandl at times perhaps pins too much faith in possibly insignificant parallels and though he fails to take into account the availability of *Frederick of Jennen* to sixteenth-century English story tellers—a consideration which might force some modification in his reasoning—I think that most of his points, when viewed against the background of the wager-cycle tradition, are satisfactorily established and aid in making less tenable the position of the advocates of *Decameron* as sole source for the wager plot in *Cymbeline*.

[47] *Op. cit.*, p. 549.
[48] Alois Brandl, "*Imogen auf den Aran-Inseln*," *Shakespeare-Jahrbuch* LIII (1917), 13-34.
[49] But note here the work of Elise Richter, "*Juan Timoneda und das Imogen-Portia-Motiv*," *Shakespeare-Jahrbuch* LXIV (1918), 141 ff.

Whether Shakespeare actually took his admittedly Boccaccian features from the *Decameron,* which in spite of the evidence against its adequacy as sole source remains probably the most satisfactory existing analogue; whether he gathered his non-Boccaccian elements from a single source or from several sources; whether he was working over an old play [50]—these are queries which I think may very well occupy the attention of students who are not satisfied with the view of the scholars quoted at the beginning of this paper.

*The University of North Carolina.*

---

[50] Suggested by W. Hertzberg (see pp. 306 ff. of the 1897 edition of *Cymbeline* in the Schlegel-Tieck translation and edition); argued by Ohle (*op. cit.*), who thought the play itself resulted from a combination of some lost version of the wager story related to *Smelts* with historical matter drawn from Geoffrey of Monmouth; C. R. Baskervill (*Mod. Phil.* XIV, 1916, 488 f.) thinks an old-play basis strongly probable; J. M. Robertson has not yet printed his reasons for believing *Cymbeline* a reworking of an old play by Peele (plus Chapman?) (*Shakespeare and Chapman*, London, 1917, pp. 218 ff.).

I have myself assembled some evidence which I think points toward an old-play source, though I do not regard it as conclusive in character. Space limitations prevent its reproduction here.

## SOME PATRISTIC CONVENTIONS COMMON TO SHAKESPEARE AND MILTON

### By George Coffin Taylor

Recent investigations in the field of Milton scholarship have very largely concerned themselves with calling attention to the possibility of Milton's familiarity with many new sources. To these researches Milton scholarship is unquestionably under a very heavy debt. The present article is written for the purpose of suggesting that it is, however, extremely hazardous to conclude that the appearance of a thought in Milton and in another writer necessarily establishes any direct relationship between Milton and the work in which this thought appears. Shakespeare is selected for treatment in this connection because he of all men was not in the habit of going to learned and out of the way sources for his material. If an interesting and outstanding conception, such for example as Milton's idea that Adam's intellectual attainments were greater even after the fall than those of any of his descendants, occurs likewise in Shakespeare, it seems reasonable to suppose that this thought had become such a commonplace in Shakespeare's day that it is next to hopeless to seek for any one particular source for this idea in Milton.

Shakespeare's use of the Bible has of course been the subject of study and investigation. The comments of the Church Fathers, best known perhaps in the works of St. Augustine, though considered in connection with Milton [1] particularly in recent years with a view to throwing new light on the meaning of *Paradise Lost,* have never been considered in connection with Shakespeare. Nor is it the purpose of this article to do so exhaustively now. Such a study would involve the analysis of the basis of a great body of Shakespeare's figurative allusions. It proposes rather to call attention to the familiarity of Shakespeare or of whoever wrote the passages which follow, with some of the highly conventionalized conceptions connected with two matters of immense importance and interest to the Fathers. Both concern origins. The first concerns the origin of this created universe, " this universal frame," as the Renaissance writers call it. The second concerns the origins of life on a very

---

[1] P. Pritchard, *The Influence of the Fathers upon Milton, with Especial Reference to St. Augustine* (Cornell University, 1925).

small portion of the world,—the earth, and of these forms of life particularly those of man, Adam and Eve.

An extraordinary case is the allusion to "Chaos" thrown off in one line in *Henry VI, III:*

Like to a

    chaos, or an unlick'd bear-whelp.[2]

DuBartas has the most extraordinary elaboration of this idea in *La Sepmaine,* where he likens God shaping up his Chaos to a bear mother licking her formless mass into the form of a cub:

> En formant l'Vniuers fit donc ainsi que l'Ourse,
> Qui dans l'obscure grotte au bout de trente iours
> Vne masse difforme enfante au lieu d'vn Ours:
> Et puis en la lechant, ores elle façonne
> Ses deschirantes mains, or' sa teste felonne,
> Or' ses pieds, or' son col: & d'vn monceau si laid
> Son industrie anime vn animal parfaict.[3]

As H. Dugdale Sykes[4] has shown Peele to be conspicuous among the Elizabethan dramatists for indebtedness to DuBartas this may be considered as added evidence of Peele's hand in *Henry VI.* It is noticeable in this connection that Shakespeare uses the word "abysm" only twice in his plays, and in both cases the word suggests the technical sense of "abyss" as used in patristic literature, where it is generally synonymous with Chaos or Hell, which next to Chaos itself is characterized by disorder. A cursory use of a Milton concordance will illustrate the frequent use by Milton of the term "abyss" in this technical sense.[5] Du Bartas uses it in the sense of Chaos:

> De ce profond abisme emmanteloit la face.[6]

That Shakespeare uses the word "abysm" in somewhat the same sense does not mean that he had been reading patristic literature. His two uses are:

---

[2] III, 2, 161.

[3] *La Sepmaine ov Creation,* pour Iaques Chouët, M. D. XCIII, p. 41, ll. 408-15.

[4] *Sidelights on Elizabethan Drama* (1924) and "Peele's Borrowings from Dubartas," *Notes and Queries,* CXLVII, 349-351 and 368-369.

[5] For the use of *abyss* in this sense see Johannes Scotus Erigina, *De divisione naturae,* II, 16-17.

[6] *La Sepmaine ov Creation,* pour Iaques Chouët, M. D. XVIII, p. 30.

> ... And shot their fires
> Into the abysm of hell.[7]

and

> In the dark backward and abysm of time.[8]

That St. Augustine [9] and other patristic writers stressed the *state of innocence* of Adam and Eve before the Fall is a matter of common knowledge. Falstaff's application of the doctrine to himself demonstrates how common that knowledge was in Shakespeare's day:

Dost thou hear, Hal? Thou know'st in the state of innocency Adam fell.[10]

The matter scarcely deserves notice in this connection, but the patristic conception that Adam was more perfect in intellect and body than any of his descendants is a more technical matter.[11] Milton has it in "Adam the goodliest of his sons since born," and elsewhere. Shakespeare had read probably no patristic literature but is familiar with the conception apparently in, "Though she were endowed with all that Adam had left him before he transgress'd." [12] It is open to anyone to believe of course if he prefers that this merely alludes to the Joys of Paradise. Shakespeare uses the word "endowments" in *Pericles,* however, in the sense of intellectual gifts.[13]

Possibly no line in Shakespeare has given rise to more discussion than the well-known *As You Like It* crux,

Here feel we not the penalty of Adam, the seasons' difference.[14]

Furness in his Variorum gives four pages of fine print to the discussion of the matter. Those who seek the solution in the Bible itself can hardly find it there. The patristic comments on the Bible however make the matter unmistakably clear. The theory

---

[7] *Antony and Cleopatra*, III, 13, 146, 147.

[8] *Tempest*, I, 2, 50.

[9] *The City of God*, John Grant. (Edinburgh, 1909), I, 363.

[10] *Henry IV*, Part I, III, 3, 186.

[11] See Sylvester's *DuBartas* (1641) *His Second Weeke, The Furies,* ll. 115 ff.

[12] *Much Ado*, II, 1, 260.

[13] *Pericles*, III, 2, 27:
> I hold it ever
> Virtue and *cunning* were endowments greater
> Than nobleness and riches.

[14] II, I, 6.

was as follows: Adam's sin had three results; first, a degrading effect upon his mental and emotional state. The passions arose in the little cosmos of man. Second, Adam's environment, the animals and the weather, became unfriendly. Third, the entire universe became slightly disarranged to Adam's discomfiture.[15] Milton has it, "the air that now must suffer change."[16]

> Some say he bid his angels turn askance
> The poles of earth twice ten degrees and more
> . . . . . . . . . .
> . . . . . . to bring in change
> Of seasons. . . .[17]

The idea that Sin threw the entire cosmic system slightly out of gear without resulting in an entire return to Chaos may also lie back of the apparently very simple bowling figure in *King John* when the Bastard says,

> Commodity, the bias of the world, —
> The world, which of itself is peised [balanced] well, . . .
> Till this advantage, this vile-drawing bias,
> This sway of motion, this Commodity,
> Makes it take head from all indifferency.[18]

These are merely a few of the allusions in Shakespeare to that elaborately worked out theological scheme of salvation with which Milton in his *Christian Doctrine* and *Paradise Lost* shows such detailed familiarity. Shakespeare's knowledge of such matters was surely not scholarly, his allusions not beyond the average playgoer of his day. These matters must have been the commonplaces of the age, a fact which those of us working into the new sources of Milton sometimes forget in attempting to establish very definite relations between Milton and those who, like him, use these conventions of the Medieval and Renaissance theologians. What Gilbert demonstrated in his article, "Milton and the Mysteries,"[19] is doubtless true of many other works or series of works in which scholars are now seeking to find the definite sources of Milton.

*The University of North Carolina.*

[15] See Sylvester's *DuBartas, His Second Weeke, The Furies.*
[16] *Paradise Lost*, X, 212.
[17] *Paradise Lost*, X, 668-677.
[18] *King John*, II, 1, 574-580.
[19] *Studies in Philology*, XVII (1920), 147-169.

## LAMB ON SPENSER

### By Frederick Hard

Charles Lamb's letter to Wordsworth, of April 28, 1815, is one of the most characteristic and delicious of his compositions. It is strange that the writer thought fit to apologize for it. He scribbles at the top of the page, " Excuse this maddish letter: I am too tired to write in formâ— " Among other good things, one finds shrewd appreciation of *Yarrow Unvisited, Yarrow Visited,* and *Poor Susan;* also an account of Mary's joke on the first line of Wordsworth's *The Force of Prayer,* " What is good for a bootless bene? "; [1] several of Lamb's irresistible puns; his canny suspicions of *Peter Bell*; his delightful account of the painting of Milton which his brother had discovered and purchased; and, finally, a passage which must be read wistfully by every one who loves both Lamb and Spenser:

> I wish you would write more criticism, about Spenser &c. I think I could say something about him myself—but Lord bless me—these " merchants and their spicy drugs " which are so harmonious to sing of, they lime-twig up my poor soul and body, till I shall forget I ever thought myself a bit of a genius! I can't even put a few thoughts on paper for a newspaper. I " engross," when I should pen a paragraph. Confusion blast all mercantile transactions, all traffick, exchange of commodities, intercourse between nations, all the consequent civilization and wealth and amity and link of society, and getting rid of prejudices, and knowlege of the face of the globe—and rot the very firs of the forest that look so romantic alive, and die into desks.

Elsewhere he describes his office as the place where " I sit like Philomel all day (but not singing) with my breast against this thorn of a Desk." And again, " The desk enters into my soul." What would we not give if Lamb could have gone to his desk the next morning and found that the Directors of India House, with super-executive wisdom, had granted their faithful clerk a fortnight's leave of absence with full pay! In that extremely hypotheti-

---

[1] Writes Lamb, ". . . in a careless tone I said to Mary as if putting a riddle, 'What is good for a bootless bean?' to which with infinite presence of mind (as the jest book has it) she answered, a 'shoeless pea.' It was the first joke she ever made."—*Letters,* ed. Lucas (Lond., 1912), I, 487. I have used this—the small octavo—edition for all of my citations from Lamb's works and correspondence.

cal case we might have had from Lamb, who thought he "could say something about him," a priceless critical essay on Spenser. Ultimately the Directors did their duty, and handsomely enough, but the inspiration of April 28, 1815, had been dissipated.

For the general reader Lamb's best criticism of Spenser is perhaps that recounted by Leigh Hunt, to the effect that Spenser "has always been felt by his countrymen to be what Charles Lamb called him, the 'Poet's Poet.'" As Pater recalls, Lamb once told Southey, in a letter, that he "never judged system-wise of things, but fastened upon particulars;" the words quoted by Hunt seem an excellent example of Lamb's ability to illuminate with a phrase. Another illustration of this faculty is his reference to "The beautiful obliquities of the Religio Medici." Possibly it is because of this "particularity," plus the fact that his comments are scattered throughout his miscellaneous writings, that the nature and extent of Lamb's interest in Spenser has received scant attention.[2] I do not wish to suggest that this failure to admit Lamb into the canon of Spenser criticism implies serious neglect. Indeed, Mr. E. M. W. Tillyard, in his *Selections From the Literary Criticism of Charles Lamb,* deliberately excludes Spenser from the list of poets criticized in his text, and explains the exclusion in his Introduction, as follows: ". . . when Lamb adjures Coleridge to attempt an epic 'by the dainty, sweet, and soothing phantasies of honey-tongued Spenser,' I feel he is not being critical. The phrase charms us by its Elizabethan echoes, but tells us nothing about Spenser we do not know already; I have not included it."[3] It is my feeling, however, that what Charles Lamb had to say about Spenser may possess a certain interest, as it were, *per se,* whether or not his comments always strike us with the force of new discoveries. Lamb's readers have become accustomed to expect the pleasure which so often accompanies his casual but arresting observations. Add to this Lamb's distinction as a critic, his pioneer Elizabethanism, his devo-

---

[2] Dr. H. E. Cory, in his *Critics of Edmund Spenser,* is limited by considerations of space to comments upon Scott, Hazlitt, Coleridge, and Hunt, as being representative of the romantic attitude toward Spenser in the nineteenth century. Carpenter's *Reference Guide* lists only two items: Lamb's poem, "To the Poet Cowper," and two letters to Wordsworth in 1806. Nor does Professor H. S. V. Jones's excellent *Spenser Handbook* contain any references to Lamb.

[3] *Lamb's Criticism,* etc. (Cambridge, 1923), p. xvi.

tion to Sir Philip Sidney,—among other traits which each of his admirers discovers for himself—and we recognize qualities which should command attention wherever he speaks seriously or familiarly of an Elizabethan. His remarks on Spenser, though occasional and unstudied, possess nevertheless certain suggested tendencies, such as a kindliness for Spenser, unspoiled by sentimentality; a delighted frankness of appreciation not inconsistent with a certain devoutness of attitude; a characteristic gusto; a humor which is wholly sympathetic; and, finally, an unusual insight into the essential reality of Spenser's imagination.

## II

The earliest specific reference to Spenser by Lamb occurs in a letter to Coleridge, about June 1, 1796. Lamb copies a sonnet which he had written in the previous summer, beginning

> The lord of light shakes off his drowsyhed.

"Drowsyhed," says Lamb, "I have met with I think in Spenser. Tis an old thing, but it rhymes with led & rhyming covers a multitude of licences." In the same letter he tells Coleridge, "I want room to tell you how we are charmed with your verses in the manner of Spencer." Ten days later, in commenting upon Coleridge's *Poems,* Lamb notes: "That in the manner of Spencer is very sweet, particularly at the close." On July 6 of the same year Lamb sends to Coleridge his lines "To the Poet Cowper," which were to be printed in the *Monthly Magazine* for December, 1796. In this poem, after a reference to the "stately-paced" verse of Milton, occur these lines:

> with lighter finger playing
> Our elder bard, Spenser, a gentle name,
> The Lady Muses' dearest darling child,
> Elicited the deftest tunes yet heard
> In Hall or Bower, taking the delicate Ear
> Of Sydney, & his peerless Maiden Queen.

This is Lamb's highest poetical praise of Spenser. It is important, I think, to point out that this was written only a few months before the great tragedy, which, it appears, was to change the whole tone of Lamb's poetry. To the letter of September 27, 1796, which informs Coleridge of the calamity, Lamb appends this postscript:

"Mention nothing of poetry. I have destroyed every vestige of past vanities of that kind. Do as you please, but if you publish, publish mine (I give free leave) without name or initial, and never send me a book, I charge you." On December 10, he alludes further to his own poetry, again writing to Coleridge: "With regard to my leaving off versifying, you have said so many pretty things . . . . At present I have not leisure to make verses, nor anything approaching to a fondness for the exercise. . . . The music of poesy may charm for a while the importunate teasing cares of life; but the teased and troubled man is not in a disposition to make that music." Later in the same letter he gives us some idea of the destruction of his own work, referred to above. "I burned all my own verses, all my book of extracts from Beaumont and Fletcher and a thousand sources; I burned a little journal of my foolish passion which I had a long time kept—

> 'Noting ere they past away
> The little lines of yesterday.'"

One wonders how much of Spenser must have appeared in the thousand sources and in his "own verses." A great deal, we may believe, to judge from a dozen or so poems written prior to the tragedy, which happened to escape destruction.

What is known to be Lamb's earliest poem, preserved in the manuscript book of James Boyer, of Christ's Hospital, is called *Mille Viæ Mortis* (1789). Whether or not the author had already come under the spell of Spenser we do not know, but the poem reflects Lamb's early tendency to archaism and perhaps a predisposition to Spenserian imitation. It begins,

> What time in bands of slumber all were laid,
> To Death's dark court, methought I was convey'd;

The King of Terrors sits upon an ebon throne, surrounded by a host of personified abstractions:

> Here pallid Fear & dark Despair were seen.
> And Fever here with looks forever lean,
> Swoln Dropsy, halting Gout, profuse of woes,
> And Madness fierce & hopeless of repose. . . .

Two sonnets to "Anna," written probably in 1795, are Spenserian in diction and figure. The first begins,

> Was it some sweet device of Faery
> That mocked my steps with many a lonely glade,
> And fancied wanderings with a fair-hair'd maid?

and contains these lines on Anna's eyes:

> methought they spake the while
> Soft soothing things, which might enforce despair
> To drop the murdering knife, and let go by
> His foul resolve.

The other begins with these lines:

> When last I roved these winding wood-walks green,
> Green winding walks, and shady pathways sweet,
> Oft-times would Anna seek the silent scene,
> Shrouding her beauties in the lone retreat.

Noticeable at once is the characteristic Spenserian inversion of the second line, together with the marked alliteration and repetition.[4] The most clearly Spenserian of Lamb's poems, however, is *A Vision of Repentance,* the date of which is uncertain; Mr. Lucas assigns it to 1796 with a query. It will suffice to quote the first stanza:

> I saw a famous fountain, in my dream,
>   Where shady path-ways to a valley led;
> A weeping willow lay upon that stream,
>   And all around the fountain brink were spread
> Wide branching trees, with dark green leaf rich clad,
>   Forming a doubtful twilight—desolate and sad.

Lamb's fondness for this poem is rather touching. He sends it to Coleridge saying, " Tell me if you like it. I fear the latter half is unequal to the former, in parts of which I think you will discover a delicacy of penciling not quite un-Spenser-like." [5] And he later expresses his disappointment that Coleridge did not praise the poem, of which he says:

You speak slightingly; surely the longer stanzas were pretty tolerable; at least there was one good line in it,
  "Thick-shaded trees, with dark green leaf rich clad"
To adopt your own expression, I call this a "rich" line, a fine full line. And some others I thought even beautiful. Believe me, my little

---

[4] See also the other sonnets from Coleridge's *Poems on Various Subjects* (1796) and from Coleridge's *Poems* (1797), in Lamb's *Works*, IV, 4 ff.
[5] *Letters*, I, 102.

gentleman will feel some repugnance at riding behind in the basket; though, I confess, in pretty good company.⁶

The expression "riding behind in the basket" alludes to the fact that Coleridge proposed to print the poem in the Appendix of the 1797 volume, where it actually appeared. Lamb printed the poem again in 1818.

With this poem we come to the close of what we may call the "early" poetical period of Lamb, and likewise to the end of the Spenserian influence upon his verse. Most of the poems written after the domestic calamity, as well as his letters and conversation, reflect, as Professor Elton points out, the fact that Lamb has settled down to a "sheer, strong-witted, secular goodness of nature."⁷ Neither *The Old Familiar Faces* (1798), nor *Hester* (1803), nor his beautiful elegy *On an Infant Dying as soon as Born* (1827),— assuredly Lamb's best and best-known poems—reflects the "Spenserian" style which he had affected in his earlier period. The same is true of the rest of Lamb's verses which are, for the most part, light in tone or casual.

In his correspondence as well as in other contacts with his friends in this earlier period, Lamb seems often to bear Spenser in mind. His adjuration to Coleridge to "attempt the Epic" by the "phantasies of honey tongued Spenser" (January 10, 1797), has already been noticed. A month later he rebukes Coleridge for failing to pay tribute to a certain poem of Southey's: "In your notice of Southey's volume you omit to mention the most pleasing of all, the Miniature 'There were Who form'd high hopes of thee, Young Robert. Spirit of Spenser!—was the wanderer wrong?'" And in the same letter (February 5, 1797) he again urges Coleridge to write a long poem, and suggests a tentative outline with indications of treatment, among the items being a section of "all manner of pitiable stories, in Spenser-like verse—love—friendship—relationship, etc."

In 1797 Lamb, in the company of Lloyd, spent a fortnight with Southey, who was then residing at Burton, a little village in Hampshire, near Christchurch. In this intimacy one may speculate upon the "divine chit-chat" which must have included discussions of

⁶ *Ibid.*, 104.

⁷ Oliver Elton, *A Survey of English Literature 1780-1880* (N. Y., 1920), II, 338.

Spenser. At all events, Southey sent to Lamb, in the year following, a manuscript of his eclogue "The Ruined Cottage," containing the following lines:

>     I led thee here,
> Charles, not without design; for this hath been
> My favorite walk even since I was a boy;
> And I remember, Charles, this ruin here,
> The neatest comfortable dwelling-place!
> That when I read in those dear books which first
> Woke in my heart the love of poesy,
> How with the villagers Erminia dwelt,
> And Calidore for a fair shepherdess
> Forsook his quest to learn the shepherd's lore,
> My fancy drew from this the little hut
> Where that poor princess wept her hopeless love,
> Or where the gentle Calidore at eve
> Led Pastorella home.

As the poem continues it becomes, as Mr. Lucas observes, practically a poetical paraphrase of Lamb's *Rosamund Gray,* which came first. I therefore take Southey's poem to be a compliment to Lamb, and in view of this the Spenser allusions in the passage quoted are perhaps worth noting as a reflection of their common interest in the poet at this time. Lamb acknowledged the manuscript (October 29, 1798), saying, "I thank you heartily for the Eclogue; it pleases me mightily, being so full of picture-work and circumstances." And in March, 1799, upon the publication of the poem, Lamb thanks Southey for a presentation volume, adding, "I have read the last Eclogue again with pleasure. . . . . I decidedly prefer this 'Ruin'd Cottage' to any poem in the book." At a later period of his relationship with Southey, Lamb makes use, in a manner far from cordial, of a quotation from Spenser, in the *Letter of Elia to Robert Southey* (1823), where he inveighs against those virtuous persons who

huddle close together, in a weak fear of infection, like that pusillanimous underling in Spenser—

> This is the wandering wood, this Error's den;
> A monster vile, whom God and man does hate;
> Therefore, I reed, beware. Fly, fly quoth then
> The fearful Dwarf. . . .

The reader will remember how Lamb's wrath subsided into apologies under the influence of Southey's temperate and well-disposed reply; and it is pleasant to record again the fact that in Southey's next public utterance upon Lamb he pays tribute to Elia's constant devotion to

>the elder sons of song
>In honouring whom thou hast delighted still.[8]

The most ardent champion of Spenser among Lamb's acquaintance, though by no means the most subtle critic, was Leigh Hunt. During the two years of incarceration which Hunt experienced after his attack upon the Prince Regent, Charles and Mary Lamb were among his most frequent and most welcome visitors. We should be very grateful if Hunt had left an account of the conversations of Lamb, " who," he says, " came to comfort me in all weathers, hail or sunshine, in daylight or in darkness, even in the dreadful frost and snow of the beginning of 1814." Aside from his sympathy and kindliness toward Hunt, it must have been infinitely diverting to Lamb to find himself in a prison cell which had been transformed into a bower by having its walls papered with a trellis of roses, its ceiling covered with clouds floating in a blue sky, and its barred windows hidden by Venetian blinds. What the talk must have been in this absurd oasis is hinted at by Hunt in a rhyming epistle to Lamb, where he relates how he and Lamb " cherished their knees " before his fire, and

>Discussed the pretensions of all sorts of writers;
>Of Shakespeare's coevals, all spirits divine;
>Of Chapman, whose Homer's a fine rough old wine;
>Of Marvel, wit, patriot, and poet who knew
>How to give, both at once, Charles and Cromwell their due;
>Of Spenser, who wraps you, wherever you are,
>In a bow'r of seclusion beneath a sweet star . . .[9]

It was Charles and Mary Lamb who bought a folio copy of Spenser for Wordsworth in 1806. The transaction is recorded in Lamb's letter of February 1:

Dear Wordsworth—
I have seen the Books which you ordered, booked at the White Horse Inn, Cripplegate, by the Kendal waggon this day 1st Feby. 1806; you will not fail to see after them in time. They are directed to you at

---

[8] *To Charles Lamb* (August 6, 1830). Cf. Lamb's *Works*, IV, 331.

[9] Published in the *Examiner* and afterwards in *Foliage*, 1818. Quoted by Lucas, *Life of Charles Lamb* (1905), I, 327.

Grasmere. We have made some alteration in the Editions since your sister's directions. The handsome quarto Spencer which she authorized Mary to buy for £2. 12. 6, when she brought it home in triumph proved to be *only the Fairy Queen;* so we got them to take it again and I have procured instead a Folio, which luckily contains, besides all the Poems, the view of the State of Ireland, which is difficult to meet with. The Spencer, and the Chaucer, being noble old books, we did not think Stockdale's modern volumes [of Shakespeare] would look so well beside them. . . . So we have used our own discretion in purchasing Pope's fine Quarto in six volumes, which may be read ad ultimam horam vitae.[10]

It is this letter which contains Lamb's entertaining account of a conversation on Spenser, which took place between himself and a young gentleman in his office ("brother to the Miss Evans who Coleridge so narrowly escaped marrying"). A very amusing confusion arose, as a result of the Young Gentleman's understanding that the subject of Lamb's discourse was the then fashionable poet, The Honourable William Spencer, instead of "an old Bard in a Ruff" who excited "dim notions of Sir P. Sydney and Lord Burleigh," who was the author of "the most perfect specimen of the Epithalamium in our language," and who "wrote a poem called the *Fairy Queen,* with the *Shepherd's Calendar,* and many more verses besides."[11] This same letter, which contains so much talk of Spenser, concludes with this comment:

---

[10] A similar copy of Spenser was among what Lamb calls "My midnight darlings, my Folios!" In his brief essay "On the Ambiguities Arising from Proper Names," he refers to "the fine folio copy of the poet's works, which I have at home." This book is described by Mr. Lucas in Appendix III of his *Life* of Lamb. I take it to be the second folio, 1617-18. The volume contains some manuscript notes by Lamb, among them, against *F. Q.*, Book III, Canto xi, Stanza xxxii, this enthusiastic comment: "Dear Venom, This is the stave I wot of. I will maintain it against any in the book." This is the stanza referred to:

> Then was he turnd into a snowy Swan,
> To win faire Leda to his lovely trade;
> O wondrous skill! and sweet wit of the man,
> That her in daffadillies sleeping made
> From scorching heat her daintie limbes to shade;
> Whiles the proud Bird, ruffing his fethers wyde
> And brushing his faire brest, did her invade;
> She slept; yet twixt her eielids closely spyde
> How towards her he rusht, and smiled at his pryde.

[11] This incident was later used by Lamb as the subject of the essay, "On

N. B. At the beginning of *Edm.* Spencer (to prevent mistakes) I have copied from my own copy, and primarily from a book of Chalmers on Shakspear, a Sonnet of Spenser's never printed among his poems. It is curious as being manly and rather Miltonic, and as a Sonnet of Spenser's with nothing in it about Love or Knighthood.

The poem referred to is the Commendatory Sonnet to Harvey, beginning "Harvey, the happy above happiest men." Lamb seems to stress the term "manly" in his comment. If this was intentional, it seems a little strange that he should have found the quality unusual in Spenser. It is true that he had previously referred to him as "honey-tongued," but he has also linked his name closely with that of Milton as an "Epic" poet, and he appears to think of him repeatedly in connection with Chaucer. Thus, in his review of Keats's *Lamia, Isabella,* etc., he remarks upon the passage where Isabella is digging for the body of her lover, that

there is nothing more awfully simple in diction, more nakedly grand and moving in sentiment, in Dante, in Chaucer, or in Spenser.[12]

The reader will remember that in Hazlitt's essay on the subject, suggested by Lamb, "Persons One would Wish to Have Seen," Lamb proposes Sir Thomas Browne and Fulke Greville, the friend of Sir Philip Sidney. Later in the discussion, Dante and Chaucer are brought up, after whom Lamb thinks of Spenser. Thus Hazlitt:

Lamb put it to me if I should like to see Spenser as well as Chaucer; and I answered, without hesitation, 'No; for that his beauties were ideal, visionary, not palpable or personal, and therefore connected with less curiosity about the man. His poetry was the essence of romance, a very halo round the bright orb of fancy; and the bringing in the individual might dissolve the charm. No tones of voice could come up to the mellifluous cadence of his verse; no form but of a winged angel could vie with the airy shapes he has described. He was (to my apprehension) rather a "creature of the element, that lived in the rainbow and played in the plighted clouds," than an ordinary mortal. Or if he did appear, I should wish it to be as a mere vision, like one of his own pageants, and that he should pass by unquestioned like a dream or sound. . . .'

---

the Ambiguities Arising From Proper Names," published in the *Reflector* (1811). The contribution is signed "X. Y. Z.," but is known to be Lamb's because of the almost verbatim reproduction of the passage in the above letter. Cf. *Works*, I, 448.

[12] Coleridge, in a marginal jotting in Lamb's copy of Daniel, mentions having seen "glaring proofs" of Lamb's "passion respecting Chaucer, Spenser, and Ben Jonson."—Cf. Appendix III, Lucas, *Life*, II, 316.

Hazlitt does not tell us what Lamb or any of the others thought of this utterance. It is fairly typical of Hazlitt and of romantic criticism generally, which has "encouraged men," as Dr. Cory sharply observes, "to take *The Faerie Queene* as an intellectual anesthetic."[13] As fragmentary and as comparatively slight as Lamb's remarks on Spenser are, I believe there is in them a quality which is at odds with the common conception of Spenser as being merely the poet of dreamland.

This is far from saying that Lamb was unimpressed with the supernaturalism of Spenser. Indeed, in his own essay *Witches and Other Night Fears,* there are several allusions which prove the contrary. Apropos of the failure of witches to resist the constituted powers, such as a "simple Justice of the Peace" or a "silly Headborough," Lamb observes,

> What stops the Fiend in Spenser from tearing Guyon to pieces—or who had made it a condition of his prey, that Guyon must take assay of the glorious bait—we have no guess. We do not know the laws of that country.

Again, it is interesting to note that the manuscript of this essay contains a last paragraph which originally ran thus:

> When I awoke I came to a determination to write prose all the rest of my life; and with submission to some of our young writers, who are yet diffident of their powers, and balancing perhaps between verse and prose, they might not do unwisely to decide the preference by the texture of their natural dreams. If these are prosaic, they may depend upon it they have not much to expect in a creative way from their artificial ones. What dreams must not Spenser have had![14]

This is about as near as Lamb comes, and he is still a great way off, to the airy-fairy conception of the dream poet.

Rather a more sober and earnest attitude of mind is discernible, I think, in these scattered comments. In *Grace Before Meat,* he asks,

> Why have we none for books, those spiritual repasts—a grace before Milton—a grace before Shakespeare—a devotional exercise proper to be said before reading the Fairy Queen?

---

[13] *Edmund Spenser: A Critical Study,* p. 443.

[14] Ms. in the Dyce and Forster collection at South Kensington. The above quoted from Lucas's note, *Works,* II, 373.

and there is a suggestion of gravity and devotion even in this casual comment from *Detached Thoughts on Books and Reading,*

> Much depends upon *when* and *where* you read a book. In the five or six impatient minutes, before dinner is quite ready, who would think of taking up the Fairy Queen for a stop-gap, or a volume of Bishop Andrewes' sermons?

In *Some Sonnets of Sir Philip Sydney,* Lamb praises a quality which he would doubtless also apply to Spenser, especially as he cites Spenser in his quotation:

> But the general beauty of them all [Sidney's sonnets] is, that they are so perfectly characteristical. The spirit of 'learning and of chivalry,'—of which union, Spenser has entitled Sydney to have been the 'president,'—shines through them.

An appreciation of Spenser's feeling for the tangible is implicit, I think, in Lamb's comments on Jonson's *The Case is Altered:*

> The old poets, when they introduce a miser, make him address his gold as his mistress; as something to be seen, felt, and hugged; as capable of satisfying two of the senses at least. The substitution of a thin, unsatisfying medium in the place of the good old tangible metal, has made avarice quite a Platonic affection in comparison with the seeing, touching, and handling-pleasures of the old Chrysophilites. . . . See the Cave of Mammon in Spenser; . . .[15]

In his essay on the *Sanity of True Genius* Lamb gives us at once the most extensive and the most subtle of his comments upon Spenser. Almost half of the space in this brief essay is devoted to an illustration from Spenser in the support of Lamb's main thesis, *i. e.,* that lesser artists usually fail to make convincing the most familiar places or characters, whereas in a great poet, like Spenser, the most extravagant dreams are ratified by the "waking judgment" of the reader.

> In the poet we have names which announce fiction; and we have absolutely no place at all, for the things and persons of the Fairy Queen prate not of their "whereabout." But in their inner nature, and the law of their speech and actions, we are at home, and upon acquainted ground. The one turns life into a dream; the other to the wildest dreams gives the sobrieties of every day occurrences. By what subtile art of tracing the mental processes it is effected, we are not philosophers enough to explain, but in that wonderful episode of the cave of Mammon, in which

---

[15] *Characters of Dramatic Writers, Works,* I, 59.

the Money God appears first in the lowest form of a miser, is then a worker of metals, and becomes the god of all the treasures of the world; and has a daughter, Ambition, before whom all the world kneels for favours—with the Hesperian fruit, the waters of Tantalus, with Pilate washing his hands vainly, but not impertinently, in the same stream—that we should be at one moment in the cave of an old hoarder of treasures, at the next at the forge of the Cyclops, in a palace and yet in hell, all at once, with the shifting mutations of the most rambling dream, and our judgment yet all the time awake, and neither able nor willing to detect the fallacy,—is a proof of that hidden sanity which still guides the poet in his wildest seeming-aberrations.

It is not enough to say that the whole episode is a copy of the mind's conceptions in sleep; it is, in some sort—but what a copy! Let the most romantic of us, that has been entertained all night with the spectacle of some wild and magnificent vision, recombine it in the morning, and try it by his waking judgment. That which appeared so shifting, and yet so coherent, while that faculty was passive, when it comes under cool examination, shall appear so reasonless, and so unlinked, that we are ashamed to have been so deluded; and to have taken, though but in sleep, a monster for a god. But the transitions in this episode are every whit as violent as in the most extravagant dream, and yet the waking judgment ratifies them.

Surely in this passage, at least, Lamb gives us one of the finest comments upon a fundamental and essential quality of Spenser's art, namely, a perception of reality that is more imaginative than mere objective realism, more profoundly truthful; and it is hardly necessary to add that this brilliant and eloquent criticism represents an intellectual and spiritual penetration quite different from the dilettante ecstasy which characterizes much of the romantic criticism of Spenser.

Two other passages in the essays invite our attention. Both are characteristic of Lamb in different moods. The first, from his amusing series of *Popular Fallacies,* "That Handsome is that Handsome Does," is unique in its familiar, not to say impudent, treatment of Spenser's *Hymn in Honour of Beauty*. It will be recalled that the uncomely Mrs. Conrady is the subject of Elia's remarks. The first part of the essay goes thus:

The soul, if we may believe Plotinus, is a ray from the celestial beauty. . . .
To the same effect, in a Hymn in honour of Beauty, divine Spenser, *platonizing,* sings:—

[668]

> "Every spirit as it is more pure
> And hath in it the more of heavenly light,
> So it the fairer body doth procure
> To habit in. . . ." [etc.]

But Spenser, it is clear, never saw Mrs. Conrady.

These poets, we find, are no safe guides in philosophy; for here, in his very next stanza but one, is a saving clause, which throws us all out again, and leaves us as much to seek as ever:—

> "Yet oft it falls, that many a gentle mind
> Dwells in deformed tabernacle drown'd
> Either by chance, against the course of kind,
> Or through unaptness in the substance found. . . ." [etc.]

From which it would follow, that Spenser had seen somebody like Mrs. Conrady.

The spirit of this good lady . . . must have stumbled upon one of these untoward tabernacles which he speaks of. A more rebellious commodity of clay for a ground, as the poet calls it, no gentle mind—and sure her's is one of the gentlest—ever had to deal with.

Certainly it would be ungracious, even in the most austere of Spenserians, to take offense at this whimsical pleasantry of a humorist who, himself, possessed one of the gentlest of minds.

The other, and final, passage which remains to be considered is one which links the two Londoners together. Notwithstanding his enthusiastic praise of the Cave of Mammon episode, or the stanza describing Leda and the swan, Lamb now tells us that his favorite passage in Spenser is that part of the *Prothalamion* which deals with the section of London which Elia calls "the most elegant spot in the metropolis,"—the Temple. In a phrase which may be a happy reminiscence of Spenser's "my most kindly nurse," Lamb affectionately refers to the Crown-office Row as the "place of my kindly engendure." He begins his essay *The Old Benchers of the Inner Temple* with Spenser in mind:

> I was born, and passed the first seven years of my life, in the Temple. Its church, its halls, its gardens, its fountain, its river, I had almost said . . .—these are my oldest recollections. I repeat, to this day, no verses to myself more frequently, or with kindlier emotion, than those of Spenser, where he speaks of this spot.

> There when they came, whereas those bricky towers,
> The which on Themmes brode aged back doth ride,
> Where now the studious lawyers have their bowers,
> There whylome wont the Templer knights to bide,
> Till they decayed through pride.

The few remaining allusions to Spenser's poetry, which exist in Lamb's published work and correspondence, are entirely incidental, such as references to Una's lamb, the Redcrosse knight, Sir Calidore, Busyrane, or such verbal echoes as "Let Gryll be Gryll," which, if significant at all, only add to the evidence of familiarity.

It would be a mistake, of course, to consider the fragmentary observations of Lamb on Spenser as forming together a definitive critical position. Such an interpretation would tend to destroy the very spirit which I have sought to preserve. Lamb's remarks herein quoted are, let me repeat, unstudied; they are not intended to support a thesis. At most, they form a faint adumbration, from broken lights, of the outline of a work which was projected but never actualized. Yet they deserve notice, I think, aside from their intrinsic and suggestive interest, as emphasizing, from a somewhat fresh point of view, Lamb's peculiarly congenial association with the Elizabethans.

*Tulane University.*

# THE READING OF RENAISSANCE ENGLISH WOMEN

By Louis B. Wright

That the great ladies of the English Renaissance were frequently learned we know from the intellectual accomplishments of such royal students as Lady Jane Grey and Queen Elizabeth, and from the activities of such lesser aristocrats as the daughters of Sir Thomas More and Sir Anthony Cooke, Lady Mary Sidney, Lady Margaret Hoby, Lady Anne Clifford, and a score of others only less well-known.[1] Of the reading and intellectual accomplishments of the average woman of the period we know less. I wish here to assemble some of the evidence of the average woman's interest in, and contact with, the literature of the time to see if we can determine what her literary tastes were, for obviously the reading public of women was an increasingly important factor in English literary circles from the middle of the sixteenth century onward.

Undoubtedly we have been prone to underestimate the literacy

---

[1] A brief survey of the learned ladies of the Renaissance is contained in the first chapter of Myra Reynolds, *The Learned Lady in England, 1650-1760* (Boston and New York, 1920). See also the introduction and notes to Dorothy M. Meads, *Diary of Lady Margaret Hoby* (Boston and New York, 1930); Rachel Weigall, "An Elizabethan Gentlewoman," *Quarterly Review*, CCXVI (1911), pp. 119-138; Evelyn Fox, "The Diary of an Elizabethan Gentlewoman," *Transactions of the Royal Historical Society.* 3rd. Series, II (1908), pp. 153-174; G. C. Williamson, *Lady Anne Clifford* (London, 1922); and George Ballard, *Memoirs of British Ladies Who Have Been Celebrated for Their Writing or Skill in the Learned Languages, Arts and Sciences* (London, 1775). A recent study of the history of women's education is Dorothy Gardiner's *English Girlhood at School* (Oxford, 1929).

William Harrison was impressed with the reading capacities of English gentlewomen. In his *Description of England* (1577) he comments: ". . . to saie how many gentlewomen and ladies there are, that beside sound knowledge of the Greeke and Latine toongs, are thereto no lesse skilfull in Spanish, Italian, and French, or in some one of them, it resteth not in me: sith I am persuaded, that as the noble men and gentlemen doo surmount in this behalfe, so these come verie little or nothing at all behind them for their parts: . . . [of the women of the court] some [occupy their time] in continuall reading either of the holie scriptures, or histories of our owne or forren nations about vs, (and diverse in writing volumes of their owne, or translating of other mens into our English and Latine toong,) . . ."—Ed. by F. J. Furnivall, New Shakespeare Society (1877).

of the Renaissance populace, whether we spoke of men or women. Mr. J. W. Adamson has recently advanced the belief that reading in the vernacular in the sixteenth century was "an art widely disseminated among the humblest social ranks irrespective of sex." [2] Many girls, he points out, learned to read from private teachers. Although girls, except perhaps in a few isolated cases, did not attend the grammar schools, both sexes seem to have attended the petty schools, where they learned to read English. Richard Mulcaster, defending the theory of education for women in his *Positions* (1581) implies that it was customary to teach girls English, as well as other tongues, for, he says, "We see yong maidens be taught to read and write, and can do both passing well; we know that they learne the best, and finest of our learned languages, to the admiration of all men"; and he adds, "I dare be bould therefore to admit yong maidens to learne, seeing my countrie gives me leaue, and her *custome* standes for me." [3] Discussing what the girl should be taught, Mulcaster comments:

To learne to read is very common, where conuenientnes doth serue, and *writing* is not refused, where oportunitie will yield it.

*Reading* if for nothing else it were, as for many things else it is, is verie needefull for religion, to read that which they must know, and ought to performe, if they haue not whom to heare, in that matter which they read. . . . Here I may not omit many and great contentmentes, many and sound comfortes, many manifoulde delites, which those wymen that haue skill and time to reade, without hindering their houswifery, do continually receiue by reading of some comfortable and wise discourses, penned either in forme of historie, or for direction to liue by.[4]

---

[2] "The Extent of Literacy in England in the Fifteenth and Sixteenth Centuries: Notes and Conjectures." *The Library*. New Series X (1929), pp. 163-193.

[3] R. H. Quick (ed), *Positions by Richard Mulcaster* (London, 1888), Ch. 38, pp. 167 ff.

[4] *Ibid.*, pp. 176-177. Several writers preceding Mulcaster had written on the education of women. See Foster Watson, *Vives and the Renaissance Education of Women* (London, 1912). Under the learned Katherine of Aragon, her preceptor, Ludowick Vives, and such men as Sir Thomas More, Sir Thomas Elyot, and Richard Hyrde, set forth ideas favoring the education of women in the learned languages. Watson (p. 159) calls Hyrde's preface to Margaret Roper's translation of Erasmus' treatise *Precatio dominica in septem portiones distributa* (tr. 1524), the "first Renascence document in English on the education of women."

One should compare Mulcaster's theories with those of Comenius as

Mulcaster's language indicates that women were in general sufficiently educated to read English works. This assumption is borne out by other allusions to women's reading.

Improvement in the education of women is one of the concerns of Edward Hake in *A Touchstone for this time present . . . Wherevnto is annexed a perfect rule to be obserued of all Parents and Scholemaisters, in the trayning vp of their Schollers and Children in learning* (1574), a work bearing a dedication to Hake's " knowne friende mayster Edward Godfrey, Merchaunt," in which he laments the depravity of the age, and among other evils, finds that girls are provided with improper reading matter which helps to keep them from better learning:

> Eyther shee is altogither kept from exercises of good learning, and knowledge of good letters, or else she is so nouseled in amorous bookes, vaine stories and fonde trifeling fancies, that shee smelleth of naughtinesse euen all hir lyfe after, . . .

Like Hake, Thomas Salter in *A Mirrhor mete for all Mothers, Matrones, and Maidens, intituled the Mirrhor of Modestie . . .* (1579)[5] condemns unwise fathers who

> doe giue them [their daughters] so sone as they haue any vnderstandyng in readyng, or spellyng, to cone and learne by hart bookes, ballades, songes, sonettes, and ditties of daliance, excityng their memories thereby, beyng then most apt to retayne for euer that whiche is taught theim, to the same maner . . . therefore I would wish our good matrone [who teaches

---

laid down in his *Great Didactic* (1628-32). Comenius is insistent on the education of girls and boys alike. Cf. J. W. Adamson, *Pioneers of Modern Education, 1600-1700* (Cambridge, 1905), p. 60.

Sir Balthazar Gerbier advertised public lectures in London in 1650 on the languages, arts, and sciences to which "not onely the Fathers of Families, but also the Mothers (mutually interested in the good education of their sonnes)" were invited.—*Ibid.*, pp. 186-187.

Perhaps the popularity of the French language text prepared by Peter Erondell, entitled, *The French Garden: for English Ladyes and Gentlewomen to walke in . . .* (1605), was a result not only of an intellectual interest among women, but a desire for the social improvement which French gave. Samuel Daniel appended a prefatory verse declaring that

> "Ladies haue long'd to match old *Holliband*,
> That they with men might parle out their part,"

and Erondell himself wrote a preface flattering English women for their studiousness and quick wits.

[5] Reprinted in J. P. Collier, *Illustrations of Old English Literature* (London, 1866), Vol. I.

young girls] to eschew such vse as a pestilent infection; ... But in steede of such bookes and lasciuious ballades, our wise matrone shall reade, or cause her maidens to reade, the examples and liues of godly and vertuous ladies, whose worthy fame and bright renowne yet liueth, and still will liue for euer, whiche shee shall make choice of, out of the holy Scripture, and other histories, both auncient and of late dayes; whiche bookes will not onely delight them, but as a spurre it will pricke and incite their hartes to follow vertue, and haue vice in horror and disdaine ... for you shall neuer repeate the vertuous liues of any such ladies as *Claudia, Portia, Lucretia*, and such like were, but you shall kindle a desire in them to treade their steppes, and become in tyme like vnto them. ...[6]

Although Salter emphasizes that woman reads and ought to be encouraged to read further, he strongly condemns allowing her to choose her own books. She should be advised to avoid moral philosophy and should have recommended to her such Christian poets as "Prudentio, Prospero, Juvenco, Nazianzeno," and their kind. On no account should she read Ovid, Catullus, the stories of Aeneas and Dido in Virgil, or of "filthie loue" among the Greek poets. Proper reading matter may be found in

... the holie Scripture, or other good bookes, as the bookes of *Plutarche*, made of such renowmed and vertuous women as liued in tyme paste, and those of Boccas tendyng to the same sence, or some other nerer our tyme; ...[7]

In the preceding passages quoted from Hake and Salter, the object of woman's training in good learning was pious or useful application of her knowledge. With the growth of Puritanism, the impetus to the acquirement of the rudiments of education grew stronger in the lower classes who regarded reading as the means to the study of the Bible and pious works, a ruling motive, incidentally, behind many of the pupils at the present time in American schools for illiterate adults. The mother was expected to read the Bible to her children and, in the absence of her husband, to conduct family worship, at which the whole household, children, servants, and apprentices were expected to attend. Hence it was a godly duty, indeed, a necessity, for mothers to know how to read. Without doubt the average middle-class woman could read and teach members of her household the rudiments of learning.[8] Unfor-

[6] *Ibid.*, pp. 10-11.
[7] *Ibid.*, pp. 15-21.
[8] A passage in Thomas Deloney's *Thomas of Reading* [1598?] seems

tunately, our records of the learning of bourgeois women are scanty. We know that Elizabeth Lucar, the daughter of a tradesman and the wife of a merchant-tailor,

> Latine and Spanish, and also Italian,
> She spake, writ, and read, with perfect utterance;
> And for the English, she the Garland wan,
> In Dame Prudence Schoole. . . .[9]

Elizabeth Wallington, wife of John Wallington, a turner in Eastcheap, was a diligent reader of the Bible, Fox's *Book of Martyrs*, and the English chronicles.[10] Doubtless the practical affairs of the home of Lady Margaret Hoby, a pious Puritan woman of Yorkshire, who left behind a diary, were not unlike those in the more prosperous tradesman's homes. In telling of her own reading and literary interests, Lady Hoby throws some light on the training of her household. When she was too busily occupied about some task to read in her herbal, her book of physic, the *Book of Martyrs*, Mr. Perkins' sermons, or some other pious or useful work, she frequently had a member of the household read: the chaplain, his wife, "one of my wemen," or one of the maids:

> . . . from thence came home and reed of Grenhame, and hard Megg Rhodes read . . .
> . . . then I was in the granerie receiuing Corne, and againe took order for supper and hard one of my women read of perkins, and after that returned to priuat praier and examenation . . .

---

to indicate that among the lower orders of servant maids, reading was not common at the end of the sixteenth century. The maids who meet fair Margaret, daughter of the banished Earl of Shrewsbury, on her way to enter domestic service, are amazed that she can read and write. In reply to their inquiries as to what she can do, Margaret replies:

". . . I can read and write, and sowe, some skill I haue in my needle, and a little on my Lute: but this I see will profit me nothing.

"Good Lord (quoth they) are you so bookish? wee did neuer heare of a Maide before that could reade and write. . . .

"I pray you (qd. another) seeing you are bookish, will you doe so much as to reade a loue-letter that is sent me, . . ."—F. O. Mann, *The Works of Thomas Deloney* (Oxford, 1912), p. 223.

Not all maids were so ignorant, and in many households some, at least, were trained by their mistresses to read.

[9] From her epitaph; quoted from Ballard, *op. cit.*, p. 26.

[10] R. Webb (ed.), *Historical Notices of Events Occurring Chiefly in the Reign of Charles I. By Nehemiah Wallington* (London, 1869), I, p. xi.

> ... After priuat prairs I went about the house and wrought amonge my Maides, and hard one read of the Booke of Marters ...[11]

The amount of pious literature consumed by the Elizabethans is amazing, and we may be sure that Lady Hoby is not an unusual creature in her inordinate interest in books of sermons,[12] an interest which led her to keep a commonplace book of sermon extracts. Death, imminent and fearful, haunted woman's consciousness. The birth of her children brought always the threat of death. Her children remained during their infancy in the shadow of a mortality frightful in its toll. Small wonder is it that the Renaissance woman kept by her side Michael Spark's *Crums of Comfort,* or some work like it. Salvation and another world were often her only consolation. Imminence of death caused Elizabeth Jocelyn (1596-1622) to write a pious little book, *The Mothers Legacie to her Unborne Childe* (1624), a book much read by her sex.[13] Some of the devotional books were addressed directly to women. Nicholas Breton, in dedicating "To the Ladies and Gentlewomen Readers" his collection of prose prayers, *Auspicante Jehoua. Maries Exercise* (1597),[14] indicates that pious material is especially suitable for woman's reading:

> ... reading in this diuine historie [the Bible] of the excellencie of Gods loue, and emong many of His elected, of some women in His especiall fauour, I could not but acquaint your good mindes, with the memoire of their names. ...

A book small enough to be carried in some convenient pocket that she might have its comfort always at hand was the anonymous *A Iewel For Gentlewomen. Containing diuers godly Prayers, fit to comfort the wounded consciences of all penitent sinners. Reade, meditate & pray and you shall find comfort to your soules* (1624).[15]

---

[11] Meads, *op. cit.*, pp. 93, 94, 175.

[12] Her diary is full of entries of pious readings. Cf. Meads, *op. cit.*, pp. 72, 87, 89, 97, 98, 111.

[13] Reynolds, *op. cit.*, p. 29. A third edition appeared in 1625. A reprint in 1852 had a preface enumerating pious works by women before 1688.

[14] Reprinted by A. B. Grosart, *The Works in Verse and Prose of Nicholas Breton.* Chertsey Worthies Library. (1879). Vol. II.

[15] Practically all the devotional books, of course, devoted space to crises peculiar to women's lives. Many prayers were designed especially for

Such books, presumably, pious women read in their odd moments. For more extended reading, there were sermons like those of Perkins and Greenham which occupied so much of Lady Hoby's time, the ever present *Book of Martyrs,* and writings of the early church fathers, like St. Augustine's *City of God,* which Anne Clifford is said to have read by the time she was thirteen, along with Eusebius, *The French Academy* by La Primaudaye, and many other useful books.[16] No one probably equalled the record of Elizabeth Carey, Viscountess Falkland (1585-1639), who mingled humane letters of the world with her piety.[17]

Not only was woman concerned in her reading with proper and useful means of attaining the kingdom of God, but she kept on her table for ready reference books designed to help mortals here below. The house-wife's first duty, from the duchess to the tailor's helpmeet, was house-wifery, which included vastly more than keeping a house in order, for she was often doctor, surgeon, and apothecary. She consulted her almanac to learn about the times for letting blood. She read in the latest herbal about the medicinal use of countless plants. Lady Hoby several times records reading in her "arbal," which may have been the *New herball* of William Turner, who kept a botanical garden at Kew, or the newer translation of Gerard's *Herbal*.[18] Lady Hoby also found interest in a book treating of mental disorders, for she records reading " Bright of Mallincocolie " (*sic*), probably Timothy Bright's *A treatise of melancholie,*

women. Cf. a later little book, Robert Aylett's *Devotions, Viz. A Good Womans, The humble mans Prayer* (1655). In the good woman's prayer, the author weaves into verse-stanzas the good women of the Scriptures whom the woman prays to be like.

[16] Reynolds, *op. cit.,* p. 32.

[17] *Ibid.,* p. 36: " She had read very exceedingly much: poetry of all kinds ancient and modern in several languages, all that ever she could meet; history very universally, especially all ancient Greek and Roman histories very thoroughly: of most other countries something, though not so universally, of the ecclesiastical very much, most especially concerning its chief pastors. Of books treating of moral virtue or wisdom (such as Seneca, Plutarch's *Morals,* and natural knowledge, as Pliny, and of late ones, such as French, Mountaine, and English, Bacon) she had read very many when she was young. Of the fathers and controversial writers on both sides a great deal even of Luther and Calvin."

[18] Meads, *op. cit.,* pp. 78, 100, 250, note 218.

*containing the causes thereof* (1586).[19] Grace Sherrington, later Lady Mildmay, relates in her *Journal* (*c.* 1570-1617) that her governess made her read in Dr. Turner's *Herball* and the "most excellent workes of chirurgerye made and set forth by maister J. Vigon."[20] The latter was a treatise by John of Vigo, translated by Bartholomew Traheron. Again she comments, "Alsoe every day I spent some time in the Herball and books of phisick . . ." Her reading was so fruitful that she left in manuscript some books of recipes and prescriptions, doubtless the sort of books kept by many housewives. When she became Lady Mildmay, she had her portrait painted in 1613 with her *Book of Simples*. The popular books on medicine, abundantly printed in the sixteenth and seventeenth centuries, found women their most conscientious readers.

Many utility books were available to the Renaissance woman. Cooks books, of course, were numerous, a fact which may throw some light on the literacy of the average housewife. The preface to *A Booke of Curious and strange Inuentions, called the first part of Needleworkes* . . . (1596), giving illustrations of lace patterns, emphasizes the fact that even maids may use the book.[21]

---

[19] *Ibid.*, p. 77.

[20] Weigall, *loc. cit.*, pp. 120-121, 125. The governess seems to have been the strict sort, typical of the school mistress recommended to godly households. Certain improper conduct between a lady and a gentleman known to the household furnished a theme for literary creation for herself and her pupil: ". . . when she beheld [the offending couple] she asked me yf I did not think it a monstrous spectacle to behold, and wished me to make one stave and she would make another untill there were four or five verses made thereupon, which she performed herselfe very wittily and sharp against such licentious behaviour."—p. 120.

[21] It commends industry in such arts as a means of improving the social position of maids:

"This worke beseemth Queenes of great renowne,
And Noble Ladies of a high degree:
Yet not exempt for Maids of any Towne,
For all may learne that thereto willing be:
Come then sweet gyrles and hereby learne the way,
With good report to liue another day.

"For many maidens but of base degree,
By their fine knowledge in this curious thing:
With Noble Ladies oft companions be,

Despite Puritan objections to idle reading—perhaps in part as a result of it—the Renaissance woman, like her modern sister, found in fiction the literature of escape which the strenuousness of her life demanded. John Lyly recognized the importanec of the feminine audience and frankly catered to it. Greene succeeded him and became, in Nashe's sarcastic comment in the *Anatomie of Absurditie,* " the Homer of women." Women in general have never subscribed to realism. Romance in strange opera lands, love stories with happy endings, these are the favorites, known to the Elizabethans as well as to us. The chivalric romance, as one might expect, remained a popular literary form with women throughout the sixteenth and early seventeenth centuries.[22] Many allusions testify to

> Sometimes they teach the daughter of a King:
> Thus by their knowledge, fame, and good report,
> They are esteemed among the noblest sort.
>
> " Then prettie maidens view this prettie booke
> Marke well the works that you therein doe finde,
> Sitting at worke cast not aside your looke,
> They profit small that haue a gazing minde:
> Keepe cleane your Samples, sleepe not as you sit,
> For sluggishnes doth spoile the rarest wit."

[22] Vives in *Instruction of a Christian Woman,* translated by Richard Hyrde and printed about 1540, after condemning filthy songs and Ovid's works, adds: "And this the laws ought to take heed of, and of those ungracious books, such as be in my country in Spain, the *Amadis,* Florisand, Tristan [of Lyons] and Celestina the bawd, mother of naughtiness; in France, Lancelot du Lac, Paris and Vienne, Ponthus and Sidonia, and Melusine; and here in Flanders, the histories of Flor [ice] and Blanchefleur. Leonella and Canamorus, Pyramis and Thisbe. In England, Parthenope, Genarides, Hippomadon, William and Melyour, Libius and Arthur, Guy, Bevis, and many other. And some translated out of Latin into vulgar speeches [i. e., languages], as the unsavoury conceits of Pogius and Aeneas Silvius, Euralus and Lucretia, the hundred fables of Boccaccio, which books but idle men wrote unlearned, and set all upon filth and viciousness, in whom I wonder what should delight men but that vice pleaseth them so much."—Watson, *op. cit.,* pp. 58-59. Later in *The Offices and Duties of an Husband,* translated by Thomas Paynell (1550), Vives further condemns romances.—*Ibid.,* p. 196. Vives' criticism is not wholly destructive, for in place of idle love stories, he suggests in his *Plan of Studies for Girls* (1523): "Let her be given pleasure in stories which teach the art of life. Let these by such as she can tell to others—e. g., the life of the boy Papirius Praetextatus in Aulus Gellius, of Joseph in the Holy Books, of Lucretia in Livy, of Griselda and others, as found in Valerius, Sabellicus,

the interest in romances of all types. In a prefatory epistle by N. W. to Samuel Daniel's *The Worthy tract of Paulus Iouius* . . . (1585) is a comment on the taste for Italian stories:

> For if Courtiers are inwardly rauished in vewing the Picture of *Fiametta* which *Boccace* limned. If Ladies entertaine *Bandel* or *Ariosto* in their Closets. If Louers imbrace their Phisition *Ouid* in extremitie of their passion: then will Gentlemen of all tribes, much rather honor your Impresa as a most rare Iewell . . .

The reading of Robert Greene's works and of chivalric romances extended even to chambermaids if one can believe a description of "A Chambermaid" in Sir Thomas Overbury's *Characters* (1614):[23]

> She reads Greenes works over and over, but is so carried away with the *Mirror of Knighthood*, she is many times resolv'd to runne out of her selfe, and become a lady errant.

Adventurous love stories are again described as the literary fare of maids by Wye Saltonstall in *Picturae Loquentes. Or Pictures Drawne forth in Characters. With a Poeme of a Maid* (1631). Of "A Mayde" he says:

> Nor should they reade books which of some fond Loues,
> The various fortunes and aduentures show;
> Nor such as natures secrets do discouer,
> Since still desire doth but from knowledge grow: . . .[24]

Again he comments, ". . . she reades now loues historyes as *Amadis de Gaule* and the *Arcadia,* & in them courts the shaddow of loue till she know the substance."[25] That the Arcadia had become the reading matter for middle class women is further attested by Thomas Powell's *Tom of all Trades, Or The Plaine Path-*

---

and other writers of the same kind—stories which tend to some commendation of virtue, and detestation of vice."—*Ibid.*, pp. 144-145. Among other authors recommended are Cicero, Seneca, Plutarch, some dialogues of Plato, the epistles of Jerome, some works of Ambrosius and Augustine, some of Erasmus, More's *Utopia*, histories of Florus, Justinus, and Valerius Maximus, the christian poets, Prudentius, Sidonius, Paulinus, Aratus, Prosper, Juvencus, and others of like character.—*Ibid.*, p. 146.

[23] Quoted by Henry Thomas, *Spanish and Portuguese Romances of Chivalry* (Cambridge, 1920), p. 229.

[24] Sig. B 1 verso.

[25] Character 19, "A Maide," Sig. E 6 verso.

*way To Preferment* (1631) in a passage on the education of women:

> In stead of Song and Musicke, let them learne Cookery and Laundrie. And in stead of reading Sir *Philip Sidneys Arcadia*, let them read the ground of good huswifery. I like not a female Poetess at any hand. Let greater personages glory their skill in musicke, the posture of their bodies, their knowledge in languages, the greatnesse and freedome of their spirits, and their arts in arreigning of mens affections at their flattering faces: This is not the way to breed a private Gentlemans Daughter.[26]

The implication is that even women in the lower social orders were laying claims to more abstract culture and greater familiarity with idle romance than Powell approved.

Other allusions indicate that romances made the favorite reading of middle and lower class women in the early seventeenth century. The goldsmith's daughter in *Eastward Hoe* (1605), the victim of Sir Petronel Flash's desertion, exclaims, " Would the Knight o' the *Sun,* or *Palmerin* of England, haue vsed their Ladies so? " Her maid adds her favorites: " Or sir *Lancelot?* Or sir *Tristam?* " (V, i).[27] The confidante in Massinger's *Guardian* declares to her mistress that she not only has read the romances but that she believes in them:

> Seek no more president:
> In all the books of *Amadis de Gaul,*
> The *Palmerins,* and the true Spanish story
> *The Mirror of Knighthood,* which I have read often,
> Read feelingly, nay more, I do believe in 't,
> My Lady has no parallel.—(I, ii).

A chambermaid described by William Browne in " Fido, an Epistle to Fidelia " is a keen student of the romances. After hearing the mistress read " one epistle that some fool had writ,"

> Her Chambermaid's great reading quickly strikes
> That good opinion dead, and swears that this
> Was stol'n from Palmerin or Amadis.

Robert Burton in *The Anatomy of Melancholy* (1621) mentions

---

[26] Reprinted by F. J. Furnivall in the New Shakespeare Society (1876), p. 173.

[27] This and the three succeeding quotations are cited by Henry Thomas, " The Palmerin Romances." *Transactions* of the Bibliographical Society of London (1916), pp. 35-40.

"many silly gentlewomen" who "are incensed by reading amorous toies, *Palmerin de Oliua,* the knight of the sun, &c."—(Pt. 3, Sect. 2, memb. 2, subs. 4).

To woman's reading of voluptuous love stories was attributed much of her moral depravity so lamented by Puritan writers. Robert Anton in *Vices Anotomie, Scourged and Corrected* (1617) complains that women both read and write bawdy verse:

> And I much wonder that this *lustie time*
> That women can both *sing* and *sigh* in rime,
> Weep and dissemble both in baudie meetre,
> Laugh in Luxurious pamphlets, like a *creature*
> Whose very *breath,* some *Ouid* did create
> With *prouocations,* and a *longing fate*
> After some stirring meates: *wiues* couet *bookes*
> Not penn'ed by Artists but the *fruits* of *Cookes*
> Prescribing *lustie dishes,* to enflame
> Their lustie fighting *broode* vnto their *game*
> *Confections* with *infections* of their *kinde,*
> Rot both their *body,* and corrupts the *minde.*[28]

John Davies in *A Scourge for Paper-Persecutors* . . . (1625), referring to *Venus and Adonis,* maintains that

> . . . the coyest Dames
> In priuate reade it for their Closset-games.[29]

Love poetry and amorous fiction, including *Venus and Adonis,* made up the library of the heroine of Thomas Cranley's *Amanda or the Reformed Whore* (1635):

> And then a heape of bookes of thy devotion,
> Lying upon a shelfe close underneath,
> Which thou more think'st upon then on thy death:
> They are not prayers of a grieved soule,
> That with repentance doth his sinnes condole,
> But amorous Pamphlets that best likes thine eyes,
> And Songs of love, and Sonets exquisit:
> Among these Venus and Adonis lies,
> With Salmasis and her Hermaphrodite:

---

[28] P. 52.
[29] Quoted by J. P. Collier in *A Bibliographical and Critical Account of the Rarest Books in the English Language* (New York, 1860), I, p. 186. Collier also notices the reference to *Venus and Adonis* cited here from Cranley's *Amanda.*

> Pigmalion's there with his transform'd delight,
> And many merry Comedies with this,
> Where the Athenian Phryne acted is.[30]

Other women of Amandas' profession were readers of prose and verse, chiefly sentimental, we are told by other writers. Thomas Lodge describes a harlot who kept a pathetic ballad over her chimney piece;[31] Humphrey Mills a little later tells of a harlot whose house was equipped "With [Martin] Parker's workes, and such like things";[32] an anonymous pamphlet near the middle of the seventeenth century, *The Yellow Book* (1656), describes Mrs. Wanton's chamber ". . . where there is nothing but four or five naked Pictures, a Song book, a Play book, a Lute, a History, two or three great Looking-glasses," and similar equipment.[33] Poetry for women seems to have become suspect, at least if they sought to write it, for Thomas Heywood in *A Curtaine Lecture* (1637) thinks " it is a question disputable " whether any virgin should " bee pleasant in lookes, free in language, wanton in carriage, to poetize, or the like," and he further enjoins maidens " to be wary in their words, and weighty in their writings, . . ."[34]

Shakespeare was the favorite reading of amorous girls of the mid-seventeenth century, to judge from an allegorical description in John Johnson's *The Academy of Loue describing ye folly of younge men, & ye fallacy of women* (1641). In a vision the author is carried through the University of Love until he comes to Love's Library, where the volumes are called

---

[30] Reprinted privately by Frederick Ouvry (London, 1869). A second edition of *Amanda* in 1639 bore the title, *The Converted Courtezan, Or, The Reformed Whore. Being a true Relation of a Penitent Sinner, shadowed under the name of Amanda.* Cranley in an epistle to the reader states that he particularly hopes that his work will appeal to women readers. It is a sentimental story in verse and prose, describing the wickedness of a fair woman whom the author saw from his own prison window and rebuked in a series of verse letters until she repented her way of life. It is the forerunner of many stories like it in the later seventeenth and eighteenth centuries.

[31] Hyder E. Rollins, "The Black-Letter Broadside Ballad," *PMLA*, XXXIV (1919), p. 301, note 30. Quoted from *Wits Miserie* (1596).

[32] *Ibid.*, p. 301, note 30. Quoted from *Night's Search* (1646).

[33] *Thomason Tracts.* Brit. Mus., E. 878. (1), pp. 7-8.

[34] Pp. 41-47.

... Tomes, or Sections, for that our Courtly Dames study onely to exect or cut off their thread-bare curtesans, and induce fresh and new furnished ones: And viewing these Tomes, saw chained up in golden linkes two Spanish Poets [sic.], Dante and Cost, and an English one called *Messenger* [Massinger], which Messenger they entertaine, hoping still to see the good and grateful newes of a well-filled purse, but if it prove contrary to their expectation, they command shaving *Shirly* to make him acquainted with Sir *Philip*, and so they flirt him into *Arcadia* to sing a lamentation for his lost Mistresse.

There was also *Shakespeere*, who (as *Cupid* informed me) creepes into the womens closets about bed time, and if it were not for some of the old out-of-date Grandames (who are set over the rest as their tutoresses) the young sparkish Girles would read in Shakespeere day and night, so that they would open the Booke or Tome, and the men with a Fescue in their hands should point to the Verse.[35]

The foregoing allusions give some clue to the literary tastes of women in general at the end of the sixteenth and beginning of the seventeenth centuries. Did professional writers realize the importance of the new reading public? The evidence is that they did. The feminine audience had reached such proportions by the last quarter of the sixteenth century that many authors were making a definite and frank appeal to women. Best known, perhaps, to modern readers are John Lyly's efforts to please the ladies with courtly fiction of good conduct. But Lyly's contemporaries were equally solicitous about having their books lie in milady's chamber.[36] A certain R. B., who signed the dedication to George Pettie's *A Petite Palace of Pettie His Pleasure* (ed. of 1576), addressing himself "To the gentle Gentlewoman Readers," openly says of his readers that "by my will I would haue Gentlewomen." Barnabe Rich, anxious to curry favor with women, in *Riche his Farewell to Militarie profession* (1581), declares he wrote "for the onely delight of the courteous Gentlewoemen bothe of England and Irelande." He makes a further conscious bid for the favor of women in *Don Simonides* (1581). William Warren in addressing *A pleasant new Fancie of a Fondlings deuice. Intitled and cald the Nurcerie of Names* . . . (1581) "to the Gentlewomen of England" refers to himself as "your poore Poet, and your olde friend."[37]

[35] Pp. 96-100.
[36] Cf. J. J. Jusserand, *The English Novel in the Time of Shakespeare* (London, 1899), p. 147.
[37] Thomas Corser, *Collectanea Anglo-Poetica*, Pt. XI (1883), pp. 359-362.

The efforts of Robert Greene to reach an audience of women in his numerous collections of love stories are obvious even to the casual turner of his pages. Such a title as *Penelopes Web: Wherein a Christall Myrror of faeminine perfection represents to the viewe of euery one those vertues and graces, which more curiously beautifies the mynd of women, then eyther sumptuous Apparell, or Iewells of inestimable valew* . . . (1587) is typical of his flattering effort to ingratiate himself, a method he pursued in title-pages, dedications, and subject matter, so that he well deserves Nashe's satirical description of him as " the Homer of women." Doubtless Nashe also had Greene in mind when he wrote further of the desire women had of hearing themselves praised by authors:

> Many of them [writers] to be more amiable with their friends of the Feminine sexe, blot many sheetes of paper in the blazing of Womens slender praises, as though in that generation there raigned and alwaies remained such singular simplicitie, that all posterities should be enioyned by dutie, to fill and furnish theyr Temples, nay Townes and streetes, with the shrines of the Saints.[38]

Writers, Nashe again comments, think " by compiling of Pamphlets in their Mistresse praises, to be called the restorers of womankind." [39]

The middle class woman, we have already observed, was a great reader of sentimental romances like those of Greene. Some of Greene's successors openly catered to her. Samuel Rowlands, author of miscellaneous works appealing to the London bourgeoisie, after addressing a jolly transcript of London life. *'Tis Merrie when Gossips meete* (1602), " To all the pleasant conceited London Gentlewomen, that are friendes to mirth, and enemies to dull Melancholy," in a prefatory address to *The Famous History of Guy Earle*

---

[38] The *Anatomie of Absurditie* in R. B. McKerrow, *The Works of Thomas Nashe* (London, 1910), I, p. 11.

[39] *Ibid.*, p. 19. A mournful commentary on the dead laureate of women is found in R. B. 's *Greenes Funeralls* (1594), ed. by R. B. McKerrow (Stratford-upon-Avon, 1922), Sonnet III, Sig. B 1:

> " He is dead, that wrote of your delights:
> That wrote of Ladies, and of Parramours:
> Of budding beautie, and hir branched leaues,
> Of sweet content in royal Nuptialls.
> He he is dead, that kild you with disdaine:
> And often fed your friendly hopes againe."

of *Warwicke* (1609) holds up Guy " To the Honourable Ladies of England " as a notable savior of women.[40]

Rowlands had an established precedent, we have seen, for dedicating a chivalric romance to women. Although romances had come to be the literary fare of the lower classes by the end of the sixteenth century, they were not abandoned by any group and remained popular with women of all classes. Indeed, a woman who has been given too little credit in the annals of her sex, a certain Margaret Tyler, came forward in 1578 as the translator of *The First Part of the Mirrour of Princely deedes and Knighthood. Wherein Is Shewed The Worthinesse Of the Knight of the Sunne and his brother Rosicleer.* . . . She appends a long epistle to the reader in which she asserts the virtue-provoking qualities of romances and the prerogative of women to read and to write them. She defends herself against critics who carp that she has not spent her time

> penning matters of great waight & sadnesse in diuinitie, or other studies, ye profession whereof more neerely beeseemeth my yeers, other some discoursing of matters more easie and ordinary in common talke, wherein a Gentlewoman may honestly imploy hir travaile. . . . But my defence is by example of the best, amongst which, many haue dedicated theyr labours, some stories, some of warre, some Physicke, some Law, some as concerning gouerment, some diuine matters, vnto diuerse Ladies and Gentlewomen. And if men may & doe beestow such of theyr trauailes vpon Gentlewomen, then may wee women read such of theyr woorkes as they dedicate vnto us, and if wee may read them, why not farther wade in them to the search of a truth. . . . But amongst all my ill willers, some I hope are not so strayght that they would enforce mee necessarily either not to write or to write of diuintie. . . . And thus much concerning this present storie, that it is neither vnseemely for a woman to deale in, neyther greatly requiring a lesse stayed age then mine is.[41]

Margaret Tyler's bold assertion of woman's equality in reading and writing is an interesting document in the history of woman's rights.

The appeal to women readers is obvious in the sequence of chivalric romances which followed Margaret Tyler's efforts in translation.

---

[40] The terms " Gentlewomen " and " Ladies " must not be taken too literally. From what we know about Rowlands and his popularity, it is plain that he was writing for the wives of tradesmen, who would be flattered, of course, by such courteous forms of address.

[41] My quotations are from the edition of 1599, which has the same preface as the edition of 1578.

For example, in L. A.'s *The Seuenth Booke of the Myrrour of Knighthood* . . . (1598) the translator calls attention to the fact that in many places he has addressed his speech, " & directed the Historie as it were particulerly to one or more Ladies or Gentlewomen." *The Ninth part of the Mirrour of Knighthood* . . . (1601) is much concerned, the title-page advertises, with " the high cheualrie of the gallant Ladyes." A little later William Webster declares in a preface " To The Faire Reader, Of The Fayrer Sex " [42] that his romance *The Most Pleasant And Delightful Historie of Curran, a Prince of Danske, and the fayre Princesse Argentile* . . . (1617) was written solely for women. John Kennedy even provides the 1631 edition of *The Historie of Calanthrop and Lucilla* (1626) with a title-page describing it as *The Ladies Delight, or, The English Gentlewomans History of Calanthrop and Lucilla*.

This is not the place to discuss the unusual interest in the literature about women in the first quarter of the seventeenth century. The controversial pamphlets in which women were in turn satirized and defended indicate that women were reading both the satires and the encomia, and were turning a hand to defend themselves.[43] From Margaret Tyler's time onward, women were asserting their literacy in definite terms. After Robert Greene, writers who hoped to earn their livelihood by their pens could no longer despise the feminine reader. Thomas Heywood, perhaps woman's staunchest literary advocate in the first half of the seventeenth century, convinced of her capacity to read and appreciate, provided for her

---

[42] Cf. Robert Hayman's dedication of his translation of the first four books of Owen's *Epigrams*, appended to his own *Quodlibets* (1628) " To The Far Admired, Admirably Faire, vertuous and witty Beauties of England."

[43] Joseph Swetnam's pamphlet *The Araignment of Lewde, idle, froward, and vnconstant women* . . . (1615), a vicious satire of women, aroused a number of defenders of the sex to reply, among whom were two or three women. Rachel Speght replied in *A Mouzell for Melastomus* . . . (1617). A certain Esther Sowernam wrote *Ester hath hang'd Haman* . . . (1617), in which she apologizes for noticing Swetnam, who was already being answered by a minister's daughter. The latter's treatise, she decided, might be too weak; hence her own reply, bearing a special dedication to apprentices to defend women against calumny. Several other pamphlets, some of which were perhaps by women, appeared. The Swetnam controversy was characteristic of the literature about women in the second decade of the seventeenth century.

such useful works as his *Gunaikeion: Or Nine Bookes of Various History, Concerninge Women* (1624) and *The Exemplary Lives and memorable Acts of nine the most worthy Women of the World* (1640). Here woman could find the biographies of virtuous and noble women, so insistently recommended over a half-century earlier by Thomas Salter. Writers no longer felt that woman's reading was limited to works of divinity and books of physic. The increase in the reading public in the later sixteenth and early seventeenth centuries was in part a result of the widening of woman's literary taste and the development of a desire for books among the women of the substantial middle class.

*The University of North Carolina.*

## *EASTWARD HOE* AND ITS SATIRE AGAINST THE SCOTS

### By Joseph Quincy Adams

*Eastward Hoe,* written, as the title-page informs us, by George Chapman, Benjamin Jonson, and John Marston, was put on the stage at Blackfriars by the Children of Her Majesty's Revels at some time in the first half of the year 1605, probably early in the summer. In the course of the play satirical girds were made at the Scottish adventurers who, after the accession of King James, flocked to London in search of political advancement, and also at the new knights freely created by a sovereign ready, it was believed, to sell the honor in order to line the royal purse. The play, no doubt, achieved at once a notable success, for in addition to its satire it was one of the most sparkling comedies of the age.

Normally a successful play would not be given to the press so long as it remained a considerable money-maker—unless the company owning it had been dissolved, or serious trouble with the authorities had led to its prohibition on the stage. In the latter case, the authors, feeling that publication was desirable, might persuade the company to release the "book" to a printer. It is significant, therefore, that *Eastward Hoe* was offered to the readers of London early in September, 1605.

A plausible cause for the quick publication of the play is to be found in the fact that the satire against the Scots aroused the ire of the Court, and led to the suppression of the Blackfriars' management and to the punishment of the authors. Jonson, according to Drummond of Hawthornden, declared that "he was dilated by Sir James Murray [a Scotchman newly knighted by James] to the King for writing something against the Scots, in a play *Eastward Hoe.*" As a result, Jonson and Chapman—apparently Marston, having taken warning, was out of London — were arrested and thrown into prison, "without examining, without hearing, or without any proof but malicious *Rumour,* hurried to bondage and fetters."

The exact time of their arrest can not be fixed, but since Jonson from prison addressed a letter to the Earl of Salisbury, who received his title on May 4, 1605, it must have been subsequent to that date. In this unfortunate lack of definite evidence, scholars are divided over the question whether the punishment of the authors came as a result of the public representation of the play at Blackfriars or of its publication some months later. Sir Edmund K. Chambers [1] and Dr. W. W. Greg [2] hold that the Scots took offense at the publication, and Mr. R. E. Brettle,[3] that the offense was occasioned by the presentation of the play. Dr. Greg, in replying to Mr. Brettle,[4] while saying "I remain unconvinced," finally admits: "Perhaps no certain conclusion is possible." It seems to me that a consideration of the evidence cited below makes it reasonably certain that the stage representation gave the offense, and led both to the punishment of the authors and the actors, and to the early publication of the play.

1. The performance of so brilliant and sensational a comedy—written by the most eminent playwrights of the day, acted by the fashionable Children of Her Majesty's Revels, at Blackfriars, a theatre patronized by the élite of London — could hardly have escaped the attention of the Court. The Scottish followers of James and the raft of newly-created knights would take far more offense at being held up to ridicule on the stage before their fellow courtiers, than at finding satirical passages in a printed play, a form of literature then held in low esteem. Only notoriety attained on the stage would lead to a wide sale of a play on the bookstalls, and hence make its publication a matter of concern to the courtiers of Whitehall.

2. Jonson declared from prison that he and Chapman were subjected to the King's high "wrath" on nothing but "malicious *Rumour*"; and in another letter he demanded that his judges trust not to "*Rumour.*" Clearly, if the printed play gave offense to King James and others, Jonson's defense is inappropriate; satirical passages in cold type could not be described as "*Rumour.*" Jonson further complains: "It hath ever been my destiny to be *misreported,*" and, he bitterly adds, "condemn'd on *first tale.*" In still another letter he asserts that "no man" could "justly complain" at the play who brought—to the theatre?—"an equal ear."

---

[1] *Elizabethan Stage*, III, 254.
[2] *Modern Language Review*, XXIII, 76.
[3] *The Library*, N. S., IX, 287.
[4] *Ibid.*, p. 303.

In none of the ten letters written by him and Chapman is there an appeal to a *reading* of the play, or the slightest hint that the evidence on which they were imprisoned was available in printed form. Only "Rumour," "misreport," and "tale" are stressed.

3. Chapman writes to the Lord Chamberlain that his Lordship would take their part if only he had "heard"—again there is no allusion to the possibility of his reading—"the words truly related, on which . . . our enemie's complaints were founded." This statement again suggests a stage representation of the comedy, and is in keeping with Jonson's allusions to "Rumour," "misreport," and "tale."

4. Marston, knowing that he was personally responsible for the objectionable passages, may have taken early alarm at the stir created by the play, and felt that it would be advisable for him to leave London. On the other hand, Chapman and Jonson, conscious of their "innocence,"[5] thought it unnecessary to flee. This may explain why, apparently, Jonson and Chapman alone were imprisoned.

5. As already stated, a highly successful play would not be released to the reading public within a few months, unless there arose some strong reason. The authors would not be inclined to publish it; indeed, Jonson writes: "The cause (would I could name some worthier, though I wish we had none worthy our imprisonment) is (the words irk me that our fortune hath necessitated us to so despised a course) a play." Chapman, too, would not desire to give the play to the press; in his *The Widow's Tears*, he expresses doubt "if any work of this nature be worth the presenting." Even Marston would object; when his *Malcontent* was published against his will, in 1604, he complains: "Only one thing afflicts me, to think that scenes invented merely to be spoken should be enforcedly published to be read." Nor were the authors free to give their play to the press. Having sold the manuscript—the "book," as it was called—to the actors, they had no right to publish it. Only the actors could surrender the play to the press; and, normally, they would not do so while it was drawing auditors to their theatre. The fact that three editions of *Eastward Hoe*

---

[5] Chapman wrote of the play: "whose chief offenses are but two clauses, and both of them not our own."

were called for by the London public between September and the close of the year indicates that on the stage the play would be a great penny-getter. And since it was so promptly released to readers, we must assume that the authors, if they were responsible for its publication, had the permission of the actors, and that both the authors and the actors were forced to the move by some necessity.

6. We can readily understand this necessity when we consider that the play was rushed to production without due license from the authorities, and that, as a result of the serious offense its satire gave to the Court, the actors at Blackfriars were prohibited from presenting plays at all. *Eastward Hoe* was now of no value to them; and if the authors desired to print the play by way of justification, the managers of Blackfriars would raise no objection. Chapman wrote to the Lord Chamberlain: " Of all the oversights for which I suffer, none repents me so much as that our unhappy book was presented without your Lordship's allowance, for which we can plead nothing by way of pardon: but your person so far removed from our required attendance, our play so much importun'd, and our clear opinions that nothing it contain'd could worthily be held offensive." Dr. Greg contends that Chapman was here referring to the failure of the authors to secure proper license for the publication of the play. But this seems highly unlikely. Chapman's use of the words " was presented without . . . allowance," clearly suggests stage presentation. His reference to the " book " is also significant, for the actors' prompt-copy was invariably so described. The Lord Chamberlain, by virtue of his position, was closely associated with the licensing of plays for performance; he had general oversight of the Office of the Revels, the governmental agency for " allowing " plays, and, as we know, sometimes licensed plays himself without referring them to the Master of the Revels. It was, of course, not the privilege of the authors to have a work licensed for the press; that was the duty of the publisher, Aspley. And, in view of the fact that the publisher was responsible for what he issued, the King, in his wrath, would certainly have punished him, if the printed play was the thing that gave the offense. Not only was Aspley unpunished, but he was allowed to put forth three editions of the work before the close of the year. Moreover, the play was duly licensed, as the entry in the Stationers' Register shows, by one " Mr. Wilson," no

doubt the "Mr. John Wilson" who licensed for the press Marston's *Sophonisba* in 1606. Sir Edmund K. Chambers [6] describes him as one of the readers formally appointed by the Archbishop or Bishop to correct and license books under their authority; and Dr. Greg calls him "the reverend gentleman who took the responsibility of licensing it." Obviously, then, Chapman could not be referring to a failure to license the play for publication. Dr. Greg thinks that the phrase "our play so much importun'd" refers "unequivocally" to the demands on the part of the public for an edition of the play. Even if the public demanded the privilege of reading the play, the authors could not hurry the "book"—the property of the Blackfriars' company—to a publisher without the consent of the actors; and, of course, the actors would not give such consent unless there was a compelling reason. On the other hand, the actors would naturally importune the authors to hasten the delivery of the finished "book" when they felt the need of a new play. Henslowe's *Diary* and *Papers* give evidence of such importunity. And perhaps we should not entirely overlook the fact that *Eastward Hoe* was being composed, as Sir Edmund K. Chambers says, as "a reply to *Westward Ho!*" a comedy presented by the rival children of Paul's in the closing months of 1604. Thus there was some reason for hurrying the stage presentation of the play. The authors, to be sure, were not charged with the responsibility of seeing that the play was licensed for stage performance, yet the "oversight" of the theatre manager in failing to secure a formal allowance would inevitably react against the authors in that it aggravated their offense. Chapman assumes the pose of regret that he and Jonson, working with a collaborator who inserted in the play pungent satire, failed to see to it that the "book" was properly licensed by the governmental agency under the administration of the Lord Chamberlain, and thus the performance before the public made to conform to the laws of the land.

7. If, as Chapman seems to say, the management of Blackfriars "presented" the play "without allowance," that management would certainly be punished. We know that those in control of Blackfriars were punished. Kirkham, the chief manager, and the others in charge of the children, were prohibited from having any further connection with the playhouse. This explains the fact that

[6] *Elizabethan Stage*, III, 168.

shortly after the *Eastward Hoe* episode, Kirkham appears, late in 1605, as one of the managers of the rival company at Paul's. It explains, too, the following statement made by Evans, who held the lease of Blackfriars: "After the King's most excellent Majesty, upon some misdemeanors committed in or about the plays there, and specially upon the defendant's [Kirkham's] acts and doings there, had prohibited that no plays should be more used there" . . . Not only was the management of Blackfriars punished, but the actors also. The playhouse was closed for a time, and the Children were denied the Queen's patronage. All this verifies Chapman's statement that *Eastward Hoe* was "presented" without allowance.

It also points to the conclusion that the release of the play to the press followed the misfortunes that attended the public presentations at Blackfriars. After their punishment, both the authors and the actors would be eager to justify themselves in the opinions of Londoners. We may assume, therefore, that the authors, with the consent of the company as owners of the play, gave the manuscript to the well-known publisher William Aspley. The "chief" passages of satire that had aroused the "wrath" of King James would, of course, be removed (Jonson and Chapman attributed those passages to Marston); otherwise Aspley would not dare to issue the play. The manuscript was duly submitted to a proper authority for license, and, with the specific statement that it was "licensed," was duly entered in the Stationers' Register. A voracious public demanded three editions before the end of the year. With the later editions, mere reprints of the first, we are not here concerned. It is the purpose of this essay to call attention to certain bibliographical peculiarities of the first edition, and the significance those peculiarities have for the satire originally contained in the play.

The first edition is extant in two issues. The first issue is found in imperfect copies in the Ashley and Wise libraries, and is represented by two leaves inserted in the Dyce copy of the second issue. Of the second issue copies are found in various libraries.

Both issues are identical throughout except for two leaves, $E_3$ and $E_4$, which in the second issue were cancelled and replaced by new leaves, in a fresh setting of type, and with the omission of a passage of seven lines attacking the Scots. The omitted passage may here be quoted. Seagull, Spendall, and Scapethrift are discussing a proposed expedition to Virginia, and the advantages of life there. Seagull assures his companions that the New World has no disagreeable features:

> Only a few industrious Scots, perhaps, who, indeed, are disperst over the face of the whole earth. But as for them, there are no greater friends to Englishmen and England, when they are out on't, in the world, than they are. And for my part, I would a hundred thousand of 'hem were there; for we are all one countrymen now, ye know; and we should find ten times more comfort of them there than we do here.[7]

Since the passage occupied the last two and a half lines of page $E_3$ verso and the first four and a half lines of page $E_4$ recto, its removal necessitated the cancellation of two entire leaves, constituting four pages of text. The printer, therefore, was called upon to reset the text of leaves $E_3$ and $E_4$ with the objectionable passage omitted, and to print the text as thus revised on two new leaves bearing similar signatures; and then the binder was instructed to tear out the original leaves and insert in their place the revised leaves.

The printer accomplished the task assigned him as best he could. He had, of course, to preserve the continuity of the text, and the proper sequence of signatures and catchwords, so that a reader would not be aware of the cancellation. And since seven type-lines were removed, he had to expand the pages, either with new text, or with a spreading of the lines in order to fill the page-forms. The person who made the deletion supplied, to compensate for the passage removed, the rather colorless clause:

> Besides, there we shall have no more law than conscience, and not too much of either; serve God enough, eat and drink enough, and *enough is as good as a feast.*

But the printer, when he set up this padding material, found that he still lacked three full type-lines. This he cared for by readjusting the spacing on the three final pages. As a result he found it necessary to use different catchwords at the foot of the inner pages $E_3$ verso and $E_4$ recto, but the changes did not affect the sequence of the text as a whole. And, of course, he inserted the proper

---

[7] In addition, the word "a nobleman," occurring a few lines later, is altered to "any other person."

signatures, so that no tell-tale evidence of the cancellation could be discerned by the reader.[8]

Scholars have assumed that this cancelled passage attacking the Scots was the main cause for the imprisonment of the authors. But since Chapman, in his letter to King James, states that the "chief offenses" were "but two clauses," it is necessary to find the second; and the Oxford editors of Jonson, as well as others, have discovered this in the phrase spoken by an anonymous Gentleman concerning Sir Petronel Flash, the butt of the satire against newly-minted knights:

> I ken the man weel, he's one of my thirty pound knights.

Since this passage was not eliminated from the play as printed (in three successive editions), since the sum of thirty pounds was the regular herald's fee for issuing a patent of knighthood, and since the pronoun "my" is used as an ethical dative, it is hard to understand how this brief clause could occasion serious offense. And hence it has been suggested that the actor, in uttering the words, may have mimicked the Scotch brogue of King James.

Even assuming the possibility of the last suggestion, and admitting the biting nature of the cancelled passage against the Scots, these "two clauses" alone seem hardly adequate to explain the great ado caused by the performance of *Eastward Hoe*. Jonson writes feelingly of "the anger of the King," and Chapman of His Majesty's "high displeasure" and "wrath." Indeed, so incensed was James that "the report was," so Jonson told Drummond, "that they should then [have] had their ears cut and noses." Further, it is doubtful whether the cancelled passage, if that passage was one of the "chief offenses" that had excited the wrath of the King and the anger of the Scottish courtiers, would have been left in the manuscript, or would have been passed by the official censor, or would have been printed by the publisher. Still further, if the passage about "my thirty pound knights" was the second of the "two clauses" that gave "chief" offense to His Majesty, it is strange that it was left untouched by the authors, the official censor, and the publisher, and that it appeared in both issues of the first edition, and in two subsequent editions.

---

[8] Except the stubs of the removed sheets, visible in several copies of the second issue.

Must we not assume that the authors, when they gave the play, with their names spread upon the title-page, to the reading public, eliminated the "two" specific clauses which had aroused the King to "stormy" anger? Would they dare, or would the publisher dare, to issue the play in the very form in which it had provoked the avenging wrath of James? Surely they eliminated the "chief offenses" before they handed the manuscript — their "unhappy book"—to the publisher Aspley.

Yet it is clear that they did not eliminate all the satire against the Scots and the new knights. The passages that gave "chief" offense ("but two clauses"), which they attributed to Marston, they would without hesitation delete. But in their keen sense of the injustice done to them, and in their confidence in the "innocence" of the "general" satire [9] they contributed to the play [10] they failed to eliminate everything that the discreet publisher, Aspley, warned by their misfortune, thought it unwise to print. Scholars have entirely overlooked the fact that after the play had been set in type, and arranged carefully in page form (with running-titles, catchwords, and signatures), but before the actual printing was started, passages of text here and there were removed, in an effort to render the play more harmless. The cancellation of the two leaves, discussed above, came later, after the printing was well under way, and represents merely the final effort of the publisher to free the play from all possible offense. That in this effort he succeeded is shown by the fact that he was allowed to issue three editions in quick succession.

Proof that passages were deleted from the play after the text had been set up and arranged in page-form, is to be found in the bibliographical irregularities of the first edition — irregularities common to both issues, and so striking in kind as to catch the eye at first glance. I shall try to present the evidence as clearly as possible, though for a full realization of its significance one should have before him a copy of the original edition.

The play was printed with an unusual effort at economy. The

---

[9] Jonson writes: "I have given no cause to any good man of grief; and if to any ill, by touching at any general vice, it hath always been with a regard and sparing of particular persons."

[10] Chapman writes: "nothing it contain'd could *worthily* be held offensive," and Jonson: "a play whereof we hope there is no man can *justly* complain."

Prologue is set on the back of the title-page; the Epilogue is forced, in small type, at the foot of the last page, where it extends three lines beyond the normal page length; the text is closely crowded; the speeches of different persons are often run together without paragraph division; songs, not without difficulty and the use of smaller type, are arranged in double columns; slugs needed for the proper "display" of stage-directions and the like are omitted; and, in short, every device to save space is employed. So niggardly a printer would not suddenly become wasteful of space without good reason, or, we may add, unless the page-forms had already been made up.

The normal number of type-lines to a page, not including the running-title and the catchword, is thirty-nine, occasionally stretched to forty. As we glance our eye over the pages, our attention is first arrested by the shortness of page $A_2$ verso, which has only thirty-seven lines, a waste of two full type-lines, only partly concealed by a wide slug before the catchword, and by lifting the catchword one line. This extravagance — and awkwardness — is continued on the next (and facing) page, $A_3$ recto, likewise of thirty-seven type-lines. Abnormally wide slugs are placed before and after the stage-direction, which is needlessly arranged in two lines instead of one. The first speech of the text is made to run over into an extra line, containing merely "Sir," by spelling out the catch-name "Golding" instead of using the usual abbreviated form "Gold." The second speech, with the catch-name "Touchstone" spelled out in full, and with wide spacing between words, may have been thus expanded in order to make the last line run over. The second speech of Touchstone, with its wide gaps before and after the internal stage-direction and its over-generous quads between sentences, seems likewise to have been deliberately spread. In all, four or five type-lines are surrendered by the printer, which, combined with the two lines surrendered on the preceding page, point to an omission of some length. When we turn to the text we discover that the authors are here engaged in satire on the Court and on knights. If I were allowed a guess, I would say that a satirical clause regarding freshly-minted knights was eliminated from the second speech of Touchstone, $A_3$ recto, at the point where the Page, having announced the coming of Sir Petronel Flash, the character designed as a satire on knights, goes out. The situation calls for satirical comment by Touchstone, and the typographical arrangement rather suggests an omission.

Our attention is next arrested by page $A_4$ verso. For one thing, the speeches of the several persons are separated by wide slugs, producing a most curious effect; for another thing, the page contains only thirty-five type-lines. Equally startling is the way in which the last portion of Girtred's second speech, in prose, is broken up into six short lines, whereas it should have been set as three lines—an exceedingly clumsy device to fill up space. When we look more closely, we observe that the first speech of Girtred, merely the expletive "Boebell," is given the dignity of a whole line (spaced with slugs before and after), whereas normally it would be run in with the speech of the next character. In all, eight type-lines have been removed from the text as originally arranged by the printer in page-form, and the omission has led to a most awkward effort to readjust the page. When now we turn to the text, we discover that again the authors are engaged in satirizing the Court, titles of knighthood, and the Scots. For instance, Mildred says to her sister, who is seeking to marry a newly-created knight: "Where titles presume to thrust before fit means to second them, wealth and respect often grow sullen, and will not follow. For sure, in this, I would for your sake I spoke not truth: Where ambition of place goes before fitness of birth, contempt and disgrace follow." This satire was left untouched. The satire eliminated, I venture to suggest, came at the place filled by the six short lines. In order that the reader may judge, I quote the lines below. Girtred is being fitted by the tailor Poldavis with a dress in the Court style, becoming her new title of "ladyship":

> *She doubled in her song.*
> Now (Lady's my comfort!)
> What a prophare Ape's here!
> Tailor Poldavis, prethee fit it,
> fit it. Is this a right Scot?
> Does it clip close? and bear up round?

The publisher did not—perhaps the typographical difficulties and the resultant costs were too great — remove all the attacks upon freshly-created knights. For instance, on page $B_1$ verso he allowed to stand a passage which I quote in order to indicate the probable sharpness of the passages he did remove. Mistress Touchstone says to her husband, the London tradesman:

Yes, that he is, a Knight! I know where he had the money to pay the Gentlemen Ushers and Heralds their fees. Aye, that he is, a Knight! And so might you have been, too, if you had been aught else than an Ass, as well as some of your neighbors. An I thought you would not ha been knighted (as I am an honest woman), I would ha dub'd you myself; I praise God, I have wherewithall.

This, surely, could not have been pleasing to King James; yet the publisher — was he primarily concerned with attacks on the Scots?—passed it over. On $C_1$ verso he was more disturbed, for here he marked a long clause for deletion. The eye instantly detects evidence that material has been eliminated from the page as originally made up. There are only thirty-seven type-lines; wide slugs separate the second speech of Quicksilver from those that precede and follow; and the first and last speeches of Quicksilver, and the two speeches of Synnedesie have obviously been spread—the catch-names are spelled out in full, and the words are widely spaced—so as to cause the last line in each case to run over. In all, six lines have been surrendered.

Further, the evidence of deletion extends to the next (and facing) page, $C_2$ recto. The eye is actually astounded by the extremely wide spacing before and after the brief speech of Quicksilver; the page contains only thirty-five type-lines; the first speech of Securitie, by spelling out in full the catch-name and by the use of wide spacing between the words, is forced to run into an extra line containing merely the word "doe." Thus, in all, we have five lines on this page deliberately sacrificed, which, combined with the lines omitted from preceding (and facing) page, makes a total of eleven lines eliminated after the page-forms had been arranged. When we turn to the text, we discover again that the authors are engaged in satire on the Court and knights. The reader will find such "clauses" as: "But he that sails in your Court Seas shall find 'hem ten times fuller of hazard, wherein to see what is to be seen is torment more than a spirit can endure"; "But he's worse than a prentice that does it, not only humoring the Lord, but every trencher-bearer, every groom that by indulgence and intelligence crept into his power, and by pandarism into his chamber." One can only guess what the wary publisher felt impelled to delete from these two pages of biting satire.

But most curious, and convincing, of all, the two facing pages, $E_3$ verso and $E_4$ recto, which were later cancelled, show *in their first state* unmistakable evidence of the omission of offensive material. $E_3$ verso is, without reason, one type-line short, and $E_4$ recto —which startles the eye with extravagant spacing before and after the stage-direction "Enter Sir Petronell"—contains only thirty-five type-lines. It is thus apparent that five type-lines of text were, with considerable difficulty and awkwardness, eliminated after the page-forms were originally made up. The further elimination of still more material (in the second issue) by means of the complete cancellation of the two leaves, came at a later time, after some sheets had been printed (constituting the first issue), and represents the final effort of the nervous publisher to free the play of dangerous matter.

If I have correctly interpreted the evidence, the printed play—even the first issue of the first edition—did not reproduce *Eastward Hoe* in the full form in which it was acted on the stage of the Blackfriars. Not only were the "chief offenses"—the "two clauses" attributed to Marston—removed, but various other clauses were eliminated, probably by the wary publisher. And this conclusion points to the belief that the anger of the Scottish courtiers and of King James was occasioned by the performance of the play rather than by its publication.

*The Folger Shakespeare Library.*

# THE DATE OF *LOVE'S PILGRIMAGE* AND ITS RELATION TO *THE NEW INN*

By Baldwin Maxwell

## I

*Love's Pilgrimage* was "renewed" and, it has been generally assumed, revised in 1635. As a result of Dyce's misreading of Malone, it was supposed that the play had been left incomplete at the time of Fletcher's death in 1625 and that it was "revised and finished" by Shirley ten years later. Although the fallacy of that view has long been noted, no evidence has, I believe, been advanced in an effort to determine the date of composition.[1] There are in the play, however, what seem to me to be two, or perhaps three, allusions to contemporary events which suggest very definitely the date at which the play must have been started.

As a general rule there is, I admit, great danger in attempting to date an Elizabethan play by topical allusions, which may well have been inserted at almost any time by a dramatist or a reviser, perhaps even by an actor. Allusions may be of little value unless there is complementary evidence of another sort. Where, however, there are references to events which follow immediately the earliest possible date at which the play could have been written, such references would seem surely to indicate the time at which the play was composed. So it is, I believe, with the references in *Love's Pilgrimage*.

As Cervantes' *Las dos Doncellas,* the ultimate source of *Love's Pilgrimage,* was not allowed for publication in Spain until August, 1613, the play certainly cannot have been composed before 1614. I am not so certain as some critics have been of Fletcher's small knowledge of Spanish, but there is good reason to believe that for the plays based upon the *Novelas Ejemplares* Fletcher used the French translation of 1615.[2] His having drawn *The Island Princess*

---

[1] Mr. W. J. Lawrence, according to Oliphant, *The Plays of Beaumont and Fletcher*, p. 435, assigns it to 1614; Professor Thorndike, in his edition of *The Maid's Tragedy* and *Philaster*, dates it "1614?"

[2] Les Nouvelles de Miguel de Cervantes Saavedra où sont contenues plusieurs rares Adventures, & memorables Exemples d'Amour, de Fidélité, de Force de Sang, de Ialousie, de mauuaises habitudes, de charmes, & d'autres

from *l'Histoire de Ruis Dias,* which was printed with the translations from Cervantes, indicates at least that Fletcher was later, if not at the time he wrote *Love's Pilgrimage,* familiar with the French version of *Las dos Doncellas.* If the French rather than the Spanish was used, *Love's Pilgrimage* could not have been started before 1615. The references to which I shall call attention, alluding as they do to events between late 1615 and the end of 1616, suggest 1616 as the date at which the play was written.

All of these allusions were to events on the continent, but that these events were closely followed and well known in England is shown by reports and letters. The accounts of these events, therefore, I quote from English sources, for the actual dates of the events are here less important than the dates at which they were discussed in England.

In Act I, scene i, Incubo says to Phillipo:

> Sir, the French,
> They say, are divided 'bout their match with us.

There can be no doubt that the reference here is to the civil war in France occasioned by the opposition of the Prince of Condé and other nobles to the double alliance with Spain arranged by the Queen Mother, whereby the young Louis XIII was betrothed to Anne of Austria, daughter of Philip III of Spain, and the Spanish prince, afterwards Philip IV, to Princess Elizabeth of France. Anne and Louis were married on November 24, 1615, Philip and Elizabeth one year later to the month. Although there had been French opposition to the alliance with Spain for some time before the first marriage, the allusion to the French being divided would best fit the period between the rebellion headed by the Prince of Condé in the summer of 1615 and the pardon accorded the rebels—all save Condé—late in 1616. That England had watched with interest the French alliances with Spain, we have the testimony of the Venetian Ambassador, who on 23 October, 1615, wrote to the Doge and Senate:

> Here they were eagerly awaiting the issue of . . . the marriages between

---

accidents non moins estranges que veritables. Traduictes d'Espagnol en François: Les six premières par F. De Rosset. Et les autres six, par le Sr. D'Audiguier. Avec l'Histoire de Ruis Dias, & de Quixaire Princesse de moluques, composée, par le Sr. Dr. Bellan. *A Paris Chez Iean Richer* . . . M.DC.XV.

France and Spain, from which will arise, in great measure, the negotiations about the prince.[3]

And how closely the sequence of events, especially the civil strife, was watched in England is revealed by the full accounts sent Sir Thomas Roe, the English ambassador to the far distant Great Mogul, by Lord George Carew. In February, 1615, Carew wrote:

> Monsieur de Silerie is gone into Spayne to consummatt the mariage of the King his master, but the event is very doubtfull, the Frenche princes beinge so opposite vnto it. The assemblye of the three Estates is dissolved . . . and France is divided into so great factions as troubles is expected.[4]

In January, 1616, Lord Carew wrote that the preceding summer the marriage of the King and the Infanta had been "as muche consummated as by proxie canne by required," and that at the moment

> The Prince of Condie, with sundrye of the peers and noblesse of France, are in armes, and the whole boddie of the Religion are ioyned with them, so as they are very stronge in horse and foote; . . . The iniquitie of the murder of Kinge Henry 4, the displacinge of corrupt councillors about the kinge, *the inconveniences which may ensue by the matche with Spayne*, and the confirmation of the former Edicts in the behalfe of the Religion, are the chiefest poyntes and motiffs of this disturbance in France: . . .[5]

In February, Carew recorded that the Duke of Vendome, Henry IV's natural son, had joined the princes to avenge the death of his father, "which, *with the mariadge with Spayne*, was one of the principallest causes thatt moved the princes to take armes."[6] In April[7] Carew writes that a general peace has been concluded, but under August he notes that on the twenty-second the Prince of Condé had been arrested, that other noblemen had fled Paris, and that "The common people of Paris, hearinge of the arrest, in furye they sacked the Marshall de Ancres [one of the principals of the Spanish party] house, and made pilladge of his goodes . . ."[8] Under September[9] Carew records the commitment of Condé to the

---

[3] C.S.P., Venetian, p. 50.

[4] *Letters from George Lord Carew to Sir Thomas Roe*, The Camden Society, vol. 76, 1859, p. 3.

[5] *Ibid.*, pp. 24-25.

[6] *Ibid.*, p. 30

[7] *Ibid.*, p. 33.

[8] *Ibid.*, p. 41.

[9] *Ibid.*, p. 45.

Bastille and the King's forgiveness of the other nobles who had been in arms against him. No other mention is made of civil discord until the account under May, 1617, of the assassination of d'Ancre, which seems to have been plotted because of the Marshall's arrogance and not because he had once been active in the Spanish alliances.

Information concerning the troubles in France was perhaps not current among the masses of London until some weeks after it had reached one so keen upon the scent of news as Lord Carew, but with the reconciliation between the King and nobles in September, 1616, and the second Spanish-French marriage in November of that year, the reference to the French being "divided 'bout their match" with Spain would seem to have no point.

Two other allusions in the play seem, with less certainty, to point to the autumn of 1616. Six lines after the mention of the Franco-Spanish marriage, Incubo asks:

> What do you hear
> Of our Indian fleet? they say, they are well return'd.

To be sure, richly laden ships from India were not uncommonly arriving in either England or Spain, but it is unlikely that Fletcher, who in the preceding speeches, and, indeed, throughout the play, so carefully keeps his Spanish locale, should here refer to an English fleet. Such fleets were, of course, so common that Incubo's question might ordinarily be thought of no value at all in dating the play. It is, however, a matter of record that in the autumn of 1616 the whole of western Europe was awaiting with interest the return of a Spanish Indian fleet to confirm rumors of the fabulous wealth it bore.

Under November, 1616, Lord Carew wrote Sir Thomas Roe: "The 19. I received letters out of Spayne. The West Indies fleet is daylye expected";[10] and in the same month the Venetian secretary wrote from London to the Doge and Senate:

> It is understood that at the island of St. Vincent there are some twenty ships of Algiers, which are awaiting the Spanish fleet to attack it. If they succeed it will be a matter of great moment in the present state of affairs, since there is a great scarcity of money both in Spain and in Flanders, and for some while they have been supporting themselves by the hope of this

---

[10] *Op. cit.*, p. 58.

fleet. The Spaniards say that His Catholic Majesty's share in it will amount to 6 millions, but it is not believed that it will even come to half that.[11]

In January of the next year Carew wrote Roe of the fleet's safe arrival at Lisbon:

> We have newes of the Lord Rosse's safe arryval att Lisbone, and thatt a fewe dayes before his cominge thether the West Indie Fleete (enforced by fowle wether) came into thatt porte richlye laden, to the valew of 20 millions of ducatts, whereof 9 millions in silver and gold was presentlye (sent) overland vnto Madrid.[12]

Such a cargo could hardly fail to excite the curiosity and kindle the imagination. One may be sure that Lord Carew and the Venetian secretary were not the only ones in London interested in its return. During the month of November, 1616, when it was said to be "daylye expected," there must have been many rumors concerning it.

There is in the play, finally, what may be an allusion to a third incident about which the streets of London must have buzzed during late October of 1616. In the same scene in which I recognize the other allusions, I, i, one of the hostlers complains of the strange way in which the horse of one of the guests has cast his shoes.

> He had four shoes,
> And good ones, when he came; 'tis a strange wonder,
> With standing still he should cast three.

Less strange but equally wondrous, perhaps, was the casting of its shoes by Lord Hay's horse in Paris shortly before the date suggested by the allusions already mentioned.

On July 12 [13] Lord Hay left London for Paris, sent by King James ostensibly to felicitate the French King on his recent marriage. The journey had been delayed to permit the Ambassador and his train to equip themselves in the utmost splendor. After describing the gorgeous dress of the embassage, Wilson recounts the following incident, which was apparently prearranged rather than accidental:

---

[11] C.S.P. Venetian. P. 358. Nov. 24, 1616.
[12] *Op. cit.*, p. 76.
[13] *Vide* Lord Carew's letter, *op. cit.*, p. 38.

And some said (how truly I cannot assert) the Ambassador's Horse was shod with Silver-shoes, lightly tack'd on; and when he came to a Place where Persons, or Beauties of Eminency were, his very Horse prancing and curveting, in humble Reverence flung his Shoes away, which the greedy Understanders scrambled for; and he was content to be gazed on and admir'd, till a Farrier, or rather an Argentier in one of his rich Liveries, among his Train of Footmen, out of a Tawny Velvet Bag took others, and tack'd them on; which lasted till he came to the next Troop of Grandees: And thus with much ado he reach'd the *Louvre*.[14]

In October "the Lord Hay retourned frome his employment in France, where he was feasted beyond belief."[15] During the remaining months of 1616 there must have been many stories current in London concerning the extravagance of his reception, the richness of his retinue, and, no doubt, the casting of his horse's shoes. If the play was being written in the autumn of 1616, as I think the allusion to the Franco-Spanish match conclusively proves, it seems not unlikely that the misfortune befalling the horse at the inn in Ossuna may have been suggested by the casting of its shoes by Lord Hay's horse in Paris.

## II

I do not insist upon the allusion to the behavior of Lord Hay's horse; it is not necessary to dating *Love's Pilgrimage* in 1616. It serves, however, as a transition to another problem—the relation of *Love's Pilgrimage* to Jonson's *New Inn*—as these lines are among those common to both plays. The similarity of the two plays is succinctly summarized by Mr. Oliphant:

... about a dozen lines in I, 1a are identical or almost identical with lines in II, 2 of Jonson's *New Inn* . . . ; while I, 1b is almost a duplicate of much of III, 1 of the same play, twenty-four out of seventy-four lines (omitting the first one and the last five) being absolutely identical with lines in Jonson's play, while only six are altogether peculiar to *Love's Pilgrimage*.[16]

Langbaine called attention to the similarity and accused Fletcher

---

[14] *The Life and Reign of James, The First King of Great Britain,* by Arthur Wilson. Reprinted in Vol. II of *A Complete History of England,* etc., 1706. P. 704. For this reference I am indebted to one of my students, Miss Kathryn Robb.

[15] Carew, *op. cit.,* p. 47.

[16] *Op. cit.,* p. 439.

of the theft, although Fletcher had been dead for four years when *The New Inn* was first presented. It has been suggested that Jonson was the renewer of *Love's Pilgrimage* in 1635 and that he at that time may have borrowed these lines from his own *New Inn*, which had been hissed from the stage six years before, and then, as an appeal from the verdict of the theater, printed in 1631. But Mr. Tennant, and he is followed by the most recent editors [17] of Jonson, believes that Jonson had no connection with *Love's Pilgrimage*, and rejects Mr. Oliphant's claim that some of the lines common to both plays show the unmistakable metrical characteristics of Fletcher. Mr. Oliphant's suggestion is " that Jonson commenced a revision of *Love's Pilgrimage*, . . . gave it up, and, when he commenced *The New Inn*, took a few of his own lines from the earlier play, and also lifted, with same alterations, the only piece of Fletcher's work he had left in the only scene he had meddled with." [18]

Mr. Oliphant uses only the argument that certain lines common to both plays show the peculiarities of Fletcher's meter. I agree; but apparently to some, such as Professor Tennant and the recent editors of Jonson, the argument has not been convincing. But there are other reasons for believing that some of the similar passages appeared first in *Love's Pilgrimage*, whence they were inserted into *The New Inn*. Both plays introduce a number of Spanish words and phrases, which, although they seem thoroughly Jonsonian, are much better suited to the earlier play where the scene is laid in Spain than to *The New Inn*, where the scene is English. Many of the Spanish terms of the latter play do not appear in the first, but one phrase is used for comic effect throughout both plays and particularly in the lines which are almost identical. In *Love's Pilgrimage*, I, i, and in *The New Inn*, II, v, the respective hosts are criticized at length for appearing *in cuerpo*. The phrase goes much more naturally with *Love's Pilgrimage*. It appears frequently in Cervantes' *Novelas*, Fletcher's source, and, apparently some years before Jonson wrote *The New Inn* Fletcher (or his collaborator), who never hesitated to repeat, had used the

---

[17] George Bremner Tennant, *The New Inn*, Yale Studies in English, Vol. XXXIV, New York, 1908; C. H. Herford and Percy Simpson, *Ben Jonson*, II, 198-200.

[18] *Op. cit.*, p. 439.

same phrase with humorous intent in *Love's Cure*,[19] where the scene is likewise laid in Spain. There, in II, i, Pachieco Alasto says to Lazarillo:

" Boy: my Cloake and Rapier; it fits not a Gentleman of my ranck to walk the streets in Querpo." Compare *Love's Pilgrimage*, I, i:

> *Inc.* Call for thy cloak and rapier
> *Diego.* How!
> *Inc.* Do, call,
> And put 'em on in haste; alter thy fortune,
> By appearing worthy of her. Dost thou think
> Her good face e'er will know a man *in cuerpo?*
> . . . call, I say—
> His cloak and rapier here!

Such a Spanish phrase may well have found its way into the English slang of the day,[20] but the other similarities in the two plays show that it was not by mere chance that it appears in *Love's Pilgrimage* and *The New Inn*. As Fletcher or one of his collaborators used it in another play, and as it appears in the *Novelas Ejemplares*,[21] the indication would seem to be that Jonson was the borrower. If there was in the horse's casting his shoes a reference (and certainly the date of *Love's Pilgrimage* suggests there was) to the behavior of Lord Hay's horse in Paris in 1616, Jonson is again the borrower, for little fun could be got from the allusion when *The New Inn* was written ten years later.

I do not argue that the passages similar or identical in the two plays were all borrowed by Jonson. It may well have been, as Mr. Oliphant suggested, that Jonson began a revision of *Love's Pilgrimage* and, having abandoned his plan, later put parts of his revision to use in *The New Inn*.

*The University of Iowa.*

---

[19] Many have placed the date of Love's Cure from sixteen to nineteen years before 1625, and almost every dramatist of the time has been advanced as a collaborating author.

[20] *A New English Dictionary* cites the passages in *Love's Cure* as the earliest noted appearance in English.

[21] I have not been able to examine the 1615 French translation.

# A NOTE ON BEN JONSON'S LITERARY METHODS

### By A. C. Howell

In his Conversations with William Drummond of Hawthornden Ben Jonson makes a statement regarding his poetry which throws an interesting light on his methods of composition. Drummond quotes him as saying, "That he wrott all his first in prose, for so his Master, Cambden had learned him."[1] If this means, as it seems to, that he first wrote his poems in prose, then worked them into verse, the statement is significant because it indicates two interesting facts about his verse.

First it is clear that Jonson's verse, composed by such a method, would be naturally sicklied o'er with the pale cast of thought, as it indeed is. Spontaneous or emotional verse is not to be looked for in Jonson, except perhaps in a few of his songs. The intellectual cast of the majority of his poems is immediately apparent. Intellectual poetry is the natural outcome of a method which puts down in prose what the poet wishes to say in order to secure clarity and precision. Time and again Jonson urged the necessity of careful revision.[2]

---

[1] Cunningham, Francis. *The Works of Ben Jonson* (London, 1871), III, 486, *Conversations*, Sec. XV, "His Opinion of Verses." All subsequent quotations except those in the *Discoveries* are from this edition.

[2] Note the following lines:

> Since, being deceived, I turn a sharper eye
> Upon myself, and ask to whom? and why?
> And what I write? and vex it many days
> Before men get a verse, much less a praise.
>
> "An Epistle to Master John Seldon," *op. cit.*, III, 301.

> For though the poet's matter nature be
> His art doth give the fashion: and, that he
> Who casts to write a living line, must sweat,
> (Such as thine are) and strike the second heat
> Upon the Muses' anvil; turn the same
> And himself with it, that he thinks to frame;
> Or for the laurel he may gain a scorn;
> For a good poet's made, as well as born.
>
> "To the Memory . . . of Master William Shakespeare," *op. cit.*, III, 289.

But another interesting sidelight on Jonson's methods of composition is to be noted as a result of this habit of writing poetry first in prose. Editors of Jonson from Whalley (Lon. 1756) to Gifford (Lon. 1816) and Cunningham (*op. cit.*) have pointed out the numerous bits of translations from the classics embedded in Jonson's work. Professors Briggs and Schelling [3] in more recent times have clearly indicated the large debt that Jonson's poetry owes to the classics; and Professor Maurice Castelain, following Schelling (Ed. of *Discoveries,* Boston, 1892), for his doctoral dissertation traced almost every line of the *Discoveries* (*ed. cit.*) to its source in Jonson's daily reading, (as the title-note itself discloses) either in the writings of such classical authors as Quintilian, Seneca, and Pliny the Younger, or in those of contemporaries such as Lipsius, Vives, Bacon, and Erasmus. As a result of the work of these investigators, we now know that many of Jonson's poems are little more than translations and adaptations from the classics,[4] and that his daily

*Indeed*, the multitude commend Writers, as they do Fencers . . . But in these things, the unskilfull are naturally deceiv'd, and judging wholly by the bulk, think rude things greater than polish'd; and scatter'd more numerous than compos'd; . . ." *Censura de poetis,*" in *Discoveries,* Par. 63, p. 35. [This quotation, and all subsequent ones from the *Discoveries,* is from the edition of Maurice Castelain (Paris, 1906).] (M. Castelain points out that this is a translation from Quintilian, *De Inst. Orat.* II, xii, 1-3.)

A *Poem,* as I have told you, is the worke of the Poet; the end, and fruit of his labour, and studye. . . . To this perfection of nature in our Poet wee require Exercise of those parts, and frequent. If his wit will not arrive soddainly at the dignitie of the Ancients, let him not yet fall out with it, quarrell, or be over hastily Angry; offer, to turne it away from Study, in a humor; but come to it againe upon better cogitation; try another time, with labour. If then it succeed not, cast not away the Quills, yet: nor scratch the Wain-scot, beat not the poor Desk; but bring all to the forge, and file, againe; tourne it a newe. . . . Indeed, things, wrote with labour, deserve to be so read, and will last their Age. " *Poesis* " Par. 130, *ed. cit.,* pp. 124-6. (The substance of part of this is adapted from Horace's Epistle to Piso, according to M. Castelain.)

[3] Briggs, W. D., " Source-Material for Jonson's *Epigrams* and *Forest,*" *Classical Philology,* XI (1916), 169-90; and " Source-Material for Jonson's *Underwoods* and Miscellaneous Poems," *M. P.,* XV (Sept. 1917), 85-120. Schelling, F. E. " Ben Jonson and the Classical School," *P. L. M. A.,* XIII (1898), 221-49.

[4] Without taking the trouble of counting the number of poems which have in them either direct translations or echoes of the classics, it is a

reading led him to set down in his notebooks large quotations translated freely from his favorite authors.

The method Jonson says he used, i. e., that of writing his poems first in prose, would easily adapt itself to the inclusion of translated bits when the sentiment of any author he had read fitted his need. Proof of this practice is abundant. It is found in his *Conversations*,[5] where he tells Drummond, "In his Sejanus he hath translated a whole oration of Tacitus."[6] He might have added that, using his own notes as the basis for the remark, the whole play is a tissue of translations from the Roman writers. Again he says in the *Discoveries*:[7]

> The third requisite in our *Poet* or Maker, is *Imitation*, to bee able to convert the substance or Riches of another *Poet*, to his owne use. To make choise of one excellent man above the rest, and so to follow him, till he grow very Hee; or so like him, as the Copie may be mistaken for the Principall, Not, as a Creature, that swallows, what it takes in, crude, raw, or undigested; but, that feeds with an Appetite, and hath a Stomacke to concoct, devide, and turne all into nourishment. Not, to imitate servilely, as *Horace* saith, and catch at vices, for vertue, but to draw forth out of the best, and choisest flowers, with the Bee, and turne all into Honey, worke it into one relish, and savour: make our *Imitation* sweet: observe, how the best writers have imitated, and follow them. . . . But, that which we especially require in him is an exactnesse of Studie, and multiplicity of reading, wich maketh a full man, not alone enabling him to know the *History* or Argument of a *Poem*, and to report it; but so to master the matter, and Stile, as to shew, hee knowes, how to handle, place, or dispose of either, with elegancie, when need shall bee.

It must be said that Jonson squared with his practice, and that he has digested and swallowed his authors, especially Martial, the "one excellent man above all the rest" whom Jonson chose to imitate. In his *Conversations* he had twice recommended[8] Quintilian, Horace, Juvenal and Martial for Drummond's reading, and Drum-

---

safe guess that almost half of Jonson's poems fall into this class. Martial seems to be his favorite; Juvenal, another; and Horace, of course.

[5] *Conversations*, XVIII, Miscellanies, *op. cit.*, 491.

[6] The speech referred to is that of Cernutus Cordus in *Sejanus*, III, 407-60 from Tacitus, *Annals*, IV, 34-35.

[7] *Poesis*, Par. 130, pp. 125-6, *ed. cit.* Castelain notes that hints for this passage were taken from Seneca's Epistle to Lucillus, LXXXIV.

[8] *Conversations*, II, 470, and IX, 476, *op. cit.*

mond notes in the first reference that Jonson had translated [9] Martial's Epigram (X, 47) beginning *Vitam quae faciunt beatorum.* In the second note Jonson had added that the poets mentioned, adding Persius, were to be read "for delight." Jonson's latest editors, in their introduction to his Poems,[10] feel that Jonson was anxious to be considered the Martial of his age, and that his book of Epigrams was in direct imitation of Martial's even the preface having its ultimate source in Martial's to his *Epigrams.* The number of poems in Jonson's *Epigrams, Book I* (so called in imitation of Martial) is almost the same as in Martial's Book I. Moreover, the first epigrams, to the reader, to the book, to the King, and to the bookseller, are reminiscent of Martial's opening epigrams and No. 36 is addressed to the "Ghost of Martial." Briggs traces many parallels. Enough has been said to prove that Jonson was a wholehearted imitator of the classics, and a believer in the practice. In fact one of the characters in Marston's revised *Histriomastix* [11] hails Chrisogonus (Jonson):

> How you translating-scholler? you can make
> A stabbing Satir or an Epigram. . . .

so that it is clear that even Jonson's contemporaries were not unaware of Jonson's proclivities as a translator. It should be remembered in this connection that plagiarism was a term unknown in its present connotation to Jonson; and although he accuses others of plagiarising,[12] he would not have considered his practice as falling within that compass.

Thus, knowing what we do of Jonson's practice, his tastes, and his reading habits, we can well imagine him sitting down to compose an elegy, an ode, or an epigram, and considering how such themes had been treated in his beloved classics. To find out, he

---

[9] This translation was discovered by Collier at Dulwich College, in Jonson's handwriting, says Cunningham (Note 2, p. 388, *op. cit.*). It may therefore be suspect. This cannot be said of the other Epigram (VIII, 77) printed on the same page. It is a gem of translation, rendering the spirit as well as the sense of the original.

[10] C. H. Herford and Percy Simpson, *Ben Jonson, the Man and His Work* (London, 1925-27), II, 349.

[11] *Histriomastix* (1610, but revised in 1599) Act II, speech of Mavortius.

[12] Epigram C., "On Play-wright," and LXXXI, "To Proule, the Plagiary."

turned, we may safely assume, to his remarkable memory,[13] or to his well-stored commonplace books, where choice bits which he had noted down in the course of his wide reading [14] were awaiting his touch. There he might find hints, or whole passages put down in his free translation, which would fit the occasion. And in this connection it is to be remembered that most of Jonson's poetry was occasional verse.

Finding the bit which he wanted, in prose, we can imagine that he used the method which Camden his master had taught him, and versified it. Let us consider a familiar example as an illustration of how he used the method—the song "Drink to me only with thine eyes." Richard Cumberland in the eighteenth century pointed out that the source of this exquisite lyric [15] is to be found in certain letters of Philostratus the Athenian (Ca. 170-245 A. D.). Our poet, reading the letters, as he did the innumerable classic writers constantly being made available in his day, was struck by the unforgettable line. When a song was called for,[16] he probably turned

---

[13] In the *Discoveries* he notes in the paragraph *Memoria* that in his youth he "could repeat all, that ever I had made; and so continued until I was past fortie; Since, it is much decay'd in me. Yet I can repeate whole books that I have read, and *Poems*, of some selected friends which I have lik'd to charge my memory with." (Par. 56, *ed. cit.*, 27-8. The force of this statement is hardly lessened when we find that it is translated from Seneca's *Controversies*.) Drummond also bears witness to his remarkable memory in *Conversations*, VII, *op. cit.*, 474-5.

[14] The subtitle of the *Timber; or Discoveries made upon Men and Matter* well indicates this commonplace book habit. The word *Timber*, of course, is connected with the Latin *Sylva*, meaning a miscellany, or collection. The subtitle reads, "As they have flow'd out of his daily Readings; or had their refluxe to his peculiar Notion of the Times." In fact, in this volume, as Castelain says, we have evidently one of Jonson's commonplace books, probably the results of his reading after the fire in 1623 which destroyed all his papers, and among other things,

"Twice twelve years stored up humanity,
With humble gleanings in divinity;
After the fathers. . . ."
"An Execration Upon Vulcan," *op. cit.*, 319.

Scholars would give a great deal to possess this series of commonplace books, for they doubtless contain the raw material of much of his work.

[15] *Observer*, No. 74.

[16] An illustration of a poem, called forth by an occasion, which exactly parallels this is the one referred to in the *Conversations*, XIV (*op. cit.*,

to his commonplace book where he found that by weaving together his jottings, he had a song ready to hand—and an immortal one. It will be noted that this theory of composition is borne out by the fact that the stanzas are taken from letters which are side by side,[17] Nos. 25 and 26 for the first two stanzas, and Nos. 30 and 31 for the last two. Similar methods were undoubtedly used in composing " An Epistle to Sir Edward Sachville, now Earl of Dorset," which Castelain has shown is practically a versification of notebook jottings [18] taken from various sections of Seneca's *De Beneficiis,* with one selection at the end from Plutarch's *De Profectibus in Virtute*; and "To Penshurst," with its echoes from a half-dozen epigrams of Martial; [19] as well as a large number of the rest of Jonson's epigrams, elegies, and odes. Truly Jonson's notebooks were an unfailing source of inspiration.

Although the fire destroyed the great bulk of Jonson's commonplace books, in the *Discoveries,* as has been shown, we have a sample, covering his later reading. If our theories of composition are true, it ought to be possible to prove them by finding these bits of versified prose (often translations or adaptations) from the *Discoveries* scattered through the plays and poems which are known to have been written in Jonson's later life. It was on this assumption that the present writer began searching. The ground had been broken by Mr. Chas. Crawford,[20] who found almost the whole of *Discov*-

---

485), in which occurs the story of how Lady Pembroke called for a poem proving that women are but men's shadows, and Jonson produced the exquisite song, "That Women are but Men's Shadows" (*The Forest,* VII, *op. cit.,* 267). It has been found that this poem is a paraphrase of a Latin poem written by Barthol. Anulus (D. *ca.* 1565).

[17] That Jonson used this practice of giving passages here and there in a work, and grouping them as they would naturally fall if he were engaged in reading a certain book, is illustrated by the order in *Discoveries,* where Castelain shows that Pars. 89, 90, and 91 are all from Machiavelli's *Il Principe,* the first two from Chapt. IX, and the last from Chapt. VII.

[18] *Discoveries, ed. cit.,* Appendix, pp. 143-150. The rest of the appendix points out other such versified gleanings from the well-stored notebooks: a passage from *Every Man in his Humor,* II, iii, 1-66, "A Panagyre on the . . . Entrance of James. . . . ; " and the Epistle Dedicatory of *Volpone.*

[19] First pointed out in detail by Andrew Amos, *Martial and the Moderns* (Cambridge, 1858), who cited many other Jonsonian borrowings from Martial. Briggs adds also an echo from Lucian's *Saturnalian Letters* in "To Penshurst."

[20] *Notes and Queries,* 9th Ser. X (Oct. 18, 1902), No. 251, p. 301.

eries, Par. 101, *Amor Nummi* [21] imbedded in *The Staple of News*, III, i and ii. Mr. Crawford and M. Castelain also cite stanza 15 from the "Epithalamion for Heirmone Weston" (*Underwoods*, No. XCIV) as a versification of *Discoveries*, Par. 97,[22] *De Gratiosis*. I have been able to add a few other bits which serve to illustrate still further Jonson's habits of composition as laid down in this paper. They are as follows:

| DISCOVERIES [23] | UNDERWOODS [24] |
|---|---|
| 111. *De Stylo*. In Picture, light is requir'd no lesse then shadow; . . . . . . . . . . | XXV<br>In picture, they which truly understand,<br>Require (besides the likeness of of the thing) |
| 112. *De Progress. Picturae*. Picture took her faining from *poetry*, from *Geometry* her rule, compasse, lines, proportion, and the whole Symmetry. . . . From Opticks it drew reasons, by which it considered, how things plac'd at a distance, and a farre off, whould appeare lesse. . . . So from thence it tooke shadows, recessor, light, and heightenings. (77-78) | Light, posture, heightening, shadow, colouring,<br>All which are parts commend the cunning hand;<br>(III, 296) |
| | XVIII |
| 23. *Scientia Liberales*. . . . It is as great a spite to be praised in the wrong place, and by a wrong person, as can be done to a noble nature. (13) | Some men, of books or friends not speaking right<br>May hurt them more with praise than foes with spight.<br>. . . . . . . . |
| 113. *Parasiti ad Mensam*. . . . There is as great a vice in praising, and as frequent, as in detracting. (81) | |
| 115. *De Stylo*. . . . He must first thinke, and excogitate his matter; then choose his words, and examine the weight of either. Then take care in placing and ranking both matter, and words, that the composition be | I find thee write most worthy to be read.<br>It must be thine own judgment yet, that sends<br>This thy work forth, that judgment mine commends. |

[21] *Ed. cit.*, p. 68-71, and cited in the Int., p. xxii. The selection is largely a translation from Seneca's Letters to Lucillus, CXV.
[22] *Ed. cit.*, p. 65.
[23] All paragraph and page numbers refer to Castelain's edition.
[24] Numbers in parentheses refer to Cunningham's edition of the *Works*.

DISCOVERIES

comely ... No matter how slow the style be at first, so it be labour'd and accurate; seeke the best, and be not glad of the froward conceits ... but judge of what we invent ... So that the summe of all is: Ready writing makes not good writing.... (84-86)

65. *Ingeniorum Discrimina*, Nota 5. ... You may sound these wits, and find the depth of them, with your middle finger. They are but cream-bowle, or but puddle-deepe. (39)

60. *Veritas Proprium Hominis.* ... For without truth all the Actions of mankind are craft, malace, or what you will. ... Besides, nothing is lasting that is fain'd; it will have another face then it had, ere long: As Eurpides saith, "*No lie ever growes old.*" (31)

116. *Praecipiendi Modi* ... Therefore a master should temper his owne powers, and descent to the others infirmity. If you powre a glut of water upon a Bottle, it receives little of it; but with a Funnell, and by degrees, you shall fill many of them. (89)

130. *Poesis*—1. *Ingenium* ... And, hence it is, that the coming up of good Poets (for I minde not *Mediocres*, or *imos*) is so thinne and rare among us: Every beggarly

UNDERWOODS

... as I would
More of our writers would, like thee, not swell
With the how much they set forth but the how well.
(III, 293)

LIX

They look at best like cream-bowls, and you soon
Shall find their depth; they are sounded with a spoon.
(III, 317)

LXIV

'Tis virtue alone, or nothing, that knits friends.
. . . . . . .
First weigh a friend, then touch and try him too:
For there are many slips and counterfeits.
Deceit is fruitful. Man have masks and nets;
But those with wearing will themselves unfold,
They cannot last. No lie ever grew old. (III, 325)

*The New Inn*, I, i
*Host.* Sir, I do teach him somewhat: by degrees,
And with a funnel, I make shift to fill
The narrow vessel; he is but yet a a bottle (II, 243)

*The New Inn*, First Epilogue
And had he lived the care of king and queen,
His art in something more had yet been seen;

## DISCOVERIES

Corporation affoords the State a Major, or two Bailiffs, yearly: but *solus Rex, aut Poeta, non quotannis nascitur.* To this perfection of Nature in our Poet, wee require Exercise of those parts, and frequent. (123)

108. *Dejectio Aulic.* A dejected countenance and meane clothes beget often a contempt; but it with the shallowest creatures: *courtiers* commonly: looke up even with them in a newe suite; you get above 'hem streight. Nothing is more short-liv'd then (their) pride: It is but while their clothes last; stay but while these are worne out, you cannot wish the thing more wretched, or dejected. (75-76)

96. *Character.* If men did know, what shining fetters, guilded miseries, and painted happinesse, Thrones and Scepters were; There

## UNDERWOODS

But mayors and shrieves may yearly
    fill the stage:
A king's or poet's birth doth ask
    an age.    (II, 384)

*The Staple of News*, I, i

*Fashioner.* Believe it, sir,
  That clothes do much upon the
    wit, as weather
Does on the brain; ...
    ... I have gallants,
Both court and country, would
    have fooled you up
In a new suit, with the best wits
    in being,
And kept their speed as long as
    their clothes lasted

Handsome and neat; but then as
    they grew out
At the elbows again, or had a
    stain or spot,
They have sunk most wretchedly.
    . . . . . .
*Pennyboy Jun.* ... I wonder, gentlemen
And men of means will not maintain themselves
Fresher in wit, I mean in clothes,
    to the highest:
For he that's out of clothes is out
    of fashion,
And out of fashion is out of countenance,
And out of countenance is out of
    wit.    (II, 281-82)

*Love's Welcome at Welbeck*

(The last speech contains the same philosophy as the paragraph in *Discoveries.* I find, however,

| DISCOVERIES | UNDERWOODS |
|---|---|
| would not bee so frequent strife about the getting, or holding of them; ... For a *Prince* is the Pastor of the people ... etc. (63) | only one verbal parallel.) The King, whose love it is to be your parent! Whose office and whose charge, to be your pastor! (III, 218) |

Other instances might be found by more diligent search, but these serve to illustrate the statement that Jonson made use of his commonplace books in his writing, versifying his prose translations [25] made from his daily readings in the classics and the learned writers of his day.

One further observation occurs to me. If, as I believe, the *Discoveries* is the raw material out of which he created his poetry, it should contain hints as to projected work of the poets. It seems fairly certain that in the numerous quotations from Machiavelli's *Il Principe,* Lipsius' *Politicorum, sive Civilis Doctrinae,* Seneca's *De Clementia,* Erasmus' *Institutio Principis Christiani* and others, found in Pars. 77 to 101, Jonson was making preparations for his projected tragedy, *Mortimer His Fall.* A perusal of the Argument prefixed to the play will almost indicate the points at which his various notes would be used.

Jonson, the thrifty student, filing his verses, being sure of the thought before he concerned himself about the manner, has left us numerous traces of his methods of literary composition, showing that he practiced in his poetry what he preached in his conversation and in his private notebooks. It is evident that he did believe in and practice imitation of the best authors, and that he first wrote his poetry in prose.

*The University of North Carolina.*

---

[25] In this connection it should be said in regard to the quotations given above, that almost without exception M. Castelain has found the originals of the passages which Jonson translated.

# THE FIRST ENGLISH TRANSLATION OF THE *PROPHECIES OF MERLIN*

By Charles Bowie Millican

Elias Ashmole (1617-1692), antiquary, astrologer, alchemist, virtuoso, and benefactor of the Bodleian, should be placed among the English translators of Geoffrey of Monmouth's *Historia Regum Britanniæ*. His translation of the *Prophecies of Merlin,* which has thus far been unrecorded by bibliographers of Geoffrey, is of interest to Arthurians as being a printed version in English of a large portion of the *Historia* some seventy years before the appearance of Aaron Thompson's translation of the whole in 1718.[1]

---

[1] The full account of the *Historia* in English will not be given until certain early partial translations are taken into consideration, such as those by Thomas Churchyard in *The Worthines of Wales* (1587), sigg. [D4v] ff., and by Richard Hakluyt in *The Second Part of the principall Nauigations, Voyages and Discoueries of the English nation* (1589), pp. 243 ff. Cognizance should also be taken of College of Arms (London) MS. Arundel XXII. (2), a description of which follows from the *Catalogue of the Arundel Manuscripts in the Library of the College of Arms* (1829), p. 32:

"A Translation of Geoffrey of Monmouth's History, into old-English, by 'Maister Gnaor.' f. 8b.

"A short prologue is prefixed (' *God that nath no bygynnyng no never schal have endyng,*') in which 'Walter archedene of Oxenforde' is said to have translated 'out of spech of brytonys into latyn' the original work. The translation begins: 'Bretayne ys the beste lond that me knowyth, and ys in the west of the ocean, by twyne France that thenne clepyd galla and erlond.'

"The translation is much larger than the original work of Geoffrey, and seems to abound in interpolations. The prophecies of Merlin are inserted in Latin (at. f. 44b.) because 'I ne can noght hem wel understonde, for y nolde nothyng saye but hyt soth were that y sayde.' In the story of Arthur at Avalon, the translator tells his own name, (f. 74c.) 'ghut he ys there as bretons lyfeth and understondeth, as they ghut understondeth and seggeth ghut fro thennes he schal come, and he may lyfe MAISTER GNAOR *that thus book made,* he nold no mor sigge of ghende thenne the prophet Merlyn seyght.'

"The copy being imperfect and ending abruptly, a former possessor supplied three paper leaves, and on the second wrote this note:—'For as much as the end of this boke is imperfect; And havinge an auncient originale written in Lattine by Gefferay of Monmouth de gestis britonum; (out of the which this semeth to be Translated,) I did examyne them

Ashmole made the translation for his friend William Lilly (1602-1681), Jack-of-all-trades and Sidrophel of Butler's *Hudibras*, with whom, according to his diary, he became acquainted through Sir Jonas Moore (1617-1679) "on a Friday night, and I think the 20th of Nov. [1646]."[2] The translation occupies pages 35 through 41 (sigg. F2-[F5]) in the following astrological treatise:

THE / VVorlds Catastrophe, / OR, / EUROPES many Mutations / untill, 1666. / The Fate of *Englands* MONARCHY / untill its Subversion. / Government of the VVorld under / GOD by the seven Planetary Angels; their / Names, Times of Government. / An exact Type of the / THREE SVNS / Seen in *Cheshire* and *Shropshire*, 3. *April* 1647. / Their Signification and Portent, / ASTROLOGICALLY handled. // By *VVilliam Lilly* Student in ASTROLOGIE: / Who is, *Amicus Patriæ, & veritatis Amator*. // To which is added, A Whip for *Wharton*. // London, Printed for *Iohn Partridge*, and *Humphrey Blunden*, and / are to be sold at the *Cock* in *Ludgate*-street, and at the *Castle* in Cornhill, 1647.[3]

Ashmole's translation runs in Lilly's book without the name of the translator, but Lilly himself in the preface tells the reader that it is from the hand of "Elias Ashmole Esquire, my noble Friend":

A work I assure you, both painfull, and full of intricate Laborinths, well becoming that sharpness of wit, wherewith he is naturally endowed: Which Version of his into our mother-tongue he hath excellently performed in significant Language, and terms of Art correspondent to the sence of the first Author: In Astrologie he is well versed, and in Antiquities no mean Student; for who shall read Merlin in the Latin Copy, shall wonder at the dexterity and sharp apprehension of this Gentleman, that being in years so young, should understand and distinguish terms and names, so obsolete, and not frequently vulgar; and yet hath he rendred them in our mother-tongue in so compliant and decent Phrase, as might well have become an Antiquary of double his years.

From Lilly's subsequent remarks we gather that Ashmole based his rendering on the edition of the *Prophecies* published, together

togeather, And fyndinge that they both vouch one Authore that is, Walter Archdecon of Oxford, and also observe on course from Brute unto Cadwalleder, therefore I have thought it good to make this addition out of the sayd Gefferay of Monmouth. Joseph Holand 1588.'"

[2] *The Diary and Will of Elias Ashmole*, ed. R. T. Gunther (Old Ashmolean Reprints, II, 1927), p. 27.

[3] Bodleian Ashmole 538. (5), 4to. See also British Museum 718. e. 20. (7) and E. 387. (1). The article on Lilly in *DNB*. states that "some" copies include Ashmole's translation.

with the commentary of Alain de Lille, at Frankfort in 1608 under the title of *Prophetia Anglicana*:[4]

> Ambrose Merlin, lived in the time of Vortiger; these are the Prophecies, for which amongst the learned he is so renowned; they were never in the English before: They were Printed at Franckford 1608, and Commented on, by one Alanus de I[n]sulis a German Doctor, who hath taken much pains to explain them, &c.[5]

The text which follows is a line for line and page for page reprint from Ashmole's own copy of Lilly's book,[6] which contains marginal notes in Ashmole's autograph. The text is ushered in by "Geffry Archdeacon of Monmouth Byshop of S.t Assaph" written in the upper margin:

---

[4] Sigg. )(2-[)(8v], beginning "SEDENTE Vortegirno Rege Britonum, super ripam exhausti stagni, egressi sunt duo dracones," etc., and corresponding to Book VII, Chapter iii, of the *Historia*, with the omission of postpositive "itaque." The special heading for the *Prophecies* is "*PROPHETIA* / MERLINI AMBROSII / BRITANNI: EX TRANSLA- / TIONE GALFREDI MO- / numetensis." The running title is "PROPHETIÆ MERLINI." The text is then repeated (pp. 1-296) with a division into seven books interspersed with the commentary of Alain. The concluding matter (pp. 297-325) does not appear in the first edition of *Prophetia Anglicana*, which was printed in 1603, also at Frankfort.

[5] Sig. A3. I have suggested the significance of Lilly's use of the *Prophecies* in my recent book, *Spenser and the Table Round* (Harvard Studies in Comparative Literature, VIII, 1931), p. 136.

[6] Bodleian Ashmole 538. (5).

( 35 )

# A
# PROPHECIE
OF
*Ambroſe Merlin*, a Britaine,

From the Tranſlation of *Gefferey*[7] of
*Monmouth:* Ænigmatically therein delivering
the Fate, and Period of the Engliſh Monarchy.

---

Vortiger (king of the Britains) sitting on the brink of an emptied Pool, there issued thence 2. Dragons one of which was white, but the other red. And when the one came near the other, they began a terrible fight & by (the vehemency of) their breath, begot fire. But the White Dragon prevailed, and chased the Red Dragon to the end of the Lake. But the Red Dragon, after he had bemoaned himselfe (thus) expulsed, made a suddaine assault upon the White Dragon, and forced him to give back. The Dragons thus contending, the King commanded *Ambrose Merline* to tell him what that Combat of the Dragons meant. Then he gushing out with tears assumeth the Spirit of Prophecy: (and saith) Wo unto the Red Dragon, for his ruin approcheth. The White Dragon shall possess his Dens, which signifieth the Saxons whom thou hast invited: but the Red Dragon designeth the Nation of *Britain,* which shall be oppressed of the White. Therefore shall the Mountains thereof be levelled as the Valleys; and the Rivers of the Valleys shall stream with blood. The purity of Religion shall be defaced; and the ruine of Churches shall be manifested. At length the oppressed shall prevail, and shall withstand the Tyrannie of strangers. For the Boar of *Cornwall* shall assist, and shall trample the necks of them under his feet. The Isles of the Ocean shall be subject to his Authority, and shall possess the French Forrests. *Rome* shall tame his Tyrannie, and his end shall be doubtfull. He shall be famous in the mouth of the multitude, and his actions shall be (as) meat to those that recount them. Six of his successors shall attain the Scepter, but after them shall a German Worm arise. The Sea-wolf shall magnifie him, whom the Affrican Forrests shall accompany. Religion shall again be defaced, and there shall be a transmutation of the chief Seats. The dignity of *London* shall adorn *Canterbury,* and the 7. Pastor of *York* shall be often in the Lesser Britanie. Anglisea shall be cloathed with the garment of the City of Legions; and the Preacher of *Ireland* shall be silent by reason of an infant growing in the Womb. It shall rain blood, and a horrible dearth shall afflict men. These things coming on a sudden, the Red Dragon shall fret, but with much ado, he shall flourish: Then shall the white Dragons calamity approach, and the build-

( 36 )

ings of his little Villages shall be overthrown. Seven kings shall be destroyed, and one shall be hallowed. The mothers bellies shall be ript open, and the children shall be abortive. There shall be a wonderfull great punishment of men, that the Natives may be restored. He that shall do these things shall become a Brazen-man; and he shall (for a long time after) keep the Gates of *London*, upon a Brazen-horse. From thenceforth the red Dragon shall return to his peculiar temperature, and shall indeavour to exercise cruelty upon himself: Therefore shall the wrath of the most high come suddenly upon him; for the fields shall frustrate the labour of the husbandman. A sudden mortality shall snatch away the people, and shall sweep a-way whole Nations. Such as be left, shall forsake their Native soil, and shall sow their corn in Forraign Countreys. A blessed King shall prepare a ship, and in a Princes Court, he shall be numbred among the 12. blessed.

There shall be a lamentable desolation of the Kingdom, and the Barn-floores full of Corn, shall be turned into unprofitable woods. The white Dragon shall arise the second time, and shall invite the daughter of Germany. Our little villages shall once more be replenished with a strange generation, and the red Dragon shall languish in the end of the Lake. Afterward shall the German Worm be crowned, and the Brazen Prince shall be humbled. A bound is set him, which he cannot pass: For, he shall remain 150. years in disquiet, but he shall be in subjection 300. years. Then shall the North wind rise against him, and shall snatch away the Flowers, which the west wind begot. Churches shall be beautified, yet shall not the sword depart. The German Worm shall hardly keep his den, because vengeance shall suddenly come upon him for his treacherie: at length, he shall flourish for a while, but the Decimation of the Normans shall offend him: for the people shall rush in upon him, in wooden horses, and Iron coats, who shall be revenged of his naughtiness. He shall restore to the former inhabitants their possessions, and the destruction of the Aliens shall (then) appear: the branches of the White Lion shall be cut off from our Territories, and the remainder of his generation shall be tenth'd. They shall undergo the yoke of perpetuall servitude; and they shall wound their mother with mattocks, and ploughs. Two Dragons shall succeed, whereof one shall be choaked by the dart of envy, but the other shall return under the shadow of a Kingly name. The Lyon of justice shall follow, at whose roaring the French Towers, and the Island Dragons shall tremble. In his days shall gold be squeezed out of the Lilly and Nettle; and silver shal be extracted out of the hoofs of the lowing beasts. The spruce Fantasticks of the times shall put on changeable garments, and their outward habits shall bewray the vanity of their mindes. The greedy hounds shall be ham-string'd, the Beasts of the Forrest shall rest in quiet, humanity shall bewail the punishment: the coyn shall be cleft, and each half shall be made round. The ravenousness of the Kites shall be consumed, and the teeth of the Wolves shall be broken: the Lions whelps shall be turned into Sea-fishes, and his Eagle shall build her nest upon Mount *Moriana*.[8] *Vendotia* shall be dyed red with her mothers blood, and the house of *Corineus*, shall slay six brothers. The Isle shall be damp with her mighty tears, whereupon all men shall be provoked to all things. Wo unto thee Normandy, for on thee shall the brain of the Lion be wasted, and his Members being torn in pieces, shall be thrown out of his Native soil. They that succeed shall indeavour to remove the Crown, but the love of new Kings shall be extol'd. For his goodness he shall be abused by the wicked, untill he become a Father. Therefore being armed with the teeth of the Boar, he shall pass over the tops of the Mountains, and the shade of the helmet: the Highlanders of *Scotland* shall be displeased,

( 37 )

pleased, and having assembled their Collaterals shall proclaim war. He shall put a bridle in the jaws of him, which shall be established in the (very) bosom of little Britany. The Eagle of the broken truce shall beutifie it, and shall rejoyce in his third building. The whelps of the roaring Lion shall awaken, and (the Forrests being forsaken) shall be hunted beneath the walls of the Cities, and shall commit great slaughter upon such as withstand them, and shall cut out the tongues of the Bulls: they shall load the necks of the roaring Lions with chains, and shall renew the ancient times. Afterward, the Regall unction shall pass from the first to the fourth, from the 4. to the 3. from the 3. to the second.

The sixt shall overthrow the wals of *Ireland*, and shall turn the forrests thereof into plain fields. He shall reduce divers kingdoms into one, and he shall be crowned with the head of a Lion. His beginning shall be in a restless, and wavering affection, but his end shall be blessed; for he shall repair the decayed Monasteries throughout the Country, and shall place Preachers in convenient places: He shall cloath two cities with two garments, and he shall bestow Virgins gifts upon Virgins, for which he shall merit the favour of God, and shall be numbred among the blessed.

A Woolf-like beast shall come out of him penetrating all things, who shall indeavour the ruin of his own Nation, for by him the Normans shall lose both the Isles, and shall be bereaved of their Pristine dignity. From thenceforth shall the ancient Inhabitants [9] return to their own Isle, for variance shall arise among the aliens. Likewise, a venerable old man, upon a white horse, shall divert the river of *Periton*,[10] and with his white Scepter shall dispose of the Mill thereon standing. *Cadwalader* shall call home the *Conani*, and shall receive the Highlanders into fellowship. Then shall there be great slaughter committed on the Forraigners, then shall the rivers stream with blood, then shall the mountains of little Britain [11] burst out, and shall be crowned with the Diadem of *Brute*. *Wales* shall be filled with joy, and the Oaks of *Cornwall* shall wax green. The Isle shall be called by the Name of Brute, and the memory of the strangers shall be forgotten.

From *Conanus* shall come a warlike Boar, who shall exercise the sharpness of his teeth, within the French Forrests: for he shall hew down all the greater Oaks, but he shall give protection to the lesser. The *Arabians*, and *Affricans* shall quake for fear of him, for the violence of his motion shall threaten the further *Spain*. A Goat of the Venerean house shall succeed him, having golden horns, and a silver beard, who shall breath forth such a cloud from his Nostrils, as that the surface of the whole Isle shal be obscured. There shal be peace in his days, and by the fruitfulness of the earth, all sorts of grain shal be multiplied.

Women by reason of their Lewdness shal be made Serpents, and every step they make shal be filled with pride. The tents of *Venus* shal be renewed, neither shal the darts of Lust leave off to wound. The Rivers shal be turned into blood, and two Kings shal fight a duel for the Lyoness of *Stafford*. Every one shal wantonize, and civility (it self) shal not forbear to admit of contraries. All these things three ages shal see fulfilled, until the interred Kings within the City of *London* shal be discovered. Famine shal again infest, mortality shal once more return, and the inhabitants shall lament the desolation of their Cities. A Boar of commerce shall unexpectedly arise, who shall bring back his scattered droves, to their forsaken Pastures. His brest shall be food to the Hungry, and his tongue shall appease the thirsty: Rivers shall flow from his mouth, which shall refresh mens dried cheeks.

Afterward a Tree shall be procreated upon the Tower of *London*, which, having only three Boughs, shall obscure the face of the whole Isle, with the breadth of its

( 38 )

leaves. From hence the North winde (its enemy) shall suddenly arise, and by its cruell blast shall snatch away the third bough thereof. The other two shall supply the room thereof, untill (by the multitude of their leaves) one shall cover another. But afterward it shall obtain the room of two, and shall sustain Birds of Forraign Nations. It shall be accounted obnoxious to the Native Birds, for through the fear of its shadow, they shall lose their flying-young.

An unprofitable Asse shall succeed, ready in punishing counterfeiters of gold, but slow in revenging the ravening of Wolves. In those daies, the Oaks throughout the Forrests shall burn, and Accorns shall grow upon the boughs of Lindens.[12]

The Severn shall run through seven Gates, and the river Osca shall wax hot for the space of seven moneths. The Fishes therein shall die by the heat thereof, and of them shall Serpents be ingendred. The Baths of Bado shall frieze, and their wholsome waters shall become poysonous. *London* shall lament the slaughter of 20000. men, and the river of Thames shall be turned into blood. Monks shall be compelled to marriage, and the noise of them shall be heard in the Mountains of the Alps. Three Fountains shall burst out in the City of Winchester, whose little brookes shall divide the Isle into three parts; he that shall drink of one, shall prolong his life, neither shall he be afflicted with any sudden feebleness. He that shall drink of the other, shall perish with hunger, and a wanness and horror shall possess his face. He that shall drink of the third, shall die a sudden death, neither shall his body be buried. But if his dead body shall be thrown upon the water, the ashes thereof shall be turned into water. Hereupon a Damosell shall come from the City of Canutus of the Forrest, to prepare a Medicine, whereby, as she shall understand all Arts, she shall dry up the obnoxious Fountains by the only vertue of her breath. Afterward, to refresh her self with the wholsome Liquor, she shall carry the Calidonian Forrest in her right hand, but in her left hand, the Bulwarks of the Walls of *London*. What way soever she shall pass, she shall leave sulphureous tracks behinde her, which shall smoak with a double flame. That smoak shall stir up the Ruthens, and shall destroy the Fishes of the Sea. She shall continue in lamentable sorrows, and shall fill the Isle with her horrible out-cry. A Stagg of ten branches shall slay her, four of which branches shall carry together the golden Diadems. But the other six shall be turned into the Horns of the wilde Oxen, which by a horrible noise shall shake the three Isles of Britainie. The Forrest of Daneum shall be stirred up, and (with a gentle voice) shall call, Come Wales, and joyn Cornwall to thee, and say to the City of Winchester, *The Earth shall swallow thee up.* Transfer the seat of thy Pastor, whither the Birds do flock, and the other Members shall follow their head.

For the day draweth near, whereon the Inhabitants shall be destroyed for the sin of perjury. The whiteness of their Wooll, and the diversity of their Tincture hath offended. Wo be to that perjured Nation, by whose means a noble City shall be destroyed. The Birds shall rejoyce at so great an increase, and two shall be made one. And a Hedghogg (laden with fruit) shall rebuild it, to the smell whereof, Birds of divers Forrests shall flock. He shall adjoyn thereto a wonderfull great Palace, and shall strengthen the same with 600 Towers. In every of which a Senator shall be appointed, who shall give Laws unto the Subjects. Therefore shall *London* envy her, and shall increase her Walls thrice so much as formerly they were. The river Thames shall incompass her on every side, and the rumour of the Works shall transcend the Alps. The Hedghog shall hide his fruits within her, and shall plot secretly (against her.)

In that day the stones shall speak, and the Sea that leads to France, shall be contracted into a narrow room. One man shall hear another from either shoar, and

the

( 39 )

the whole Isle shall be enlarged: The wonders of the deep shall be revealed: France shall quake for feare. After these things a Hearn shall proceed from the forrest *Callaterium,* which shall fly about the Isle the space of two years; by her night clamour shee shall call the other birds, and all other birds shall associate her: they shall fall upon mens Tillage, and shall destroy all manner of grain. A famine shall pursue the people, and a dire mortality shall ensue the famine: but when so great mortality shall be ceased, a detestable fowl shall betake himself to the utmost bounds of Wales, and shall raise it up to a high mountain, and in the top thereof shee shall plant an Oak, and shall build her nest in the boughs thereof, three egges shall be layd in the nest, from which a Fox, a Wolfe, and a Beare shall come. The Fox shall devour his mother, and shall beare an Asses head. Therefore being become a Monster, he shall affright his brethren, and shall banish them into *Normandy*: but they shall excite the shorn Boar against the Fox, and being returned in a ship, they shall encounter with the Fox; who, so soon as the combat shall begin, will fain himselfe dead, and shall move the Boar to pity him,: a while after he shall go to the dead Carkase, and whilst he shall stand over it, he shall breath upon the eyes, and face thereof: But he not forgetfull of (his former falshood) shall bite his right foot, and shall tear it quite from the body; and also at one leap shall snatch to him his right eare, and his tayle, and shall hide himselfe in the holes of the mountains: therefore the deluded Boar shall require the Wolfe, and the Beare, to restore unto him his lost members, who (as they shall begin the Quarrell) shall promise him two feet, and two ears, and a tayl, and of them they shall compose the Boars members: so he shall be pacified, & expect the promised restauration. In the interim the Fox shall come from the mountaines, and shall change himself into a Wolf; and as if he were to have some discourse with the Boar, he shall go craftily to him, and shall wholly devour him. Then shall he transforme himself into a Boar, and (as if he wanted his members) he shall waite for his brethren, and after that they shall be come, even them also shall he suddenly slay, and shall be crowned with the head of a Lion. In his dayes a serpent shal be engendered, which shal endeavour the destruction of all mortalls; he shall by his length environ London, and shall destroy all the passengers. A Bull of the Mountain shall assume the head of the Wolf, and shall cleanse his teeth in the shop of *Sabrina*: he shall gather to him the Highlanders and the Welch who shall drink the Thames dry. The Asse shall call a Goat with a long beard, and shall change his shape: therefore shall the Bull be displeased, and having called the Wolfe, the horned Bull shall make at them; and the more to manifest his cruelty, he shall devour their flesh and bones: but he shall be burnt in the top of *Urianus*. The embers of the fire wherein he shall be burnt, shall be changed into Swans, which shall swim as well upon dry ground as on the water. Fishes shall swallow Fishes, and men shall devour men: but old age comming on, submarine lights shall be ingendered, and they shall devise submarine deceipts. They shall sink shipping, and they shall gather much money. The River Thames shall flow again, and the united rivers shall exceed the bounds of the Channell: it shall overflow the neighbouring townes, and shall overturne the opposite mountains. It shall incorporate with the fountain *Galabes,* full of deceit and naughtiness; whence shall arise seditions, provoking the *Vendotians* to wars. The Oakes of the Forrests shall unite, and shall encounter with the stones of the *Geuvisey*. The Crows and the Kites shall devour the bodies of the slain. The Owle shall build her nest upon the walls of *Gloucester*; and in her nest shall an Asse be generated. The Serpent of *Maluernia* shall educate him, and shall hatch more trecheries. Having got the Crown he shall soar on high, and with a horrible noise

shall

( 40 )

shall affright the people of the countrey: in his daies the mountaines of *Pachacius* shall stagger, and the Provinces shall be deprived of their Forrests: for a Worme of a fiery breath shall suddenly come, who shall burne the trees with his sent-out vapour. Seaven Lions shall come out of him, disgraced by the heads of Goats: they shall destroy women by the stinch of their nostrils, and shall make wives wantons. The Father shall not know his own Son, because their wives shall play the beasts. Therefore shall a Gyant of wickedness rush upon them who by the sharpness of his eyes shall terrifie all. The Dragon of *Worcester* shall rise against him, and shall strive to rout him out, but an encounter being made, the Dragon shall overcome, and the ungodliness of the victor shall be repressed; for he shall subdue the Dragon, and having put off his garment, shall remain naked. The Dragon shall carry him aloft, and with his tayle (erected) shall beat the naked Gyant. But the Gyant reassuming his vigour, shall break his jaws with a sword: at length the Dragon shall fold himself under his tayle, and (poysoned) shall die.

The Boar of *Tolenesius* shall succeed him, and by his terrible tyranny shall oppress the people. *Gloucester* shall cast out the Lion, who shall disquiet the Serpent with severall Wars. He shall tred him under his feet, and shall affright him with his open jaws. At length the Lion shall contend with the Kingdom, and shall climb upon the backs of Noble men. The Bull shall rush into the strife, and shall smite the Lion with his right foot. He shall drive him throughout all the parts of the Kingdom, but he shall break his horns in the Wals of *Exon*. The Fox of *Kaerdubalus* shall be revenged of the Lion, and shall wholly devour him with his teeth. For the Serpent of *Lincoln* shall surround him, and by a horrible hissing shall intimate his presence to many Dragons. The Dragons shall gather together, and shall tear one another in pieces. The winged shall oppress those that want wings, and shall fasten their poysoned claws upon their Eye-lids, the rest shall consent to combating, and shall one kill another. These being dead, a fifth shall succeed, and shall break the remainder by sundry devices; he shall crush the back of one in pieces, and (with his sword) shall separate his head from his body. Having put off his garment, he shall ascend another, and shall throw upon him the right & left side of his tayl. One that is naked shall keep him at a distance, when one that is cloathed shall not deterr him. He shall torment the rest upon the back, and shall drive them to the uttermost part of the Kingdom. A roaring Lion (and one to be feared for his outragious cruelty) shall suddenly come. He shall reduce fifteen Provinces into one, and he alone shall enjoy the people. A Gyant shall shine with a white colour, and shall germinate a white people. Pleasures shall make Princes feeble, and the Subjects shall become savage. A Lion (with his belly full of blood) shall arise among them, a sickle shall be given him in the corn, which (whilst he shall grieve in anger) shall be oppressed of him. A Carter of York shall quiet them, and (his master being thrust out) he shall ascend into the Cart which he drove, and shall threaten the East with a drawn sword, and he shall fill the Track of his Cart wheeles with blood. Afterwards a Fish shall be procreated in the Sea, which being allured by the hissing of the Serpent, shall copulate with him, betwixt whom three glistering Buls shall be generated; who (having eat up their pastures) shall be turned into Trees. The first shall carry a viperous whip, and shall turn his back of him that is born after him. The second brother shall endeavour to snatch the whip from him, but he shall be rebuked by the youngest. They shall turn away their faces mutually from one another, untill they shall poure forth a poysoned cup. A Prince of the Highlanders shall succeed him, whom (also) the Serpent shall seek to destroy. He shall apply himself to Tillage, so that the Countries shall be white with Corn. The Serpent shall indea-

vour

( 41 )

vour to diffuse poyson, to hinder the growth of the grass and corn. The people shall waste by reason of a deadly famine, and the Wals of their Cities shall be made desolate. The City of *Gloucester* shall be given for a Medicine, which shall render sustenance to those that be under the lash, for she shall bear the ballance of the medicine, and the Isle shall be renewed in a short space. After which, two shall sue for the Scepter, to whom the horned Dragon shall submit himself. Another shall come armed, and shall ride the flying Serpent; being naked he shall sit upon his back, and shall cast the right side of his Tayl upon him. The neighbouring Nations shall be awakened by his clamour, and shall startle other Nations. Therefore shall the second be united to the Lion, but (dissenting betwixt themselves) they shall encounter one another; and (after mutuall wounds) they shall lie down together, but the fierceness of the Lion shall prevail. There shall one suddenly come with the Timbrell & Harp, and shall asswage the fierceness of the Lion, therefore shall the people of the Kingdom be pacified, and shall provoke the Lion to Justice. Being setled in his Throne, he shall think of Rewards; but his power shall extend into the Highlands. Therefore shall the Northern Provinces be sorrowfull, and shall open the doors of the Temples. The Standard-bearer-Woolfe shall raise Troopes, and shall environ *Cornwall* with his tayle. A Souldier (in a Cart) shall withstand him, who shall change that people into a Boar. Therefore the Boar shall waste the Provinces, but he shall be drowned in the deep of Severn. A man (in Wine) shall be as a Lion, and the lustre of his Gold shall dazle the eyes of the beholders: He shall gild his silver-wine-bowles, and shall trouble sundry Wine-presses. Men shall be drunk with Wine, and having laid aside the thought of heaven, shall be wedded to the Earth. The Stars shall with-hold their influence from them, and shall confound their wonted motion. The Heavens being thus averse, their Corn-fields shall be dryed up and the dew of heaven shall be denyed them. The roots and branches shall change their offices, and the novelty thereof shall be miraculous. The splendour of the Sun shall languish by the paleness of *Mercury*, & it shall be dreadfull to the beholders. *Mercury* of *Arcadia* shall change his shield, and he shall call *Venus* the Helmet of *Mars*; the Helmet of *Mars* shall cast a shadow, and the rage of *Mercury* shall exceed its limits. Hard-hearted *Orion* shall unsheath his Falchion. *Phœbus* of the Sea shall disturb the Clouds. *Iupiter* shall leave off his appointed course, and *Venus* shall forsake her Orb. The malice of *Saturn* shall be poured down grievously, and with his crooked Sythe shall he destroy mankinde. The 12. Houses of heaven shall bewail the absence of the Planets. The *Twins* shall leave off their accustomed Imbraces, and shall exchange Summer for Winter. The Scales shall hang uneavenly, untill the Ram support them with his crooked Hornes. The Scorpions tayl shall engender Lightening, and the Crab shall contend with the Sun. The Virgin shall ascend the back of the Archer, and shall obfuscate the pure and beautifull Flowers. The Orbe of the Moon shall trouble the Zodiack, and the Pleiades shall gush out with tears. The Offices of *Ianus* shall no more be restored, but (the Gate being shut) he shall lurk in the Creeks of *Ariadne*. In the twinckling of an eye shall the Seas arise, and the Ashes of the dead shall be renewed. The Winds shall contend with a terrible sufflation, and shall terminate their sound amongst the Stars.[13]

*New York University.*

[7] " surnamed Arthurius saith Wm of Newborough " (part of the outer marginal commentary).
[8] " Welch Morinwyr " (*ibid.*).
[9] Inhabitauts.
[10] " Petoriton " (part of the outer marginal commentary).
[11] " Armorica " (*ibid.*).
[12] " Linden trees " (outer marginal commentary).
[13] " Concerning this Prophesie, heare wt Will: of Newborough, (whoe liued in ye Tyme of this Geoffry of Monmouth,) saith——" (part of the lower marginal commentary).

# THREE JACOBEAN DEVIL PLAYS

## By Russell Potter

It is a truism that old conventions die hard, that there is nothing new under the sun. Masefield catches the ear of the twentieth century by going back to 1385 and the *Canterbury Tales;* Picasso and Gauguin astound and shock by going back to primitive negro art; O'Neill startles Broadway by reproducing something of the swift movement of the Elizabethan stage. Only a few years ago Stephen Leacock lamented in the public press that the devil is dead, and three centuries ago Thomas Dekker, Elizabethan prentice, craftsman, and playwright, wrote in his *A Knight's Conjuring:* " I swore by Hellicon (which he could never abide) that because 'tis out of fashion to bring a Divell in on the stage, he should (spite of his spitting fire and brimstone) be a Divell in print."

Now, the " divell " referred to by Dekker is not the epic Lucifer of Milton's poem, nor the aweful Mephistopheles of *Faustus,* but the devil of popular legend and fancy, the devil of the Friar Rush legends and the later mystery plays. This devil of English comedy is a descendant of a long line of more or less disreputable forebears. In 1568 John Weir estimated that there were seventy-two princes of evil (he names each one) ruling over 7,405,926 demons.[1] Quite early he became so indispensible a property of legend and folk-tale that he was confused in the popular mind with elf and dwarf, satyr and Puck and Robin Goodfellow, etc.[2] Quite early—long before he found his way into the religious plays—he became a comic figure. The story of Morgan Jones and the Devil, as related by Thomas Wright in his Friar Rush and the Frolicsome Elves,[3] will perhaps best serve to illustrate this conception of the devil. The legend of the Changeling Monk is another good example,[4] and many similar folk-tales might be cited, for, as Lowell observed in his essay on Witchcraft, " there is no end of such stories."

---

[1] Lecky, *History of the Rise and Influence of the Spirit of Rationalism in Europe,* (N. Y., 1880), Vol. I, p. 107.

[2] In Piers Plowman, for example, Puck (or Puke) is the great Devil himself; in *A Midsummer Night's Dream* he is a merry elf.

[3] Thomas Wright, *Literature and Superstition* (2 vols., London, 1846), Vol. II, pp. 35 ff.

[4] Reprinted by G. C. Coulton in his *A Medieval Garner,* pp. 105-108.

It is this devil of the folk which found his way onto the English comic stage through the rather restricted avenue of the mystery play, and there is ample evidence that from an early time his stage appearance was dictated by the crowd's conception of its " dear delight," by its love of the incongruous, the ludicrous, the comically impossible. In the accounts of the Draper's Company at Conventry occur many memoranda of payments made for " hose with heare," " Heare for the demons cote and hose and mending the devyls hede," " a staff for the demon," etc. In the Newcastle play of Noah's Ark the devil swears to Noah's wife " by my crooked snout." In the Digby Conversion of St. Paul occur the stage directions: " Here to enter the dyvel with thunder and fire," " Here shall entere anothere devyll called mercury, with a fyering, coming in hast, cryeing and rorying," " vanyshe away with a fyrye flame and a tempest." And in the Smith's pageant, we know, the devil was equipped with a painted vizor (which needed frequent repairs and repainting) and wore a dress made of leather and colored in all probability black. And it is this devil of the Englishman's childhood [5] the passing of which Dekker lamented in the prose tract above referred to.

But the devil was not dead, dramatically speaking, during the first sixteen years of the seventeenth century; in three plays he is very much alive: *Grim the Collier of Croydon, or the Devil and His Dame,* Dekker's own *If This Be Not A Good Play the Devil is In It,* and Jonson's *The Devil is an Ass.* In these plays no conjuror is needed to call up the devil; in each of them the action originates in the infernal regions. In *Grim* the first stage direction indicates a " place for the devils' consistory." St. Dunstan enters and delivers a long soliloquy; then, overcome by drowsiness (induced perhaps by his speech), he lies down and sleeps. Whereupon " lightning and thunder; the curtains drawn on a sudden; Pluto, Minos, Aeacus, Rhadamanthus, set in counsel; before them Malbecco's ghost guarded with furies." In Dekker's play the opening scene is also in hell, or rather upon the banks of the Styx,

---

[5] Reginald Scot, writing in his *Discovery of Witchcraft* (1584), recalls the fact that " in our childhood our mother's maids have so terrified us with an ugly devil, having horns on his head, fire in his mouth, and a tail in his breech, eyes like a basin, fangs like a dog, claws like a bear, a skin like a nigger and a voice roaring like a lion."

with a lively debate between Pluto and Charon to start with. In Jonson Satan and Pug enter at the beginning of the first scene, Satan coming in like the roaring devil of the old plays: "Hoh, hoh, hoh," he cries, "hoh, hoh, hoh, hoh, hoh."

Now, although the first of these plays is separated from the last by almost a score of years, stage conventions seem to have changed but little, so far as the devil and his minions are concerned, from the days of Timothy Tattle, "who was wont to say there was no play without a fool and a devil in it," to the latter and more sceptical days of Jonson himself. This devil was easily recognized by his "saucer eyes," [6] by his fondness for roaring and rolling his "r's," [7] by his "true, hellish smoky hue," [8] by the thunder and lightning or fireworks with which his entrances and exits were not infrequently marked.[9] There were times, of course, when the dramatist varied the conventional formula,[10] and he had good

---

[6] Referred to in *The Virgin Martyr*, III, i; *Return from Parnassus*, IV, ii; *Goblins*, IV, i; *The Gamster*, III, i; *A Very Woman*, II, ii.

[7] In *Monsieur Thomas* (III, iii), Tom is singing ballads to the maid. The maid replies in a song inviting him to climb up to her. He does so, with considerable difficulty, and when he is scrambling over the parapet, "Madge with a Devil's vizard roaring, offers to kiss him, and he falls down." Richard Carew in his *The Excellency of the English Tongue* (?1595-96, reprinted in Smith's "Elizabethan Critical Essays" Vol. II, p. 292) says that the Spanish language is "magesticall, but fullsome, running too much on the O and terrible like the devill in a playe." But Tobie in the Night Walker (II, i) asserts that devils have a "kind of tone like crickets!"

[8] *Return from Parnassus*, IV, ii: W. Spelman in his "A Dialogue between Two Travellers" (c. 1580), speaking of the robber on the Swarte Ritter, says: "His face was as black as a devill in a playe" (Roxburgh Club ed., p. 42).

[9] There are to found many examples of this. The convention, well founded in the mystery plays, had a long life. In Dekker's play, when Ruffman wants to exhibit "a thousand Balles of wildfire, flying around the Aire," there occurs the stage direction, "Fire-works on Lines." In Heywood's *Silver Age* the prince of hell may be called Pluto but his minions are English devils and his hell is the hell-mouth of the old plays: "Flashes of fire; the Divels appear at every corner of the stage with several fireworks . . . fireworks all over the house" (p. 159 of the Pearson edition).

[10] In *The Birth of Merlin* the devil enters "in a man's habit, richly attired, his feet and his head horrid." In *Wily Beguiled* Robin Goodfellow plans to frighten Sopho: "I'll put me on my great carnation-nose, and wrap me in a rowsing calf-skin suit." In Middleton's *Black Book* Lucifer

precedent for this in the conduct of the devil himself, for it was well known that the devil could assume any shape he chose, even that of an angel. Just how the devil sometimes managed to possess one is jestingly illustrated in *The Sisters* (II. i) when Antonio tells the proud sister: "Thou hast drunk a devil," and she replies: "I did not see him in my cup." The speech is reminiscent of the popular medieval legend of the young nun who carelessly swallowed a devil that was sunning himself on a lettuce leaf in her salad. Finally, it may be remarked, the devil carries away damned souls or is beaten off by the vice down to the very last.

As suggested above, no magician or conjuror of human proportions is needed in these three plays, and this fact serves to differentiate them from other devil dramas of the time. Here the devils exist in their own right, just as they do in Machiavelli's Belphagor and in the Friar Rush legends. In *Grim* Belphagor, who has been sent to the earth to find out if all women are as shrewish as Malbecco reports, is himself the magician. Disguised as a Spaniard and calling himself Castiliano, he comes to London, having determined to marry Honorea, the Earl of London's dumb daughter. His proposal to release her speech is accepted; but St. Dunstan is found with the dumb maiden, offering up prayers for her recovery. There follows immediately a trial of magic skill, evidently a popular device by this time,[11] which ends in the triumph of Castilano's black magic over the white magic of Dunstan. Castiliano causes Dunstan's harp to sound of its own accord, yet when Dunstan takes it into his hands he cannot strike a note from it. Then, Dunstan routed, the infernal magician frees Honorea's tongue, only to receive a sharp rebuff. "Mercenary fugitive,"

---

says one of the pimps "had a head of hair like one of my devils in Doctor Faustus." In *The Antipodes* (III, v) the mad Peregrine gets into the stage property room and finds "divells visors, and their flame painted skin coates." In Jonson's *Staple of News* (II) Gossip Mirth recalls plays in which "Iniquity came in like Hokus-pokus, in a juggler's jerkin, with false skirts, like the knave of clubs." And in *A New Trick to Cheat the Devil* (IV, i) occurs a bit of vaudeville diablerie which must have been popular with the crowd. At the end of the antic dance which is the feature of this interpolation, Slightall calls the devil back: "Enter the Divell like a Gentleman, with glasse eyes."

[11] Popularized in *Friar Bacon and Friar Bungay* and *John a Kent and John a Cumber*.

"presumptuous Spaniard," she calls him, and then turns on her father. At the end of her first speech all agree with Lacy: "I would to God her tongue were tied again."

In the end the women prove too much for the devil, just as they prove too much for his man, Akercock or Robin Goodfellow, who has followed him from hell and who leaves London to play the same rôle in the sub-plot that his master is playing in the main one with this great difference: he ends on excellent terms with the Collier of Croyden. When Belphagor's time is up, the earth swallows him just in time to release him from the intricate maze of trouble which he has got himself into. St. Dunstan is left to deliver the semi-epilogue; and thus Christian white magic triumphs in the end.

*Grim* is founded on Machiavelli; *If This Be Not a Good Play the Devill is In It* is founded on the old story of Friar Rush, popular in continental folk-lore as the devil who, disguised as a cook, corrupted a whole monastery.[12] But in the play there appear a number of additions. It is as though the dramatist, seeing a "good thing" in the Friar Rush story, had determined to improve upon his last by "going the original one better." Here we have not one devil sent to corrupt mankind, but three! Shackle-soule is sent to the friary, Ruffman to the court, Grumshall to the market-place. No sooner have the devils been dispatched than the scene begins jumping from monastery to the court to the market-place. It is a diabolical confusion, although the dramatist does try to give some semblence of unity to his diverse plot by sending the subprior (who refuses to yield to temptation) to the court to complain and by bringing the king (when he is hard pressed by war) to the monastery for refuge. However, the devils are all successful in the end and the play is closed with a purely extraneous scene of diabolerie in which the puritans are rather pointedly ridiculed.

Four years before the appearance of Dekker's devil play [13] Ben Jonson had denied the devil a place in comedy, relegating him to the limbo of "ridiculous and exploded folies" and castigating those who would retrieve and keep alive such "relics of bar-

---

[12] Cf. C. H. Herford: "Literary Relations of England and Germany," (Cambridge, 1886), pp. 293-322.

[13] Cf. E. K. Chambers, *Elizabethan Stage* (Oxford, 1924), Vol. III, p. 368.

barism."[14] But the devil was far too engaging a figure in comedy and far too deeply entrenched in popular favor to be so summarily dismissed; and nine years after he wrote this dedication Jonson admitted this himself and, in the full maturity of his powers, placed on the stage a devil comedy of his own, a comedy which, it need hardly be said, adds nothing to his fame—*The Devil is An Ass*.[15] Pug gets Satan's permission to visit the earth, although the prince is very sceptical of his lieutenant's powers—in Satan's first speech Jonson takes the opportunity of satirizing eight popular beliefs of the time—and is decidedly jealous of his reputation.[16] Jonson, however, is not content to rework an old legend and let it go at that. He is ever the satirist, the critic of society, and seizes this as another opportunity to flay the vices and follies of his time. Pug is not so great an ass as is Fitzdottrel, the Londoner of means and boundless credulity who is thoroughly gulled by Meercraft, one of the "projectors" who thronged London in Jonson's day. Meercraft has a plan by which the "drowned lands" of England are to be reclaimed, and promises to make Fitzdottrel duke of them. Here is the situation that Jonson loved to create: a dupe, an imposter, and a comic butt. Here, however, the dupe becomes himself an imposter, thus giving the dramatist another target for his satire. Fitzdottrell, in order to regain the deed to his land, which Wittipol refuses to give up, pretends to be possessed of a devil; and this time it is the pompous justice, Sir Paul Eitherside, who is the dupe and who is quite seriously convinced that he is dealing with a real case of possession.[17] But when word is brought to him that Pug has disappeared from his cell in Newgate, leaving only his clothes and an odor of brimstone behind him, Fitzdottrell confesses his counterfeiting and Meercraft is left holding an empty sack into which he had hoped to stuff the Londoner's ducats.

[14] See his dedication to *Volpone*.
[15] See Herford and Simpson's *Ben Jonson* (Oxford, 1925), for a brief but most able discussion of this play.
[16] Satan warns Pug: " . . . The state of hell must care Whom it employs in point of reputation, Here about London."
[17] Shakespeare, it will be recollected, had already had his laugh at the expense of those who believed in possession and exorcism. Dr. Pinch (*Comedy of Errors*) is a case in point, and in *Twelfth Night* (III, iv; IV, ii) the laughter is even sharper.

Now, the existence of these three plays, all of which were on the boards and were more or less popular during the first sixteen years of the seventeenth century, indicates the continued favor with which the public greeted its old favorite, the stage devil. Each is based on current folk-lore or legend; and each was evidently written to meet the box-office demand. Furthermore, it may be noted that each is distinctly satirical in tone. The satire of *Grim* is that of its original. Much of Dekker's satire is rather without point, for he failed to "bring it up to date"; but the raillery which is tucked onto the end of the play is unmistakable. Jonson's comedy so closely approaches that anomaly called the "play with a purpose" that his satire quite outstrips his Pug and centers on the projector and his gull. Nevertheless, Jonson's play, poor as it is, is the best of the three, and his satire, as might be expected, is by far the most trenchant.

*The Institute of Arts and Sciences,*
  *Columbia University.*

# A PIRACY OF POPE'S *ILIAD*

## By R. H. Griffith

Pope made choice of the subscription method for publishing his translation of the Iliad, and issued his work in installments,—Volume I in 1715, II in 1716, III in 1717, IV in 1718, and V and VI together in 1720. In the history of this publication two points were occasions of puzzlement to me when I was preparing the *Bibliography* of Pope, Part I (1923), and for some time afterward. One point is, why was the year 1719 skipped over? And the other is a discrepancy in Dr. Johnson's account of a pirated edition of the Iliad. Now it looks to me that the two points are connected. To take up the latter point for discussion first. Dr. Johnson, in the *Life* of Pope, writes:

> It is unpleasant to relate that the bookseller [Bernard Lintot], after all his hopes and all his liberality, was, by a very unjust and illegal action, defrauded of his profit. An edition of the English "Iliad" was printed in Holland in Duodecimo, and imported clandestinely for the gratification of those who were impatient to read what they could not yet afford to buy. This fraud could only be counteracted by an edition equally cheap and more commodious; and Lintot was compelled to contract his Folio at once into a Duodecimo, and lose the advantage of an intermediate gradation. The notes, which in the Dutch copies were placed at the end of each book, as they had been in the large volumes, were now subjoined to the text in the same page, and are therefore more easily consulted. Of this edition [Lintot's duodecimo, 1720] two thousand five hundred were first printed, and five thousand [Lintot's duodecimo "Second Edition," 1720-1721] a few weeks afterwards; but indeed great numbers were necessary to produce considerable profit.

Dr. Johnson may have examined a copy of the pirated edition or he may have drawn all his information from Lintot's account-book, to which he had access. Professor Courthope, too, may have seen a copy, but the account of the transaction set out in his *Life* of Pope looks like a paraphrase of the Doctor's, slightly marred by misinterpretation; he writes:

> Lintot's spirited enterprise was exposed to rough weather through fraudulent competition. A pirated edition of the first four books was produced in Holland, to meet which he was obliged to withdraw the folio he had printed, and to produce the volume in duodecimo, but his confidence never failed him, and the new issue contained seven thousand five hundred copies, a standing proof of the vast increase in the number of

readers since the time of the Revolution. It is satisfactory to find that the publisher's courage met with its due reward. Lintot made his fortune from the speculation, and both he and his son served in the office of High Sheriff of Sussex.

At the time of publishing my *Bibliography* thus much was all I knew of the Dutch piracy of the Iliad. I had no copy; and since Dr. Johnson's time no bibliographer or cataloguer had, so far as I could trace the matter, described the edition or even seen it. Not long ago I procured a half set, Volumes I-III; and subsequently the Bodleian Library, at Oxford, became possessor of Volumes II-VI (and of a Volume I dated 1729). On the basis of these volumes I present a few notes to the readers who are interested in Pope books.

From Dr. Johnson's account I inferred that the Dutch edition appeared first in 1720; but in fact, part of it appeared earlier. Johnson uses (properly) the word "book" to mean one of the twenty-four cantos into which the Iliad is divided, each of Pope's volumes containing four "books," or cantos. What Courthope means by "book" is uncertain. If he means canto, he implies the Dutch bookseller issued his Volume I in 1715; but then he is wrong, if present knowledge is definitive. If by "book" Courthope means volume, he implies that the Dutchman published Volumes I-IV in 1718, and then he is nearly right, though it's hard to believe Courthope knew the facts; certainly Lintot did not "withdraw the folio edition" in 1718 or for many years later.

The Dutch adventurer was T. Johnson, Bookseller at The Hague. Before 1718 he had already poached in Pope's preserves (or Lintot's, to stick to the facts), and he was to continue to do so for twenty years to come. Indeed, he was the greatest pirate publisher of the day, greater than Henry Hills, Jr., or even Edmund Curll, who has commonly been reputed the greatest and most flagrant among book pirates. T. Johnson had already included Shakespeare, Congreve, Addison, and numerous others among the authors whose works he printed and vended in London in spite of laws. In 1716 he had pirated Pope's *Rape of the Lock,* calling his the Fifth Edition.[1] In 1736 he pirated the *Essay on Man* and other things.[2]

---

[1] In the *Bibliography* of Pope, see Book No. 62 (p. 55) and the note affixed.

[2] *Ibid.,* Book No. 391 (p. 313).

As for Pope's Iliad, T. Johnson appears to have held back until Lintot had issued three volumes (1715-16-17). In 1718 he placed on sale these three volumes in a pocket size, and in 1719 added Volume IV. To stop his infractions was difficult, impossible indeed; he and his shop at The Hague were outside English jurisdiction. For this reason Lintot, I think, as soon as he learned of Johnson's infringement, persuaded Pope to agree to postpone the issuance of the fifth installment till 1720, when it and the final (sixth) volume could be issued together, and when he might also have his own small size edition printed and ready to be placed on sale as soon as the cream of the trade had made its purchases of the folio issues, thus beating The Hague bookseller to market.

This is not the place for a detailed bibliographical description of the Dutch edition, but two or three points will be of interest. The volumes are small octavos, *i. e.*, the signatures are in eight's, though Dobell (Cat. 95, June, 1930) in describing the Bodleian copy called them duodecimos. The titlepage of each of the six volumes carries the monogram of T. Johnson. The imprint in Vols. I-IV is: *London. Printed by T. J. for B. L. & other Booksellers.* In Vols. V-VI it is: *London. Printed by T. Johnson.* In my set Vols. I-III are dated 1718; in the Bodleian set Vol. IV 1719, and V-VI, 1721. The illustrations are, in Vol. I, a frontispiece bust of Homer (a copy of Lintot's copperplate reduced and reversed), a plate of coins at the end of the Preface, a folding-plate in the Essay on Homer, and a folding-plate map of Greece at the end of the volume; in Vol. II, a frontispiece portrait of Pope (as in Book No. 103), and a folding-plate map of Troy after the titleleaf; in Vol. III, a frontispiece bust of Homer (repeated from Vol. I); and in Vol. V (Bodleian copy) a folding-plate in the latter part of the volume.

Much change in matter is not to be expected. In Vols. I-III, three footnotes are added, I, p. 81; I, p. 106 ("M. Boivin has lately given a curious draught of this Shield, which shall be inserted in the XVIII. Book," referring to the illustration in Vol. V); and on p. 14 (prose) of Vol. II; at the end of Vol. II is a "Catalogue of English Plays," much the same as that described under Book No. 62 (*Bibliography* of Pope, p. 55).

Johnson's comment upon his own piracy is worth quoting in full;

it is headed, "The Booksellers Advertisement On this new Edition:"

This excellent Translation of Homer's Iliad, being so universally esteemed by all those that have any taste of Learning or Poetry, it will undoubtedly be very acceptable to the publick to have a neat Edition of it in small portable volumes: For not only such as cannot well afford to go to the expense of six volumes in folio, will be glad to have the same thing in as many pocket volumes at less than a quarter of the price; but even those that have generously contributed by their subscriptions to give that encouragement so justly due to the ingenious Author for publishing this work, & thereby have acquired the large volumes for their Librarys, will be well pleased to have also these little volumes for their ease & conveniency to carry about with them either in Town or Country.

There has been a good deal of care & pains taken to have this Edition correct as well as neat, & it is hoped with so good success that the Reader will find very few faults of any consequences. A few small literal slips of a *c* for an *e*, an *n* for an *u*, an ſ [*s*] for an *f* or the like, when they do not alter the sense, will be easily pardoned by a candid Reader, especially if he has any experience of printing & correcting the press. Those that have that experience know how difficult, or next to impossible it is to have any book, or even a single sheet, wrought off absolutely without a fault; & those that have not should be sparing in their censures till they have tryed to correct 30. or 40. sheets only for the press, & seen their success. Such a tryal would be an excellent school of patience & moderation, & might also be usefull in many other respects. Many of the great men of the XVIth. century (the most glorious for learning since that of Augustus) thought it worth their pains to correct for the press; & then even the Printers themselves were men of considerable learning; which is the reason why the Books printed in that age are generally more correct & more esteemed by men of judgement, than most of those that have been published since by Printers & Correctors very unlike those above mentioned.

But to return to our present Edition, it has been thought necessary for its greater beauty to leave out that prodigious number of Capitals, which disfigures the page, by an abuse introduced, thro' want of taste, into English books more than any other. Care has been taken to have the copper plates better & neater done than those of the folio Edition, & some are added which, 'tis hoped, will not be disagreeable. What other improvements are made the curious Readers will find by comparing this with the former Edition. If the care & pains taken on this work be agreeable to the judicious & curious Readers, it will be very gratefull to their most humble servant,

the Bookseller.

T. Johnson did not stop with printing Pope's Iliad once. The Bodleian copy of Volume I is different from my copy; it is dated

1729 on the titlepage, and a collation [3] shows that it is printed from a new setting of type in part, if not entirely. The half-title of my (1718) copy reads: *Homer's Iliad. In English Verse;* the Bodleian (1729) copy repeats this and adds: *A New Edition, carefully revised & corrected by the Author in a great many places.*

We have yet to learn how many editions pirate Johnson issued, and whether or not he made his further compliments to Pope by pirating the Odyssey also.

*University of Texas.*

---

[3] For great courtesy and much helpful correspondence I have most sincerely to thank Mr. Stephen Wright, of the Bodleian Library.

# SHENSTONE'S HEROI-COMICAL POEM

## By Richmond P. Bond

The Augustan age in England stimulated the growth and flowering of the mock-heroic poem. The most skillful and perhaps the most interesting type of mock-heroic was the "heroi-comical"—a type that claimed the *beau monde* as its *milieu*, a type that elevated "Snuff, Patches, Paste, and Billet doux" to heroic proportions and portrayed the life of Society with a smiling accuracy. Such teacup epics represent a bygone mode; Pope's famous burlesque has far overshadowed, and rightly, the other jests of Homer in harlequin.

The two favorite subjects of the heroi-comical poem were the social incident and the invention of a social object; Pope's *The Rape of the Lock* and Gay's *The Fan,* respectively, were the principal instigators of these vogues.[1] Among the poems that celebrated some happening in the whirl of Society there are *The Battel: or, Morning-Interview,* by Allan Ramsay, 1716, *The Rape of the Smock,* by Giles Jacob, 1717; *The Assembly,* by Richard Barford, 1726; *Clarinda,* by James Ralph, 1729; *The Fall,* by James Thurston, 1732; *The Pettycoat,* 1738; *Pamela,* 1744. Among the poems devoted to the subject of inventing an article regarded as important in high life we have *The Petticoat,* by "Joseph Gay," 1716; *The Kite,* by Phanuel Bacon, 1722; *The Patch,* by Francis Hauksbee, 1723 (?); *The Shuttlecock,* by Anthony Whistler, 1736; *The Thimble,* by William Hawkins, 1744. Shenstone's unpublished heroi-comical poem, *The Snuff-box,* belongs to this second class.[2]

Snuff and snuff-boxes were as important to the eighteenth-century belle and beau as the fan and the cane. Pulverized, scented tobacco was used in great quantities within and without the fash-

---

[1] The episode of the patten in Gay's *Trivia* was also influential in the establishment of the invention type. Related to the heroi-comical poem was the kind that treated a game; cf. Concanen's *Match at Foot-Ball* (1720), Somervile's *Bowling-Green* (1727), Mathison's *Goff* (1743), Love's *Cricket* (1744?), and Whitehead's *Gymnasiad* (1744).

[2] This was not, of course, Shenstone's only effort in burlesque poetry; besides the famous Spenserian parody, *The School-Mistress,* a mock pastoral, "Colemira," appeared in his *Poems upon Various Occasions* (Oxford, 1737), pp. 11-14.

ionable world. Satire and taxes were not sufficient to drive out snuff; it was Time, as usual, that did the trick. Meanwhile, the proper style was cultivated for the handling of the pungent grains and the display of the receptacle. The art of cunning workers in gold, silver, enamel, and gem produced boxes that pleased the vanity of the fop and the fair. Here was an ideal article: it offered opportunity for varied and rich ornamentation; its correct manipulation denoted an acquaintance with the *bon ton;* and it served as a convenient container for the divine snuff itself.[3]

The British Museum contains a long poem in Shenstone's handwriting (Add. MS. 15,913); it was purchased at Upcott's sale in 1846. On the flyleaf Isaac Reed's name and the date 1800 appear; Reed wrote, "This is an original unprinted poem by *William Shenstone,* Esq., in his own hand writing—See what is said of it by M$^r$ Graves in his 'Recollection' p: 90." On folio 1, above the "Advertisement," in another hand there is this severe sentence, " This Poem of the Snuff-box—tho' not without some good Lines— disgusts by being too close an imitation of Pope's Rape of the Lock—& is quite a Juvenile performance." Folio 1 *verso* is given to the motto:

> Hi Motus animorum, atq, haec certamina tanta
> Pulveris exigui jactu compressa quiescunt.

The poem itself, "The Snuff-box, an Heroi-comical Poem written MDCCXXXV," occupies folios 2-25; there are six cantos and 845 lines, a score of which have been cancelled. The revisions are mostly in pencil and are not important. On folio 25 *verso* there is the Horatian tag, " Hæc ego mecum Compressis agito labris, for my Prise Sentences." [4]

The poem begins:

> Speak gentle goddess! since you best can show
> How *human* Loves from *heavenly* causes flow!
> The wond'rous influence trivial toys retain,
> And Fate dependent on a single grain!     [f. 2]

---

[3] Numerous references to snuff and snuff-boxes may be found in eighteenth-century literature. James Arbuckle's *Snuff* (1719), is particularly illuminating. See also *Pandora's Box: a Satyr against Snuff* (1718); there is a good passage on the snuff-box and the custom of having a picture within the lid, pp. 6-10.

[4] *Serm.*, I, 4, 137.

Melissa the belle shows disdain for all her lovers, including Lorenzo.

> What dire suspense awaits yᵉ lovely Dame!
> Can mortal Fair reject each various claim?
> What can she more? relentless & unkind,
> In bright *Lorenzo* she rejects them join'd. [ff. 2v-3]

The palace of Vanity is described.

> Here crystal wainscots paint th' enamour'd queen;
> Where'er she moves, unnumber'd selfs are seen.
> Each radiant Pannel diff'rent grace bestows;
> And ev'ry grace, when view'd, sublimer grows.
> Here she extatick wanders o'er her charms;
> Sees gods enslav'd, & goddesses in Arms!
> Much to this Queen yᵉ world it's Poets owes;
> The Belles, their Peace; their every care, yᵉ beaux.
> *Art's* various charms, from her protection, rise;
> And *Science* wanders earth, & air, & skies.
> She arm'd with smooth deceit yᵉ sons of men;
> The tongue, yᵉ glass, yᵉ pencil, & yᵉ Pen!
> Light seems yᵉ Dome, as visionary dreams;
> As fairy turrets, or poetick schemes.
> The lucid crystals form a waving Sea;
> Move with each wind, & every gale obey:
> Oft envious Eol ends her rising Joys;
> Ruffles a charm, & all her peace destroys. [ff. 3-3v]

Vanity visits the earth in various disguises in order to exert her potent influence. She appears at Melissa's toilette and flatters the beautiful maid, for whom "youth may justly *sigh,* but sigh in *vain.*" Her advice is to let "grandeur move, & splendour fire" the mind, to forsake the "lowly plains" for the gay court.

> Shall gems & Lace embellish Love in vain?
> And solid merit recommend the swain? . . .
> For you young nobles shall their stars renew;
> And garters shine more ravishingly blue;
> Your radiant Eyes yᵉ distant Sun supply;
> Your radiant chariot wᵗʰ his carr shall vie;
> Charms, bright as yours, may Rank, may titles claim:
> What means, my Fair, Lorenzo's vulgar Flame?
> She ceas'd; yᵉ Nymph enraptur'd sees, & hears,
> Shine yᵉ gilt coach, & neigh yᵉ Flanders mares.
> The sumptuous watch surveys wᵗʰ brilliants crownd,
> And Coronets on evry trifle found,
> Gold-clocks in chains more fiercely pleasd to see.
> Shock barks—& sets a thousand nobles free. [ff. 5v-6]

In the second canto the slighted Parliament of Heaven convenes.

> Here y̲e̲ grave Pow'rs from noisy courts w̲t̲h̲ draw,
> To mix a Liquor, or contrive a Law:
> To human bliss, or heav'nly joys wish well;
> Drink George's health, or toast a favrite Belle.
> A falling state, or broken glass bemoan;
> Or burst w̲t̲h̲ Laughter, at an *Eastern* throne. [f. 6v]

Venus is the first speaker; she objects to the submission of the gods to "one terrestrial Fair." She tells of a "beauteous flow'r"; its "fragrant branches drop divine perfumes" and its "wither'd Leaves" have proved of "sovereign Influence in rejected Love." Minerva volunteers to conduct the compound to the fair. The gods collaborate to "raise y̲e̲ fair Design." Apollo recommends amber, and Plutus promises to provide the golden ore. One of the attendant Cupids has three of his purple plumes enshrined in the amber gum; Minerva selects this specimen and thus comforts the "Veteran, wounded in his sovereign's Cause."

The third canto begins thus:

> Cupid o'er human minds resistless reigns;
> Fierce in his joys, unrival'd in his Pains.
> Not *Jove*, when hypocrites his shrine adore;
> Not *Juno*, when her altar smokes no more;
> Not *Bacchus*, when y̲e̲ schools inhibit wine;
> Not *Mars*, when peacefull mortals nurse y̲e̲ vine;
> Not *Phoebus*, when from Pope's distinguisd brows
> *Dennis* w̲d̲ rend y̲e̲ Laurels, *He* bestows;
> Revolve such vengeance, or such Pangs decree,
> As owe their source, relentless Boy! to thee. [f. 9v]

The spurned, desponding Lorenzo asks aid of Cupid, who, resolving to have a hand in the scheme, contributes the diamond with which to decorate the box. Here the story of Brillante furnishes a long digression; she had refused Apollo and after death was formed into the gem that "wounding all, itself untouch'd remains."

In the fourth section, Venus, expert in essences and draughts, prepares the deadly grain; she scents the product with two whole drops.

> Now to the Phial Beauty's queen repairs;
> The Phial, Source of all Melissa's cares!
> Killing y̲e̲ drops, y̲e̲ soft-ey'd virgins shed;
> Their Squirrel missing, or their Lover dead;

> Killing yᵉ drops, Pæonian Pens distill;
> When Ignorance guides, or Caprice joggs yᵉ Quill.
> But Drops like these require'd a skill divine;
> Ah! far more killing, mighty Ward! yⁿ thine! [ff. 16-16v]

The gods again convene and debate the design to be painted on the "powerfull toy."

> Then *Momus* rose—contemn'd each various plan,
> And wᵗʰ insulting accents, thus began.
> "Tis strange yᵗ courts, where female councils join
> To vanquish female art, shou'd want *design*.
> If to a female Eye, Ye Pow'rs, be known
> No Arts, no charms, so pleasing as their own;
> And if, with mortal Dames, by intrest fir'd,
> The giver pleases, when yᵉ gift's admir'd;
> If constant Flatt'ry, wᶜʰ all Nymphs embrace,
> Still wins yᵉ Heart, wⁿ level'd at the Face;
> To gain our End, wᵗ Picture can surpass
> That sweet bewitching toy, a Looking-glass?" [f. 17v]

This plan is approved, though grudgingly by Jove. The next canto opens thus:

> Now to Love's Queen the glitt'ring toy was givn;
> Form'd by yᵉ peerless mechanist of Heav'n!
> A Rim of gold yᵉ breathing amber bounds;
> And, chas'd with matchless art, yᵉ Lid surrounds.
> Around yᵉ brilliant, streams a vivid blaze;
> Destin'd e'er while to meet wᵗʰ rival Rays!
> The Hinge alone was wrapt in dark disguise;
> The curious Hinge eludes all mortal Eyes.
> No prying Artist cᵈ its Joints explain;
> And *microscoptick* art was try'd in vain! [f. 18v]

Venus tests the vows, sighs, and prayers of the beaux and decides to award the trinket to Lorenzo. A tea scene is described, which is followed by a digression on Thea the gossip.[5]

In the last canto the belles tell fortunes; Melissa issues cautions against "each soft approach of Love". Lorenzo appears and produces the toy, which "wᵗʰ glory rang'd yᵉ Room."

> Now had yᵉ Box, by snowy Hands conveyd,
> Engag'd yᵉ wonder of yᵉ scornfull Maid:
> While from each grain incentive odours rise,

---

[5] Cf. Nahum Tate's *Panacea: a Poem upon Tea* (1700), and the anonymous *Tea* (1743).

She strives in vain to slight y^e radiant Prize
And views y^e giver with no scornfull Eyes.
Fate guides her hand—y^e lovely victim stains
Her ruby Lip w^th four well-tinctur'd grains!
Thrice screams her bird; & Shocks resounding voice
The sympathetick spinnet thrice replies:
Quick to y^e distant clock y^e voice resounds;
And y^e press'd Bell returns three languid Sounds.
To her dear *Cynthia* Vanity repairs;
Who answers all her Love, & equals all her Cares.

[ff. 24v-25]

Richard Graves referred to *The Snuff-box* and other poems of the same stamp as servile imitations of the *Rape* in which the authors "copied from books, and not from real life." Accordingly, Dodsley did not insert that poem in Shenstone's works, but Graves thought "as it has some merit, it might, as a curiosity, be an agreeable present to the many admirers of Mr. Shenstone."[6] Graves also mentioned "a little mock-heroic poem called 'The Diamond'" as one of the imitations of Pope's masterpiece and as the poet's "first production worth mentioning."[7] The preface to *The Snuff-box,* the "Advertisement, MDCCL," affirms the youthfulness of the piece, gives the author's criticism of it, and mentions *The Diamond*.

The following Poem was written amongst y^e Author's earliest compositions; tho' y^e Plan was afterwards extended, in order to include some separate Pieces which now make part of it. This may serve to account for y^e perplexity & Air of constraint y^t appears throughout y^e Fable. It was not transcrib'd by him as worthy any one's Perusal, except his own; and *that* only as it calls to Mind the particular *Place* and *time* of *Life*, at w^ch it was written. What *little* Merit it has, must depend rather on y^e *particular* ornaments y^n any symmetry in y^e *whole;* to w^ch it has no pretension.

NB. All y^t relates to the Diamond was a separate Poem, & tends to render this more confused, & unaccountable.

[f. 1]

Moreover, Shenstone wrote to Lady Luxborough, March, 1750/51:

Mean time y^e complaint you make of y^e present want of Amusement gives me an occasion to pour in Floods of my *written* Impertinence. The Progress of Taste I meant to shew you long ago: The Snuff-box (which by

---

[6] *Recollection of Some Particulars In the Life of the late William Shenstone, Esq. In a Series of Letters* (1788), p. 90.

[7] *Ibid.*, pp. 88-89.

interweaving another poem or two is now I see a mere Piece of Patchwork) appears before you for no other Reason in ye world but yt it happens to be transcribed in ye same Book with ye former; & is interested in my desiring you not to read a Line of it.[8]

Of these separate pieces that made *The Snuff-box* seem a patchwork, the poem called *The Diamond* is without doubt the most important.[9] This work was not printed until fifteen years after Shenstone's death. It was sent by an unknown lady to Thomas Hull, who printed it in his *Select Letters . . . of 1778*.[10] This lady in her accompanying letter claimed to be no judge of the merit of the poem but judged from its authorship that it was "not destitute." She had been pleased by Hull's revival of Shenstone's name, and she wished to make some acknowledgment; "for should not the *Diamond* have Brilliancy enough for the Public, yet it may not be an unwelcome Amusement to a private Friend, to remove the Dimness."[11]

---

[8] Bodl. MS. Montagu d. 18, f. 97. See also B. M. Add. MS. 28, 958 f. 110, and Thomas Hull's *Select Letters between the late Duchess of Somerset, Lady Luxborough, Miss Dolman, Dr. Whistler, Mr. R. Dodsley, William Shenstone, Esq, and Others . . .* (1778), I, 116-117.

[9] A short poem, "The Snuff-Box," which appeared in Shenstone's *Poems upon Various Occasions* (1737), pp. 56-57, was probably a sort of first draft or even a by-product. It has in common with the much longer poem of the same title an allusion to Parnell, who "has divinely sung" how "from the plastic Hand *Pandora* sprung," which is obviously a reference to Parnell's *Hesiod; or, the Rise of Woman*. Another poem in this miscellany, "Cupid and Plutus," pp. 53-54, has phrasal resemblances to *The Snuff-box*.

[10] II, 193-212. Hull had been friendly with Shenstone and indebted to him for important suggestions in the composition of the tragedy, *Henry the Second; or, the Fall of Rosamond* (1774). The dedication of the play to Shenstone prompted the lady to forward *The Diamond*, which had been in her possession for some years.

[11] II, 190-191, Letter XLIV, dated Dec. 28, 1774, signed "M." She wrote to Hull a second time, II, 213-214, Letter XLV, Jan. 16, 1775, signed "Mrs. W." Hull had apparently written to her and compared the manner of the poem with that of the *Rape;* she replied that she prefered the former, "even against POPE, and this because I think there is greater Delicacy of Sentiment: but what else could be expected from a Mind, the Characteristics of which were refined Sensibility, and unbounded Benevolence?" In this connection it is interesting to note the title of a poem that appeared the next year: *Shenstone; or, The Force of Benevolence.*

Shenstone at the end of *The Diamond* wrote, " This was written before the *Snuff-Box,* at the time I lived at *Harborough,* perhaps about the Year 1734, and has a more simple Plan than the other; but has little or nothing to recommend it besides." A reading of the poem, in three cantos and 340 lines, will make clear how obviously it was the basis for the later work. Notwithstanding many omissions and additions, *The Diamond* was practically incorporated in *The Snuff-box.* Canto I of the former can easily be seen in Canto III of the latter; Canto II of the shorter poem went into Cantos V and VI of the longer. The digressions on Brillante and Thea are in both poems. In *The Diamond* the protagonists are named Lamira and Myrtillo; the brilliant is the deciding factor in the winning of the belle. Despite its comparative brevity *The Diamond* is not better organized, and the verse is inferior to that of *The Snuff-box.*

There is no reason to charge Shenstone with excessive modesty in his criticisms (given above) of *The Snuff-box.* He frankly regarded it as a youthful performance; he recognized its lack of symmetry and its patched nature. Nor was he wrong in preferring the " *particular* ornaments." The poem is a juvenile exercise in an established *genre;* it lacks the organization of other poems of the type; it is not comparable to *The Rape of the Lock.* It was, however, probably good practice for the production of later levities. Often the poet has neatly caught a Popean trick; there are many good lines and passages. The mild burlesque tone proper to the heroi-comical poem is at times captured; the mirror of Society is here not dim. And, after all, may we not vouchsafe gentle Shenstone the fun he had in writing *The Diamond* and *The Snuff-box?*

*The University of North Carolina.*

# THE HERMIT AND DIVINE PROVIDENCE

## By Arthur Palmer Hudson

There is a tale illustrating the workings of divine providence which attracted the monks of the Middle Ages, a dreamy English Platonist of the Restoration period, a most conspicuous high priest of the New England theocracy, a convivial parson-poet of the circle of Pope and Swift, and the arch-skeptic of the eighteenth century (perhaps of all time). This long-continued and varied appeal would suggest a story with an interesting literary history and a remarkable degree of flexibility for theological application. Such is the Parable of the Hermit, which appears in the *Gesta Romanorum* (*ante* 1326),[1] in Doctor Henry More's *Divine Dialogues* (1668),[2] in Cotton Mather's *Magnalia* (1702),[3] in Thomas Parnell's *Poems* (1721),[4] and in Voltaire's *Zadig, histoire orientale* (1741).[5] Several other treatments of the story will be mentioned later; these are the most important.

With incidental glances at the relations of these literary versions to one another and to traits of the folk-tale, it is the purpose of this paper to suggest the values of the five treatments as indexes of the intellectual outlooks and artistic powers of the story-tellers.

In order to present the salient features of the story and to lay a basis for comparison, I give the following brief synopsis of it as it appears in the *Gesta Romanorum*:

---

[1] No. LXXX, trans. Charles Swan, with a Preface by E. A. Baker (London, n. d.).

[2] *Divine Dialogues, containing Sundry Disquisitions and Instructions concerning the Attributes of God and His Providence in the World*, Collected and Compiled by the Care and Industry of Franciscus Palaeopolitanus, Second Edition (London, 1713), pp. 165 ff.

[3] *Magnalia Christi Americana; or, The Ecclesiastical History of New-England, from Its First Planting in the Year 1620, unto the Year of Our Lord, 1698*, First American Edition, from the London Edition of 1702, 2 vols. (Hartford, 1820), I, 172-3.

[4] Ed. George A. Aitken, *The Poetical Works of Thomas Parnell, with Memoirs and Notes* (London, 1894), pp. 100 ff.

[5] *Oeuvres complètes de Voltaire, Nouvelle édition avec notices, préfaces, variants, table analytique, les notes de tous les commentateurs et des notes nouvelles conforme pour le texte à l'édition de Beuchot* (Paris, 1879), XXI, 86 ff.

A devout hermit who dwelt in a cave was led, by seeing an innocent shepherd put to death and the real author of the crime in question escape, to doubt the justice of God's providence. He therefore set out to see what the world was like. He was soon joined by an angel in the form of a man. At the end of the first day of their travels, the two spent the night with a soldier, who entertained them with generous hospitality. Before departing the next morning, the angel approached the cradle in which slept the only child of the soldier, and strangled it. The hermit was, of course, horrified. "Never can this be an angel of God!" he exclaimed. At the end of their second day's journey the two were feasted and lodged by a convivial citizen of another city. On their departure the angel stole the citizen's "superb golden cup." On the same day, crossing a bridge under guidance of a kindly pilgrim, the angel repaid the pilgrim by pushing him into the stream below, where he was drowned. "It is the devil!" cried the hermit. That night the two travelers were given lodging in a pig-sty by the ungracious master of a house. In the morning the angel requited this hospitality by presenting the master the "superb golden cup." Here the hermit said to himself, "Now I am certain that this is the devil," and sought to part company with the angel. But the latter stayed him and made him listen to an explanation of these strange events.

God had allowed the shepherd to be slain because He had foreseen that the shepherd was about to commit a mortal sin and die unrepentant. Now he dwells in bliss. The guilty man, however, is to suffer eternally. The angel slew the child to save its father from parsimony and covetousness on behalf of his heir. He stole the cup to save the owner from intemperance. He drowned the pilgrim to save him from a meditated mortal sin. He gave the cup to the person who had lodged them in the swinehouse as a consideration for hospitality; the master "will hereafter reign in hell." Thus the hermit was admonished "to detract not from the Almighty. He knoweth all things well."

Analyzing the five versions of the story in a manner suggested by the systematic method that has long been employed in Finland in the study of popular traditions,[6] we have the following scheme:

---

[6] See, for example, Archer Taylor, "The Black Ox, a Study in the History of a Folk-Tale," *FF Communications* No. 70 (Helsinki, 1927).

## The Narrative Proper

| Elements | Gesta Romanorum | More |
|---|---|---|
| Setting: | "Remote cave." | A "cell." |
| Inciting Force: | Unjust execution of a shepherd leads Hermit to doubt justice of God. Resolved to "do as other men do." | "Jealousies touching the due administration of Divine Providence." Hermit resolves "to see how things went abroad." |
| Real Character of Expositor of Providence: | Revealed to the reader and to the Hermit: "An angel in the form of a man. | Not revealed either to reader or to Hermit: "A young man." |
| Incidents in Order: 1 | Angel strangled only son of "a certain soldier" who had entertained him and Hermit. | Young man "stole away a guilt cup from the Gentleman of the House." |
| 2 | Angel "purloined a superb golden cup" from a hospitable host. | Young man rewarded an unhospitable host with the cup. |
| 3 | Angel threw an obliging pilgrim guide from a bridge into a stream. | Young man "strangled the child of their so courteous host." |
| 4 | Angel rewarded pigsty hospitality of a surly householder by giving him the golden cup. | Young man pitched over a "stone-bridge" and drowned a servant guide sent by host. |
| 5 | Hermit: "Now I am certain that this is the devil. . . . I will travel with you no longer." Angel explained. "Detract not from the Almighty." | Hermit "would travel with him no longer. Hermit reveals angelic character. "Sent to ease his mind of anxiety touching the Divine Providence." |

The Narrative Proper (*cont.*)

| Mather | Parnell | Voltaire |
|---|---|---|
| Unspecified. | "Far in a wild," "cave," "moss his bed." | Unspecified. A chance meeting. |
| "Vexed with blasphemous Injections about the wisdom of Divine Providence." Invited by an angel to see "hidden judgments of God." | "That vice should triumph, virtue vice obey. This sprung some doubt of Providence's sway." "To clear this doubt." | Zadig, not the hermit, "full of despair and secretly accusing Providence." |
| Revealed to reader but not to Hermit: "An angel in human shape." | Not revealed either to reader or to Hermit: "youth," "complexion fair," "graceful ringlets." | Not revealed to reader or to Zadig: "A hermit," "white beard[ed]," reading book of fate. |
| Hermit's companion "took away a valuable cup from their Host." | "Younger guest purloined the golden goblet." | Hermit stole from the host a golden basin "garnished with rubies and emeralds." |
| Companion "bestowed cup upon a very wicked host." | "Young companion paid [a miser host] profusely with the precious bowl." | Hermit paid a rich miser with the golden bowl. |
| Angel threw from bridge into stream "servant of a Godly man" by whom they had been "lovingly treated." | Young companion "writh'd the neck" of his pious, frank, and sober host's only child. | Hermit "evidenced his esteem and affection for" a kind, philosophical host by setting fire to his house. |
| Angel "did unaccountably kill" the only child of a "very Godly man who had most courteously treated them." | Youth pushed from "Long arms of oaks [that] an open bridge supplied" a servant that "show'd the way." | Hermit drowned the nephew and sole hope of a poor widow, their late hostess, who had sent the boy to guide them over a bad bridge. |
| Companion would have left his guardian, but Angel addressed him, "Understand now the secret judgments of God." | "Detested wretch." But here youth resumed angelic nature: "Then know the truth of government divine." | Zadig denounces. Hermit turns into angel Jesrad. Explains divine unity, harmony. "Cease to dispute with what should be adored." |

### The Explanation

| Action. | Gesta Romanorum | More |
|---|---|---|
| Child was killed: | To save the father from becoming covetous and parsimonious for the child's sake. | To save the father from doting too much on the child, to the peril of his own soul. |
| The cup [bowl] was stolen: | To save the owner from intemperance. | To save a charitable man from intemperance that would have destroyed his benevolences to society. |
| The cup [bowl] was given to a miser: | As a "valuable consideration for hospitality." But the miser will "reign in hell." | "As a Plague and Scourge" to the "harsh, unhospitable Man, . . . that he may fall into intemperance." |
| The obliging guide was killed: | To save him from a meditated mortal sin. | To prevent him from slaying his master for his money. |

This analysis leaves out of account two incidents, and the corresponding explanations, not common to all five versions. In the *Gesta* story it is explained that Providence willed that the shepherd should be unjustly put to death because it was foreseen that he was about to commit a sin and die unrepentant. The guilty man, for whose crime the shepherd was executed, is to suffer eternally. In Voltaire's *Zadig,* the angel Jesrad explains that his reason for setting fire to the house of his host was that the latter might find, beneath the ruins, a great buried treasure.

With possible exceptions, to be noted later, the *Gesta Romanorum* version of the story is the oldest in English literature. Speculations as to the date of composition and authorship of the *Gesta* as a whole have varied from those of Warton, Madden, Eschenberg, and others, placing it as probably before 1326 and connecting it with Pierre Bercheur (Berchorius), a native of Poitou, who was prior of the Benedictine convent of St. Eloi, at Paris, and who

EXPLANATION (cont.)

| Mather | Parnell | Voltaire |
|---|---|---|
| Substantially the same—to save the father from the sin of covetousness. | "To save the father. ... The child half-weaned his heart from God." | To keep him from killing his aunt and his prince; also, lest, living, he should be slain by his own son and wife. |
| "For the Advantage of his Interior," i. e., to save him from intemperance. | To save the owner from intemperance. | To teach a vain man the lesson of wisdom and prudence. |
| As a "present reward of his good works." | To make "compassion touch his grateful soul." | To teach the miser to exercise hospitality. |
| To keep him from carrying out "a bloody design to have slain his master." | To prevent him from murdering his master. | [Only one person, the nephew of the widow, is slain in this version.] |

died in 1362,[7] to Gaston Paris' more recent opinion that it was written down without doubt in England towards the end of the thirteenth century.[8]

The story of the hermit is not in the *Early English Versions* referred to above, but it was known in Anglo-Latin versions of the *Gesta*.[9] It occurs in the French collection of the *Gesta Romanorum* edited by M. G. Brunet.[10] The Latin sources of the two transla-

---

[7] See *The Early English Versions of the Gesta Romanorum, Formerly Edited by Sir Frederick Madden for the Roxburgh Club, and Now Re-Edited from the MSS. in the British Museum (Harl. 7333 and Addit. 9066) and University Library, Cambridge (Kk. 1.6), with Introduction, Notes, Glossary, &c.,* by Sidney J. H. Herritage, EETS, Extra Series, XXXIII (London, 1879; repr. 1898), pp. viii-x.

[8] *La poésie du moyen âge, Leçons et lectures*, Première série, Sixième édition (Paris, 1906), p. 154.

[9] Summarized by Herritage, *op. cit.*, in an appendix containing brief accounts of stories in the Anglo-Latin versions.

[10] *Le Violier des histoires romaines, ancienne traduction française des*

tions, English and French, are obviously close together. It appears with some minor variations in the pre-fifteenth-century Spanish *Libro de los enxemplos* as No. CLXI.[11]

The consensus of scholarly opinion as to the origin of the story of the hermit is that it is oriental, ultimately from Hebrew folk tradition.[12] Gaston Paris states that the most remote sources to which the occidental versions of the Middle Ages can be traced are intimately connected with the immense cycle of tales which concern the hermit life of the Fathers of the Desert.[13]

As to the moral intent of the story and the conduct of the narrative, the *Gesta* chapter title, "Of the Cunning of the Devil, and of the Secret Judgments of God," and my brief summary are almost sufficient to characterize it. The moral is naively monkish enough. The story is told with scarcely a line of picturesque description and with hardly an image. There is no effort at character portrayal. The mental and emotional reactions of the characters are of the simplest. The story is one of bare incidents. Moreover, as the reader must have observed from my summary, though it is straightforward, it has no regard for narrative suspense or climactic arrangement. The angel announces himself as such. His first act is his most terrible. In short, whatever the traditional original may have been, this is a tale stripped for homiletic action. Such, too, are the characteristics of the French and Spanish versions.

These characteristics, moreover, almost perfectly describe the various traditional versions of the story gathered from popular sources in several quarters of Europe,[14] or, for that matter, any typical folk-tale. A comparison between this body of popular versions and the best literary treatments of the theme, as to style and manner of variation and evolution, might show interesting differ-

*Gesta Romanorum, nouvelle édition, révue et annotée* (Paris, 1868), Ch. LXXVIII.

[11] Published in *Biblioteca de autores españoles*, Vol. 51 (Madrid, 1912), p. 485 ff.

[12] W. A. Clouston, *Popular Tales and Fictions: Their Migrations and Transformations*, 2 vols. (Edinburgh and London, 1887), I, 20 ff.; Brunet, *op. cit.*, p. 193.

[13] *Op. cit.*, pp. 153-169.

[14] The story belongs to type Mt 759 in the Aarne-Thompson system of classifying folk-tales. See *FF Communications*, Nos. 74, 25, 37, 90.

ences between the manner of growth of a tale in tradition and in literature; but limitations of space prohibit more than a suggestion of this aspect of the subject in my examination of the remaining four literary treatments selected for study.

Dr. Henry More (1614-1687), the author of the second version of the story under consideration, " represents the quintessence of Cambridge Platonism." [15] His *Divine Dialogues,* modeled on the Platonic scheme and representing in its *dramatis personæ* the personalities and the views of More's circle, is his best-known and most typical work.[16]

It is apparently not known where More found the source of his " Parable of the Hermit." There are several possibilities. There is, of course, first, the *Gesta,* well known in its Latin form before its complete translation in 1703. Axon remarks that More's story " follows very closely that given in the *Gesta.*" [17] But More did not follow closely, as a glance at my tabular analysis will show. According to both Axon and Warton,[18] two other versions were accessible to More—in James Howell's *Letters* and in Sir Percy Herbert's *Certaine Conceptions.* A fourth possibility is Bradwardine's *De Causa Dei,* of which more later.

The " Parable of the Hermit " is in the " Second Dialogue." [19] Philotheus, Bathynous, Sophron, Philopolis, Euistor, Hylobares, and Cuphophron are discussing the " two main Heads of Objections against Providence.... *The Evils that are in the World,* and *The Defect of Good."* After a somewhat lengthy discussion of the problem of evil, Euistor interrupts with the remark that Philotheus has solved that of " The Defect of Good," and adds, " The other

---

[15] E. A. George, *Seventeenth Century Men of Latitude, Forerunners of the New Theology* (New York, 1908), p. 109.

[16] M. F. Howard, ed., *The Life of the Learned and Pious Dr. Henry More, Late Fellow of Christ's College in Cambridge, by Richard Ward,* etc. (London, 1911), Introduction, pp. 14 ff.

[17] William E. A. Axon, " The Literary History of Parnell's ' Hermit,' " in *Memoirs of the Manchester Literary and Philosophical Society,* Third Series (London, 1882), VII, 144 ff.

[18] Thomas Warton, *History of English Poetry from the Twelfth to the Close of the Sixteenth Century,* ed. W. C. Hazlitt, 4 vols. (London, 1871), I, 257 ff.

[19] *Op. cit.,* pp. 165 ff.

which is the more ordinary, never seemed to me to have the least force in it, since I met with the story of the *Eremite* and the *Angel*." Upon the insistence of the others that he interpolate the story in Philotheus's discourse, Euistor relates it. At the conclusion Philotheus remarks that it is "so much to the purpose that it is plainly superfluous to add any more words touching this Theme." But the gentle author of the *Dialogues* apparently reconsidered Philotheus's judgment, for, later on, he reflects again on the moral, in part as follows:

> The affairs of this world are like a curious, but intricately contrived Comedy; and we cannot judge of the tendency of what is past, or acting at present, before the entrance of the last act, which shall be in righteousness and triumph; who, though she hath abided many a brunt, and has been cruelly and despitefully used hitherto in the World, yet at last, according to our desires, we shall see the knight overcome the giant.

Whatever one may think of the fundamental theological doctrine which the parable illustrates, its moral and spiritual elevation above the *Gesta* version is obvious at a glance. And, though perhaps More was little more interested in the artistic possibilities of the story than was the unknown compiler of the *Gesta,* there is an equal heightening of narrative effect. This is achieved by concealing both from the Hermit and the reader the angelic nature of the former's companion, until the climax of the story is reached, and by making the arrangement of incidents climactic. There is, too, a more effective sequence between the purloining and the giving of the cup. Finally, of course, the increased impressiveness of the story is due to the frame in which it is placed—a group of grave platonic gentlemen who

> reasoned high
> Of Providence, Foreknowledge, Will, and Fate—
> Fixed fate, free will, foreknowledge absolute,

and humanized their austere discourse with the sweet lenitive of story-telling.

Our next treatment of the story, in point of time and, possibly, in point of literary relationship, is that by Cotton Mather (1663-1728). Commenting upon providential compensations for the failure of Sir William Phips's expedition against the French in Canada, among them "that his voyage to Canada diverted from his country an Horrible Tempest from an Army of Boss-Lopers," Mather adds concerning his hero:

> Unto this purpose likewise, he was heard sometimes applying the Remarkable Story reported by Bradwardine.
>
> There was an *Hermit*, who being vexed with Blasphemous Injections about the Wisdom of Divine *Providence*, an Angel in Human Shape invited him to travel with him, *that he might see the hidden Judgments of God.* Lodging all night at the House of a Man who kindly entertained them, the Angel took away a valuable Cup from their Host, at their going away in the Morning, and bestowed this Cup upon a very *wicked Man*, with whom they lodged the night ensuing. The Third Night they were most lovingly Treated at the House of a very Godly Man, from whom, when they went in the Morning, the Angel meeting a Servant of his, threw him over the Bridge into the water, where he was drowned. And the Fourth, being in like manner most courteously Treated at the House of a very Godly Man, the Angel before Morning did unaccountably kill his only *Child*. The Companion of the Journey being wonderfully offended at these things, would have left his *Guardian:* But the Angel then thus Addressed him, *Understand now the Secret Judgments of God! The first Man that entertained us, did inordinately affect that Cup which I took from him; twas for the Advantage of his Interiour that I took it away, and I gave it unto the Impious Man, as the present Reward of his good Works, which is all the Reward that he is like to have. As for our* Third *Host, the Servant which I slew had formed a bloody design to have slain his Master, but now, you see, I have saved the Life of the Master, and prevented something of growth unto the Eternal Punishment of the Murderer. As for our* Fourth *Host, before his Child was born unto him, he was a very liberal and Bountiful Person, and he did abundance of good with his Estate; but when he saw he was like to have such an Heir, he grew Covetous; wherefore the Soul of the Infant is Translated into Paradise, but the occasion of Sin is, you see, mercifully taken away from the Parent.*
>
> Thus General *Phips*, though he had been used to Diving in his time, would say, *That the things which had befallen him in this Expedition, were too deep to be Dived into.*[20]

The Bradwardine whom Mather mentions as authority for his story is Thomas Bradwardine (1290?-1349), archbishop of Canterbury, to whom Chaucer playfully refers in the Nun's Priest's Tale, on a point very like the one the story of the hermit illustrates:

> In scole is greet altercacioun
> In this matere, and greet disputisioun,
> And hath ben of an hundred thousand men,
> But I ne can not bulte it to the bren,

---

[20] *Op. cit.*, I, 172-3.

> As can the holy doctour Augustyn,
> Or Boece, or the bishop Bradwardyn,
> Whether that Goddes worthy forwiting
> Streneth me nedely for to doon a thing, *etc.*[21]

My search for the story in Bradwardine resulted in finding it in his *De Causa Dei, contra Pelagium, et de virtute causarum, Lib. I, Cap. 13 Quòd actiones voluntariae divinae prouidentiae supponuntur,* p. 281.[22] In a marginal gloss Bradwardine cites as his authority for the story Jacobus de Vitry, and again gives him credit for it in the body of the story—"quod narrat Iacobus de Vitriaco." This version of Jacques de Vitry (d. 1240) is told in his Exemplum CIX.[23] Bradwardine follows Jacques de Vitry about as closely as Cotton Mather follows Bradwardine; there are no significant differences among the three versions.

In comparison with the *Gesta* and the More versions, Mather's (in common with Jacque de Vitry's and Bradwardine's) has a more striking climax—the killing of a host's child. My reproduction of Mather's version in full renders it unnecessary to comment further upon his narrative management, or upon his point in using it and his interpretation. Though he tells the story vigorously and concisely and gives us a fillip with his remark "'twas for the Advantage of his Interior that I took it [the cup] away," it is clear that he is not interested in its full artistic possibilities.

The finest artistic treatment of the apologue in English is Thomas Parnell's "The Hermit," a poem in heroic couplets, published in Pope's edition of Parnell's poems in 1721. Concerning Parnell's source there is disagreement of scholarly opinion. Warton, who wrote a fine dissertation upon the *Gesta Romanorum,* the

---

[21] Lines 417-424.

[22] The title-page reads: Thomae Bradwardini, Archiepiscopi olim Cantuariensis, *De Causa Dei, Contra Pelagium, et de Virtute causarum, ad suos Mertonenses, Libri Tres: Iussu Reverendiss. Georgii Abbott Cantuariensis Archiepiscopi; Opera et Studio Di. Henrici Savilli, Collegij Mertonensis in Academia Oxoniensis, Custodis, Ex scriptis Codicibus nunc primum editi.* Londini, ex Officina Nortoniana, Apud Ioannem Billium. M.DC. XVIII.

[23] Published in *The Exempla or Illustrative Stories from the Sermones Vulgares of Jacques de Vitry,* ed. Thomas Frederick Crane, *Publications of the Folk-Lore Society,* Vol. XXVI (London, 1890), p. 50 (Latin text) and p. 179 (translation).

first on the subject in English literary history, states that Tale LXXX " is the fable of Parnell's Hermit. . . . But Parnell was indebted for most of the plot and plan of his poem to a narrative in Sir Percy Herbert's *Conceptions.*" Later he adds, apparently contradicting himself, " Parnell seems to have chiefly followed the story as it is told by this Platonic theologian" (More).[24] Clouston expresses the opinion that " Parnell doubtless found it in the English translation of the ' Gesta Romanorum' published in 1703." [25] Axon accepts Pope's statement that Parnell found the story in Howell's *Letters,* and traces Howell's source to Herbert's *Certaine Conceptions* (1652).[26]

If Warton's implied statement that he had read Howell's and Herbert's versions of the tale is correct, the contradiction in his remarks about Parnell's relation to these two and to More is to be resolved, I think, in favor of More. Whatever Howell's and Herbert's versions may have been, the "happier arrangement of circumstances" (in comparison with the arrangement in the *Gesta*) which he finds in Parnell's poem is exactly that which is found in More's version. Of course, as has been pointed out before, both More and Parnell may have got the story from Howell or Herbert.

Parnell's poem begins with a brief but charming description, reminiscent of the Spenserian manner, of the hermit's habitation and his mode of life. There is not, however, as in the *Gesta* version, a specific occurrence to make the hermit doubt the justice of God. His life

> Seem'd heaven itself, till one suggestion rose;
> That vice should triumph, virtue vice obey,
> This sprung some doubt of Providence's sway.[27]

This discrepancy is present in both More's and Mather's versions. There is, then, in comparison with the ultimate source, some loss of concreteness in the motivation of the pilgrimage. But this is more than compensated for by Parnell, as it is not by the others, by the fine simile of the still forest pool disturbed by a stone, which suggests the agitation of the hermit's soul; by the romantic account of the beginning of the pilgrimage; and by the picturesque relation of the first morning's journey, in the course of which the hermit

[24] *Op. cit.*, pp. 257-259.
[25] *Op. cit.*, p. 24.
[26] *Op. cit.*, pp. 145-146.
[27] Text, Aitken, *op. cit.*, p. 100.

met the fair youth. The description of the youth, who is scarcely more than a lay figure in More and Mather, is ample and suggestive. Unlike the *Gesta* narrator, but in line with More, Parnell skilfully presents him, not as an angel from God, but as a beautiful young man. The advantage of concealing his angelic identity for the sake of the dramatic denouement, and yet making him appear so beautiful that the revelation seems credible to the hermit, is obvious. Parnell manages this point with much greater skill than does More.

The changes in the ordering of events and in the relations one to another of the persons concerned—made in the interest of a closer-woven plot and heightened narrative effects—all follow More. The episode of the golden cup, not, as in the *Gesta,* the strangling of the child, comes first. The palace of the hospitable host is splendidly described, and the suggestion of the incongruity between the host's christian charitableness and his sybaritic inclinations is made more skilfully than in the *Gesta* or in More. Again, in the fine figure of one suddenly spying a snake, the hermit's horror of the theft is presented with a vividness totally lacking in other versions.

Following a description of a storm that might have served as a worthy model for a similar scene in Chatterton's " Ballad of Charity," the hermit and the youth are presented as applying for refuge, not to a vaguely surly master of a mere abstract house, but to a solitary miser fortified in a mysterious, tree-shadowed, turreted seat. Here, though at first unheeded, they are given the mean best that the miser has and are lodged, not in a pig-sty, but in the miser's own habitation. The cup is left with the miser, as in the other versions, but to more humane ends. The hermit's wonder over this act is finely suggested.

The horror of the scene in which the youth strangles the sleeping child is intensified by the preceding description of the idyllic beauty and peace of the home and the simple piety of the family life. It will be remembered that cheerfulness and magnificence, merely asserted, not suggested, are the circumstances in the *Gesta* story; the circumstances are almost as general in More's version. With this fiendish act, too, is connected, as in More, but not as in the *Gesta,* the drowning of the guide. It is while the hermit is fleeing in horror and the youth is following him, from the stricken house, that the two are guided, across the swaying oak-limb bridge, over the wild torrent (a mere bridge, or " stone-bridge," and a stream in the other versions), and the final opportunity for apparent perfidy comes:

> The youth, who seem'd to watch a time to sin,
> Approached the careless guide, and thrust him in;
> Plunging he falls, and rising lifts his head,
> Then flashing turns, and sinks among the dead.

At first struck dumb by this diabolical act, the hermit masters his rage and fear sufficiently to burst out wildly, "Detested wretch!" But the youth suddenly transforms himself into an angel, as in More's version, calms the good old man, and proceeds to explain everything.

Parnell's handling of the story is thus tremendously enhanced by the youth's surprising revelation. This surprise, as has been shown, has been cannily reserved and carefully prepared—much more carefully than by More—all along, and is presented at the right dramatic moment.

The explanation of events, following this revelation, though managed with greater eloquence and plausibility and with a nicer regard for the correspondence between the motivating circumstances of the angel's actions and those actions themselves, than More's explanation, impresses the modern reader, however, as a more artistic rather than a more convincing attempt to justify apparent misfortunes sent by Providence. Parnell seems to be conscious of the inhumanity of his own theology at one point, where, perhaps out of deference for the reader's instinctive feelings, he makes the angel say that the death of the infant appeared to members of the family to have been the result of some sort of spasm, not of visible external violence. More makes no such concession. On the whole, Parnell's attempt to "vindicate the ways of God to Man" is as inadequate as Pope's deism in the *Essay on Man,* though it implies more faith; and it is scarcely more persuasive than More's.

The merit of Parnell's poem, however, is to be judged not on the basis of its theology, as More's must largely be judged, but on the basis of its poetic charm. Parnell treats it not as a subordinate means but as an independent entity worthy of artistic treatment for its own sake. He has succeded in investing the outline of a story with a beauty that results from perfect harmony of parts and a discriminating embellishment. There is a nice balance between description and incident, between reflection and action. Setting and atmosphere, painted or suggested with the finished artistry of eighteenth century poetry, are just what they should be, no more and no less. There is in them just enough of restraint to keep them from being too romantic for a moral tale, and just enough of color and feeling to humanize the story. The plot is closely knit—even more deftly in minor connections than More's; all of its effects are carefully prepared for with a craftsmanship that hides itself. The psychology of the hermit, though simple, is well adjusted to the moral purpose of the story without loss of humanity. Finally, though as Johnson pointed out, there are some weak lines, nevertheless such lines as "The moss his bed, the cave his hermit cell," " And beasts to covert scud across the plain," "And long and lonesome was the wild to pass," and such images as those already alluded to, exhibit exquisite mastery in details that eighteenth century poetic art chose to treat.

In a note to Voltaire's version of the hermit story in *Zadig,* his editor repeats Fréron's charge that Voltaire took this chapter almost word for word from Parnell's "Hermit," but points out that there were several French versions antedating Parnell's.[28] On Fréron's charge Gaston Paris remarks, "Il avait raison . . . certains traits ne permittent pas de douter que la narrative de l'écrivain français ne remonte pas directement au poème anglais."[29] A brief inspection of my analyses of the respective versions will discount if not refute the charge. In *Zadig* it is the hermit who teaches the lesson to Zadig; and there is an important difference in the handling of the manslaughter motif, and an addition of an entirely independent incident. Moreover, the explanation of events is not entirely reserved for the denouement, for the hermit gives Zadig apparently satisfactory reasons for purloining the cup, for bestowing it upon another, and for setting fire to the house of a hospitable host, immediately after these acts; and he reveals his angelic nature in the midst of his explanation of his reason for killing the widow's nephew.

The chapter "L'Ermite" bears such an important relation to the purpose of the romance that it requires a brief explanation. Zadig had just won victory in the tournament—a victory which entitled him to the hand of the beautiful queen Astarte. Weary from

[28] *Op. cit.,* p. 86.  [29] *Op. cit.,* p. 153.

the exertions of the tournament and the agitations of love, he fell into a profound slumber. While he was asleep, his despised enemy, Itobad, the green knight, stole his armor. He awoke to discover that he had apparently lost a mistress and a kingdom.

> A murmur against providence escaped him, and he was tempted to believe that everything was governed by a cruel destiny that oppressed the good and prospered the green knights. . . . He was skirting the banks of the Euphrates, full of despair and secretly denouncing Providence, which was always persecuting him.[30]

It was in these circumstances that he met the venerable, white-bearded hermit reading the book of fate. The adventures with the hermit may be said to constitute the climax of the romance, for while Zadig is on his knees adoring Providence and submitting himself to her, "The angel cries from aloft: 'Take your way toward Babylon'"; and he thereupon returns, conquers his enemy, regains his mistress, and wins the kingdom.

It has been well said that "*Zadig* has for its object to show that Providence leads us by ways of which the secret belongs alone to her, and against which our reason, blind and unsubmissive, often rebels." [31] Like most of Voltaire's romances it has a philosophical aim. Voltaire, it may be recalled in this connection, wrote his *Éléments de la philosophie de Newton* to destroy Cartesianism. The hermit's explanation of the events of the story is an eloquent exposition of universal harmony in accordance with Newtonian physics—the sort of declamatory determinism that one finds in Pope and many other eighteenth century English writers. This is a part of it.

> "But," said Zadig, "is there only good, and no evil?" "In that case," Jesrad replied, "this world would be another world, the concatenation of events would constitute another order of wisdom; and this order, which would be perfect, could be only in the eternal abode of the Supreme Being, whom no evil can approach. He has created millions of worlds, of which not one can resemble another. This immense variety is an attribute of his immense power. There are no two leaves of a tree upon this earth, nor two globes in the infinite meadows of heaven, which are exactly alike, and all that you see upon this little atom where you were born has become a being fixed in place and time according to the immutable laws of that

---

[30] *Op. cit.*, pp. 86 ff. My own translation.
[31] *Biographie universelle (Michaud) ancienne et moderne,* . . . *nouvelle édition*, Paris, n. d., article "Voltaire," vol. XLIV.

which embraces all. Men think that this child who has just perished fell into the water by chance, that it was by chance that this house was burned up; but there is no chance: all is trial, or punishment, or recompense, or foresight.[32]

It will be noticed that the problem of evil is treated here in a manner characteristic of the eighteenth century; it is associated with the idea of the universe as a *continuum*. Perhaps the most notable English exposition of "the theory of plenitude" is Archbishop King's *De origine mali* (1702, translated and published in 1731). This treatise sets forth the theory that the universe is a *continuum*; that it pleased God (or the Supreme Being) to make a graduated scale; that this gradation implied imperfection and evil; but that God desired a world of infinite fulness and variety. The theory influenced Pope's *Essay on Man*, directly, or indirectly through Bolingbroke.[33] It undoubtedly influenced Voltaire too.

Within its limited scope this paper has sought to assemble evidence concerning an interesting minor problem of literary borrowings. It presents one version of the story of the hermit (Cotton Mather's) which seems to have escaped comment. It suggests characteristic ways in which literary versions of a story, in contrast to folk-tales, elaborate the elements of plot, character, and setting. If it has succeeded in recalling attention to this interesting old story itself, to a few artistic treatments of it that do not deserve to be entirely forgotten, and to the characteristic ways in which markedly different minds of different ages and countries have reacted to a fundamental idea, it has accomplished what it set out to do.

*The University of North Carolina.*

---

[32] *Op. cit.*, p. 90. My own translation.

[33] For an interesting discussion of the effects of the theory on English literature, see A. O. Lovejoy's "Optimism and Romanticism," *PLMA*, XLII (1927), pp. 921 ff.

# THE IMPORTATION OF FRENCH LITERATURE IN NEW YORK CITY, 1750-1800

By HOWARD MUMFORD JONES

Since an American interest in French literature dates almost from the beginning of American letters, a vast deal of spade work is necessary, especially in the earlier periods, before we can arrive at a just estimate of the amount and character of that interest. Especially is this spade work necessary if one is to avoid rash generalizations about the influence of French thought in the United States which are now unhappily too current. In the effort to ascertain the facts in a limited area, I have gone through the files of New York newspapers from 1750 to 1800 as copies have been available to me [1] with a view to culling out and studying important

---

[1] In the William L. Clements Library at the University of Michigan. The files of no library in the country are complete, but the papers in the Clements Library are sufficiently rich to allow a fair "sampling" process. The list follows. In making this list I have not thought it necessary to indicate the innumerable changes of title, or to take up space by stipulating missing issues. The initials in parentheses are the abbreviations used in the text:

(DLR) *The Diary; or, Loudon's Register* (printed by S. Loudon), Dec. 12, 1792–May 5, 1798. Scattering issues.

(GNYJ) *Greenleaf's New York Journal, & Patriotic Register* (printed by J. Greenleaf). Issues for Nov. 1 and Dec. 13, 1794.

(Her) *The Herald: A Gazette for the Country* (printed by George Bunce & Co.), June 4, 1794–Sept. 30, 1797.

(GUS) *Gazette of the United States* (printed by John Fenno), Jan. 2, 1790–April 10, 1790 (when the paper was transferred to Philadelphia).

(IJ) *The Independent Journal; or, the General Advertiser* (printed by J. M'Lean), March 1, 1786–Dec. 29, 1787; and three issues in 1788.

(NYDA) *The New-York Daily Advertiser* (printed by Francis Childs), five issues between May 16, 1785 and Nov. 1, 1787; becomes *The Daily Advertiser*, April 1, 1788, when the file is almost complete to 1791, poor for 1792, complete for 1793-1794, scattering from 1795 to 1799, and complete from 1799 to 1800.

(NYDG) *The New-York Daily Gazette* (printed by J. & A. M'Lean), three issues in 1789, 1791, 1794.

(NYEP) *New-York Evening Post* (printed by Henry De Forest), scattering issues, 1750-1752.

items. An element of great interest is the booksellers' lists of imported books, from which we catch some idea of the interest in French authors in colonial and revolutionary New York. As no one who has not gone through the files of colonial newspapers can realise how extensive a variety of titles is to be found in the booksellers' advertisements, I have thought it wise to report my findings *in extenso*.

At this distance it is of course impossible to identify all the items, to determine whether a particular title represents a book in French or in English, or to speak with confidence of the edition

(NYG) *New-York Gazette, or Weekly Post-Boy* (printed by James Parker), scattering issues from 1750 through 1768. (The title of this paper varies more widely than perhaps that of any other).

(NYGW) *The New-York Gazette: and the Weekly Mercury* (printed by Hugh Gaine), scattering issues from 1768 to 1772; and fairly representative issues from 1773 to Aug. 4, 1783.

(NYJ) *The New-York Journal; or, The General Advertiser* (printed by John Holt), scattering from 1768 to 1788; a fairly representative file from Jan. 12, 1775 to Dec. 21, 1775.

(NYM) *The New-York Mercury* (printed by Hugh Gaine) (becomes *The New-York Gazette: and the Weekly Mercury, q. v.*), a few issues in 1754-55; a good file in 1756; scattering issues, 1757-1759.

(NYMP) *The New-York Morning Post* (printed by Morton and Horner), issues in November, 1783, and January, 1787.

(NYP) *New-York Packet* (printed by S. Loudon), 16 issues, 1784-1789.

(NYWJ) *New-York Weekly Journal* (printed by J. P. Zenger; afterwards by his heirs), January–March, 1750.

(NYWM) *The New-York Weekly Museum* (printed by Harrisson and Purdy), three issues from 1788 to 1793, a good file from March, 1794 to June, 1797, scattering issues, 1799–1800.

(RNYG) *Rivington's New-York Gazetteer: or, The Connecticutt, New-Jersey, Hudson's River, and Quebec Weekly Advertiser* (printed by J. Rivington), April, 1773–Nov., 1773; Jan., 1774–Nov., 1774; Feb., 1775–Nov., 1775.

(RRG) *The Royal Gazette* (printed by J. Rivington), 20 issues from Dec., 1777 to June, 1783; and a good file, July 4, 1781 to Dec. 29, 1781.

(Spec) *The Spectator* (printed by Hopkins), issues from Oct. 4, 1797, to Dec. 28, 1799.

Needless to remark, I have given the first printer in each case. Only the first appearance of advertisements is cited.

or place of publication. Sometimes the bookseller is content with generalization. Thus Henry De Forest announces as "just published" (NYEP, 2/12/50) "the Manner of receiving a *Free-Mason, as it was discovered at Paris. Translated from the French, in English....*" More characteristically, Garrat Noel is content to announce the arrival of French Bibles, Testaments, and Grammars (NYJ, 2/18/68), John Applegate's Vendue House advertises merely "French and English books" (NYJ, 6/15/69), or Samuel Loudon advertises "A neat assortment of French books, some new and a few second-hand." (NYGW, 7/25/74).[2] More specific are James Inglis advertising an auction of a "small but valuable collection of curious books," including some "in the French language on anatomy, physic, surgery, chymistry, philosophy, etc. with a variety of polite books." (NYGW, 3/6/80); J. Fellow, who says in 1794 that he has imported books from London including "many valuable classics in ... the French ... in the latter a variety of Dictionaries, Grammars, Idioms, Exercises, Fables, etc." (DLR, 1/3/94); and Caritat, the French bookseller, who says that his bookstore and circulating library at 125 Broadway contain "French maritime atlasses the most accurate extant, French books on Religion, Morals, Politics, Finances, Commerce, Agriculture, History, Geography, Arts, Sciences & Belles Lettres, by the best writers, some of which are either new works or of the best & newest editions." (NYDA, 6/5/98). Eighteenth-century spelling is uncertain, proof-reading was not of the best, and the absence of French accent marks adds to the confusion, so that identification is often impossible or difficult.[3]

---

[2] In 1773 Noel and Hazard, and Loudon, rival booksellers, advertise a large shipment of books, but only *Gil Blas* is specifically French (NYGW, 7/5/73). Valentine Nutter merely offers French dictionaries (NYJ, 1/4/76). William and James Hay advertise French schoolbooks (IJ, 9/6/88), and so on.

[3] Thus I have not been able to identify "Viaud's Voyages," advertised by Hugh Gaine (NYGW, 3/6/75); or the "Memoirs of the Marchioness de Louvoi" (NYMP, 1/26/87)—can this last be the *Mémoires, ou Essai pour servir à la histoire de F. M. Le Tellier, Marquis de Louvois*, possibly by Chamlay, and published at Amsterdam (!) in 1740? Instances of ludicrous spellings will presently appear; it requires an act of faith to

Fortunately we are not always left to puzzle over the advertising phraseology of the eighteenth century; other items are specific. I know no better way to picture the extraordinary cosmopolitanism of New York reading taste in these fifty years than to quote the items in order with explanatory comment.[4] Accordingly I begin. In the fifties, information is mainly from the *New-York Mercury*; and represents importations by two booksellers, Garrat Noel in Broad Street, and Hugh Gaine, printer of the paper. In 1752 Noel was advertising a wide variety of books, including French grammars and dictionaries, and an " Age of Lewis XIV "—clearly Voltaire's *Siècle de Louis XIV* (NYM, 11/13/52). In the supplement to this issue Gaine lists Vertot's *Revolutions of Sweden and Denmark,* " Telemachus " (*Télémaque*), " Fontenell's Plurality of Worlds," and " Charles the 12th "—obviously, Voltaire's.[5] The next month Gaine lists these as " just imported " and also gives the *Spectacle de la Nature* (7 vols.)[6] and Rollin's *Belles Lettres*[7] (4 vols.) (NYM, 12/11/52). The next year (NYM, 1/4/53) Gaine was selling *Gil Blas,* " Fontain's Fables," Voiture's works

identify, as one must, " Epruve de Sentiment, by Darnau " as the *Epreuves du sentiment* of François-Thomas de Baculard d'Arnaud (IJ, 1/10/87).

[4] While numerical summary would save space, it would not give the effect of richness and variety which is as necessary as statistical analysis to clothe the skeleton of the past. Thus when R. L. Hawkins insists in his *Madame de Staël and the United States* (Cambridge, 1930) on the cultural poverty of the United States at the turn of the century, and accuses others of exaggerating its richness, he seems to me to lack the kind of historical picture I am trying to give.

[5] René-Aubert Vertot (1655-1735) was popular in colonial America, specifically his *Histoire de la conjuration de Portugal, Histoire de les révolutions de Suède, Révolutions romaines,* and *L'Histoire des chevaliers hospitaliers de Saint-Jean de Jérusalem,* books which paved the way for Rollin or accompanied the latter's works.

[6] By the Jansenist N. A. Pluche, and published in 9 vols. in Paris in 1732. There were various translations published in London, for which see the British Museum Catalogue.

[7] Faÿ has commented (*L'Esprit Révolutionnaire en France et aux Etats-Unis,* Paris, 1925) on the extraordinary vogue of Rollin in the colonies and the place of Rollin in colonial education. His popular ancient history did much to fix the pattern of republican Roman virtue which helped to create the Order of the Cincinnati and name the upper legislative house the Senate. See Faÿ, pp. 26, 143, 307.

in two volumes, the "Jewish Spy"[8] in five volumes, and Maintenon's Lettres. In September (NYM, 9/24/53) Noel has imported half a column of books, including Rollin's "Arts & Sciences" and Rabelais in five volumes. Three issues later Gaine counters with Boyer's French Dictionary and Grammar, Telemachus in French, "Fontain's Fables," Voiture, and the *Memoirs of a Man of Quality* (2 vols.), which I take to be Prévost's novel (NYM, 10/15/53). His advertisement for December 17 adds nothing to his list. By October 7, 1754 (NYM), Noel[9] is selling an octavo edition of Pascal's "Thoughts"; and the next week Gaine has added "Fontenell of Oracles" to his French stock (NYM, 10/15/54). The next year sees no change (NYM, 2/10/55; 6/16/55). But in March (NYM, 3/1/56) Noel advertises "M. L'Abbe Lambert's Curious Observations on the Several Nations of Asia, Africa and America" (2 vols.), Vertot on the revolutions of the Romans, and Rabelais in five volumes "with very neat cuts"; and in June (NYM 6/7/56) he has Boyer for sale, and also Vauban on fortifications; the best that Gaine can offer is a "History of France" "by way of question and answer." Shortly after Gaine had advertised (NYM, 7/18/57) a book on Count Saxe's plan for new-modelling the French army, available papers dwindle away. And as papers for the sixties are not rich let me add here that Noel imports a life of Madame Pompadour in 1766 (NYJ, 12/5/66) and a shipment of French Bibles and "Le Dran on Surgery"[10] in 1768 (NYG, 2/15/68).

In the seventies, either because more data are available, or because of increasing interest, the variety of these importations is much greater. To begin with, Noel and Hazard advertise in 1771

---

[8] The famous *Lettres juives, chinoises et cabalistiques*, 1738-69, by Jean-Baptiste de Boyer, Marquis d'Argens, are perhaps meant.

[9] "At the Sign of the Bible in Dock-street near Coentie's Market" Noel continued to advertise Rollin during the winter (NYM, 2/25/54). A list of about 150 importations by Gaine (NYM, 5/13/54) adds nothing.

[10] The works of H. F. Le Dran were much translated. This may be *Consultations on most of the disorders that require the assistance of surgery*, translated by A. Reid, London, 1766; or *Observations on Surgery*, translated by J(ohn) S(parrow), 3rd edition, 1768; or *Operations in Surgery of Mons. Le Dran*, translated by Gataker, 4th ed., London, 1768. We badly need some studies of the influence of French medicine upon America.

(NYGW, 10/28/71) " books for those who teach or want to teach French," including Boyer, Perrin, Chambaud, Nugent, and others, French Testaments, Epistolary Correspondence in French and English, *Télémaque,* and the like. In 1772 (NYGW, 5/18/72) Rivington has for sale " Les Oevres (*sic*) de Fontenelle, de Racine, de Boileau & de Montesquieu & Les Moeurs & Eclaircesment (Voltaire?); Bossu's " Travels in Louisiana "; " Letters on the English Nation " (Voltaire's *Lettres Philosophiques*), " Les Charactres de Bruyere," " Les Memoires de Mareshall Feuquires,"[11] " Les Oeuvres de Rousseau et de Fontaine," " Les Oevres (*sic*) de Belidore."[12] In a later issue (NYGW, 8/10/72) Noel and Hazard advertise Tissot " on health,"[13] M. Grosley's " Tour to London or New Observations on England and its inhabitants, translated from the French by Mr. Nugent," a life of Théodore Agrippe D'Aubigné, Madame Riccoboni's " Letters from the French." The next year Rivington (RNYG, 5/6/73) advertises Voltaire's works, Chambaud's French dictionary " so much wanted by the students in that language "; and " has lately received a very large quantity of books; French, Italian, and in other polite languages " (RNYG, 7/29/73). In the autumn he devotes space to the novels of d'Arnaud,[14] saying " They are translated from the French of Mons. d'Arnaud, the most favourite novelist at this time existing in any country; there is scarcely any translation of the kind held in competition with them, and there is no reading them without feeling the most sensible compassion for the principal characters."

An unusual advertisement appears in the same paper in September (RNYG, 9/16/73), when John Donaldson of London says his

[11] Isaac, Marquis de Feuquières (1618-88), whose *Mémoires contenant ses maximes sur la guerre* was printed at Paris in 1770.

[12] This is Bernard Forest de Belidore, an army engineer, whose *Œuvres diverses sur l'artillerie et le génie* (Paris, 1764) is probably meant.

[13] Probably the much translated work of Samuel August André David Tissot, *Advice to the People in General with regard to their Health,* translated by J. Kirkpatrick. Editions appeared in London in 1765, 1766, 1768, etc.

[14] The novels of François-Thomas de Baculard d'Arnaud (1718-1805) were collected as *Epreuves du sentiment,* and included various exercises in the " sombre " vein. Particular titles are *Fanny ou la Nouvelle Paméla, Sidney et Lilli, Lucie et Mélanie.* Rousseau said of them: " M. d'Arnaud écrit avec son coeur."

London shop, " at the corner of Arundel Street in the Strand " is the " only shop for cheap Books," and, to attract American trade, gives a table of comparative prices. His list of titles is highly indicative of what was likely to be bought: Vertot's Knights of Malta, 5 vols.; Vertot's Revolutions of Rome, 2 vols.; The Adventures of Gil Blas; the Memoirs of Sully, 5 vols.; Montesquieu's Spirit of Laws, 2 vols.; Rousseau's Emilius, 3 vols.; Marmontel's Moral Tales; and various French medical works. The next year Rivington lists by title some of d'Arnaud's novels, of which " a very few are left " (RNYG, 1/20/74), and Hugh Gaine advertises " Voltair " in 24 vols. (NYGW, 7/25/74).[15]

The troubles of 1775 did not check the importation of books. In February (NYM, 2/6/75) Valentine Nutter offers a group of English titles, Voltaire's " Peter the Great " and his " Charles 12." In March Gaine is selling Viaud's voyages, Rollin's *Belles Lettres,* and Voltaire's *Works* (NYGW, 3/6/75). Nutter repeats his advertisement (RNYG, 3/9/75), and Rivington offers Crévier's " History of the Roman Emperors " (10 vols.)[16] in the same issue. In April an American edition of *The Spirit of Laws* is planned (NYGW, 4/3/75): Montesquieu is one " so honourably mentioned by the Continental Congress," the translation is by Mr. Nugent, and 300 subscribers are wanted in " various parts of the country."[17] Rivington outdoes himself: in the summer (RNYG, 8/3/75) he is selling all the writings of Montesquieu, Fontenelle's " whole works," " Nature Displayed " (*Spectacle de la Nature?*), Molière's plays (bilingual), the works of Crébillon *fils, Gil Blas,* the inevit-

---

[15] Sentimentalism was perhaps having its effect. Rivington (RNYG, 3/24/74) advertises " The American Scarron, or the Story of Aeneas and Dido burlesqued," " replete with wit and comicality," but " free from the gross impurity justly complained of in Charles Cotton of England, and the Scarron of France, who, though extremely droll and facetious, were exceedingly indelicate."

[16] Jean-Baptiste-Louis Crévier (1693-1765), a pupil of Rollin, continued his Roman history as *Histoire des empereurs jusqu'à Constantin,* 1750-1756, in 6 volumes.

[17] Hugh Gaine was to print it.—One enigma of this year I refer to the decent obscurity of a footnote: in August (NYGW, 8/14/75) the New York Society Library advertises for the return of certain borrowed books, including " Cluemelle on Husbandry." Is this French, or a misprint for Columella?

able *Télémaque,* the works of Boileau, and two important military publications, the Polybius of Folard (7 vols.) and the "whole works of the famous Belidore" in eight.[18] In October he advertises for the benefit of the French schools in New York.[19] The war does not hamper Rivington's activities. In 1777 (RRG, 12/27/77) he advertises exercises for turning English into French by "Alex. Scott," "member of the University of Paris," various French grammars and aids, *Télémaque* (bilingual), *Gil Blas* in French, the *Contes Moraux* of Marmontel, "Le Paysan Parvenu,"[20] and "Moral and Entertaining Dialogues" in French and English "for foreigners." In 1778 Benjamin Davies and Son advertise a shipment of books (RRG, 10/24/78) including Bougainville's *Voyages* and Marmontel's *Incas de Peru;* and in another issue (RRG, 10/31/78) Sévigné's Letters and "Gil Blas". Rivington's last advertisement for the year (RRG, 11/11/78) includes Crévier's History of the Roman Emperors, Raynal's History of North America and the West Indies, Bossu's Travels through Louisiana, Helvétius's "Treaty of Man," Tissot on Health, and Montesquieu's "Spirit of laws."

If it be argued that the British occupation of the city helped to increase an interest in things French, it does not appear that there is any decrease of interest in the eighties. Montesquieu's Letters,[21] a book of travels in France and Turpin on war are early advertisements. Valentine Nutter sells Ross's French Grammar, Boyer's French dictionary, Voltaire's works (24 vols.) and Voltaire's English Nation (*Lettres Philosophiques*) in 1780 (NYGW, 1/16/80). In the following summer Rivington (RRG, 6/4/81) lists his usual dictionaries and grammars, items by Marmontel, Mde. de Sévigné,

---

[18] Jean-Charles de Folard (1669-1752), *Commentaire sur Polybe,* Paris, 6 vols., 1727-30, had the honor of being discussed in a critical work by Frederick the Great. Both publications were known in America. On Belidore, see footnote 12.

[19] Boyer's large and small dictionaries, Entick's Pocket French and English Dictionary, Chambaud's Grammar, Idioms and Fables, Fontenelle, *Gil Blas* & *Télémaque,* Molière, Boileau, Montesquieu, the *Spectacle de la Nature,* La Fontaine, Racine, and Crébillon *fils.*

[20] Marivaux, published 1735-36.

[21] Hugh Gaines' advertisement, NYGW, 1/16/80. Turpin de Crissé's *Essay on the Art of War* was translated as early as 1761 by J. Otway, London, 2 vols. The second advertisement of Gaine is in NYGW, 3/20/80.

Fénelon, and Le Sage, and the "Memoires of Cardinal de Retz ... recommended warmly by Lord Chesterfield" and "to be had in both French & English." He also sells, among the "New Pamphlets" Raynal's *The Revolutions of America*, "an entire new work, commencing with the year 1763 and deduced to the present time, a most curious work, and much read by the Literate."[22] In July (RRG, 7/21/81) he advertises books by Turenne and Marmontel;[23] and two days later (NYGW, 7/23/81) Gaine is selling Abbé Millot's *Elements of General History*. In the autumn (RRG, 10/3/81) Rivington includes among his "Novels and Books of Entertainment" Madame Riccoboni's "Letters from Eliza de Valiere to Louisa de Cantelen" (2 vols.), Marmontel's "Incas, or the Destruction of the Empire of Peru" (2 vols.), *Gil Blas* in English or French, and "Emilius" in four volumes. In the same month (NYGW, 10/22/81) Hugh Gaine is offering Bougainville's *Voyages*, Charlevoix's "Voyage to North America," Tissot on health, and Cambray (i. e., Fénelon) on education; and Valentine Nutter lists his usual French school books. But an even more impressive list is Rivington's October offering (RRG, 10/27/81):

Voltaire complete in 40 vols.
Tales of Fontaine
The Jewish Spy
Moliere's Works
de Retz's Memoirs
Madam Maintenon's Memoirs
Book of Common Prayer in French
Letters of Ganganelli [24]
Marmontel's Letters of the Incas, or Kings of Peru
The Wars of ... the Marquis Feuquiere
The Spirit of Folard, by the King of Prussia [25]
The Whole Works of Rousseau in 11 volumes
The Emilius of Rousseau
Folard's Polybius
Works of Moliere (all his comedies)

---

[22] He offers an American edition of Raynal for $1.00 in the autumn (RRG, 9/5/81).

[23] *Belisarius*, Marmontel's philosophic romance of 1767.

[24] Jean-Vincent-Antoine Ganganelli, as Clement XIV, abolished the Jesuit order in 1773. The *Lettres intéressantes* (Paris, 1775) are probably a forgery; as are also the *Nouvelles Lettres*, 1776-7.

[25] A commentary on Folard's *Polybius*, listed below. See note 18.

Gisbeare on Tactics (Essais de Tactique) [26]
Campaigns of the Famous Duke de Noailles
The Bachelor of Salamanca
Memoire Military (sic) &c . . . of the Great Duke of Berwick
Voltaire's Age of Louis XIV
The Fortunate Peasant, a novel [27]
Raynal's East & West Indies, 7 vols.
Buffon's Natural History, 35 vols.,

and in addition Sherlock's "Letters and Travels" in French (also in English) and the Trial of de la Motte for high treason. In November (RRG, 11/7/81) Jeremiah Tronson advertises Montesquieu and Millot; Henry Guest (RRG, 11/14/81) offers books at auction, including Rousseau; and Andrew Barclay (RRG, 11/17/81) advertises a long list, including grammars, Rousseau's *Works,* Raynal's "British Settlements in North America with the History of the Present War," Ganganelli's "Letters," a history of France by "Machiaval," Rousseau's *Emilius,* Sully's *Memoirs,* "Bruyer's Works," Tissot on health, and Molière. Rivington later (RRG, 6/21/83) repeats some of his old titles, adding the "Letters of Ninon de l'Enclos" and "Rouchefaucault's Maxims." [28]

The last half of the eighties proves extraordinarily rich in titles. In 1785 Woolsey and Tronson (NYP, 7/7/85) advertise the Abbé de Mablay's work on the United States, with notes by the translator, and also Raynal's History of the Indies. January, 1786, opens with *Tales of the Castle* (5 vols.) by the Countess of Genlis, sold by A. M'Lean (IJ, 1/11/86); the same bookseller also advertises Raynal's Montesquieu, Marmontel and Le Sage a little later (IJ, 4/19/86). In May (IJ, 5/27/86) Gaine has removed to a new store and lists an almost identical group of titles. Rivington adds the Works of Florian to his list (IJ, 5/27/86), and later acquires *Tales of the Castle* and *Adelaide and Theodore* by Mde. Genlis (IJ, 12/9/86). Gaine advertises *Manon Lescaut* (IJ, 12/30/86). The next year opens with Voltaire, T. Allen having imported "in the last vessel from Europe" the "Memoirs of M. de Voltaire" in French, and his *Philosophical Dictionary* (IJ,

---

[26] I have not yet been able to identify this item.

[27] Marivaux' *Le Paysan Parvenu.*

[28] Gaine repeats his advertising in August (NYGW, 8/4/83), listing Montesquieu's Roman Empire and Spirit of Laws, Vertot's Revolutions of Sweden and Revolutions of Rome, and Buffon's Natural History.

1/3/87). That same month Rivington repeats most of the items on the long list already quoted, adding, however, the "Memoires of the Duc de Bourgogne" (2 vols.), "L'Isle Inconnu," "Epruve (*sic*) de Sentiment by Darnau" (D'Arnaud), "Les Moeurs" (Voltaire?), the "Works of Regnard" in 2 vols., the works of D'Astoriche [29] in 10 vols., and a "Theorie d'Education," not to speak of "Jewish Letters, written by the Marquis d'Argens, favorite of the last and greatest King of Prussia," and a "Dictionarie de Physique, with all the new Philosophical Discoveries since the year 1773," "all the best tragedies of the great Corneille," the dramatic works of "Mons. Bellay" [30] (8 vols.), *The Devil on Two Sticks* of Le Sage, a French New Testament, a volume of "Morale Tales, diverting Histories and Romances, collected from the works of Mons. Le Sage, the admirable author of Gil Blas," a "Theatre d'Education" (4 vols.), and various language books. John Gaine is selling "Manon L'Escaut, a French Story" subtitled "A Fatal Attachment" that same month (NYMP, 1/26/87), and Hugh Gaine advertises the "Memoirs of the Marchioness de Louvoi" [31] in the same issue. Rivington has acquired new titles in May: Chastellux's *Travels* (IJ, 5/3/87), Necker on Finance (3 vols.), and various language books (IJ, 5/3/87). Allen proposed an American subscription edition of Chastellux in June (IJ, 6/6/87). Almost simultaneously Samuel Campbell was selling Voltaire's *Universal History* (NYP, 6/5/87) and various others. In September (IJ, 9/1/87) Rivington capitalized a current interest by announcing a life of Turgot, "a favorite work, adapted to the perusal of Gentlemen in Congress," and continued to push *Télémaque* in French and English, "with various others in French & English . . . to teach the French tongue." Later (IJ, 11/28/87) he advertised Monk's life of Voltaire. The next year (NYDA, 2/1/88) S. and R. Campbell advertise a new shipment of books, including Goguet's(?) *Origin of Laws, Arts and Sciences* (3 vols.), Montesquieu's *Spirit of Laws,* and "Beauties of the countress (*sic*) de Genlis." Hugh Gaine offered the Monk life of Voltaire and a life of Turgot in May (NYDA, 5/1/88), the Camp-

---

[29] I am unable to identify this.

[30] Pierre-Laurent Buyrette, called Dormant de Belloy, 1727-1775, whom Grimm severely condemned. His *Œuvres Complètes* appeared in 1779.

[31] This defies search, but see note 3.

bells received Fourcroy's *Elements of Natural History and Chymistry,* a new enlarged edition, and Bonnet's *Inquiries concerning Christianity* (NYDA, 6/6/88); in September Rivington was advertising Mazzei's *Recherches historiques et politiques sur les Etats-Unis de l'Amérique Septentrionale* (IJ, 9/6/88), and Thomas Allen was selling Voltaire's *Philosophical Dictionary,* Voltaire " on toleration," Rousseau's " Eloisa " (4 vols.), " Emilius " (3 vols.) and La Rochefoucauld's *Maximes* in November (NYDA, 11/28/88). Curiously enough, the revolution year of 1789 is not productive of new titles: Rapin's *History of England* (NYDA, 1/22/89), Millot's *Elements of Ancient and Modern History* (NYDA, 7/24/89), and Burlamasque (Burlamaqui) on natural law (NYDA, 8/5/89) being representative.

But the political tensity of the nineties is faithfully reflected in the advertising. Voltaire's *Letters on the English Nation* appeared in January (NYDA, 1/20/90); Hugh Gaine offers Necker's *Religious Opinions,* Vatel's *Law of Nations,* and Millot's *Elements* in the spring (NYDA, 3/4/90), and T. Allen sells Buffon's *Natural History* in nine volumes " with above 300 copper plates," Voltaire's *Essay on Universal History* and his *Charles XII* (NYDA, 5/4/90). In June (NYDA, 6/18/90) S. Campbell sells the " Memoirs and Travels of Count de Benyowsky," [32] Grosier's(?) *Description of China,* and Mirabeau's *Secret History of the Court of Berlin.*[33] Rivington is importing French law books in November (NYDA, 11/11/90), including Vatel, and also Volney's " Travels in Egypt." Allen equals this next spring (NYDA, 4/15/91), and adds the " King of Prussia's Works in 13 vols." [34] As a mark of the vogue of Voltaire it is interesting to note Allen's advertising of the " Posthumous Works " of the great Frederick, translated by Thomas Holcroft (NYDA, 5/10/91)—the work contains pieces " relative to Voltaire " and the *philosophe* group. Allen says Necker's treatise on religious opinion is " an offering . . . made at

---

[32] *The Memoirs and Travels of M. A., Count of Benowsky,* supposed to be translated from the French, appeared in London in 1790. There is said to be, at the least, a large admixture of fiction in the book.

[33] Campbell is still advertising Buffon in the autumn, together with the *Memoirs of Sully* (5 vols.). (NYDA, 10/8/90.).

[34] Another of Rivington's encyclopedic lists appears in April (NYDA, 4/15/91), including Spanish, Italian, and French books.

the shrine of religion by a man of business" (NYDA, 8/9/91); and he advertises "Books in French" by Frederick the Great, Le Sage, Fénelon, Buffon, and Raynal, and a life of Voltaire in September (NYDA, 9/7/91). Dupaty's "Travels Thro' Italy," "a work considered as one of the most pleasing books of observations that ever came from a writer of sensibility" is advertised (NYDA, 9/22/91), as are other French travel books (NYDA, 12/30/91), and the close of the year is made interesting by the announcement of new books at the New York Society Library (NYDA, 9/9/91), including "Mollier's" Works, Anderson's *France,* Bossu on the epic, Tissot on health, de Retz's *Memoirs,* Mirabeau's "Economical Tables," and various others.

The year 1793 reveals little new—a French voyage to Africa and a translation of Lavater (NYDA, 1/19/93), Young's *Travels through France,* Rochon's voyage to East India, and various linguistic works (NYDA, 1/19/93), travels (NYDA, 2/29/93) and minor items. But the Revolution soon engrosses the booksellers. Rivington announces the publication of "A Review of the proceedings at Paris . . . written by Mr. Fennell" (NYDA, 4/4/93), and adds Florian's "new Tales," and the letters and tales of Madame de Cambon. April 17 (NYDA, 4/17/93) he has imported Necker's "essay on the true principles of executive power in great states," and "A Comparative Display of the different opinions of the most distinguished British writers on the French Revolution," [35] as well as a new novel by Madame de "Chambon" and Mirabeau's "Speeches in the National Convention." Interest grew. In the winter (NYWM, 2/15/94) "Le Livre Rouge," a list of private pensions paid from the French public treasury, is advertised. In June [36] (NYWM, 6/21/94) the "memoirs of the Queen of France," "including her armours (!) and intrigues," with a motto from Brantôme, is advertised. Next month (NYDA, 7/3/94) L. Wayland has received a shipment of French school books, Buffon's *Natural History* in 52 volumes with colored plates, Nugent's French dictionary, Raynal, and other works; and the next day Childs advertises John Moore's "Journal during a residence in France"

---

[35] The contributors include Burke, Mackintosh, Paine, Rous, Christie, Priestley, "Mrs. M'Aulay", Mary Wollstonecraft, and others.

[36] Barlow's writings and a book by Priestley are advertised by Francis Childs and J. Fellow (NY Herald, 6/16/94).

(NYDA, 7/4/94). The influx of émigrés desiring to learn English is soon felt: Rivington advertises (NYDA, 7/10/94) a list "for students in language, both Englishmen and Frenchmen," including a number of bilingual items. In August, T. Allen (NYDA, 8/1/94) counters with a similar list, and a new history of the French Revolution, and Mrs. Williams' "Letters of the French Revolution." [37] In September (NYDA, 9/3/94) F. Childs has received from London Young's *Travels in France,* the "memoirs of Doumouriar," *Domestic Anecdotes of the French Court,* Vauban on fortifications, and " Francomania . . . or the travels of the devil & folly in France, Liege, &c," and Courtney's travels in France. An interesting October item (NYDA, 10/2/94) is Robespierre's report on the institution of National Morality and Festivals, a book serving "to convince the world that the calumny of Atheism (*sic*) thrown on that nation is only the efforts of their enemies." In December (NYDA, 12/15/94) a bilingual (?) "Faits et dits memorables de l'histoire Ancienne et Moderne" is to be published; and later Moreau de St. Mery & Co. advertise their new store, stocked with "French, English, German & Latin books," where they will receive subscriptions for the French Gazette published in New York. But they "will not go into tedious detail," though they "purchase French books" (NYDA, 12/29/94).

Unfortunately, files for 1795 are not available. In 1796, however, Volney's *Ruins of Empires* is advertised (NYWM, 4/2/96); also such items as *The Devil on Two Sticks* (bilingual), a book on the Queen of France, and "Tales of Past Times" (bilingual) (NYWM, 10/22/96).[38] The next year John Harrisson, author of the foregoing advertisement, has an amusing item which reflects the conflict (NYWM, 3/25/97): "In spite of Deism, Tom Paine, and the Devil, the following very valuable book is offered for sale. . . . The Pious Christian." Erskine's "Views of the War," which has gone through "24 editions in London" is advertised in May (DLR, 5/19/97). Mde. de Genlis' *Knights of the Swan* in Beresford's translation is sold in June (NYWM, 6/3/97), also *The Foresters,* "altered from the French by Miss Gunning," and Moore's *Journal* and his *View of the French Revolution* attract

---

[37] A four-volume edition which included correspondence by Doumourier (*sic*), Pache, Bournonville, Miranda, and Valence.

[38] And Volney's *Ruins.*

attention (NYWM, 6/17/97). A new edition of *Télémaque* is proposed in September (DLR, 9/28/97). The decade draws to an impressive close with the following list (with prices) offered by John Fellows (DLR, 3/24/98):

Œuvres Posthumes de Frederic II, 15 tomes, $15.
Supplement a la Collection des Oeuvres de J. J. Rousseau, 6 tomes, $3.00.
Theatre a l'Usage des jeunes Personnes, par Mme de Genlis, 4 tomes, $2.00.
Histoire Litteraire de Voltaire, by Luchet, 4 vols, $2.00.
Tusculanes de Ciceron, 2 vols. $1.75
Entretien de Ciceron sur la Nature des Dieux, 2 vols. $1.75.
Les Offices de Ciceron, $1.10.
Lettres de Ciceron, $.87.
Phillippique de Demosthene, et Catilinaires de Ciceron, $.87.
Les Livres de Ciceron de la Viellesse (et) de l'Amitie, $.87.
Les Oeuvres d'Horace, (Latin & French), 2 vols. $1.50.
Journal de (John) Moore, 2 tomes, $3.00.
Elemens de la Languange Anglaise, $.62.
Traite de la Cochenille, 2 tomes, $2.00.
Traite de l'Orthographe Francaise, $.75.
Mirabeau on Lettres de Cachet, 2 vols. $3.25.
Mary Wolstonecraft, History of the French Revolution, $2.00.
Philosophical Dictionary, by Voltaire, $1.00.
French Revolution, by Rabaut & others, 2 vols. $2.25.
Condorcet on Human Mind, $1.00.
[Paris edition of Joel Barlow's "Voyage of Columbus", "elegant," $1.25.]
Millot, Elements of Ancient History, 2 vols. $4.00.
Letters of certain Jews to Voltaire, $1.75.
Natural Ideas opposed to Supernatural, by the Marquis d'Argent (*sic*), $1.00.
Volney, Law of Nature, $1.00.

In September Caritat advertises "Rousseau's Celebrated Confessions" and "some works of considerable merit in French" such as Condorcet's "Library of the Man in Public Affairs" (8 vols.), Mirabeau's "Correspondence with his Constituents" (16 vols.), "Children's Friend," Telemachus, etc. (NYDA, 9/8/98). These he sells; but he has added to his circulating library Adam's "Complete History of France," "Memoirs of Living Authors," Gifford's "Residence in France," Chastellux's "Travels in America," Bonhote's "Parental Monitor," the Countess of Genlis' "Letters of a Governess to her Pupils," Forlaix's "Memoirs," and various other titles. Florian's *Galatea,* " a pastoral Romance, imitated from the celebrated Cervantes" and translated, is advertised in 1799 (NYDA, 11/21/99), and Caritat concludes the year with two interesting advertisements. On December 17 (NYDA, 12/17/99) he announces Saurin's "Sermons" (6 vols.), Fourcroy's Chemistry, Liancourt's "Travels," French dictionaries, Mirabeau's "System of Nature" and his speeches, and an "extensive collection of the latest & best novels." And on December 27 (NYDA, 12/27/99) he has published the "Beauties of the Studies of Nature Selected from the works of Abbe de Saint Pierre."

Imperfect as these data are in one sense, there is little reason to suppose that they are not typical and representative. They offer certain interesting conclusions. In the first place, one is struck by the prodigious interest in the teaching of French shown by the steady advertising of grammars, dictionaries, and the like,[39] an interest probably increased in the nineties by the influx of émigrés from Europe and the West Indies. But as New York was, even in 1750, something of a polyglot city, it is important to note in the next place that most of the important seventeenth- and eighteenth-century authors, whether in the original or translation, were available to readers in New York in these fifty years. But the distribution of emphasis is here significant. In no case, with the exception of Fénelon and La Rochefoucauld (who does not figure importantly in the lists) are thinkers of a conservative stamp much read. Bossuet and Massillon do not appear; we have instead Fontenelle, Pluche, Vertot—liberals and rationalists—in the seventeenth century; and a heavy representation of rationalist thought in the eighteenth century. It is, however, curious that Diderot and D'Alembert seldom figure in the book lists. The leading authors, in the order in which works by them or about them appear, are by a rough count (excluding the advertisement of the London book-

---

[39] The interest in learning French is further shown by the number of advertisements of persons offering to teach the language, of which I have collected 53 from these papers; advertisements in French, of which these papers yield 11; and various articles on the needs of knowing French. These counts represent only the *first appearance* of a particular advertisement, as is the case with book advertisements. In addition, advertisements of dancing masters, fencing masters, and *cicéroni* frequently stress the fact that the teacher knows the language.

seller, and including items I have attributed to them): Voltaire, 30; Rousseau, 11; Fénelon, 11; Le Sage, 11; Montesquieu, 8; Raynal, 8; Mde. de Genlis, 8; Mirabeau, 5; Molière, 5; and Frederick the Great, Fontenelle, Rollin, Millot, Buffon, Necker, and La Fontaine, 4 each. Aside from the striking preponderance of Voltaire items, perhaps the most significant fact in this list is that Rousseau is no more important than are Fénelon and Le Sage—a truth which should give us pause when next we read brilliant generalizations about Rousseau's direct influence in America. Undoubtedly, however, sentimentalism is well represented by the novels of Mde. de Genlis, Florian, d'Arnaud and Marivaux. Two other conclusions suggest themselves: a moral objection to polite French literature has not yet importantly obtruded itself in a half century which imported Rabelais, La Fontaine's *Tales,* Crébillon, and which delights in Voltaire, the rationalism of writers like Condorcet, and the scepticism of Frederick the Great. Lastly, the striking contemporaneity of much of this interest must be significant—books are imported in many cases almost upon publication. When we recall the difficulties of trans-Atlantic communication, the smallness of the reading population of New York, and the remoteness of Europe, we must be impressed by an interest so varied and so vivid as that here sketched.

*University of Michigan.*

# SOME NOTES ON PIERCE EGAN

## By George L. Marsh

Pierce Egan the elder, "glorious Pierce," the author of *Life in London, Boxiana, The Life of an Actor,* etc., was not a great writer; but he was a very conspicuous writer during the Regency and the reign of George IV. *Life in London* fathered at least seven plays during its first year of existence. The Cruikshanks made drawings for it and other works by Egan. Thackeray recorded pleasant memories of Tom and Jerry, the roystering heroes of *Life in London*.[1] Yet for many years there has been scarcely any notice of Egan except in two German studies of his influence on Dickens,[2] and some discussion by F. W. Chandler in his *Literature of Roguery*[3] and by Harold Child in Chapter VI, Volume XIV of the *Cambridge History of English Literature*.[4] Under these circumstances, then, it seems not amiss to make some additions and corrections to the recorded knowledge of Egan.

First I wish to call attention to a book by him that is not mentioned in the *Cambridge History* bibliography just referred to or in the article on Egan in the *Dictionary of National Biography*[5] or in the British Museum Catalogue. The book is an octavo of about 500 pages, with the following title page:

> Sporting Anecdotes, / original and selected; / including / numerous characteristic portraits / of / persons in every walk of life, / who have acquired Notoriety from their Achievements on / the turf, at the table, / and in the / diversions of the field, / with Sketches of the various / Animals of the Chase : / to which is added, an Account of noted / pedestrians, trotting matches,

---

[1] In an article on George Cruikshank in the *Westminster Review*, XXXIV (1840), 1 ff., and "De Juvente" (No. 8 of *Roundabout Papers*) in the *Cornhill Magazine* (1860), II, 501-512.

[2] Arnold Berndt, *Entstehungsgeschichte der "Pickwick Papers,"* Greifswald (1908); Wilhelm Dibelius, "Pierce Egan and Dickens," Herrig's *Archiv* (1910), CXXIV, 306-317.

[3] Vol. II (1907), 380.

[4] "Caricature and the Literature of Sport" (1917), pp. 245 ff.; bibliography, p. 601 (very inadequate).

[5] Vol. XVII (1889), 142-144.

cricketers, &c. / the whole forming a complete Delineation of the / Sporting World. / By Pierce Egan. / London: / Printed for Sherwood, Neely, and Jones, / Paternoster-Row. / 1820.

Opposite the title page is an excellent engraving in eight parts representing different sports—fox hunting, fishing, horse racing, bird shooting, archery, cock fighting, walking, and pugilism; with the artist and engraver indicated thus:

    J. R. Cruikshank [6] Inv$^t$.                  P. Roberts Fecit.

There is an elaborate "Dedication, To the Sporting World," dated, "London, Jan. 1, 1820," and signed "Pierce Egan," written in that worthy's characteristic style, with lavish use of italics, capitals, and other devices for strident emphasis.

The book is a curious hodge-podge, devoid of the slightest pretense of systematic arrangement, consisting of some hundreds of bits, each with its own heading, ranging in length from a joke or anecdote of a few lines to a good many pages. It begins (after the dedication) with nearly sixteen pages about Captain Barclay, to whom Egan had dedicated the first two volumes of *Boxiana*. Then follow four pages on "The Mocking-bird of America," concluding with a poem; four more pages on "The Moorish Wrestlers, with some Account of their Equestrian Performances"; a paragraph (half a page) on the "Voracity of the Heron"; a short poem entitled "Nabob and Tiger"; a page on the weights that race-horses should carry in proportion to their inches; three pages on "The Late Duke of Hamilton"; a poem called "The Bull Bait." So much to illustrate the hap-hazard arrangement. Some of the longer sections are on training for various sports; a "Description of the Automaton Chess Player Exhibited in Spring Garden, London, in 1819"; "Ancient and Modern Coursing. By Major Topham"; "Portrait of a Professed Gambler"; a considerable section on "Pedestrianism." The poems inserted at intervals include a "Sporting Adventure of Courteous King Jamie. By M. G. ['Monk'] Lewis, Esq."; a portion of "Tom Crib's Memorial to Congress. A Sporting Satirical Effusion, attributed to the pen of

---

[6] Obviously Isaac Robert, elder brother of the now more famous George, is meant. Both he and George had made drawings for *Boxiana* and were soon to do so for *Life in London*.

Mr. T. Moore " [an undoubted work of Moore's]; " The Old Shepherd's Dog," by Peter Pindar; " Influence of the Post-Horse," from Bloomfield's " Farmer's Boy "; and a poem by Egan himself which he later put into volume III of *Boxiana*. Many sources of the material are acknowledged: from *The Examiner* (meaning, no doubt, Leigh Hunt's celebrated Sunday newspaper) an " Account of Cavanagh, a celebrated Fives Player "; " Sporting in the United States. From 'A Year's Residence,' &c., by W. Cobbett "; numerous extracts (or in some cases apparently summaries) from books of travel; and several paragraphs on pugilists from the editor's own *Boxiana*—with due acknowledgments.

It seems odd that this book should have been overlooked in the principal sources of information regarding Egan, and that the British Museum should have no copy of it,[7] for it is mentioned as one of Egan's works on the title page of *Life in London,* which is said to be " By Pierce Egan, Author of Walks through Bath, Sporting Anecdotes, Picture of the Fancy, Boxiana, &c." (I quote from the British Museum copy, " Printed for Sherwood, Neely, and Jones, Paternoster-Row. 1821.") Moreover, a review of *Life in London* in the *European Magazine* for November, 1820 [8] (LXXVIII, 436-438), contains the following sentences: " It is unnecessary to say one word on Mr. Egan's previous literary achievements. Boxiana and the Sporting Anecdotes will form the monument of his talents ' aere perennius ' while taste and science exist in the world."

On the last page of the British Museum copy of *Life in London* (mentioned above) is an advertisement of *Sporting Anecdotes* as a work of Egan's, quoting from a review of the book in " Baldwin's London Magazine, August and September, 1820." This *London Magazine* review [9] is an elaborate and amusing discussion under the title, " The Jewels of the Book," of which I feel confident that Keats's friend, John Hamilton Reynolds, was the author because of various bits of internal and circumstantial evidence of perhaps doubtful appropriateness in this article.[10]

---

[7] Or at any rate had none in the summer of 1928.

[8] Evidently applying only to parts then issued; the work was not completed till the summer of 1821.

[9] Vol. II, pp. 155-164, 268-276.

[10] Nevertheless, without going into the matter fully I wish to call atten-

Unknown though *Sporting Anecdotes* seems to have been to writers of modern works of reference and literary history,[11] however, it has made a number of appearances in sales catalogues. I have not found mention of the 1820 edition, of which mine is a copy; but a New York edition of 1823 in two volumes is recorded in Temple Scott's *Book Sales of 1896* and *Book Sales of 1897;*[12] and I find a London edition of 1825, "enlarged and improved," mentioned in both the sources just cited as well as in Temple Scott's *Book Sales of 1897-8*[13] (published 1899), and in the *Catalogue of the Literary and Artistic Properties of the late Evert Jansen Wendell*.[14] This last work gives full details indicating that Robert Cruikshank's frontispiece dated 1820 was reproduced in the 1825 edition, and that there were also "colored plates [not in my 1820 copy] by Cruikshank and Alken, and woodcuts by Bewick and others." This 1825 edition is also mentioned in Brunet's *Manuel du Libraire*[15] and in *English Books 1475-1900, a Signpost for Collectors*, by Charles J. Sawyer and F. J. Harvey Darton.[16] These writers, in speaking of Egan's *Anecdotes of the Turf*, etc. (1827), say: "This is not the same book as the author's Sporting Anecdotes, the best edition of which is that of 1825, which has but two coloured plates."

tion to the editorial mention (p. 122) of "our *fanciful* contributor, Mr. Egan's encomiast" (Reynolds's little book, *The Fancy*, had been reviewed in the previous number of the magazine, pp. 71-75); to the fact that the reviewer of *Sporting Anecdotes* pays much attention to Habberfield, of Tothill Fields, who appeared as Abberfield in Reynolds's fragmentary poem, "Tothill Fields," in *The Fancy*; to comment on "poor deceased Mr. Corcoran" (p. 268), the name Reynolds gave the pretended author of *The Fancy*; and to indications of special friendliness to Keats both in the editorial remarks (p. 123) about "Mr. Egan's encomiast" and in the body of his article (pp. 270, 273).

[11] F. W. Chandler, *op. cit.*, p. 380, does indeed include this with his list of Egan titles obviously taken from the title page of *Life in London*, which is the only work he discusses.

[12] Both volumes published by Bell, London, and Macmillan, New York, 1897. See number 4377 in the list for 1896; 1318 in the list for 1897.

[13] Number 4379 in the list for 1896; 1317 in the list for 1897; 171, 1423, 2172, 2219, in the list for 1897-8.

[14] American Art Association, New York (n. d.), Part VI, number 7563.

[15] Vol. I (1835), p. 122.

[16] Westminster, Chas. J. Sawyer Ltd., 1927, p. 234.

Temple Scott's *Book Sales of 1896* and of 1897-8, cited above, introduce a complication by mentioning an 1804 edition of *Sporting Anecdotes*,[17] naming Egan as the author, but not indicating the publisher. If this date is correct and Egan the author of the volume of 1804, his activity as a writer began at least eight years earlier than has previously been known; but in any case the book of 1820 cannot have been a reprint (unless in some small portions) of any book of 1804, since most of the "anecdotes" of 1820 are definitely dated within a short time before that year. Certainly both the contents of the book and the contemporary comments on it indicate plainly that it was a "new thing" in 1820. Moreover, there has been such a tendency to list under Egan's name any anonymous or pseudonymous work with a title resembling any of his titles, that I should not be surprised to learn sometime that the earlier *Sporting Anecdotes* has only its identity of title to connect it with him.

The tendency just mentioned is especially worth noting in the case of what was perhaps the most popular of the numerous imitations of *Life in London*—*Real Life in London*, "by an Amateur." Since it has never been learned who wrote this book, and "there was a suspicion that Egan was its author,"[18] it is natural and proper that library catalogues, bibliographies, etc., should mention it in connection with Egan; but I have not found due recognition of his positive description of the work as "a bare-faced piracy, published in sixpenny numbers, calculated to deceive the 'good folks' in the country, and which also proved a great injury to the Proprietors of the original Work."[19] In spite of this, however, one reads on the backs of the two volumes of an attractive reprint of *Real Life in London* issued by Methuen & Co. in 1905, "by Pierce Egan," though the title pages more properly bear, "by an Amateur." Even in the British Museum Catalogue we find in brackets after the phrase just quoted, "i. e. Pierce Egan the elder." *Real Life in London* is a considerably more elaborate and extensive work than its prototype, with more serious guidebook elements and less of the extraordinary slang and exuberance of Egan. My impression

---

[17] No. 4378 in *Book Sales of 1896;* 745 in *Book Sales of 1897-8.*
[18] *D. N. B.*, XVII, 143.
[19] Pierce Egan, *The Finish to the Adventures of Tom, Jerry, and Logic*, as reprinted by Reeves & Turner, London (1889), p. 7.

is that no person who really reads both *Life in London* and *Real Life in London* would be likely to think them by the same author.

The *D. N. B.* article on the elder Egan contains one serious error of date in relation to *Life in London,* saying that the first number (it was issued in parts) appeared July 15, 1821. Of course this date should be 1820; I have already mentioned a review of some of the parts of *Life in London* in a magazine of November, 1820. Moreover, the *D. N. B.* article exposes its own error when it mentions *Real Life in London* as being started as an imitation in May, 1821.

Returning briefly to *Sporting Anecdotes,* I wish to record my recognition of the fact that the book is but a journalistic potpourri of no literary merit except perhaps for some of the bits from good authors that I have mentioned in part. Nevertheless, it contains material of real value for an understanding of the social background of the time; and Egan himself was a writer of such immense popularity—ephemeral though it proved to be—as to deserve any supplement to our knowledge of him that can be provided.

*The University of Chicago.*

# PLANCHÉ'S FAIRY EXTRAVAGANZAS

## By Dougald MacMillan

In a previous brief study of the early burlesque of James Robinson Planché [1] I called attention to the existence of his fairy extravaganzas, which are, in many ways, his most important contribution to the history of English burlesque drama. The use of fairy tales, like that of classical myths, was not new to the English stage in Planché's day; but the well worn stories of the White Cat or Riquet with the Tuft had not in the eighteenth century been used to the same extent as classical stories by the writers of burlettas and pantomine openings. Planché may, safely I think, be said to have given the fairy tale its definite and prominent place on the Victorian stage. The many imitators of Planché's work carried on in classical burlesque and fairy extravaganza the tradition set by Planché, chiefly through the brilliant series of pieces produced by Madame Vestris at Covent Garden and The Lyceum. As the classical burlesques merit attention, so do the fairy extravaganzas call for analysis. An understanding of Planché's pieces will go far toward producing a fairly complete picture of a type of comic drama immensely popular in Victorian London. To accomplish this end, I should like to point out the subjects, sources, and characteristics of these fairy pieces.

Twenty-two of the extravaganzas are little more than dramatizations of French fairy tales, chiefly those of Perrault and Madame D'Aulnoy. The first three were written during the period of collaboration with Charles Dance, the others by Planché alone.[2] Many of the titles are familiar to everyone and the unfamiliar ones are mostly those that Planché made himself to fit his plays, departing deliberately from the titles by which the stories are commonly

---

[1] " Planché's Early Classical Burlesques," *SP*, XXV, 340.

[2] The list follows: *Riquet with the Tuft, Puss in Boots, Blue Beard, The Sleeping Beauty in the Wood, Beauty and the Beast, The White Cat, Fortunio and His Seven Gifted Servants, The Fair One with the Golden Locks, Graciosa and Percinet, The Bee and the Orange Tree, The Invisible Prince, The Golden Branch, The King of the Peacocks, The Island of Jewels, King Charming, The Queen of the Frogs, The Prince of Happy Land, The Good Woman in the Wood, Once Upon a Time There Were Two Kings, The Yellow Dwarf, The Discreet Princess*, and *Young and Handsome*.

known. In handling the stories Planché, almost without exception, adhered strictly to the story as it is told in his original. The most noticeable exception to this rule which he made for himself is in the case of *The Yellow Dwarf,* where he has given the tale a happy ending, an obviously necessary change if the piece were to succeed with the holiday audience.[3] In practically every case the dramatist tells us the source of his story, and he usually points with pride to the fact that he has carefully followed his original as far as the actual story goes; he was also much interested in getting the audience to appreciate this faithfulness on his part and in destroying the current misconceptions of his sources, misconceptions that had their origin in the "garbled nursery versions" of the tales that circulated under the title "Tales of Mother Goose" (from Perrault's *Contes de ma Mère l'Oye*), in which the stories were obviously "written down" to small children and deprived of all their subtlety and humor, qualities that are easily discernable in the French originals and in Planché's own translations of them. Though he was probably not as successful in this as the excellence of his object and his own sincerity might have deserved, he certainly succeeded in making his versions of the tales pleasing to the audience and very popular. This is amply proved by the fact that the pieces held the stage for twenty years, many of them in individual cases running from the night of their first production to the openings of their successors at the next holiday season.

It will be observed that Planché, who, when his works are viewed as a whole, displays astonishing versatility, in these extravaganzas has taken his subjects from a very limited field. Except for a few instances all of the important and best extravaganzas have for their plots stories taken from classical mythology or from French fairy tales. He chose his subjects with due care and developed them to the best of his ability, always endeavoring to give the stories their true interpretation, while, at the same time, he made them into amusing nonsense for the delight of his audiences. The humor is derived not from a perversion of the tales or from a distortion of the characters, but from a delicate, whimsical handling of the themes, behind which one can always feel the intelligent sympathy that he has for the original treatment of the subject.

[3] This, by the way, is one of few fairy tales that end tragically with the death of the lovers.

This is particularly true in the case of the fairy pieces. In *Riquet with the Tuft* he has attempted to tell the story in an amusing fashion and at the same time to preserve the subtle pathos of the character of Riquet, the hunchback with the ugly body and beautiful mind, the pathos that is a true part of the tale as it is told by Perrault. And the same quality is seen in *The Yellow Dwarf*, where the character that gives the play its title has much in common with Riquet, though he lacks the pathetic sweetness of disposition that makes the latter character appealing. The same is true, perhaps in less degree, of the other plays. The Greek gods may participate in all sorts of buffoonery, but they remain gods to the end and act their parts in the usual stories as we have been accustomed to see them. This faithfulness to the story is one of the points in which Planché's burlesques differ from those of his contemporaries, who were usually content to pervert the tales whenever it was necessary by so doing to please the galleries and the managers. In spite of the atrocities of his friends, Planché usually remained true to his ideal of a good story faithfully retold, that he might not do an injustice to his source. And his success proved, frequently in spite of the qualms and fears of managers, that he was right, that the people liked best the old stories told as they were used to hearing them from childhood, with the added spice of clever dialogue and pretty scenes to tickle the adult palate. In the preface to *Telemachus*, Planché says, "In this instance as in every dramatization of a popular subject that I have been concerned in, the well known plot was invariably preserved with the most reverential fidelity, whatever liberties might be taken with the details. . . . Whether this be a merit or not is, of course, a matter of opinion, but it is upon that principle that I have worked throughout my career, and believe that it has been most essential to my success."[4]

It has been necessary in this discussion of the subject matter of Planché's plays to touch on the subject of sources of plots, but this matter must be taken up for more detailed consideration. As is apparent at a glance, few of Planché's plots are original and those few are not among his best works. His ability seems to have enabled him to readjust stories already well known,—sometimes

[4] *The Extravaganzas of J. R. Planché* (London, 1879), I, 174.

too well known, it seemed,—rather than to invent and construct plots of his own. Even in his original plots, as in *The Irish Post* (1846) or in *Who's Your Friend* (1843), there is little true originality; yet these pieces interest one by the sprightliness of their dialogue and the prettiness and delicate good taste of their construction. The result is that he naturally turned more and more from the presumably original productions of his earlier years (at that time, too, came the acknowledged rearrangements and adaptations) to the carefully constructed plays bearing old names and telling old and loved tales.

Beginning with *Riquet with the Tuft,* comes the series of burlesques based upon French seventeenth and eighteenth century fairy tales. The sources of these plays offer more interesting material for consideration., The authors whom Planché used as sources are five: Perrault, Mme. D'Aulnoy, Mme. le Prince de Beaumont, Mlle. de la Force, and Mme. de Murat.

*Riquet with the Tuft,* the first of the fairy pieces, is based on the French "*Comédie Féerie,*" *Riquet à la Houppe,* by Saurin and Brazier, which Planché had seen in Paris in 1821.[5] The story is from Perrault's "*Contes des Fées.*" Planché says that *Riquet with the Tuft* "is the only piece of this class [i. e., based on a fairy tale] for any portion of which I am indebted to the French stage."[6] *Puss in Boots* bears on the title page the statement: "Founded on the well known TALE of that extraordinary Animal, as unfolded by the best authorities." Planché's translation of Perrault's tale [7] is called *Master Cat; or, Puss in Boots.* The other plays based on stories from Perrault are *Blue Beard, The Sleeping Beauty in the Wood,* and *The Discreet Princess,* based on "*L' Adroite Princesse*" in Perrault's *Les Contes de ma Mère L'Oye.*[8] The titles are all translations of Perrault's own titles.

Fourteen of the fairy extravaganzas have for their sources tales by Madame D'Aulnoy.[9] All of the tales used as foundations for

---

[5] J. R. Planché, *Recollections and Reflections* (London, 1872), I, 44.

[6] *The Extravaganzas,* I, 211.

[7] *Fairy Tales* by Perrault (London, 1867).

[8] *The Extravaganzas,* V, 103.

[9] They are: *The White Cat, Fortunio and his Seven Gifted Servants* (from *Belle-Belle; ou, Le Chevalier Fortune*), *The Fair One with the Golden Locks, Graciosa and Percinet, The Bee and the Orange Tree, The Invisible*

the plays are also included in Planché's published translations of Madame D'Aulnoy's fairy tales.[10]

The three remaining plays from French sources in this group are *Beauty and the Beast,* from Madame le Prince de Beaumont's *La Belle et la Bête; The Good Woman in the Wood,* from Mlle. de La Force's *La Bonne Femme;* and *Young and Handsome,* from the Countess de Murat's *Jeune et Belle.*

In each case Planché has followed the version of the story as it appears in his own translations of the works of the various authors, always giving a complete story, and sedulously avoiding the "garbled nursery versions" which were well known to his audiences and had been the inspiration of Christmas pantomimes before his day. This avoidance of the nursery tales is more apparent in the spirit of his work than in the actual story itself. One of the characteristics of the original French tales is their humor, which appears in the comments of the author on the actors in the story, and their apparently unconscious criticism of the life around them, that of the court of Louis XIV. Both of these qualities have disappeared from the nursery tales as we, and Planché's audiences, know them. In the original tales, behind his perfect seriousness, we feel the intention of the narrator to poke fun not at the characters in the tales but at the readers of them. This subtle satire contributes largely to their charm. It is something of this air that Planché has tried to preserve in his stage versions of the tales, as in his translations he has tried to

---

*Prince* (from *Le Prince Lutin*), *The Golden Branch, The King of the Peacocks* (from *La Princesse Rosette*), *The Island of Jewels* (from *Le Serpentin Vert*), *King Charming or The Blue Bird of Paradise* (from *L'Oiseau Bleu*), *The Queen of the Frogs* (from *La Grenouille Bienfaisante*), *The Prince of Happy Land or the Fawn in the Forest* (from *La Biche au Bois*), *Once upon a time there were Two Kings* (from *La Princesse Carpillon*), and *The Yellow Dwarf.* In cases where the titles of the plays differ from those of the tales, I have given the titles of the latter in parentheses.

[10] After the fairy extravaganzas has become established on the stage, Planché translated a number of the French fairy tales on which they are based: *Fairy Tales by the Countess D'Aulnoy* (1885) and *Four-and-twenty Fairy Tales selected from those of Perrault and other popular writers* (1888). Cf. Kurt Kruger, *Die Märchen der Baronin Aulnoy* (Leipzig, 1914). See also *Le Cabinet des Fées* (Geneva, 1785), vols. II and III. Of the translation of Madame D'Aulnoy I used the 1888 edition.

keep the original flavor, substituting for the atmosphere of Louis's France that of Victoria's England.

In technical method the fairy pieces resemble quite closely their classical predecessors which I have discussed elsewhere.[11] That this method is much like that which was used in the eighteenth-century ballad operas and burlettas is at once apparent. In Planché, however, is found a closer coördination between songs and spoken dialogue than in most of the earlier plays. The extravaganzas are in this respect certainly better put together than such pieces as Planché's own earlier works and, in general, the productions of his contemporaries and imitators.

The characters that appear in these little plays are in most cases not developed with any attempt at distinct portrayal. In the fairy pieces, however, there are two exceptions, more remarkable because they are unexpected in drama of this frivolous sort. Riquet with the Tuft and Gam-Bogie, the yellow dwarf, stand out among the other characters of the extravaganzas as exceptional, first in being physically unattractive and in having in their characters and positions a touch of pathos. Riquet is a deformed, repulsive looking prince with a clever mind and a happy disposition. This is not a startlingly original conception, but the character has a sincerity that is unusual in burlesque. He describes his case thus, in a song:

> I'm a strange looking person I own,
>   But contentment forever my guest is;
> I'm by habit an optimist grown,
>   And fancy that all for the best is.
> Each man has of troubles his pack,
>   And some round their aching hearts wear it;
> My burden is placed on my back,
>   Where I'm much better able to bear it.

And so on to much the same effect, reaching the conclusion:

> Thus on all things I put a good face,
>   And however mis-shapen in feature,
> My heart, girl, is in the right place,
>   And warms towards each fellow creature!

The character is, in a manner, appealing; and one is truly glad when the fair princess has him in the end.

---

[11] See article cited above. In general they consist of verse dialogue interspersed with songs.

*The Yellow Dwarf* is the one of the fairy extravaganzas which has a tragic ending. The dwarf, Gam-Bogie, in his efforts to keep Allfair, the beautiful lady, in his possession brings about, unintentionally, the death of the two lovers, Allfair and Melidorus. In Madame D'Aulnoy's tale the lovers remain dead but are transformed into two palm trees growing side by side. Planché revivifies them at the end of his play and adds a last, grand scene, for obvious reasons. Gam-Bogie is represented as vicious and vindictive. Most of his speeches are typical of the dialogue of burlesques, but at the end of the play he reveals his character in the speech made after the violent death of Allfair. It is a parody of part of Othello's speech, in the fifth act, in which he curses himself.[12]

> And caused her death to whom I was devoted
> Oh, heavy trial! Verdict: Serves me right!
> Whip me ye devils—winds come, blow me tight!
> Roast me in flames of sulphur—very slow!
> Oh, Allfair—Allfair! Dead—O, O, O, O!

It must be remembered that this appears in a Christmas extravaganza, in which local slang was regarded as humorous; but the conception of the remorse and disappointment of the dwarf is apparent. And the actor, Robson, was able to make a serious impression with it. The language is, despite the slang and the ridiculous rhyme, if anything, perhaps less extravagant than that in *Othello,* whence many of the phrases are taken.

These two characters, however, in which there is some attempt to portray depths of emotion, are exceptions. The characters are not of first importance in the extravaganzas, and most of them are conventional but pleasing. Their most satisfactory quality is, perhaps, the tenacity with which they "stay in character" until the action of the play is over and they address the audience in the finale. Unlike most of his contemporaries, Planché expected his actors not to indulge in "gags" or private jokes with the audience but to play their parts in the drama that they always take seriously regardless of the ridiculousness of their speeches or the effect on the audience. In this laudable object this serious writer of burlesque was not always entirely successful.

The dialogue of most of the extravaganzas is in pentameter

---

[12] Cf. *Othello,* V, ii, 277-282.

couplets. There is some prose in *Puss in Boots* and a good deal in *Riquet with the Tuft*. It is, however, the usual couplet that appears most frequently. Such an abundance of this meter, not especially well written or much varied, is apt to become tiresome, but the audience is saved from tedium by the frequent introduction of songs.

Though I have already cited examples of these songs in my discussion of the classical burlesques and have no desire to multiply examples, a few might be quoted from the fairy extravaganzas to show the continuity of Planché's practice. An example of a type still found in musical comedy, the plaintive, sentimental song, is found in *Graciosa and Percinet*. Graciosa is tied to a tree in the forest to be devoured by wild beasts. After the following song her fairy lover appears and, of course, saves her.

> True love can ne'er forget;
> Long here I should not fret
> Were I still, Percinet,
>   Your darling one;
> This very day you said,
> When first your bow you made
> If I required your aid,
>   You'd to me run.
> But " "out of mind when out of sight,"
> I'm afraid the proverb's right;
> Of your promise you'll think light,
>   And brown I shall be done.
> True love can ne'er forget;
> Long here I should not fret
> Were I still, Percinet,
>   Thy darling one! [13]

Another type is found in which the words are parodied after the words of their originals. An example comes from *Fortunio and his seven Gifted Servants*, though almost any other extravaganza would yield as good results. Here the parody is upon "The Days that we Went Gypsying," once popular. I quote only the first stanza.

> Oh, the days that we got tipsy in, a long time ago,
> Were certainly the jolliest a man could ever know!
> We drank champagne from glasses long, and hock from goblets green,
> And nothing like a cup of tea was ever to be seen.

---

[13] *The Extravaganzas*, II, 320.

All night we passed the wine, nor dreamed of hyson or pekoe
In the days that we got tipsy in—a long time ago.[14]

One other matter relating to these extravaganzas, their moral purpose, I have presented in an article on that phase of the subject.[15] Here it remains only for me to express my profound conviction that, though these pieces of Planché's and others like them are frequently arrant nonsense, in them one finds often a truer key to the spirit of their age than in the works of persons of considerably greater literary respectability; and in the history of the stage of the early nineteenth century they must be considered.

*The University of North Carolina.*

---

[14] *The Extravaganzas*, II, 202.
[15] "Some Burlesques with a Purpose, 1830-1870", *PQ*, VIII, 255.

# COOPER AND *THE NORTH AMERICAN REVIEW*

## By Gregory Paine

### I

In the early decades of the nineteenth century the literary magazine that was most influential in the creation and encouragement of American literature was *The North American Review*. Its first number was published in Boston in 1815 when the post-Revolution poets, essayists, and novelists, like Trumbull, Barlow, Dwight, Freneau, Dennie, and Brown, had not been succeeded by new writers, aware of changing ideas and tastes in literature. Irving, it is true, had been warmly praised for his *Salmagundi* and *Knickerbocker's History*, but his *Sketch Book* was to appear several years later. Bryant, Cooper, Halleck, and others were yet to become known, and Longfellow, Hawthorne, and Emerson had not matriculated in college.

The early editors of the *Review*, who wrote the articles themselves, with a few contributions by others, were brilliant young men, cultured, educated, and traveled, later attaining eminence in various fields. The first editor was William Tudor, Jr., Harvard graduate, traveler, later merchant and diplomat, who had successfully edited *The Monthly Anthology* from 1804 to 1811.[1] Associated with him was Willard Phillips, Harvard graduate and tutor, later lawyer, judge, and legislator, succeeding Tudor as editor, and contributing during his life about thirty-five articles. Assisting Phillips as editor was Jared Sparks, Harvard graduate and tutor, later Unitarian clergyman, historian, biographer, Harvard professor and president (1849-52). From 1824 to 1830, succeeding Edward Everett, Sparks was editor. Another manager, though not an editor, was Richard Henry Dana, Harvard graduate, later lawyer, orator, editor, and author, who secured Bryant's "Thanatopsis" for publication. In 1818 the editorship was assumed by Edward T. Channing, Harvard graduate and later professor of rhetoric and oratory, the brother of the eminent William Ellery Channing. His

---

[1] See F. L. Mott's *A History of American Magazines* (New York, 1931) for a sketch of *The Monthly Anthology*. This book, however, does not contain a discussion of *The North American Review*, which Professor Mott is reserving for his second volume.

labors for the *Review* yielded about eighteen articles. His brother, Dr. Walter Channing, later an eminent physician, contributed several articles. The most successful early editor was the distinguished Edward Everett (Jan., 1820—Oct., 1823), Harvard graduate and professor, later president (1846-49), clergyman, orator, congressman, governor of Massachusetts, ambassador to England, U. S. Senator, and secretary of state. His elder brother, Alexander Hill Everett, was a Harvard graduate, lawyer, state senator, and diplomat, whose interest in the *Review* stimulated the writing of seventy-five articles, and the assumption of the duties of editor from 1830 to 1835. In the early years of the *Review* John G. Palfrey contributed several articles; and succeeding A. H. Everett as editor, he served until 1842. After graduating from Harvard, he became a Boston clergyman, and was later a professor of theology at Harvard, an orator, and a writer on religious and political topics.

Among the contributors who occasionally wrote on literary topics were Grenville Mellen, Harvard graduate, later lawyer and litterateur of New York; Lewis Cass, eminent for his services to the West as soldier and territorial governor, who wrote on Indian and Western subjects; William Howard Gardiner, Harvard graduate and lawyer, who contributed ten articles; O. W. B. Peabody, assistant-editor to his brother-in-law, A. H. Everett, Harvard graduate, lawyer, Unitarian clergyman, journalist, and biographer.[2]

Although these editors and contributors were usually Boston and Harvard men, they were generally free from the provincialism and controversial spirit that vulgarized Francis Bowen, editor from 1843 to 1852. The early contributors were akin in spirit to the first editor, William Tudor, who wrote: " I tried to abstract myself from the narrow prejudices of locality, however I might feel

---

[2] Information about early editors is found in volume CCI (1915) of *The North American Review*, which contains biographical sketches and portraits, and a historical sketch by Julius H. Ward (Jan., 1915, pp. 123-34). Further information is found in the volumes of the incomplete *Dictionary of American Biography*, and in the several older cyclopedias of American biography and literature, especially Duyckinck.

Since the articles in the early volumes were unsigned, we are compelled to accept the attribution of authorship by William Cushing in his *Index to North American Review* (Cambridge, Mass., 1878) and accepted by W. F. Poole in the third edition of his *Index to Periodical Literature*, printed in 1882.

them."[3] On the other hand, the spirit was nationalistic, almost to the point of chauvinism. Goaded by the animadversions on the United States by British travelers and by the reviewers for the British and Scottish quarterlies, especially *The Edinburgh Review,* the editors attempted to stimulate achievement in American letters and scholarship. The first number contained articles by Tudor on " Books Relating to America," and on " The United States and England," in which the prevailing custom of depreciating America was valiantly rebuked. Succeeding volumes were heavy with articles in praise of American democracy, religious institutions, historic successes, the abundant possibilities of the West, and the rich promise of American life.

With apologies and misgivings, however, the writers discussed the barrenness of American literature. For the third number Dr. Walter Channing wrote an able article on " The American Language and Literature," in which he deplored " the dependence of Americans on English literature, and their consequent negligence of the exertion of their own intellectual powers."[4] In the next number he continued the argument in the " Literary Delinquency of America," confessing to his fellow-Americans that " we have wanted literary enterprise, and been sadly deficient in genuine intellectual courage."[5]

Other writers demanded the creation of a national literature. Bryant, flattered by the publication of " Thanatopsis " in 1817, and a few other poems in succeeding issues, contributed an article entitled " An Essay on American Poetry," in which he solemnly proclaimed that " National gratitude—national pride—every high and generous feeling that attaches us to the land of our birth, or exalts our characters as individuals, ask of us that we should father the infant literature of our country."[6]

Upon assuming the editorship in 1820 Edward Everett sounded a more optimistic note in asserting that " Our literary character is advancing with our political and civil progress; we produce more

[3] Algernon Tassin, " The Magazine in America," *Bookman,* XLI (April, 1915), 141.

[4] *NAR,* I (Sept., 1815), 314.

[5] *NAR,* II (Nov., 1815), 35.

[6] *NAR,* VII (July, 1818), 198. See also Tremaine McDowell's " Bryant and *The North American Review,*" *American Literature,* I (Mar., 1929), 14-31.

and better books every year."⁷ Two years later, in reviewing *Bracebridge Hall,* Everett condemned Irving for treating un-American themes.

> He has shown with what ease and freedom he can write on English scenery and manners, after two or three years passed in England; and this is agreeable. We are not saying that the Sketch Book and Bracebridge Hall are not pleasing, finely written works; but we do say that . . . they can be read through and through, without causing a thrill in the heart of a countryman.⁸

In 1821 John C. Gray, Esq., addressed the Phi Beta Kappa society in Cambridge, Massachusetts, on the subject of American literature, and the *Review* promptly published his oration. He closed his peroration on the necessity for a native American literature with the challenge: "Why then may we not one day aspire to the character of a people universally literary, to a distinction which has hitherto been the exclusive glory of Athens."⁹

In the early years of the *Review* the contributors scorned much of the foreign fiction, and pleaded for American novels, native in scenic setting, in the use of historic incidents, in the representation of national life and character, perhaps poetical in style, but true to life. In 1817 Edward T. Channing deplored that

> novels, like every thing else in literature, have fallen too much into the hands of men whom nature never formed for authors; men void of genius, ignorant of life, getting their marvels and love from wild romance or idle pastoral, and mixing all up in a way of vulgar tawdriness, to entertain boys and girls, who have more sensibility perhaps, but not a jot more of experience than the authors themselves.¹⁰

The optimistic Edward Everett was, on the other hand, almost ecstatic in his praise of the progress of novel writing. Since 1814 Scott had been producing native, historical fiction that especially pleased Everett.

> It is enough [he writes] to mention the names of Edgeworth and Walter Scott in England; of Rousseau and Madame de Staël in France; of Wieland, Goethe and Schiller, in Germany; and of Fascolo in Italy, to show, that scarce a branch of modern literature has more great names to boast of, than that of novel writing. . . . We have now the masterly sketches of history, the most discriminating views of national character, the deepest

---

⁷ *NAR*, XI (July, 1820), 85.  
⁸ *NAR*, XV (July, 1822), 214.  
⁹ *NAR*, XIII (Oct., 1821), 487.  
¹⁰ *NAR*, IV (Mar., 1817), 403.

lessons of morals, and the finest bursts of eloquence, under the name of a romance, a novel, or a tale.[11]

Inspired by the story of *Yamoyden,* a long poem narrating the adventures of King Philip, John G. Palfrey, with New England provincialism very uncommon in the *Review* contributors, asserted " the unequalled fitness of our early history for the purpose of a work of fiction," and said, " whoever in this country first attains the rank of a first rate writer of fiction, we venture to predict will lay his scene here [in New England]." [12]

## II

The pronounced Americanism of the editors of the *Review,* their demand for a native American literature, and their eagerness to welcome American fiction by new writers, accounts for their favorable criticism of many of James Fenimore Cooper's early novels.

This American novelist lavishly described the scenery of the wilderness, narrated the stirring incidents of colonial history, pictured the life of the higher and lower classes, and argued the privileges of political democracy.

Cooper's first novel, *Precaution* (1820), was unnoticed, and probably unread, by the reviewers, for, with its English setting and characters, it had no American elements.[13] His second novel, *The*

---

[11] *NAR,* XI (Oct., 1820), 272.

[12] *NAR,* XII (April, 1821), 480.

[13] The following reviews and notices of Cooper's writings appeared in *The North American Review:*

*The Spy.* By William Howard Gardiner. XV (July, 1822), 250-82.
*The Pilot.* By Willard Phillips. XVIII (April, 1824), 314-28.
*The Pioneers; The Last of the Mohicans.* By W. H. Gardiner. XXIII (July, 1826), 150-97.
Reference to Cooper's romances in a review by Lewis Cass. XXVI (April, 1828), 373-76.
*The Red Rover.* By Grenville Mellen. XXVII (July, 1828), 139-54.
References to Cooper's writings in reviews by Jared Sparks, XXX (January, 1830), 15-17, and by Alexander Hill Everett, XXXI (July, 1830), 36-40.
*The Water-Witch.* By Oliver William Bourne Peabody. XXXII (April, 1831), 508-23.
References to Cooper's romances in a review by William Hickling Prescott. XXXV (July, 1832), 190-91.

*Spy*, received extended notice by W. H. Gardiner.[14] Although he wrote in the ponderous judicial manner of the reviewers for the English and Scottish quarterlies, Gardiner produced an excellent critical article, indicating faults and merits of *The Spy*, and suggesting new themes for the young novelist. Having "long been of the opinion," he says, "that our native country opens to the adventurous novel-writer a wide untrodden field, replete with new matter admirably adapted to the purposes of fiction," and hoping that "the modern historical romance shall be erected in all its native elegance and strength on American soil, and of materials exclusively our own," Gardiner welcomes *The Spy* as "a work, which, with numerous and great blemishes, has yet redeeming merits to give it a respectable station in the ranks of historical romance." He finds that Cooper "possesses inventive faculty to the highest degree," that his "particular talent . . . seems to lie in describing action and hitting off the humors of low life," and that Harvey Birch is a "finely conceived character." On the other hand, he notes that Cooper's capital defect is "excessive minuteness which leaves nothing for the imagination to supply," that Cooper is "not endowed with power of moving the softer affections," and that he has the "faults of inexperience and haste." Cooper must have

> Paragraph reference to *Sketches of Switzerland* by John Gorham Palfrey. XL (July, 1836), 280.
> *Gleanings in Europe*. By Francis Bowen. XLVI (Jan., 1838), 1-19.
> *Homeward Bound*. By Francis Bowen. XLVII (Oct., 1836), 488-89.
> *Naval History*. By Alexander Slidell Mackenzie. XLIX (Oct., 1839), 432-67.
> *Ways of the Hour*. By Francis Bowen. LXXI (July, 1850), 121-35.
> *Works*. By Francis Parkman. LXXIV (Jan., 1853), 147-61.
> *Works*. By Henry Theodore Tuckerman. LXXXIX (Oct., 1859), 289-316.

[14] *NAR*, XV (July, 1822), 250-82. In the chapter on "The North American Review," in his *Literary Criticism in America* (New York, 1931) George E. De Mille attributes the authorship of this review to another Gardiner. He says, "The author, whom I take to have been the John Sylvester [John] Gardiner, who was rector of Trinity, Boston, from 1805 to 1830, was, of all the contributors to the *Review* during the first decade of its existence, by far the best critic" (p. 27). Since Mr. De Mille gives no evidence, I cannot accept this. Cushing attributes only *one* review to John Sylvester John Gardiner, a review of Bishop Taylor's *Discourses*.

read with pleasure this sentence: " He has the high praise, and will have we may add, the future glory, of having struck into a new path—of having opened a mine of exhaustless wealth—in a word, he has laid the foundation of American romance, and is really the first who has deserved the appellation of a distinguished novel writer." [15]

A most significant paragraph is the one in which Gardiner sets forth the possibilities of Indian romance.

> At the present day, enough is known of our aborigines to afford the groundwork of invention, enough is concealed to leave full play for the warmest imagination; and we see not why those superstitions of theirs . . . may not be successfully employed . . . to light up a new train of glowing visions, at the touch of some future wizard of the West . . . and if we may credit their best historian, the indefatigable Heckewelder, not a little of softer interest might be extracted from their domestic life.[16]

In his review of *The Pilot*, published two years later, Willard Phillips praises the author for creating a new American fiction.[17] Referring to the earlier *Spy*, as well as to *The Pilot*, he claims that Cooper "has produced works, which deserve to be, and will be, a permanent part of our literature; and in a province where few adventurers have preceded him with any tolerable success." [18] He commends Cooper for writing popular literature which is " thoroughly American, containing frequent allusions to our history, manners, and habits . . . which strike deep into the feelings of American readers. . . . On the subject of our naval skill and prowess . . . we are yet real enthusiasts. This is a string to which the national feeling vibrates certainly and deeply; and this string the author has touched with effect." [19]

Two years later Gardiner contributed to the *Review* a forty-eight page review of *The Pioneers* and *The Last of the Mohicans,* including references to *Lionel Lincoln*.[20] He recognizes that Cooper has a " sort of magical authority over the spirit of romance," and " we

---

[15] *Op. cit.*, p. 281.

[16] *Ibid.*, p. 256. For a discussion of Cooper's Indian tales see my article on " The Indians of the Leather-Stocking Tales " in *Studies in Philology*, XXIII (Jan., 1926), 16-39.

[17] *NAR*, XVIII (April, 1824), 314-28.

[18] *Ibid.*, p. 315.

[19] *Ibid.*, p. 329.

[20] *NAR*, XXIII (July, 1826), 150-97.

are borne along by the author through a crowd of romantic incidents and marvelous adventures, without stooping from the flight to consider the reality of things as they exist in the same places at the present day [Boston in *Lionel Lincoln*]." [21] But notwithstanding this recognition of Cooper as a romancer, Gardiner shows his predilection for realistic fiction. He says he presumes that *The Pioneers* is a favorite with Cooper, and " on this point we have the pleasure to agree with him," and although " The Last of the Mohicans, we believe, has generally been the most popular of these two books, . . . we still hold to The Pioneers." [22] He prefers the realistic characters in *The Pioneers,* for he says, " The Leatherstocking [in *The Pioneers*] is a natural, and yet poetical being, not only far above the ordinary run of fictitious personages, but even superior to the scout" [in *The Last of the Mohicans*], and Chingachgook in *The Pioneers* " is very much such a humble, long haired, half civilized, and drunken Indian as we have often seen, with some little remnant of his ancient glories about him." [23]

This is not the place to discuss Cooper's creation of Indian characters, but it may be said that Gardiner's and more especially Lewis Cass's denunciations of Cooper's Indians were based upon their demand for realistic characterization. Grenville Mellen, in his review of *Red Rover,* rejoices that Cooper has abandoned Indian tales, for " our complaint is, that we are overdoing the matter," and greets "him the more heartily on his own element," for "the quarter-deck is his home." [24]

In reviewing *The Water-Witch,* O. W. P. Peabody compares Cooper with Scott, declaring that Cooper is not an imitator of Scott, except " in his adherence to truth and nature; and we wish that such imitation were more common than it is." [25] He praises Cooper's power of description, and admits that it is not " altogether just to condemn " his Indians. But Peabody strikes one discordant note in exhibiting a New England sensitiveness to Cooper's Yankee characters. Former critics had made no comment upon such characters as Harvey Birch and David Gamut as Yankees; the Boston and Cambridge contributors saw no offense—for there was none—in a New Yorker's portrayal of eccentric New England

[21] *NAR*, XXIII (July, 1826), 152.
[22] *Ibid.*, pp. 195, 197.
[23] *Ibid.*, p. 195.
[24] *NAR*, XXVII (July, 1828), 139-54.
[25] *NAR*, XXXII (April, 1831), 511.

characters. But Peabody seems decidedly provincial when he writes, "We may possibly subject ourselves to the imputation of being unreasonably sensitive; but a decent regard to the New England character impels us to declare that it has never been our fortune to encounter any Yankee, in any novel, who has the slightest claim to be considered as a fair specimen of the genus." [26]

From 1838 to 1850 the *Review* published four reviews of Cooper's works, all marked by vitriolic denunciation. Three dealt with *Gleanings in Europe, Homeward Bound,* and *Ways of the Hour,* and were written by Francis Bowen; the fourth was a review of the *Naval History* by Alexander S. Mackenzie. Francis Bowen's review of *Gleanings in Europe* was his first contribution to the *Review,* written while he was an instructor at Harvard; but during his prolific journalistic life he contributed a hundred articles and reviews which mark the decline of the *Review* to its lowest depths. As philosopher and historian, he was " always definite in his contentions," against the theory of evolution, against the revolutionary cause of Louis Kossuth in 1851 (which cost him the McLean professorship of history at Harvard), and against the tariff laws, although he was a protectionist. He seemed completely unaware of the transcendental movement and of the Concord-Cambridge writers. In the words of J. A. Ward, ". . . there is no hint throughout the ten years of his service that the active minds in New England were at that time in a social and spiritual ferment, or that *The Dial* was taking the lead in live discussions." [27]

Under Francis Bowen's heavy hand Cooper's works were bludgeoned with denunciatory pronouncements. " Mr. Cooper's cardinal sin," he says, " is negligence "; his sketches are " evidently thrown off in a hurry "; his " most decided failure is in the description of female personages "; " he cannot catch the tone of polite conversation "; " the main action of the story is often incredible, and the lesser incidents . . . are frequently forced and unnatural "; " he has presented the aborigines of this country in far too flattering colors "; *The Pilot* is his best sea-novel, because " it is not strained to produce striking events, or to get up an effective picture of movements at sea "; *The Red Rover* " borders on romance "; and *The Water-Witch* has many " absurdities of plot." Cooper's *Gleanings in Europe* shows that he " has certainly seen something of the

[26] *Ibid.*, p. 518.        [27] *NAR*, CCI (Jan., 1915), 129.

world, whether it has been to his advantage or not," but "its meagreness is such, as to render it difficult to tell what it does contain." "On trifling occasions his ire is roused, and manifested with a bitterness of expression, which, when contrasted with the insignificance of the matter in question, appears wholly unreasonable and absurd." After pointing out many of Cooper's real or imagined defects, Bowen writes: "We have spoken freely, though with no captious spirit, of the defects of Mr. Cooper's writings, for the beauties are so evident, and have been so well attested by the wide-spread popularity of the works that they needed no particular notice."

There is no indication that Bowen regarded Cooper as prejudiced against New England, although he considered his New England characters as only half successful. He says that "Billy Kirby, the wood-chopper from 'Varmount,' with his huge frame, indolent good-nature, boastful speech, and readiness to turn his hand to any employment, is a successful sketch. And the bustling, pragmatical 'Squire Jones,' with his inordinate self-conceit, and officious habits, the *factotum* of the village, shrewd in some things, but a most practicable dupe in others, will be easily recognized by any denizen of a New England town. Still, the real Yankee remains to be sketched by some limner of a more delicate touch, and nicer tact than Mr. Cooper." Bowen advises Cooper to turn again to tales based on native material. "There are copious materials for fiction," he says, "in the adventurous history of the pilgrim settlers, and their immediate descendants, by using which, he will do better service to his countrymen and more honor to himself, than by retracing the worn tracks of European novelists, or speculating upon political topics of ephemeral interest."

Bowen's brief notice of *Homeward Bound* was unnecessarily severe, as the following extracts show:

> Professing to be a sturdy republican, he [Mr. Cooper] has exhausted his powers of invective upon the manners and characters of his countrymen, who are, taking his own descriptions for truth, ignorant of the first principles of social refinement, and no better than a nation of brutes and savages. If such are the friends of Republicanism, she may well pray Heaven to save her from them.
>
> Mr. Cooper's works, for the past three or four years, seem to have been written under no higher inspiration that than of spleen. They abound in uncalled-for political disquisitions filled up with bitterest scorn and

hatred. They are deformed by perpetual outbreaks of a spirit, which might be expected to show itself in the pages of a ruthless partisan, careless of truth in aiming at the reputation of an opponent whom he wishes to ruin.[28]

Twelve years later, Bowen reviewed Cooper's last novel, *Ways of the Hour*.[29] In this review he gives no evidence that he had read *The Pathfinder, The Deerslayer, Miles Wallingford,* and the other excellent tales written by Cooper in the last decade of his life.

> Mr. Cooper as a novelist is but the ghost of his former self. He committed literary suicide at least ten years ago . . . with the publication of *The Monikins*. Of the novels which have come after it . . . they are written by a shade of Mr. Cooper, who represents very fairly his bad taste, his garrulity, and his prejudices. . . . They are ebullitions of ill nature, petulant manifestations of an irritable and scolding temperament.[30]

The review of Cooper's *Naval History* by A. S. Mackenzie appeared in October, 1839. The accounts of Cooper's version of the battle of Lake Erie, of the bitter enmities between Commodore Perry and his second in command, Commodore Jesse Elliott, and between their partisans, the facts about the libel suits which Cooper won against his libelers, are told at considerable length by Lounsbury and other biographers, and are too long to be related here. The attitude of the *Review,* as indicated by the notorious Mackenzie, was that of resentment against Cooper for refusing to disparage Elliott. What reader today knows about Elliott? But for writing impartial history and biography, for attempting to state the truth, Cooper fell afoul of the partisan editor of the formerly impartial magazine. It is not surprising that throughout the remaining years of his life Cooper regarded *The North American Review* as unfair and prejudiced, like the hated *Edinburgh Review*.

If the length of this article permitted, one might study with interest the more judicial and inclusive criticism of Cooper's complete works, written after his death by Francis Parkman and Henry Theodore Tuckerman, and published in the *Review* in 1852 and 1859. In spite of the fair estimates by these capable critics, however, the narrow sectionalism of *The North American Review* under Palfrey and Bowen continued for many years to prejudice readers against the most nationally-minded novelist of his time.

*The University of North Carolina.*

---

[28] *NAR*, XLVII (Oct., 1838), 488-89.
[29] *NAR*, LXXI (July, 1850), 121-35.
[30] *Ibid.*, pp. 121 ff.

# LITERATURE FOR AN AUDIENCE

By George F. Reynolds

(1)

Classifications in literature are, especially in empressionistic critical circles, now much out of favor. Indeed, since Polonius's "tragedy, comedy, history, tragical-historical, tragical-comical-pastoral," a good many more classifications than his have seemed rather ridiculous. Yet there is one not generally recognized, which, resting on a few simple differences, assists, I think, toward fairer judgments, clarifies some critical problems, and is therefore worth considering.

This classification, to state it briefly, is that between literature for people assembled as an audience, and literature for the individual reading alone. Of course many critics have considered the influence of an audience, especially upon drama; for example, Bacon (*De Augmentis,* tr. Wats, 1640, 107): "The minds of men are more patent of affections congregate than solitary"; A. W. Schlegel (*Lectures on Dramatic Art and Literature,* chapter II): "almost inconceivable is the power of a visible communion of numbers"; and Poe (*Marginalia,* 384): "One half the pleasure experienced in a theater arises from the spectator's sympathy with the rest of the audience, and especially from his belief in their sympathy with him." Numerous more recent writers, especially actors, managers, and practicing theatrical critics (for instance, H. Glover, *Drama and Mankind,* 17, 21; Clayton Hamilton, *Studies in Stagecraft,* 259-261; George Nathan, *The Critic and the Drama,* 57-58) have emphasized the importance of the audience in drama. Contrarywise, J. E. Spingarn (*Creative Criticism,* 84) after a long historical treatment of critical opinion on the subject, dismisses the influence of the audience on itself as of little consequence, and says that the less a playwright thinks of his audience the better. I am not forgetting these contributions. But what appears to have escaped much observation is the considerable number of literary forms intended for an audience, and the light they collectively throw upon certain problems. Some now exist only in books—for them scarcely a form of life; for instance, the folk-ballads; some, like the oration, have though still practised almost succumbed to the influence of the printed page; others, like the story for vocal telling, have, at least in our civilization, become merely trivial. To be noted in passing, also, though largely omitted of necessity in the following treatment, are the related forms which the crowd not only listens to but participates in—I name the important and the unimportant together—the college yell, hymns and patriotic songs, liturgies, etc.; and also those kinds of dancing, music, and pictures (movies) for the crowd. All have in common not unilluminating characteristics, for all are planned to be apprehended by people in groups. The group is a conditioning influence upon them, and the suggested classification of art for an audience, and specifically literary art, is therefore not merely a critical figment arbitrarily imposed, but fundamental. It seems, however, pretty much neglected, or, worse, misunderstood.

(2)

The misunderstanding lies in confusing the audience for this sort of literature with the psychological "mob" or "crowd" which M. LeBon described in his *The Crowd,* and which numerous students like Professor Brander Matthews (*A Study of Drama,* chapter IV) and his disciple, Mr. Clayton Hamilton (*The Theory of the Theater,* 33) have accepted as a true account of the theatrical audience. Maybe groups do actually exist in which as the psychologists say the conscious personalities of the individuals composing it are swallowed up in the mob-mind—fortunately it is not necessary for mere students of literature to decide whether this is true or not. But we may safely assert that such groups seldom or never arise in the theater. Many circumstances prevent such a development, but one is enough to mention: people never, unless like Mr. Partridge unbelievably unsophisticated, forget that they are witnessing a play. If they did so forget they would themselves join in the action to aid the distressed heroine or call the police. They never do; so much at least of individual consciousness remains and so little does the mob state of mind arise. Oratory and religious and patriotic songs may on occasion, when this element of play and pretence is lacking, produce a nearer approach to such a mob state of mind as the psychologist describes, but since in most situations they do not, they may be considered, like the drama and the story, literature for an audience rather than for a mob.

[811]

To deny that the audience is a mob is not however to say it has no special psychology of its own. I am inclined to think that it has—that there is an audience, as well as, less surely, a mob state of mind. (Mr. Everett Martin in his *The Behavior of Crowds*, 23 ff., distinguishes between the behavior of an audience and a "crowd.") In an audience, for example, though quite aware that we are in a theater at a play, we endure without conscious discomfort drafts, bad air, restricted positions which if we were alone would make us acutely miserable. Moreover some of our perceptions are heightened. We laugh, applaud, make inferences, keep silence in unison with a thousand others. Anybody ever practically concerned with the production of plays is convinced of the reality of the audience influence upon itself. But some literary critics deny it, and the point need not here be insisted upon. Undeniable remain the differences which arise from reading by ourselves and listening in company with others. In the one circumstance we read at any rate we please, turn back to clear up vague parts, skip at our pleasure, repeat what we specially enjoy, stop and resume when we wish to. In an audience we must keep up with what is going on, comprehend it at once or not at all, depend upon the author for contrast and relief. In art for an audience the audience is itself part of the material in which the author works, modifying his style, his devices, his technic. Mr. Spingarn would have a playwright forget his audience. To preserve his artistic integrity perhaps he should forget their tastes, opinions, and prejudices. But to neglect an audience in the points I am emphasizing is almost as absurd as to write in Chinese for Englishmen. Respect for one's medium is one of the few unquestioned principles of criticism. Therefore, however impatient one may be of classifications in general, and however doubtful as to the reality of mob and audience states of mind, the difference between literature for a solitary reader and for an audience may still be accepted.

(3)

Logically, I suppose, some of the differences between these types of literature should now be cited in proof, but it will save space to do not merely this but to present them in connection with other larger matters. For instance, I have claimed that recognition of these types makes possible a fairer critical judgment. Literary critics as a rule have been scornful of literature for an audience. Professor Gummere ("Primitive Poetry and the Ballad," *Modern Philology*, I, 1903, 193 ff.) noted the injustice done to the old ballads by criticism generally, and it is a commonplace to brand oratory as "rhetorical," "wordy," "vulgar." Often this is deserved, of course, but often it is not, though the reason for it is clear enough. Literary criticism is a function exercised mainly by a person reading alone. He forms his principles and standards on the basis of this solitary reading, and then applies them to all literature which he encounters, most of which, indeed, in this age of printed books, is intended for such reading. So, quite naturally, he approaches literature for an audience in the same way; very often he even tests it by the effect it has upon him when he reads it by himself. Most of the time he can scarcely do otherwise. But by not allowing, even imaginatively, for the difference in circumstances, he is clearly unfair. It is, shall we say, like looking at a painting in a red light. When he is by himself he is undisturbed by outward impression. His attention may be held by an only mildly interesting story, provided it has other attractive features. He enjoys sometimes being puzzled, and if he is a skillful reader finds delicately suggestive phrasing more delightful than outright statement. His cultivated taste tends continually toward the finished, the subtle, even the precious. He is likely to admire concisely expressed ideas. On the other hand an individual member of an audience is in the midst of distraction and will not, indeed cannot, listen at all unless the material presented has so compelling an interest that all the audience attends to it. Though intense, the attention of this group is at best wavering and unstable. The audience resents being puzzled—unless it understands that is part of the game, it must have time to grasp ideas, it has no ear for subtleties. The careful effects which please the solitary reader do not touch even the same person when he first hears them in an audience—perhaps he cannot hear them. All this may sound as if literature for an audience was much limited in its possibilites. Its advantage lies in the depth and power of its effects. The intent audience leaps as it were to a resounding phrase, a repeated expression, a sharp contrast, a swift climax, a bold figure (to illustrate at least the last, notice Hamlet's "to take arms against a sea of troubles ") which trouble the solitary reader or perhaps leave him cold. These devices of audience art are just as legitimate for it and just as skillfull as are the devices of individual art for its special purpose. But the critic reading alone is apt to call them cheap because to him too obvious, or when he does praise some piece of literature for an audience to do so for qualities which could equally well appear in literature for an individual, and which as likely as not hinder rather than help it in its intended purpose. No one would condemn a sonnet, an essay, or a novel because it fails to impress an audience to whom it is read—most such forms fail completely; that a ballad or a speech or a play does not please a solitary reader, is, it seems only fair to say, equally beside the mark.

This is not to claim, of course, that every speech or play which is successful with an audience is therefore great literature. Not every novel that enthralls an individual reader is great either. That reader even after an all night session with it, may toss it to quick oblivion. Permanence of value rests on other grounds, the same for literature of all kinds whether for an audience or for the solitary reader—truth, universality, significant form, and all the rest. Nor am I now discussing whether literature for an audience is more or less likely than literature for an individual to possess these admirable qualities. That is another question; each form has its own peculiar merits and defects. I am only emphasizing the necessity of considering literature for an audience in the light of its special circumstances.

(4)

A precise instance or two will make the point clear. One striking device of literature for an audience is repetition in one form or another. It shows in the responses of the litany, even in most college yells, in the patterns of dances for an audience, in the parallel constructions of oratory, in the refrains of hymns and of the old ballads, in the repeated phrases, business, situations of drama. And it generally forms the very basis of stories for telling. In Jesus's parable of the talents, for example (*Matthew*, xxv, 14-30), why is the second servant, the one with the two talents, included? He adds nothing to the idea; the first with his five and the third with his one furnish the necessary contrast. The second servant shows conspicuously the methods of art for an audience; the details about him, prolonging the crisis, serve to heighten expectation, and give the parable much of its effectiveness. This triple structure is common to most successful after-dinner anecdotes and to many folk-tales; for example The Three Bears and The Little Red Hen. Yet to the solitary reader, unless imaginatively he makes himself into an audience, the second step in the triple situation seems rather a waste of words, mere surplusage.

This is the effect sometimes of another device in art for an audience. Mr. C. E. Montague in his paper "The Literary Play" (*Essays and Studies by Members of the English Association*, vol. II, 1911) notices the provision in the orations of Fox and Bright of apparently "infantine redundancy and tautology" and in Ibsen's plays of "idle-looking little trivialities, perhaps about cigarettes and coffee," which Montague rightly recognizes as intended as "breathing-spaces for the audience's attention," necessary moments of relief from strain. Unless these are provided—he notes their absence in Phillips's *Paolo and Francesca*—the audience is unable to grasp the meaning of the successive situations in the swift progress of the play, or, held tense too long—as perhaps in Maeterlinck's *Intruder*—is likely to break out into hysterical shuffling or even laughter. Such a passage for relief occurs, for example, in act I of *The Doll's House,* the placing of the Christmas tree after Krogstad's call, though Ibsen with craftsman's economy also uses it to show Nora's apprehension. Sometimes such apparently trivial passages, instead of letting down the tension, prolong it and even intensify it, as Helmer's talk to Mrs. Linde about knitting after she has advised Nora to tell him everything. Duncan and Banquo's conversation (*Macbeth,* I, 6) concerning the pleasant location of Macbeth's castle may be considered to illustrate either of these uses. On the Elizabethan stage its tranquil beauty followed without a pause Lady Macbeth's sinister planning for Duncan's murder. The purely "literary" critic praises this passage for its poetry; the antiquarian notes that it complies with the so-called Law of Re-entry; examined from the point of view of literature for an audience, it affords an excellent example of a passage unnecessary for the plot but highly useful in the emotional sequence of the play.

(5)

The two characteristics of literature for an audience just discussed are after all only devices. A third, however, brings up one of the most hotly disputed matters concerning drama; that is, its essential element. Is this surprise—the shock of the unexpected, as Dumas and Scott thought and practised; or suspense—waiting for we know not what (most people will say off-hand their interest is in learning "how the story comes out"); or expectation—eagerly looking forward to something we *almost* foresee? Coleridge ("Characteristics of Shakespeare's Dramas," *Collected Works,* IV, 61) noted Shakespeare's preference for expectation rather than surprise: "As the feeling with which we startle at a shooting-star compared with that of watching the sunrise at the pre-established moment, such and so low is surprise as compared with expectation." And Lessing (*Hamburg Dramaturgy,* No. 48): "Whoever is struck down in a moment, I can only pity for a moment. But how if I expect the blow, how if I see the storm brewing and threatening for some time about my head and his?" These are opinions based on drama; other forms of literature for an audience similarly show the greater force of expectation. The triple structure of the parable, the refrain of the hymn and the litany, the parallel construction of the oration, the repeated phrases and situations in a play—devices I have already called attention to—get their effectiveness largely from the expectation they create. So do the hints and omens and forebodings and prophecies of tragedy. The baleful openings of *Macbeth* and *Hamlet,* the oracle of *Oedipus,* the hints of disaster in such different sorts of modern plays as *The Second Mrs. Tanqueray* and *Riders to the Sea* are useful because they create expectation. The familiar "law" of comedy that the audience should be in on the joke points in the same direction. It is also notable how interest in any play increases as soon as the audience glimpses an approaching situation, whether made to do so by, for instance, a revolver casually displayed in a drawer, the completion of arrangements for a practical joke, the determination of somebody to do something decisive, or the threat of some immediate catastrophe. Similarly an orator has the keenest attention when the situation by itself or by his own devising makes it appear that each successive word may bring him either disaster or victory. Only when a group of people is thus made to look ahead, waiting intently for something dimly foreseen, does it become a real audience; only then is the essential element of art for an audience shown to be present.

(6)

What will bring about such expectation is another much debated matter. Conflict, turning of the will, crisis, putting a man "up against something"—these are the more precise answers so far as drama is concerned of in turn Brunetière and his many followers, and Stuart Sherman, William Archer, and Henry Arthur Jones. But none of these answers has satisfied everybody or explained all successful plays. Perhaps this is because critics in searching for what is "dramatic" have really been trying to distinguish what will create and hold the attention of an audience. Indeed some definitions of drama are scarcely less precise: Nathan (*The Critic and the Drama*, 33): "Good drama is anything that interests an intelligently emotional group of persons assembled together in an illuminated hall"—but why "illuminated hall"; to exclude circuses? And Barker (quoted by Moderwell, *The Theater of Today*, 154) "A play is anything that can be made effective upon the stage of a theatre by human agency. And I am not sure that this definition is not too narrow." These definitions would include oratory, lyrics, and stories adapted for the crowd, and they should. Professor Brander Matthews's thesis in his *Development of the Drama* that in sloughing off these elements, present in Greek plays, the drama has progressed can hardly fail to give one pause. There seems to be something dubious about a progress from Sophocles to —shall we say—Pinero. Of course this is a progress toward realism, or at least that ideal of it expressed by Ibsen—that the play should as presented seem actually occurring, and for the first time. But if anything is sure it is that this ideal of realism has been the ideal of drama only for a relatively few years, and that it is by no means the only ideal for drama now; the newer expressionistic drama denies it as clearly as does the drama of the Greeks and the Elizabethans. To say, therefore, that oratory—if it is *dramatic* oratory, and lyric poetry—if *dramatic* lyric, and epic—if *dramatic* epic (and by "dramatic" I mean here "suited for an audience"), are necessarily excrescences to be sloughed off, is to fail to recognize the essential oneness of literature for an audience. *Cyrano de Bergerac,* to cite a single modern instance, successful surely if any play has been, combines incident, the usual stuff of drama, with oratory (the tirades), lyrics (the ballades), and narrative (the trip to the moon), and makes it perfectly clear that these are still harmonious and effective elements in drama as art for an audience. Perhaps the sloughing off has been impoverishment rather than development.

(7)

All of which suggests, further, that the much disputed " dramatic illusion " is after all only another name for audience spirit. The criticism of twenty-five years ago, obsessed by realism, identified dramatic illusion with an illusion of reality, but this is obviously not the effect aimed at in many great dramas of the past or present, and it is seldom attained, as I have already pointed out, even in dramas which do try for it. But this does not seem to make much difference. What does matter is whether the group of listeners is made to respond together as an audience. If this happens, even though the play is fantasy, impossible farce, or bald melodrama, there is illusion and to spare; if it does not exist, all the realistic detail in the world will not create any kind of dramatic illusion with anybody.

(8)

In this attempt to show that literature for an audience is a valid and useful classification, I have by intention only scratched the surface of the subject, and I have dealt mostly with drama, since it is the most important form of such literature today. Even so slight consideration shows, I think, that study and criticism of such literature can fairly be carried on only with its special circumstances in mind. That is, all the plays we study should, so far as possible, be acted or at least read before an audience, and, when this is not possible, imagined in such a setting. Until we have done this we can say little that is profitable concerning any play.

Further consideration of these various forms of literature for an audience will show other likenesses as well as distinct differences. One important difference is, for example, in style. To discuss this properly would require considerable space; here I may only mention these two facts: that in drama the competent playwright omits in dialogue what can more effectively be said by gesture or by settings—he leaves, as Sidney Grundy advised, gaps to be filled by his collaborating actors and scene-designers; and that he crystallizes his ideas at frequent intervals into phrases immediately comprehensible but pregnant with meaning. Not observing one or both of these necessities, Browning and Tennyson, in trying to write plays for audiences, showed rather how effective poets they are for individual readers. It would be difficult to find better proof than their plays of the desirability of recognizing literature for an audience as distinct from literature for the solitary reader.

*University of Colorado.*

# GOETHE AND BANCROFT

## By O. W. Long

One of the most important contributions to American intellectual life in the early nineteenth century was the romantic impulse which impelled a group of scholars to pursue their studies in foreign countries. George Ticknor, Edward Everett, Joseph Cogswell, and George Bancroft, as students at Göttingen between the years 1815 and 1820, were the pioneers in this movement. Their return to pursuits in various fields of knowledge, and the dissemination of their views of European life and culture in several of the prominent journals, lent a powerful inspiration to the progress of learning. The diaries and correspondence of this group who met many celebrities abroad, including Goethe in Weimar and Jena, furnish many parallels of record and impression. No one of them, however, was so deeply impressed by Goethe as was George Bancroft.

After graduating with distinction from Harvard in 1817, Bancroft, upon recommendation of Edward Everett, his former tutor in Greek, was sent by the Harvard Corporation the following year to Göttingen to complete his training. He studied with several of the leading scholars of that time, with Eichhorn, Dissen, Heeren, and Blumenbach, and received the doctor's degree in 1820, at the age of less than twenty years. The following semester was spent in Berlin, and after a period of travel, he returned home in 1822.

Although Bancroft entered upon his university life in Göttingen with a slight knowledge of German,[1] he devoted considerable attention, in addition to his major subjects, history and the classics, to the study of the German language and literature, an interest which he continued until many years later. Immediately after his arrival in August, he writes that the first month or two must be passed in learning the German language "for conversation," for which purpose he is spending an hour each day with his tutor, George Friedrich Benecke, the professor of English and German. He continued his study with Benecke through the autumn, was

---

[1] James Russell Lowell, referring in his address before the Modern Language Association in 1890 to the early struggle of German in this country, adds: "Mr. George Bancroft told me that he learned German of Professor Sidney Willard, who, himself self-taught, had no notion of its pronunciation." Cf. *PMLA.*, V, 51.

soon prepared to send his friend, the Reverend Andrews Norton, a specimen or two of "the high language of Germany, if it did not sound so flatly like blasphemy or vulgarity in English," [2] and progressed so rapidly that, in June of the following year, he was bold enough to deliver a sermon in the language in the vicinity of Göttingen.

Bancroft's earliest impressions of Goethe were based on anecdotes that were current in Göttingen, and on direct reading of his writings. In the home of Blumenbach, the natural scientist, he heard stories of the poet's "love of good living and good company," [3] and of his disappointment in the reception of his treatise on optics. The journal for September 15 records the reading of Schiller's historical writings and several works of Goethe.

> I am only more and more astonished at the indecency and immorality of the latter. He appears to prefer to represent vice as lovely and exciting sympathy, than virtue, and would rather take for his heroine a prostitute or a profligate, than give birth to that purity of thought and loftiness of soul, which is the peculiar duty of the poet to raise, by connecting his inventions with the actions of heroes, and embodying in verse the merits of the benefactors of mankind.

Nor was Bancroft's prejudice diminished as he continued his reading during the year. The following March he states frankly:

> I do not love Goethe. He is too dirty, too bestial in his conceptions. There is nothing of a noble, high, enthusiastic soul in him. His genius is admirable. His knowledge of life wonderful. But the whole is spoilt by the immorality of his writings, by the vulgarity of his characters. It may be, that all this happens in the world, but at any rate, this remains a blot on his fame, which all the waters of the ocean cannot make white and which justify in his censures a moral man, who cannot find in him a single work of genius.[4]

---

[2] Letter to Pres. Kirkland, Aug. 15 and Sept. 12, 1818, and to Norton, Oct. 17 and 26, 1818, Bancroft MSS. *Mass. Histl. Soc.*

[3] Journal, Aug. 30, 1818. Cf. M. A. DeWolfe Howe, *Life and Letters of George Bancroft* (N. Y., 1908), I, 38. A curious entry appears in Bancroft's Journal for Jan. [n. d.] 1819: "I hear that Goethe married about seven years ago, & I believe a mistress, by whom he had had a son. The woman was very disgusting in her manners, and after being married a short time, died of intemperance, i. e., of drinking gin." A similar story was included in Bancroft's letter to Andrews Norton, June 21.

[4] Journal, March 28, 1819, Bancroft MSS.

As was true of all American students in Germany, Bancroft took advantage of his vacations in making excursions to various cities, and in meeting men of eminence. September 4, 1819, he started on a tour of six weeks which carried him as far east as Prague. In Dresden he met Cogswell, with whom he was to be intimately associated in later years, and at Jena in the forenoon of October 12 he met Goethe for the first time. The interview was informal, in the garden, where, as Bancroft reports, the poet was clad in a "most unseemly manner," in dress which was "somewhat that of a sloven," and the conversation was principally on America, literary topics, and on English poets, particularly Byron. The visit is described in Bancroft's journal and in subsequent letters.[5] He wrote to President Kirkland:

> Goethe received me with unusual kindness, and spoke of America, as if our country was one of the objects that most interested him in his old age. I got him to talk about the present race of English poets. He spoke of Byron with quite as much admiration as even John Randolph can ever have felt for him. Goethe is now exceedingly old, yet vigourous, dignified and active. He talks with liveliness and quickness, yet never relaxes from a high air of majesty, which is meant to inspire every one with proper awe, though not more than half of it is genuine gravity of character, the other moiety being nothing more than the importance excited by the feeling of being prime minister to the Duke of Weimar.[6]

Bancroft promised to send Goethe a book on the early inhabitants of North America,[7] and journeyed the following day to Weimar, where he was received by Kräuter, secretary of the library, and was entertained in Goethe's home. He found Ottilie "witty and agree-

---

[5] Cf. Howe, I, 67-68, Biedermann, *Goethes Gespräche*, II, 448 f. and unpublished letters of Nov. 20, 1819, to Pres. Kirkland and of May [n. d.], 1820, to Bancroft's sisters.

[6] Letter, Nov. 20, 1819.

[7] Cf. L. L. Mackall, "Briefwechsel zwischen Goethe und Amerikanern," *Goethe-Jahrbuch*, XXV, 19. The particular work was, as Mackall points out in "Goethe's Letter to Cogswell," *Essays offered to Herbert Putnam* (New Haven, 1929), p. 325, a volume of *Transactions of the Historical & Literary Committee of the American Philosophical Society* (Phila., 1819), containing "An Account of the History, Manners, and Customs, of the Indian Nation, who once Inhabited Pennsylvania and the Neighbouring States," by the Rev. John Heckewelder, a German translation of which appeared at Göttingen in 1821.

able ... knowing always what to say," and the son "rather a stupid and ignorant fellow."

In September of the following year Bancroft received his degree. He had become displeased with Göttingen, in which he found "a want of religious sentiment, an absence of moral feeling," the people unsocial, and many of the men of letters "altogether without manners."[8] Berlin with such scholars as Boeckh, Buttmann, Wolf, Hegel, and Schleiermacher, offered, he believed, more advantages. He therefore spent a semester at Berlin, and later, on March 7 and 12, visited Goethe in Weimar.[9] The first of these visits is fully described in Bancroft's journal.[10] He found him this time more formal and less interested in affairs of the world, though he spoke of the progress in America, and again displayed his fondness for Byron, referring especially to *Manfred* and *Don Juan*. He was silent concerning German poets, but praised Humboldt's *Agamemnon* and Schlegel's translation of Shakespeare. The visit a few days later was brief. Goethe expressed an interest in Bancroft's future welfare, and mentioned Cogswell, to whom he had forwarded books.[11] "Weimar is the only place I know of, worthy of commemoration for its staid morality," wrote Bancroft afterward to Andrews Norton,[12] who was constantly warning him against the vice of Europe, and many years later, when Bancroft represented his country at Berlin, he took pride in telling the Queen of Prussia that he had seen Goethe.[13]

After a year of travel, in the course of which, May 22, 1822, he had his memorable visit at Monte Nero with Byron, to whom he mentioned Goethe's comparison of *Manfred* and *Faust*, Bancroft returned home.[14] Although disappointed in not being granted

[8] Journal, Dec. 3, 1820.

[9] According to Goethe's diary, it was "Herr Beresford aus der Gegend von Boston," who visited him. Cf. *Goethe-Jahrbuch*, XXV, 19. This, as Mackall points out, *Essays offered to Herbert Putnam*, p. 324, was Bancroft.

[10] Cf. Howe, I, 97 f. and *Goethes Gespräche*, II, 500 f.

[11] For Goethe's relations to Cogswell, cf. Mackall, *Goethe-Jahrbuch*, XXV, 6 f.

[12] July 18, 1821.

[13] Cf. Howe, II, 177.

[14] Byron's statement that he had known something of *Faust* through Monk Lewis is well known. Cf. H. S. White, "Goethe in Amerika," *Goethe-Jahrbuch*, V, 223, and the *Life, Letters and Journals* of George Ticknor, I, 165, for Byron's remarks to Ticknor in Venice, Oct. 20, 1817.

permission to lecture at Harvard on history, he accepted an appointment as tutor in Greek, which position he held for one year, preaching some of the time in the leading churches in the vicinity of Boston. He had made the most of his opportunities in Europe, had returned with enthusiasm for German scholarship and German methods of education, but was regarded affected and artificial in manner, and needed, as Emerson stated, "a great deal of cutting and pruning."[15] He attempted to reform the curriculum, but encountering difficulties in a conservative institution, was glad at the close of the year to withdraw with Cogswell to Northampton, where the two established the famous Round Hill School. With this institution he was associated until 1831, when he began his historical pursuits and public career.

Although Bancroft is known chiefly as an historian and a diplomat, he devoted much time in his early life to poetry and to writing essays on German literature. His private library, rich in historical subjects, contained the works of Herder, Goethe, Schiller, and Heine. In Germany, as we have seen, he began his studies in German literature, even translating some of the poems of Schiller and Goethe, and during his connection with Round Hill he published in some of the leading journals many articles on literary subjects. His first contribution, a review of *Schiller's Minor Poems,* appeared in October, 1823, in the *North American Review.*[16] His early liking of Schiller is somewhat reflected in the following:

> Goethe reflects in his poems the feelings of others; Schiller felt deeply himself, and knew how to embody his feelings in verse. In whatever age or country Goethe places his invention, he instantly adapts himself to its manners and tone; Schiller always preserves under all changes of scene the peculiar characteristics of his own mind. The person of Goethe is never seen through his verse; that of Schiller presents itself constantly. It is the German poet in Spain, in Switzerland, in France; seizing on all opportunities of paying tribute to excellence, truth, and liberty. We may learn from Goethe what the world is; but Schiller teaches us what it should be.

---

[15] Letter to John B. Hill, Jan. 3, 1823, Bancroft MSS, N. Y. Pub. Lib.

[16] XVII, 268 f. Bancroft's review contains translations of five of Schiller's poems, three of which are included in his *Literary and Historical Miscellanies,* pp. 206, 210, 239. Dec. 15, 1824, Mrs. Hemans wrote to Bancroft: "I have heard your translation of Schiller's beautiful 'Ideale' spoken of in high terms, and should highly prize a copy of it, if you would be kind enough to favor me with one."

On February 9 of the following year Bancroft wrote to Jared Sparks, who had succeeded Everett as editor of the *North American*, "I have been cheating myself of my cares by making little translations from Goethe." In March he wrote: "On Goethe I am seriously employed, and hope to give some translations, which shall at least find their way into the albums of the ladies;" and in June: "Goethe shall be done soon. I have the ideas all warm in my head but must let them ferment a little more, that I may write coolly and judiciously."[17] He was then preparing his well-known essay, "The Life and Genius of Goethe," which was published in the October number.[18] The essay, which is Bancroft's most important contribution on the subject, shows that his earlier attitude of condemnation is somewhat modified. He reviews the various factors which influenced Goethe's poetic progress, commends him for his devotion to the pursuit of letters, and gives unqualified praise to his genius and his style. Certain works are cited as indication of great power of one who was master in his art, special reference being made to *Iphigenie, Tasso,* and the poems, several of which he translates.[19] *Faust* is a work of genius, though it is not of "a purely moral tendency," and in America the *Elective Affinities,* Bancroft states, would be considered "a false and dangerous libel on human nature." He closes by stating:

> But the works of Goethe are not without lessons of practical morality. . . . Though Goethe has so often delineated imaginary woes, and carried his readers into a world of fiction, yet it is the tendency of his writings

---

[17] Feb. 9, March 26, and June [n. d.], 1824, Sparks MSS, Harvard Library.

[18] *North Amer. Rev.*, XIX, 303 f. A separate reprint, Boston, 1824.

[19] The poems, "My Goddess," "Mignon," "The Violet," "The Angler," "Song of the Captive Count," "The Salutation of a Spirit," "Joy," and "The Eagle and the Dove," with two additional, "The Mournful History of the Noble Wife of Asan Aga" and "The Divine," are reprinted in the *Literary and Historical Miscellanies,* pp. 231 f. "The Salutation of a Spirit" is included in Longfellow's *Poets and Poetry of Europe* (Phila., 1845), p. 294. Mrs. Hemans wrote Bancroft, April 11, 1825, "I never saw the 'Angler' nor the 'Violet' so lightly and buoyantly rendered before, and I have to thank you not only for your translation of, but your observations upon that striking little piece, 'The Salutation of a Spirit,' which have thrown a light over its purpose, and developed a beauty I had not till now been aware of." Bancroft MSS.

to promote a love for the arts, for activity, for truth. They do not merely teach us to be satisfied with the world, but to bear with it, by showing how rich it is in the means of acquiring virtues, and of performing just and benevolent deeds.

The correspondence between Bancroft and his publisher in connection with this essay is interesting, and makes us query whether, after all, Bancroft's views were accurately presented. He sent his manuscript in July to Sparks, who, it seems, not infrequently took liberties with his contributors,[20] stating that it had cost him much time in the making, and requesting that it should not be altered without consultation before it was printed. However, the essay appeared with various changes which Sparks explained as "trifling," to which Bancroft replied:

> I know not how you can call the changes you made in the unfortunate article so trifling; for while I had been expecting to derive much pleasure from the appearance of it, I have felt only chagrin. And I cannot persuade myself, my disappointment is not well founded. Do you not know, you changed one assertion from a negative to a positive one, thereby saying something, which I do not believe, & which makes the words at least unmeaning. . . . You altered, what you would not have altered, had you understood, why and in what spirit it was written. And the change in two cases out of three, though few, materially affect both the meaning and the style of the most labored parts. I say labored parts, and I am free to add, labored with the most success, and the most *truth and nature*. The matter is of little moment, only in so far as the whole article is of little moment, and my desire to be esteemed as a writer a childish vanity.[21]

During his residence in Germany in 1825, George H. Calvert sent Goethe a copy of Bancroft's article, thinking, as he stated, that the poet might like to read what was written about him in the New World.[22] But Goethe had a few hours previously received a copy from a friend in Berlin, to whom he expressed his appreciation:

> It is in every case noteworthy to see how the effects of a long life work through the world, and also gain gradually here and there in influence, according to the times and circumstances. I had to smile when I was obliged to regard myself in so distant and besides so republican a mirror.

---

[20] Cf. John S. Bassett, *The Middle Group of Amer. Historians* (N. Y., 1917), p. 156.

[21] Nov. 17, 1824, Sparks MSS.

[22] "Weimar in 1825," *Putnam's Mag.*, VIII, 259, and *First Years in Europe* (Boston, 1866), pp. 165 f.

Moreover, this essay has a good effect upon everybody; so much intellect and insight, joined with a youthfully cheerfull enjoyment in writing, excites a certain sympathetic, pleasing feeling. He was able to fill out pleasingly even the gaps where particular information failed him and in general to round out the whole with euphemy.[23]

From 1827 to 1829 Bancroft contributed to the *American Quarterly Review* a series of articles on German literature, basing his remarks on various publications which appeared in Germany, and giving an outline of the development of the literature from its early period. He points out the essential characteristics of the most prominent writers, and in the third of the series,[24] published in September, 1828, pays his respects to Goethe. He refers to the poet's position of supremacy in the world, his sound judgment, brilliant imagination, wide range of ideas, and his optimism. "The author of *Werther*," writes Bancroft, "is the very last man who would have killed himself for love; the poet who has delineated Tasso's exquisite sensibility, was never a misanthrope or a hypochondriac." Nevertheless, Bancroft would condemn certain productions for ethical reasons. The *Roman Elegies* are of "heathenish voluptuousness," and the details of *Faust* are "often gross and offensive." One year later, in reviewing Henry E. Dwight's *Travels in Germany*,[25] Bancroft recalled with pride his personal contact with Goethe, and concluded his remarks by pronouncing the poet one of the greatest geniuses in history.

If Bancroft had written nothing further on Goethe than the publications thus far included, we should credit him with an intelligent appreciation, at times, even a scholarly analysis, of Germany's greatest poet. As we have observed, however, there is often in his opinions of Goethe's personality and of some of his writings a discordant note which is distinctly emphasized in the course of years. In 1838 John S. Dwight, one of the most enthusiastic exponents of German literature, published his *Select Minor Poems from the German of Goethe and Schiller*.[26] This was favorably reviewed by

---

[23] Cf. Mackall, *Goethe-Jahrbuch*, XXV, 20, 36. Mackall states that Varnhagen von Ense presented Gothe with a copy of the essay. The translation of Goethe's letter is given in Howe's *Bancroft*, I, 182.

[24] IV, 157 f.

[25] VI, 200 f.

[26] Contributed to Ripley's *Specimens of Foreign Standard Literature*, vol. III.

Bancroft the following year in the July number of the *Christian Examiner*,[27] but it gave him opportunity for one of the most scathing attacks on Goethe's character in the history of criticism. Contrasting Schiller and Goethe, he states that the latter had no philosophy, no creed, no principles. In youth Goethe was "indifferent to God, and reverential only toward rank and the Bourbons," in maturity, when his country was invaded, he "quietly studied Chinese or made experiments in natural philosophy," and is the representative of the morals and character of the "broken-down aristocracy." On matters of public opinion, he was silent, being "one of the most wary, calculating, circumspect people of all times." He is "far inferior" to Voltaire in genius, industry, and morality. His conception of freedom, as expressed particularly in three lines of *Tasso*, is his reply to Jefferson and the doctrines of the American Revolution. His works bear evidence that he had "no faith in reason, in affections, in God, in man, or in woman." *Wilhelm Meister* and *Elective Affinities* are products of the poet who "not only had no morals, but scarcely a knowledge of what morality consists in." Bancroft continues:

> It is this ignorance of morals, which gives to Goethe's works one of their peculiarities: insincerity. He is an artist, and not a man. He imitates, he reproduces, he does not create, he does not build up.
>
> In this want of sincerity lies also the secret of his want of popularity. Goethe is at once dissolute and illiberal. The poet knew in his old age, that he never could become popular. His chances at popularity are diminishing. Twaddle will not pass long for wisdom. The active spirit of movement and progress finds in his works little that attracts sympathy. The conservative loathes him; for there is nothing fixed and permanent and vital in his principles. To rest on him is like trusting in a gale to a dragging anchor, that has caught only in a quicksand.
>
> In everything that relates to firmness of principle, to love of truth for truth itself, to humanity, to holiness, to love of freedom, to virtue, Goethe holds perhaps the lowest place. What man of his genius is comparable to him for baseness? Byron, Voltaire, we had almost said Shelley, soar far above him in moral worth and generous feelings.

After his long tirade, Bancroft admits that Goethe is a master in the art of writing, of which his prose and shorter poems furnish the best illustration. He then turns to a discussion of Dwight's translations, and to his favorite poet, Schiller.

[27] XXVI, 360 f.

The "Studies in German Literature" which Bancroft published in his *Literary and Historical Miscellanies* in 1855, is largely a repetition, with slight variations, of what he had contributed in former years to the reviews. His discussion of Goethe was probably written many years earlier and expanded when he was preparing his essay for 1824, and more especially, his merciless criticism of 1839. In its present form, however, it is Bancroft's last published comment on the subject, and expresses, in the final paragraph, not only what he had practically stated years previously, but the opinion of Goethe which he doubtless held throughout his life:

> At the close we must again concede to Goethe that quality which distinguishes Scott, and in which Shakespeare was of all English writers pre-eminent—Truth in his descriptions. This, combined with the beautiful style and artistic skill of an accomplished master, will preserve through all the vicissitudes of taste the fame of a poet, whom universal consent would revere as one of the greatest of all time, if he had connected the culture of art with the service of humanity.[28]

Although not always consistent in his views, and changing decidedly his attitude between 1824 and 1839, it is evident that Bancroft had unlimited admiration for Goethe's genius and his commanding position in the world of letters. But it was the moral aspect of the poet, as revealed in some of his writings, that created the deepest impression on Bancroft. This point of view was manifest, as we have seen, in his journal when he first began reading Goethe, and remained with him throughout the years. He did much to make Goethe known in America, but the poet's views of life and those of the young New England Puritan were essentially different.

*Williams College.*

---

[28] P. 205.

## SPARSUS, A FRIEND OF PLINY

### By G. A. Harrer

It so happens, due to a paucity of historical material from the period, that friends of Pliny, to whom he addresses his *Letters,* are often little more than names. At times the contents of the letters sent them may give something about them, or Pliny may refer to them in other letters, or now and then other writers may mention them. A man like Tacitus, the historian, who is one of Pliny's addressees, is of course well known, but many others, although apparently men of standing in their day, are now unknown. Under such conditions inscriptions sometimes give welcome supplements to our stock of information. This is the case with reference to a man named Sparsus.

To Sparsus Pliny addressed two of the letters of his collection, Book IV, 5, written about 104 A. D., and Book VIII, 3, written about 108. There is no positive proof that these letters were sent to one man, Sparsus; but identity has been reasonably assumed from identity of name, a very rare name. Both the letters are concerned with one subject, literary efforts of Pliny. With the one, Pliny is sending a long oration which he has read during two days to a group of admiring and learned friends, and has now evidently prepared it for publication and wants Sparsus to read it. In the other letter Pliny has learned of Sparsus' good opinion of some book he has written, and he is on the point of sending him another oration to read. Sparsus is treated certainly as an equal of Pliny. He seems to have been one of the many well-to-do friends of Pliny who professed a taste for literature.

Martial wrote one of his *Epigrams* (Book XII, 57, written about 101 or 102 A. D.) for a Sparsus, who may be considered identical with Pliny's friend.[1] The cognomen *Sparsus* is very unusual. Some five men [2] altogether are known of this name for the first three centuries of the Roman Empire, and none of them is of the time of Pliny and Martial except the man, or men, they address. Martial's friend too is wealthy, and the great difference between his estate and Martial's is the cause of the composition of the poem.

---

[1] This was suggested by L. Friedländer (edition of Martial, Leipzig, 1886) in a note to the poem.

[2] *Prosopographia Imperii Romani,* vol. III, 574, s. v. *Sparsus,* and Pauly-Wissowa, *Real-Encyclopädie,* vol. XIII, Sp. 1890.

'You ask me, Sparsus,' says Martial, 'why I go off to the country to Nomentum? There is no place for a poor man to be at peace in Rome. You may enjoy your *rus in urbe,* but for me here *ad cubile est Roma.*'

The Pliny letters in question are addressed simply to a Sparsus, *Sparso suo.* So the manuscripts give the reading with no essential variations.[3] Only one manuscript, *codex Ashburnham R. 98(37), olim Riccardianus, saec. IX/X,* gives, not in the text, but in an index of the persons addressed, *adiuliumsparsum,* as the man of *Letters* IV, 5. Sparsus then may have been a *Iulius.* However, H. Keil in his great edition of Pliny [2] did not so much as refer to this *nomen,* nor did Mommsen in his *Index Nominum* to Keil's edition. More recently, however, Merrill [5] and R. C. Kukula [6] in their editions have trusted in the index of the Ashburnham Ms. and have addressed IV, 5, *Iulio Sparso.* On this question of the name, and on the question of the identity of Sparsus much may be learned from the reading of a recently discovered inscription.

The inscription is a Military Diploma, first published by I. Welkov,[7] and edited again by R. Cagnat.[8] Military Diplomas may be called honorable discharges from service in the Roman army. They are essentially laws given by the emperors, and therefore are regularly very accurate and dependable in statements of fact. They are dated by the emperor's reign and by the consuls. The Diploma in question was given by Domitian in his eighth tribuniciam power, and when M. Otacilius Catulus and Sextus Iulius Sparsus were consuls, November 7, 88 A. D.[9]

---

[3] See in the edition by C. T. Merrill (Leipzig, 1922) the critical notes on IV, 5.

[4] Leipzig, 1870.

[5] *Op. cit.*

[6] Leipzig, 1912.

[7] *Bull. de l'Inst. Archeol. Bulgare,* IV (1926/1927), p. 69 ff. I have used a photostatic copy of the photographic facsimiles given in Welkov's article. So far as his explanations were of use to me, I have had available a translation of the Bulgarian made for me by Miss Nada Tchomoneff in the Library of Congress.

[8] Cagnat used Welkov's edition, and published his study in *Syria,* IX (1928), pp. 25-31. The text of the Diploma is given also in *L'Année Épigraphique* (1927), 44.

[9] Harrer and Griffin, *Fasti Consulares, American Journal of Archeology,* XXXIV (1930), pp. 3-7.

It is highly probable that the Sextus Iulius Sparsus here mentioned is the friend addressed by Pliny. The identity in the *nomen* and in the unusual *cognomen,* the fact that the date of the inscription falls in the life-time of Pliny's friend, a time when a contemporary of the age of Pliny might well have been consul, are the chief bases for this conclusion.[10] It may be added that the Sparsus of the inscription was of Senatorial rank as were many of Pliny's circle.

What information then about Sparsus does the new inscription supply? It gives his name in full, Sextus Iulius Sparsus, his position as consul, which carries with it his rank as Senator.[11] The date of his consulship, in November, 88, probably means that he was consul for the last two months only in that year, and certainly shows that he was a *consul suffectus,* not one of the *consules ordinarii,* who began their term on the first of January and had the honor of giving their names to the year. As the qualifying age for the consulship was 35 at this time, Sparsus must have been born not later than 53 A. D., and so was at least six or seven years older than Pliny, whose birthday was in 62. The year of Sparsus' consulship was the year of the praetorship of Tacitus, the historian. It is therefore to be assumed that these men were acquainted. So much for the man.

It is now obvious that the inscription, giving the name Sextus Iulius Sparsus, attests the correctness of the index to the Ashburnham codex on the *nomen*,[12] and very nicely supports those editors, Kukula and Merrill, who had showed their belief in the value of the index.

*The University of North Carolina.*

---

[10] To a considerable extent the evidence is also good for an identification with Martial's friend. *Cognomen*, period, high position assumed from the great wealth of the man of the poem, all agree for inscription and epigram.

[11] B. Stech, in his *Senatores Romani* [Vespasian to Trajan inclusive] (Leipzig, 1912), having only the information in Pliny and in Martial about Sparsus, did not venture to list him as a Senator, or even to mention him as possibly of that rank.

[12] See too an unpublished thesis by Henrietta Underwood, *Inscriptional and Palaeographical Evidence on the Addressees of Pliny's Letters* (University of North Carolina, 1930), pp. 35 and 65.

## NOTES ON MATHURIN RÉGNIER'S *MACETTE*

### By J. Coriden Lyons

The long list of possible literary sources of Régnier's *Macette* has been a favorite field of discussion: particular attention is due the studies of M. Joseph Vianey and M. Ferdinand Brunot.[1] The succession of prototypes of this celebrated satire usually starts with the hag of Ovid's *Amores*[2] and includes Juan Ruiz's Trotaconventos and the Celestina.

Both Vianey and Brunot take due account of the possible classical influences on the development of the character of the *entremetteuse*. Such a character, in the classics and in obvious direct imitations of the classics, is pictured as a sorceress and magician. Where then, asks M. Brunot, did Régnier draw the inspiration of making his Macette a hypocritical lip-worshipper in the Christian faith?[3] He sees the answer in the far-flung influence of the *Celestina* and in actual observation of such types in real life.

To the already over-long list of possible sources of *Macette*, I should like to add the *Légende de Pierre Faifeu* of Charles de Bourdigné. This seems to have been first printed in 1532.[4] In chapter eight of this work, we read of a prank which Faifeu played on "Seur Macée la dévotte." The name and the suggestion of religious bigotry tempt one to make a more careful comparison of the two works.

While the old woman of the Faifeu story is far from being the complete character that Régnier created, certain of her traits remind one constantly of Macette. She is elderly and *dévotte*, and abuses her influence over the rather simple mother of Pierre Faifeu to prejudice her against her wayward son. She is not pictured as

[1] Joseph Vianey: *Mathurin Régnier* (Paris: Hachette, 1896). Ferdinand Brunot: *Macette, édition critique* (Paris: Soc. Nouv. de Librairie et d'Edition, 1900).

[2] Elegy XIII.

[3] *Op. cit.*, introduction, xxiii ff.

[4] On the *Légende de Pierre Faifeu* and the date of its appearance, see article by Abel Lefranc, *Rev. des Etudes Rabelaisiennes* (1905), 219 ff. and 327.

an *entremetteuse,* but such a further development in her character is suggested by the prank that Pierre plays on her in order to destroy her influence over his mother. He secretly hides a *fille de joye* in Macette's room and accuses the old woman of hypocrisy in his mother's presence. Macée denies the charge indignantly and demands a visit to her room: there is found the girl who confirms Faifeu's charge. All there remained for Régnier to do was change the apparent secret profession of Macée into a reality in order to have, in germ, all the character elements involved in the type of Macette.

There is no intention on the part of the writer to insist that Régnier knew the *Légende de Pierre Faifeu* and drew on this episode for the creation of his type. Such a knowledge seems impossible to prove. Even if he had been acquainted with the earlier poem, his own credit would not be diminished, for he created a work of art from a very crude model. It is interesting, however, to find the name Macée applied to a similar type almost a hundred years before the composition of Régnier's immortal satire.

The general conception of Macette belongs to all ages and all countries and Régnier's merit lies in having given elegant expression to a familiar idea. However, the influence of Pietro Aretino is so likely that it is impossible to overlook it. Both Vianey and Brunot have taken cognizance of this influence, the former emphasizing it and the latter minimizing its importance in favor of the *Celestina,* observation of actual life, and Ovid. Brunot seems to think that the *Roman de la Rose* had more probable influence on the evolution of Macette than the works of Aretino. My own feeling is that M. Vianey is right, that the works of Aretino exercised the preponderant literary influence on the development of the character of Macette.

Both Vianey and Brunot refer quite generally to the influence of Aretino's *Ragionamenti* and *Cortigiana* on *Macette*.[5] While such general comparisons have their value it would be desirable to bring out some more specific points of contact. I believe these

[5] The *Ragionamenti* were first printed in 1534, in an edition which pretends to have been printed in Paris, but which Brunot believes was actually made in Venice. The *Cortigiana* was first printed in 1535, and *Macette* in 1612.

points of contact can be shown to exist between the last third of Régnier's poem,[6] in which Macette prescribes the rules by which the girl will win fame and fortune as a courtesan, and that one of the *Ragionamenti* which is called *l'Educazione della Pippa*.[7]

Régnier was too much of an artist to follow exactly, point by point, the advice which Aretino makes his older woman give the younger. The ideas of the French satirist are much more condensed than those of his model, and a single line often fixes a character trait which is developed in several pages in the older work. However, the general nature of the instruction is the same in the two works. The young girl is reminded that a courtesan who allows her heart to be affected is on the road to ruin, and her success is dependent on her maintaining a cold-blooded indifference to everything except the possibilities of mercenary gain. The coins of a merchant ring as true as those of a man of position and, since all men are the same under their habiliments, the wise courtesan chooses the one whose purse is fattest. In both authors the older woman informs the girl that all classes of men are fair game, but cautions her against paying attention to the exaggerated promises of conceited, foppish courtiers, and recommends particularly churchmen with well-lined money-bags. Régnier says all this and more in a few lines, whereas Aretino causes the old woman to elaborate on the merits and defects of sundry classes and nationalities of men.

In another of the *Ragionamenti*[8] there is pictured an *entremetteuse* who relies on apparent religious devotion to enable herself to win the confidence of maidens who are the objects of lovers' desires. It is quite possible that this dialogue also contributed to the conception of Macette. In each case the old woman frequents the churches, pretends humility, and is in reality much amused by the gullibility of humanity.

It is a foregone conclusion that Régnier knew Aretino's works. The *Ragionamenti* have had frequent editions in Italy from 1535

[6] *Oeuvres Complètes de Mathurin Régnier* (Paris: Lemerre, 1875). 110-113.

[7] The *Ragionamenti* are divided into two parts of three days (or dialogues) each. The one referred to here is Part II, First Day. I have used the edition of Turin, 1536.

[8] Part II, Third Day.

down into the nineteenth century. They were most popular from the time of their appearance on through the sixteenth century.[9] Régnier made at least one and probably a number of trips to Italy: the first of these was probably in 1589 in the company of the Cardinal de Joyeuse. We learn from his *Satires* that he spent a considerable length of time in Rome, and what we know of Régnier's temperament and interests inclines us to believe that he frequented especially those circles of Roman society in which the works of Aretino would have been likely to find most favor.

An interesting parallel can be established between Régnier and Joachim du Bellay, who visited Italy thirty-odd years before the former did. Each was attached to a distinguished personage in the Church hierarchy, each was an adept at satire and chose to exercise this skill upon the foibles of Roman society of his day. The similarity in condition of life and temperament is striking, and we can easily imagine that they frequented the same circles of society. Du Bellay even composed a poem which is reminiscent of *Macette,—La Vieille Courtisane*.[10] We are quite willing in this case to accept Brunot's conclusion that there is not close enough similarity between the two poems to establish Du Bellay as a possible source for Régnier's character. But it is significant, we believe, that Du Bellay was thoroughly familiar with the works of Aretino and recognized him as the authority in this type of literature,—as is shown by the following lines he caused his old courtesan to utter:

> "Bref, tout cela qu'enseigne l'Aretin,
> Je le sçavoy: et sçavoy mettre en oeuvre
> Tous les secrets que son livre descoeuvre:"[11]

---

[9] In the preface to Vol. II of his translation of the *Ragionamenti* (Paris, 1923) Guillaume Apollinaire offers a bibliography of the editions of this work which he regards as incomplete. However, he mentions twenty editions and reprints of the *Ragionamenti* between 1534 and the end of the century. Interestingly enough, he mentions an edition of the *second part* of the *Ragionamenti* in 1584, just five years before it is calculated that Régnier made his first trip to Italy.

[10] *Poésies de Joachim du Bellay* (Paris: Garnier, 1919). Vol. II, 384-400.

[11] Ibid, 391.

Our conclusion is, in brief, that Vianey was perfectly right in believing Artetino's works, and especially the *Ragionamenti*, to be the direct literary source of Mathurin Régnier's *Macette*. The effort of this article has been to bring out with a certain additional degree of clarity the especial facts about the two works which establish this connection almost beyond the shadow of reasonable doubt, as well as to suggest Bourdigné's Macée as a possible ancestor of the type of Macette.

*The University of North Carolina.*

# A NOTE ON STENDHAL AND VICTOR HUGO

## By William M. Dey

In a volume published recently by M. Pierre Jourda,[1] we find the following passage quoted from the *Mémoires* of Rochefort concerning Victor Hugo's opinion of the *Rouge et le Noir:*

> J'ai tenté de lire ça, me dit-il (*Victor Hugo*); comment avez-vous pu aller plus loin que la quatrième page? Vous savez donc le patois? . . . Chaque fois que je tâche de déchiffrer une phrase de votre ouvrage de prédilection, c'est comme si on m'arrachait une dent . . . M. Stendhal ne peut pas rester parce qu'il ne s'est jamais douté un instant de ce que c'était qu'écrire.

In view of this passage, it is interesting to note several opinions found in the *Correspondance de Stendhal*[2] concerning Victor Hugo and his work. Given the character and the nature of the two men, it was inevitable that they should have a certain feeling of hostility toward each other. Stryienski[3] quotes a letter in which Sainte-Beuve describes to Albert Collignon a meeting of Stendhal and Victor Hugo in 1829 or in 1830, arranged by Mérimée. It was the first, and probably the last, meeting of the two men. A part of the letter follows:

> . . . . Quelle singulière soirée! Hugo et Stendhal chacun comme deux chats sauvages, de deux gouttières opposées, sur la défensive, les poils hérissés, et ne se faisant la patte de velours qu'avec des précautions infinies. Hugo, je l'avouerai, plus franc, plus large, ne craignant rien, sachant qu'il avait affaire dans Stendhal à un ennemi des vers, et de l'idéal, et du *lyrique*; Stendhal plus pointu, plus gêné, et (vous le dirai-je?) moins grande nature en cela.
>
> Mérimée, qui avait ménagé le rendez-vous, ne le rendait peut-être pas plus facile, et il n'aidait pas à rompre la glace; elle ne fut jamais brisée, ce soir-là, et je ne sais pas même s'ils se revirent. L'impression de Hugo ne fut pas très favorable.

---

[1] Pierre Jourda, *Stendhal raconté par ceux qui l'ont vu* (Paris: Librairie Stock, 1931), pp. 184-185.

[2] Paupe et Cheramy, *Correspondance de Stendhal (1800-1842)*, 3 vol. (Paris: Charles Bosse), 1908.

[3] Casimir Stryienski, *Soirées du Stendhal-Club* (première série) (Paris: Mercure de France, 1904), pp. 189-190.

There are three important passages of the *Correspondance* in which Stendhal refers to Victor Hugo; namely, in letters dated January 1, 1823,[4] February 10, 1829,[5] and (day and month not given), 1829.[6] These passages are quoted in the order mentioned:

(1) *Odes et Poésies sacrées* (*sic*), par M. Hugo, un volume.

Faire correctement des vers est devenu un métier dans la littérature française. Un jeune homme, en travaillant constamment, pendant quatre ans, à apprendre par cœur et étudier les vers de Racine et de Delille, parvient, en général, à faire des vers corrects et assez bons au premier coup d'œil; le mal est qu'à peine en a-t-on lu quinze ou vingt l'on se sent une très grande envie de bâiller.

Voilà ce que n'a pas dit le n° 74 de l'*Edinburgh Review* dans son excellent article sur la poésie française. Nous avons à Paris quatre mille jeunes littérateurs qui font bien le *vers français*; il y en a trois ou quatre, peut-être, qui sont parvenus à faire passer leurs pensées dans leurs vers; ce n'est pas une petite affaire. Sur ces quatre mille poètes, beaucoup ont des pensées; mais comment les rendre dans la langue de Racine? Dès qu'ils ne peuvent plus parler de *Muses*, d'*Apollon*, d'*Hélicon*, d'*inspiration*, de *mélancolie* et de *souvenirs*, ils n'y sont plus.

. . . . . . . . . . . . . . . . . . .

Du reste, l'*Edinburgh Review* s'est complètement trompée en faisant de M. de Lamartine le poète du parti *ultra*. Ce parti si habilement dirigé par MM. de Vitrolles et Frayssinous, cherche à adopter toutes les gloires. Il a procuré à M. de Lamartine neuf éditions de ses poésies; mais le véritable poète du parti, c'est M. Hugo.

Ce M. Hugo a un talent dans le genre de celui de Young, l'auteur des *Night Thoughts*; il est toujours exagéré à froid; son parti lui procure un fort grand succès. L'on ne peut nier, au surplus, qu'il ne sache fort bien faire des vers français; malheureusement, il est somnifère.

(2) Ce soir, on joue *Henri III* de M. Dumas. C'est un acheminement au véritable Henri III politique. Ceci est encore Henri III à la Marivaux. Victor Hugo, ultra vanté, n'a pas de succès réel, du moins pour les *Orientales*. Le *condamné*[7] fait horreur et me semble inférieur à certains passages des *Mémoires de Vidocq*.

(3) M. Victor Hugo n'est pas un homme ordinaire, mais il *veut* être extraordinaire, et les *Orientales* m'ennuient; et vous?

Stendhal was not fond of poetry, although one of his early

---

[4] Paupe et Cheramy, *op. cit.*, II, pp. 283-284.
[5] Paupe et Cheramy, *op. cit.*, II, p. 493.
[6] Paupe et Cheramy, *op. cit.*, II, p. 518.
[7] *Le dernier jour d'un condamné.*

aspirations was the desire to acquire the reputation of being the greatest French poet. He wrote to Baron de Mareste in 1820, à propos of Byron, that verses bored him, as being less exact than prose.[8] He admired Lamartine and Musset, but he considered Hugo as the representative of the pompous and exaggerated style for which he had great disdain.

*The University of North Carolina.*

---

[8] Stendhal, *Souvenirs d'égotisme, autobiographie et lettres inédites*, publiés par Casimir Stryienski (Paris: Charpentier et Fasquelle, 1892), p. 273.

# GUTIERRE DE CETINA: NOTES ON THE DATE OF HIS BIRTH AND THE IDENTITY OF DÓRIDA

## J. P. Wickersham Crawford

The earliest composition of Gutierre de Cetina which can be definitely dated is the fifty-sixth sonnet in Señor Hazañas y la Rua's edition, addressed to the Marquise del Vasto on her arrival at Milan:

> Cual en la deseada primavera
> Suelen venir a nos Favonio y Flora
> Cual se suele mostrar la bella aurora
> Ante el rector de la celeste esfera;
> Cual en aquella dulce edad primera
> Diana en selva se mostró a deshora:
> Tal vos, excelentísima Señora,
> Parecéis a este pueblo que os espera.
> Alégrate hora pues, Liguria mía;
> Que si grande ocasión para gozarte
> Deseabas hallar, hoy es el día.
> Si de dolor te queda alguna parte,
> Sea por no haber visto en compañía
> De la nueva Diana al nuevo Marte.

The Marquise, Maria d'Aragona, was as beautiful and as frequently celebrated by the poets of her day as her famous sister-in-law, the Marquise of Pescara, Vittoria Colonna. Her husband, Alfonso d'Avalos, "bellissimo fra tutti gli huomini del mondo, e fortissimo sopra tutti i capitani," in the words of Paolo Giovio, the hero of the Emperor's Tunisian and other campaigns, had been named by Charles the Fifth Governor General of the State of Milan in 1536, but the Marquise had remained in Naples where she was lauded by the poets as an "esempio di bellezza e castidade." She rejoined her husband at Milan in the spring of 1538, and in his sonnet Cetina expresses the welcome of Liguria to its new mistress.

If we were to judge wholly from the evidence of Cetina's verses, it would appear that the poet's youth was occupied almost exclusively in love-making. So far as we know, his first love affair was with a Sevillan lady whom he calls Dórida, to whom he addressed many sonnets and other compositions, and to whom he bids a tender farewell in his second epistle, promising her his eternal love. But on the banks of the Pisuerga, probably at Valladolid, he became enamoured of another lady whom he calls Amaríllida:

>¡Ay, mísero pastor! ¿Dó voy huyendo?
>¿Curar pienso mi ardor con otro fuego?
>Cuitado, ¿a dónde voy? ¿Estoy ya ciego
>Que ni veo mi bien, ni el mal entiendo?
>¿Dó me llevas, amor? Si aquí me enciendo,
>¿Tendré do voy más paz o más sosiego?
>Si huyo de un peligro, ¿a dó voy luego?
>¿Es menor el que voy hora siguiendo?
>¿Fué más ventura el Betis por ventura,
>Que es agora Pisuerga? Aquél no ha sido
>Tan triste para mí como éste agora.
>Si falta en Amaríllida mesura,
>¿Cómo la tendrá Dórida, sabido
>Que lleve ya en el alma otra Señora?        (*Son. XXI*)

Cetina's position was embarrassing, because Amaríllida as well as Dórida had a right to charge the poet with fickleness. With grief and humiliation he seeks to justify himself in his tenth epistle, addressed to Amaríllida. How can he be blamed, he asks, if Love has broken the bond that united him to Dórida for nine or ten years? He confesses that he cannot forget his old love, but asserts that this only serves to make more intense his new passion.

In a recent article [1] Signor Eugenio Mele and Señor Alonso Cortés have shown that in all probability Amaríllida may be identified as Doña Marina Siguriosa, a lady whose name serves as caption for the two hundred and fortieth sonnet. Their love affair lasted at least three years for the poet writes in the fifth *canción* (*34-42*):

>Amaríllida mía, ¡oh tú, que sola
>Doquiera que yo sea,
>En el alma me estás! hoy tres veranos
>Se cumplen que en las bodas de Erithrea
>En el bailar ganaste el premio sola,
>Por lo cual Alba se mordió las manos:
>Tú, moza sin consejo
>Eras, yo, no tan viejo
>Que aun andaba sirviendo a mis hermanos.

---

[1] *Sobre los amores de Gutierre de Cetina y su famoso madrigal* (Valladolid, 1930), pp. 11-14.

If we can accept internal evidence of this sort, and there seems to be no reason to reject it, Cetina was in love with Dórida for nine or ten years, followed by the love affair with Amaríllida for at least three years before his journey to Italy which we have seen must have taken place as early as 1538. No statistics are available as to when young men first fall in love, but if we assume sixteen as a reasonable age, it follows that Cetina must have been at least twenty-eight years old when he reached Milan, or in other words, that he must have been born at least as early as 1510.

Until recently the accuracy of Francisco Pacheco's statement in his *Libro descripción de verdaderos retratos* that Cetina was born in 1520 has not been definitely challenged. We have a right, however, to examine this date in the light of other evidence when we remember that Pacheco, who was born in 1564, could not have known Cetina personally and that his statement was based upon hearsay. Señor Rodríguez Marín[2] states that the poet was born at Seville, "si no el año de 1520, como dicen sus biógrafos, pocos antes." Don Lucas de Torre argues with good reason that the date 1520 assigned for Cetina's birth does not accord with the data regarding the poet's family discovered by Señor Hazañas y la Rua, and that the references to his love for Dórida extending over nine or ten years indicate clearly that "su nacimiento debió verificarse años antes de lo que se supone, a menos de concederle una extraordinaria precocidad."[3]

The reader of Cetina's verse is naturally curious regarding the identity of Dórida, the Sevillan lady to whom he was devoted for nine or ten years, and who was by no means forgotten when he was living at Valladolid and in Italy. In the fourth sonnet he definitely challenges his own friends as well as the literary ferrets of the future to guess his secret:

[2] *Luis Barahona de Soto. Estudio biográfico, bibliográfico y crítico.* Madrid, 1903, p. 128.

[3] "Algunas notas para la biografía de Gutierre de Cetina," *Boletín de la Real Academia Española*, XI (1911), pp. 390-391. He assumes that Amaríllida was an Italian lady, Countess Laura Gonzaga, whom Cetina met at Milan, and therefore in his calculations he does not include the period of at least three years which the poet spent with her at Valladolid before going to Italy.

>     Al pie de un monte que divide a España
>    De Francia, do más alto el cuello asoma,
>    En las faldas de aquel que el nombre toma
>    Del ladrón más sutil, de mayor maña;
>       En un valle hermoso a do la extraña
>    Cabeza el blanco monte abaja y doma,
>    No lejos de la fuente por quien Roma
>    Dió nombre a la región que en torno baña;
>       Cerca de do perdió el francés famoso
>    La gloria de que aun hoy soberbio viene,
>    Allí nació la causa del mal mío.
>       Después lo crió el Tago, y de envidioso
>    Pisuerga lo robó; Betis lo tiene.
>    Intendame chi può, che m' intend'io.

It was pointed out many years ago by Morel-Fatio [4] that the mountain here referred to is the Moncayo and that the pass is Roncesvalles. Mele and Alonso Cortés [5] have recently called attention to certain inconsistencies in this description, but they agree that it must refer to Pamplona or a town in its immediate neighborhood.

In the fourth *canción* addressed to the river Guadalquivir, Cetina describes the vicissitudes of his love for Dórida (*152-158*):

>     Cuando estaba más blanda y cuando dura,
>    Yo, que andaba engañado en mi locura,
>    Todo lo atribuía a buena suerte;
>    El nudo estrecho y fuerte,
>    Que sólo entre los dos ligó Himeneo,
>    Y en verme en posesión, menos cuidoso
>    Me hicieron del daño que hora veo.

Possibly this means that the poet was engaged to marry Dórida when he left Sevilla to go to Valladolid. At all events, it is she whom he mentions in the sixth epistle addressed to Isabela di Capua, Princess of Molfetta, in which he describes his old love for Dórida whom he symbolizes as the "elm" (*olmo*) as contrasted with his new love for the "laurel" (*lauro*) who is almost certainly the beautiful Countess Laura Gonzaga. This insistence upon the word "olmo" in a number of compositions addressed to Dórida

---
[4] *Revue critique d'Histoire et de Littérature*, XXX (1896), pp. 131-136.
[5] *Op. cit.*, p. 10.

led Señor Icaza to conjecture that her real name was Olmedo or del Olmo.[6]

Another intimate friend of Cetina was Don Luis de Leiva, who inherited the title of Prince of Ascoli from his father Antonio de Leiva, but not his great talents. Cetina, assuming his usual poetic name Vandalio, addressed several compositions to Lavinio (Leiva), and the latter who, like all noblemen of his day, could turn off a sonnet when sufficiently provoked, answered occasionally in kind. Each was well acquainted with the secrets of the other's heart, and each seems to have relied upon the other for counsel.

In the one hundred and twenty-second sonnet, directed to Don Luis de Leiva, Cetina writes in an apologetic tone regarding his fickleness:

> Lavinio, si el hallarme el alma ajena
> Del ardor en que había hábito hecho,
> Te hace de mi fe mal satisfecho,
> Sin saber la ocasión que el hado ordena;
> La historia de disculpa y razón llena,
> Que me tiene ya en lágrimas deshecho,
> Podrás leer do hallarás que el pecho
> El objeto mudó, mas no la pena.
> Baste, pues, un recaudo al más honrado:
> La más justa ocasión para mudarme
> Que pudo un corazón mudar cuidado.
> Sólo una razón hay para culparme;
> Que las alas de bajo vuelo usado
> No debieran tan alto levantarme.

In the eighth verse, he merely repeated what he wrote to Amaríllida in the tenth epistle (*31-33*):

> Verdad es que mudé la fantasía;
> El objeto mudé, mas no la pena:
> Hora muero por ti; por ella ardía.

Possibly the Key to the secret of Dórida's identity may be found in the eighty-ninth sonnet:

> El que está como yo tan desvalido,
> Tan sujeto a su mal, tan desmayado,
> No puede su dolor mostrar pintado,
> Ni con palabras ser bien referido.
> Liviano es aquel mal (ya lo has leído)

---

[6] *Sucesos reales que parecen imaginados de Gutierre de Cetina, Juan de la Cueva y Mateo Alemán* (Madrid, 1919), p. 64, n. 1.

> Que el seso puede en sí tener guardado;
> Pero muy más liviano el que contado
> Puede ser de la suerte que es sentido.
>     No quieras pues, pastor, importunarme
> Que te muestre en dibujo mis pasiones
> Para que la ocasión se entienda luego;
>     Que como por la luz se saca el fuego,
> Se puede de tan altas ocasiones
> Entender quien las causa y condenarme.

The line " Liviano es aquel mal (ya lo has leído)" is undoubtedly a covert allusion to the lady's name, and when we recall that in the sonnet just quoted above, addressed to Don Luis de Leiva, he seeks to justify his change of heart, it is at least a fair conjecture that Dórida was a relative of the Prince of Ascoli.

For centuries the Leiva family had been prominently identified with the history of Navarre and Guipuzcoa. One might be tempted to spin a romantic story of Cetina's wavering attachment for one of the daughters of Don Sancho Martínez de Leiva, uncle of Don Luis, who after a successful campaign against France, was appointed in 1524 Governor of Fuenterrabia [7] and Captain General of Guipuzcoa, but it would be difficult to choose between his six daughters, Juana, Costanza, Ana, Francisca, Isabel and María, and besides, the identification would not rest upon fact.

*University of Pennsylvania.*

---

[7] Alonso López de Haro, *Segunda parte del Nobiliario genealógico de los Reyes y Títulos de España* (Madrid, 1622), p. 396.

# NOTES ON THE GRACIOSO AS A DRAMATIC CRITIC

## By Sturgis E. Leavitt

The *gracioso* of the *siglo de oro* seldom fails to express himself in a picturesque and original manner, though it must be admitted that sometimes this is his principal recommendation. On other occasions, however, his humor adds color to pronouncements of considerable moment. But when the wit figure enunciates judgments far beyond his experience, we may well suspect that the author is prompting from behind the scenes. Is not this the case when the *gracioso* appears in the rôle of a dramatic critic?

The poor taste of the Madrid audience in matters of drama, for example, is set forth with such feeling by Redondo in Alarcón's *Mudarse por mejorarse* that his remarks seem to reflect an actual experience on the part of the much be-deviled dramatist.

> Comedia vi yo, llamada
> De los sabios extremada,
> Y rendir la vida al quinto;
> Y vi en otra, que a millares
> Los disparates tenía,
> Reñir al quinceno día
> Con Jarava por lugares;
> Y sus parciales, vencidos
> De la fuerza de razón,
> Decir: «Disparates son,
> Pero son entretenidos.»
> Representante afamado
> Has visto, por sólo errar
> Una sílaba, quedar
> A silbos mosqueteado;
> Y luego acudir verías
> Esta cuaresma pasada
> Contenta y alborotada
> Al corral cuarenta días
> Toda la corte, y estar
> Muy quedos papando muecas,
> Viendo bailar dos muñecas
> Y oyendo un viejo graznar.[1]

The prominent part which the *gracioso* plays in the *comedias* of the period and the familiarity with which he treats his superiors

---

[1] *Biblioteca de Autores Españoles*, XX, 104.

were common conventions and offered easy targets for criticism. Tirso de Molina, for one, voices his objection to this sort of literary promotion, and even uses the *gracioso* himself to present the protest.

> ¿Qué comedia
> Hay, si las de España sabes,
> En que el gracioso no tenga
> Privanza, contra las leyes,
> Con duques, condes y reyes,
> Ya venga bien, ya no venga?
> ¿Qué secreto no le fían?
> ¿Qué infanta no le da entrada?
> ¿A qué princesa no agrada?[2]

In *Los favores del mundo,* Ruiz de Alarcón seems to be employing the *gracioso* to speak his mind on the same subject.

> Si el cielo no lo remedia
> La sátira encaja aquí:
> Mas no ha de haber cosa en mí
> De lacayo de comedia.
> ¡Cual a la corte pusiera
> Algún poeta, si el caso
> Y el lacayo en este paso
> De la comedia tuviera!
> ¡Cuál pusiera yo a su Alteza!
> ¡Qué libremente le hablara,
> Y qué poco respetara
> Su poder y su grandeza!
> ¡Luego me apartara dellos,
> Cuando a graves cosas van
> El y mi amo y Don Juan!
> ¡Mal año! por los cabellos
> De otra parte me trajera,
> Y en todo el caso me hallara,
> Que el Príncipe aun no fiara
> Quizá a los dos, si pudiera.
> Y estando en lo mas famoso,
> Grave, fuerte y apretado,
> Saliera el señor criado
> Con un cuento muy mohoso,
> O una fábula pueril

---

[2] *Amar por señas, Ibid.,* V, 462. Cf. also Gascón in *El prudente celoso, Ibid.,* V, 620, and Fuencarral in Castillo Solórzano's *El Marqués del Cigarral, Ibid.,* XLV, 317.

> De la zorra y el león,
> Y la mas alta cuestión
> Concluyera un hombre vil.[3]

With regard to the convenient soliloquy indulged in by master and servant alike, Rojas has one of his comic figures ironically tell us that its use could be extended even further.

> Yo solamente no tengo
> A quien le cuente mis males;
> Pues vaya de soliloquio,
> Que en cuantas comedias se hacen
> No he visto que las criadas
> Lleguen a soliloquiarse.[4]

Another dramatic device which seems to have evoked considerable comment from the much coached *gracioso* was the happy ending in which marriage arrangements were made for every available couple in the play. Sometimes the servant is so impressed by this practice that he announces the end of the piece even before the first act is finished.

> Y pues con tanta gloria
> Dama y galán se han casado,
> Perdonad, noble Senado,
> Que aquí se acaba la historia.[5]

Or the prospect of marriage convinces him that the second act is the final one.

> Y si el galán y la dama
> Están ya desengañados,
> Aquí acaba la comedia.[6]

As a rule, however, ironical remarks about the wholesale-marriage plan are reserved until the last act.

> ¡Aguarda!
> Ya sabrán vuesas mercedes,
> Que en el punto que se casan

---

[3] *Ibid.*, XX, 8.
[4] F. de Rojas, *Donde hay agravios, Ibid.*, LIV, 165.
[5] Calderón, *A secreto agravio, secreta venganza, Ibid.*, VII, 599. Cf. Mengo in Vélez de Guevara's *La luna de la sierra, Ibid.*, XLV, 183; and Copete in Cubillo de Aragón's *El señor de noches buenas, Ibid.*, XLVII, 149.
[6] Calderón, *Mañanas de abril y mayo, Ibid.*, IX, 288.

> Las damas de la comedia,
> Es señal de que se acaba. . . .[7]

It might seem that this ridicule of practices in which the author himself indulged to a greater or less extent was evidence that the writer in question did not take himself any too seriously. But this hardly seems to be the case. Some examples of dramatic criticism by proxy may be only humoristic touches with no underlying motive; but in other instances, notably with such independent thinkers as Ruiz de Alarcón and Tirso de Molina, the intention is undoubtedly adverse criticism of a technique to which they did not fully subscribe.

*The University of North Carolina.*

---

[7] Calderón, *Saber del mal y del bien, Ibid.*, VII, 35. Cf. also Beltrán in Pérez de Montalván's *Ser prudente y ser sufrido, Ibid.*, XLIV, 585.

# HARTZENBUSCH'S "SANCHO ORTIZ DE LAS ROELAS"

## By N. B. Adams

Juan Eugenio Hartzenbusch is remembered chiefly for a few original dramas, a large collection of verse fables, for editions of seventeenth century classics, and for excellent service as librarian of the Biblioteca Nacional. His record in these fields is readily available, but one aspect of his dramatic activity is often overlooked or passed over with no more than bare mention: his adaptations of plays of the older Spanish theatre. According to the bibliography compiled by the dramatist's son, supplemented by Fernández-Guerra, Hartzenbusch adapted no less than thirteen native plays and has to his credit also numerous translations and *arreglos* of foreign pieces. Indeed it may be said that the playwright was introduced to the stage by one of his seventeenth century dramatic forbears, for Hartzenbusch's first play to appear in a public theatre was an adaptation of Rojas' *El amo criado* (Teatro de la Cruz, April 24, 1829). His adaptations were spread over a period of thirty-three years, and included plays of Lope, Tirso, Calderón, Rojas, Moreto, Coello and Bances Candamo.

If further proof of Hartzenbusch's interest in the theatre of the Siglo de Oro were needed, it would be furnished by his editions of the plays of Tirso, Calderón, Ruiz de Alarcón and Lope de Vega. Since the four volumes of Lope (B. A. E. XXIV, XXXIV, XLI and XLII) appeared from 1853 to 1857, it would seem natural to assign Hartzenbusch's particular interest in *La Estrella de Sevilla*, which he attributed to Lope without question, to that general period.

It also seems probable that Hartzenbusch's son was right in ascribing the first (fragmentary) adaptation of *La Estrella* made by the diligent dramatist and editor to the early eighteen-fifties.

The fragment of this *refundición*[1] consists of only a hundred lines, the first scene and part of the second, but some idea of the changes to be made by the adapter can be deduced from the omission of the slave girl Matilde, don Iñigo Osorio, don Manuel and

---

[1] Published by E. Hartzenbusch Hiriart, in *Bibliografía de Hartzenbusch*, (Madrid, 1900), pp. 162-166.

Pedro de Caus from the list of *personas*. These omissions would imply a number of alterations in Act II, Scenes i, ii and iv, and Act III, Scenes i, ii, vi and xi, though the place of Pedro de Caus could, of course, be easily taken by one of the Alguaciles.

If we can judge by the surviving fragment this adaptation was in general to follow the original *Estrella de Sevilla* quite closely. The first scenes of the two are identical in substance, though only five lines were preserved intact by the adapter. The second scene has been abbreviated and not a single line of the original left untouched. The adapter evidently disapproved (or thought his audience would disapprove) of the rather fulsome verbiage and *culterano* style of the seventeenth century *Estrella,* and the language of the King in Hartzenbusch's version is flattened to resemble that of any *bon bourgeois* of the mid-nineteenth century. Readers will probably remember Sancho's first impression of Estrella:

¿Quién es la que rayos son
Sus dos ojos fulminantes,
En abrasar semejantes
A los de Júpiter fuerte,
Que están dándome la muerte,
De su rigor ignorantes?
Una que, de negro, hacía
Fuerte competencia al sol,
Y al horizonte español
Entre ébano amanecía.
Una noche, horror del día,
Pues de negro, luz le daba,
Y él eclipsado quedaba;
Un borrón de la luz pura
Del sol, pues con su hermosura
Sus puras lineas borraba.[2]

Hartzenbusch's King Sancho is far more prosaic in his utterance:

A una dama saludé
Absorto de admiración.
Llamáronme la atención
Sus gracias, su tierna edad,
Su apacible gravedad,
Sus ojos . . . ¿Cómo se llama,
Don Arias, aquella dama
Con prendas para deidad?[3]

[2] B. A. E., XXIV, 138.    [3] E. Hartzenbusch Hiriart, *op. cit.*, p. 165.

If the whole of the adaptation was to be as flavorless as this sample, which is quite representative of the fragment, one cannot regret very keenly that the work was not completed. Fortunately a line such as "llamáronme la atención" is not characteristic of Hartzenbusch at his best.

Possibly he realized that his beginning was not auspicious. At any rate he abandoned the original *Estrella* and made a new adaptation of an already existing adaptation; that is to say, he re-adapted the version of Cándido María Trigueros, which had been first played, with great success, on January 22, 1800, in the *Cruz*. The title was not *La Estrella de Sevilla,* but *Sancho Ortiz de las Roelas.*

It is not our purpose to endeavor to shed new light on this version, already discussed at some length by Menéndez y Pelayo.[4] It seems to us significant, however, that Hartzenbusch, who began as a Romanticist, (*Los Amantes de Teruel*, 1837, *Doña Mencía,* 1838, *Alfonso el Casto,* 1841, *Honoria,* 1843), should be veering toward neo-classicism in the eighteen-forties (*Floresinda,* 1844) and around 1850 should be choosing to adapt a neo-classic *Sancho Ortiz de las Roelas* rather than a far more romantic *Estrella de Sevilla.* Hartzenbusch was certainly changing his manner if not his literary principles, as we hope at some future date to show further by comparing the successive versions of *Los Amantes de Teruel.*

Of Hartzenbusch's *Sancho Ortiz,* Menéndez y Pelayo says:[5]

El texto castellano que actualmente se representa, y siempre con el favor del público, no es ya la tragedia de Trigueros, sino una nueva refundición que hizo D. Juan Eugenio Hartzenbusch, conservando del drama primitivo todo lo que sin violencia podía adaptarse a la escena moderna.

This statement of the great literary historian might readily be misunderstood. It would seem to imply that Hartzenbusch made a new adaptation of the primitive form of *La Estrella;* but such is not the case. He merely reworked Trigueros' adaptation, making modifications which we shall now consider.

On the whole the versions of the two authors are quite similar. Both omit the first and part of the second act of the original *Estrella,* and begin the action with King Sancho already violently

---

[4] In *Obras de Lope de Vega,* vol. IX (Madrid, 1899), pp. xxxvi-lxxii.
[5] *Op. cit.,* p. lxxv.

in love with Estrella. In both the unities are observed; Trigueros makes the unity of time very clear by having the King say:[6]

> Id con Dios, y dejad tiempo
> de admirar vuestras hazañas,
> que me tiene sorprendido
> ver en un día tantas.

In the Hartzenbusch version, he says:[7]

> ¡Válgame Dios, y qué día
> tan confuso y tan turbado!

Hartzenbusch transfers to his version a large proportion of Trigueros' lines, including, of course, the famous words of Estrella, quoted by the King to Arias:

> — Soy, dijo a mi furor loco,
> para esposa vuestra, poco,
> para dama vuestra mucho.[8]

These phrases were often attributed to Lope by those unfamiliar with the original *Estrella*.

In general it may be said that Hartzenbusch endeavors to make Trigueros' *style noble* less oppressive, to make his language less pompous and less *conceptuoso*. A significant detail is the near-suppression of Trigueros' (and the original author's) many plays upon the name *Estrella*.

In both plays, as their title implies, the interest is centered in Sancho Ortiz, and the unity of action is more closely observed than in *La Estrella*. While the two plays are neo-classic in style as well as in plan, that of Hartzenbusch is rather less poetic, even though Trigueros' inspiration failed him all too often. Both refer to

---

[6] Act V, sc. ix.

[7] Act IV, sc. i.

[8] One is likely to recall Doña Sol's words to Don Carlos (*Hermani*, Act II, sc. ii):

"Trop pour la concubine, et trop peu pour l'épouse."

This sentiment had been repeated so often in *siglo de oro* plays that the *gracioso* of Calderón's *No hay burlas con el amor* says (Act III, sc. v):

> "Que soy grande para dama,
> Y para esposa soy chica:
> Eso, a reyes de comedia
> No hay condesa que no diga."

Sancho's murder of Bustos as a *desliz* ( ! )—a good rhyme for Ortiz, obviously, but a most infelicitous term.

Hartzenbusch compressed Trigueros' five acts into four by fusing Acts III and IV of his predecessor into his own third act. It will be remembered that Hartzenbusch similarly made a four-act play of his own *Amantes de Teruel* in 1849.

While in general Hartzenbusch follows Trigueros with considerable fidelity, there are numerous differences of detail, of which only a few can be suggested here. In Trigueros' play the announcement of Bustos' death is made to Estrella very abruptly; in Hartzenbusch it is much more tactfully presented. In Trigueros' Act II, Scene vii, Estrella asks Sancho what induced him to kill Bustos, and finally says: "Was it the King?" No such suggestion comes from her in Hartzenbusch's version. Hartzenbusch considerably reduced the soliloquy of Sancho in prison, and emphasized less his longing for Estrella's "dulces brazos." He also failed to mention the heroism which Trigueros assigns to the King, giving him the words:[9]

> Todos, menos yo, son héroes
> en esta dichosa patria:
> también yo ser quiero hablando
> tan héroe como el que calla.
> Matadme a mí, sevillanos,
> que yo solo fuí la causa
> de esta muerte.

Hartzenbusch, evidently realizing that this claim to heroism was quite unjustified, very properly omitted it.

The greatest difference between the two versions, however, is in the ending. Trigueros, with his rigorous sense of propriety, felt that all thought of marriage between Estrella and Sancho was impossible. He has Estrella say:[10]

> Viva Don Sancho felice,
> pero no viva en la casa
> en donde ha sido el origen
> de tan funesta desgracia.

Sancho agrees that union with his beloved would also be torment to him. To console him, she says:

[9] Act V, sc. ix.    [10] Act V, sc. ix.

and he replies:
>     No os olvidaré, Don Sancho,
>
>     Tanta será mi desgracia.

Hartzenbusch viewed the matter differently, and the final words of his version are significant. When the King urges Sancho and Estrella to marry, Sancho says:

> Estrella, fuerza es hablar.
> *Estrella:* Callar y huir es mejor.
> *Sancho:* Yo no he de engañar tu amor.
> *Estrella:* El se quisiera engañar.
> *Sancho:* No: yo de tu hermano fuí . . .
> *Estrella:* ¡Ah! no alces el triste velo:
> él te perdona en el cielo,
> y yo te perdono aquí.

In other words, the matter is left in some doubt, but the implication is that time will close the wounds and that the two can be united.

One cannot say definitely why Hartzenbusch made this change. He may have felt that love was stronger than a sense of propriety; perhaps he had the *Cid* in mind.

The most surprising feature of Hartzenbusch's adaptation, when we consider his love of the seventeenth century drama, is that he did not occasionally abandon Trigueros to drink at the original source, and that his *Sancho Ortiz* is not closer to what he regarded as Lope's original. One can understand why the exigencies of staging would necessitate a rearrangement of the scenes of the primitive drama; but they did not demand that most of its freshness and vigor should be sacrificed. The most convenient explanation would be that Hartzenbusch was in 1852 an Academician and that he had lost a taste for the exuberance and enthusiastic expression which characterized the Siglo de Oro drama and also his own earlier productions.

*The University of North Carolina.*

# A SPANISH PLAY ON THE FAIR ROSAMOND LEGEND

## By S. A. Stoudemire

Spanish Romantic dramatists were peculiarly fond of historical and legendary themes, with medieval stories of Spain furnishing a large number of their plots. Often the history of France or Italy offered a subject, but rarely does one find a play making use of English history. Hence, it is of particular interest to observe that Don Antonio Gil y Zárate (1793-1861), an eclectic dramatist who passed through the usual preliminary stages of classicism, Moratinian comedy, translations and adaptations of French plays before finally reaching romanticism, has two plays dealing with English history. One, *La familia de Falkland* (1843), deals with the wars between the Royalists and the Populists (1642-1649) in which Sir Lucius Cary Falkland distinguished himself as a Royalist leader. In the other, *Rosmunda* (1839), Gil y Zárate reworks the well-known story of Henry II of England and his mistress, the Fair Rosamond Clifford.

There is little in the records of twelfth century England to substantiate the popular story concerning Henry and Rosamond. No chronicler of that period has given even a close approximation of the legend as it was known in the seventeenth century. Giraldus Cambrensis says that the King put away his wife, Eleanor, and that he lived in open adultery with another woman.[1] Finally the story reached the proportions of a lengthy and romantic legend. Unfortunately, there is no study which traces the story from its beginnings through all the ramifications and points out the parts that are historical and those that are legendary. A synopsis of the legend in its present form indicates the extent to which it has grown at the hands of numerous chroniclers. Henry II of England, about the year 1156, deserted his Queen, Eleanor of Aquitaine, the divorced wife of Louis VII of France, and frequently visited the Fair Rosamond, the daughter of Walter de Clifford. His mistress had been established in a beautiful garden, similar to a maze, at Woodstock, where only the King could reach her. Even

---

[1] Giraldus Cambrensis, *De Instructione Principum* (London, 1846), III, 21-22.

he had to follow a strand of silk to find the heart of the bower. Queen Eleanor, upon learning of the mysterious woman and her more mysterious retreat, decided to investigate. She discovered the silken clue and followed it to the heart of the maze. There she tortured Rosamond and told her that she must die from a poison bowl or under a dagger. Rosamond sought to justify herself, but was finally forced to drink the poison.

One wonders why such a picturesque legend has not been more popular with the chief writers of England. The story, however, has not been entirely neglected, for it has been made the theme of various literary works, which will perhaps be studied in some future monograph. Some of the treatments of the legend are fairly well known. Thomas Deloney's ballads, "The Faire Lady Rosamond"[2] and "The Imprisonment of Queen Elenor"[3] have no historical purpose as did the medieval chronicles. The first of Deloney's ballads is important in that it seems to have added to the legend the episode of the poison bowl. Another old ballad, "Queen Eleanor's Confession,"[4] reprinted by Bishop Percy, touches on the poisoning of Rosamond. These ballads treat only an isolated feature of the story and in no sense the whole. Cervantes makes an anachronistic reference to Rosamond in *Persiles y Sigismunda*,[5] in which he reviles her as a base and wanton creature. Addison's *Rosamond*[6] (1706) is a delightful comic opera. The author follows the popular version, but his attitude calls for a different ending. Consequently, the conclusion cannot be a horrible death. The poison proves to be a sleeping potion and the dead come to life. Henry is cured of his polygamous tendency and returns to Eleanor. Then they both agree to the sentiment:

> Who to forbidden joys would rove,
> That knows the sweets of virtuous love?[7]

---

[2] T. Deloney, *Works*, ed. F. O. Mann (Oxford, 1912), pp. 297-302.

[3] *Ibid.*, pp. 397-399.

[4] T. Percy, *Reliques of Ancient English Poetry*, ed. H. B. Wheatley, 3 vols. (London, 1910), II, 164-168.

[5] Cervantes, *Persiles y Sigismunda*, ed. Schevill and Bonilla, 2 vols. (Madrid, 1914), I, 94.

[6] J. Addison, *Rosamond, Complete Works* (London, 1854), vol. I.

[7] *Ibid.*, p. 81.

Thomas Hull's *Henry II or the Fall of Rosamond*[8] (1773) is a typical eighteenth century tragedy. The dramatist has followed the story rather closely, although some of the characters are not in keeping with the legend. The tragedy is given a poignant note since Clifford, Rosamond's father, is depicted as one of the King's closest friends. Rosamond, too, is treated in a kindly manner by the dramatist; she is not the wanton of legend, but an innocent girl who loves Henry for himself and not because he is the King of England. The whole plot is made up of the machinations of an abbot, a figure not common to the legend, who is playing one person against another for his own benefit, namely, to become Archbishop. In this version Rosamond dies of the poison and Eleanor becomes remorseful after her disastrous deed.

It seems unlikely that Gil y Zárate was influenced by any of the works mentioned above. The date of Tennyson's *Becket* (1879) makes any influence on the Spanish playwright impossible. Of the few works on the Rosamond legend, Gil y Zárate seems to have used several details to be found in Bonnechose's *Rosemonde*.[9] In this play the page, Arthur, tells Eleanore that Henri, using the name Edgar, is enamored of a woman whom he keeps hidden in the garden. Upon learning this, the Queen swears to kill her unknown rival. At this point Clifford, a powerful nobleman, returns after an absence of six years, and is told of the King's disgraceful conduct. The Queen tells Clifford to bring his daughter, Rosemonde, to the palace for she wishes to arrange a noble wedding for her. Henri returns from a victorious invasion of Ireland, and at once visits his mistress. He confesses to her that Edgar is not his real name, but he refuses to disclose his identity. Clifford begs Henri to give up this woman and return to Eleanore, but the King is obstinate and swears that he is going to marry her. Clifford becomes furious and wants to know when he can see the King's mistress, and Henri answers him, "This very day." At this point Arthur carries an anonymous letter to Rosemonde decreeing her death. Clifford enters and is grief stricken to see that

---

[8] T. Hull, *Henry II or The Fall of Rosamond, Modern Theater*, selected by Mrs. Inchbald (London, 1811), IV, 337.

[9] E. de Bonnechose, *Rosemonde*, tragédie en cinq actes, représentée pour la première fois, sur le premier Théâtre Français, le 28 octobre, 1826 (Paris: Lecaudey, 1826).

his daughter is the King's mistress. Rosemonde, too, is overcome when she learns that her lover is the King. Henri rushes into the bower, swearing that in spite of everything he intends to marry Rosemonde. Eleanore, touched by Rosemonde's sorrow, is willing to pardon her until she hears of her husband's matrimonial project. In order to protect his paramour, Henri orders both Clifford and Eleanore seized. Eleanore, however, comes upon the fleeing Rosemonde in the garden and stabs her. Henri, rushing after his mistress, encounters a soldier who tries to stop him. The King kills this man and in the moonlight sees that it is Clifford. Henri now refuses to entertain the thought of either love or friendship for Eleanore.

There can be little doubt that this is the immediate source for Gil y Zárate's *Rosmunda*. In both of these works several striking features are to be found that do not occur in other literary treatments of the legend or in the chronicles. Henry's use of a fictitious name, Edgar in Bonnechose and Alfredo in Gil y Zárate, is a device common to these two alone. Gil y Zárate also has borrowed from the French writer the character Arturo. In the French tragedy Arthur is a young page attached to Eleanore, while in the Spanish play Arturo is Rosmunda's absent lover. In both plays Rosamond is again pictured as a young and innocent girl, and not as the wanton of the legend.

It is obvious, however, that Gil y Zárate has not followed the French source slavishly. The most striking change is that he has made the tragedy into a *comédie larmoyante*. In fact, the characteristics of the *comédie larmoyante* that occur in Gil y Zárate's drama may be definitely traced to the play by Bonnechose. Although the latter work is called a tragedy, it assumes such proportions only in the last short act. The persons are indeed noble, but their actions are never as elevated and lofty as is commensurate with tragedy. Throughout the whole work there is a feeling of sentimentality and tearfulness that leads one to believe that if the author had caused the King to return to his wife he would have made a better play. As has been pointed out, the tragic ending has been changed by Gil y Zárate to a happy one, where the King once more realizes the loveliness and virtue of his wife and returns to her.

Gil y Zárate's *Rosmunda,* in four acts and in verse, is the story of an erring husband brought to his senses. Although part of the main plot is based upon Bonnechose's tragedy, new turns have been added to the story. He never once hints that there exists a liaison between Henry and Rosmunda. The legendary bower becomes the country home of the Cliffords, and Eleanor is not forced to exert her wits in seeking out her husband's mistress. She merely enters the country place and has her servants carry the girl to the palace. It is there that she attempts to poison her, but is foiled by Arturo. Elfrida, Rosmunda's mother, not ordinarily included in the legend, has an inconspicuous part in Gil y Zárate's play.

The setting is changed entirely and the characters are not in keeping with those of history or legend. Eleanor is pictured as a calm and gentle wife who desires to regain the love of her wayward husband. Rosmunda is the epitome of virtue, and listens with only one ear to the pleading of Alfredo (Henry), because her thoughts are of Arturo, who has not appeared for two years. Henry becomes the magnanimous gentleman, and feels keen remorse for trying to seduce an innocent girl. Gil y Zárate, it may be said, abhorred even a suggestion of immorality, and here he has tried to remove every trace of wrongdoing. In making such a change he has really evolved a new plot and created new characters. In the end, when Henry and Eleanor are reconciled, Rosmunda could not be ignored and, therefore, Arturo's role of page in Bonnechose is changed for the sole purpose of disposing gracefully of Rosmunda.

In conclusion, it seems that Gil y Zárate was well acquainted with the Rosamond story and has undoubtedly taken suggestions from Bonnechose's tragedy. The fact remains, however, that he has exercised the same liberty in treating this legend that he displays in each of his *dramas históricos*. He justifies his procedure in his study of the theater when he says, " Es lícito al poeta fingir sucesos que nunca han existido, y quitar o añadir a los hechos históricos lo que le haga al caso." [10]

*The University of North Carolina.*

---

[10] A. Gil y Zárate, *Manual de literatura*, primera parte (Madrid: Boix, 1842), p. 271.

www.ingramcontent.com/pod-product-compliance
Lightning Source LLC
Chambersburg PA
CBHW080408300426
44113CB00015B/2436